After Heidegger?

New Heidegger Research

Series Editors:

Gregory Fried, Professor of Philosophy, Suffolk University, USA

Richard Polt, Professor of Philosophy, Xavier University, USA

The *New Heidegger Research* series promotes informed and critical dialogue that breaks new philosophical ground by taking into account the full range of Heidegger's thought, as well as the enduring questions raised by his work.

Titles in the Series:

After the Greeks, Laurence Paul Hemming (forthcoming)

After Heidegger?, edited by Gregory Fried and Richard Polt

Correspondence 1949–1975, Martin Heidegger, Ernst Jünger, translated by Timothy Quinn

Existential Medicine: Essays on Health and Illness, edited by Kevin A. Aho (forthcoming)

Heidegger and the Environment, Casey Rentmeester

Heidegger and the Global Age, edited by Antonio Cerella and Louiza Odysseos

Heidegger in the Islamicate World, edited by Kata Moser and Urs Gösken (forthcoming)

Heidegger and Jewish Thought, edited by Micha Brumlik and Elad Lapidot (forthcoming)

Heidegger in Russia and Eastern Europe, edited by Jeff Love

Heidegger's Gods, Susanne Claxton

Making Sense of Heidegger, Thomas Sheehan

Proto-Phenomenology and the Nature of Language, Lawrence J. Hatab

The Question Concerning the Thing: On Kant's Doctrine of the Transcendental Principles, Martin Heidegger, translated by Benjamin D. Crowe and James D. Reid (forthcoming)

After Heidegger?

Edited by
Gregory Fried and Richard Polt

ROWMAN &
LITTLEFIELD
INTERNATIONAL
London • New York

Published by Rowman & Littlefield International Ltd
Unit A, Whitacre Mews, 26–34 Stannary Street, London SE11 4AB
www.rowmaninternational.com

Rowman & Littlefield International Ltd. is an affiliate of Rowman & Littlefield
4501 Forbes Boulevard, Suite 200, Lanham, Maryland 20706, USA
With additional offices in Boulder, New York, Toronto (Canada), and Plymouth (UK)
www.rowman.com

British Library Cataloguing in Publication Data
A catalogue record for this book is available from the British Library

ISBN: HB 978-1-7866-0485-9
PB 978-1-7866-0486-6

Library of Congress Cataloging-in-Publication Data is Available

ISBN 978-1-78660-485-9 (cloth: alk. paper)
ISBN 978-1-78660-486-6 (pbk: alk. paper)
ISBN 978-1-78660-487-3 (electronic)

∞™ The paper used in this publication meets the minimum requirements of American National Standard for Information Sciences—Permanence of Paper for Printed Library Materials, ANSI/NISO Z39.48–1992.

Printed in the United States of America

Contents

Abbreviations

The following abbreviations for texts by Heidegger are used in this volume. When both a German text and a translation are cited, the German pagination is followed by a slash and the English pagination. When no translation is cited, any translation is the author's own. The abbreviation "tm" indicates that a translation has been modified, and "em" indicates that emphasis has been modified.

BEING AND TIME

SZ = *Sein und Zeit*. Tübingen: Niemeyer, 1953. Later editions share the same pagination, which is also provided in the English translations and in the *Gesamtausgabe* edition (GA 2). The first edition was published in 1927.

MR = *Being and Time*. Tr. John Macquarrie and Edward Robinson. New York: Harper & Row, 1962.

SS = *Being and Time*. Tr. Joan Stambaugh, revised by Dennis J. Schmidt. Albany: State University of New York Press, 2010.

GA = *GESAMTAUSGABE*

All volumes of Heidegger's *Gesamtausgabe* are published in Frankfurt am Main by Vittorio Klostermann. The date of publication, or dates if there is more than one edition, is followed by the date of original composition in parentheses. A translation is listed when available.

GA 1 = *Frühe Schriften*. Ed. Friedrich-Wilhelm von Herrmann. 1978 (1912–1916).

GA 3 = *Kant und das Problem der Metaphysik*. Ed. Friedrich-Wilhelm von Herrmann. 1991, 2010 (1929)./*Kant and the Problem of Metaphysics*. 5th ed. Tr. Richard Taft. Bloomington: Indiana University Press, 1997.

GA 4 = *Erläuterungen zu Hölderlins Dichtung*. Ed. Friedrich-Wilhelm von Herrmann. 1981, 2012 (1936–1968)./*Elucidations of Hölderlin's Poetry*. Tr. Keith Hoeller. Amherst, NY: Humanity Books, 2000.

GA 5 = *Holzwege*. Ed. Friedrich-Wilhelm von Hermann. 1977 (1935–1946)./*Off the Beaten Track*. Tr. Julian Young and Kenneth Haynes. Cambridge: Cambridge University Press, 2002.

GA 6.1 = *Nietzsche* I. Ed. Brigitte Schillbach. 1996 (1936–1939)./*Nietzsche: Volumes I and II*. Tr. David Farell Krell. New York: HarperOne, 1991.

GA 7 = *Vorträge und Aufsätze*. Ed. Friedrich-Wilhelm von Herrmann. 2000 (1936–1953).

GA 8 = *Was heißt Denken?* Ed. Paola-Ludovika Coriando. 2002 (1951–1952)./*What is Called Thinking?* Tr. J. Glenn Gray. New York: Harper & Row, 1968.

GA 9 = *Wegmarken*. Ed. Friedrich-Wilhelm von Herrmann. 1976, 1996, 2004 (1919–1961)./*Pathmarks*. Ed. William McNeill. Cambridge: Cambridge University Press, 1998.

GA 11 = *Identität und Differenz*. Ed. Friedrich-Wilhelm von Herrmann. 2006 (1955–1963).

GA 12 = *Unterwegs zur Sprache*. Ed. Friedrich-Wilhelm von Herrmann. 1985 (1950–1959)./*On the Way to Language*. Tr. Peter D. Hertz and Joan Stambaugh. New York: Harper & Row, 1971.

GA 13 = *Aus der Erfahrung des Denkens*. Ed. Hermann Heidegger. 1983, 2002 (1910–1976).

GA 14 = *Zur Sache des Denkens*. Ed. Friedrich-Wilhelm von Herrmann. 2007 (1927–1968)./Partial translation: *On Time and Being*. Tr. Joan Stambaugh. New York: Harper & Row, 1972.

GA 15 = *Seminare*. Ed. Curd Ochwadt. 1986, 2005 (1951–1973)./Partial translation: *Four Seminars*. Tr. Andrew Mitchell and François Raffoul. Bloomington: Indiana University Press, 2003.

GA 16 = *Reden und andere Zeugnisse eines Lebensweges*. Ed. Hermann Heidegger. 2000 (1910–1976).

GA 17 = *Einführung in die phänomenologische Forschung*. Ed. Friedrich-Wilhelm von Herrmann. 1994, 2006 (1923–1924)./*Introduction to Phenomenological Research*. Tr. Daniel O. Dahlstrom. Bloomington: Indiana University Press, 2005.

GA 18 = *Grundbegriffe der aristotelischen Philosophie*. Ed. Mark Michalski. 2002 (1924)./*Basic Concepts of Aristotelian Philosophy*. Tr. Robert

D. Metcalf and Mark Basil Tanzer. Bloomington: Indiana University Press, 2009.

GA 19 = *Platon: Sophistes*. Ed. Ingeborg Schüßler. 1992 (1924–1925)./*Plato's "Sophist."* Tr. Richard Rojcewicz and André Schuwer. Bloomington: Indiana University Press, 1997.

GA 20 = *Prolegomena zur Geschichte des Zeitbegriffs*. Ed. Petra Jaeger. 1979, 1988, 1994 (1925)./*History of the Concept of Time: Prolegomena*. Tr. Theodore Kisiel. Bloomington: Indiana University Press, 1992.

GA 21 = *Logik. Die Frage nach der Wahrheit*. Ed. Walter Biemel. 1976, 1995 (1925–1926)./*Logic: The Question of Truth*. Tr. Thomas Sheehan. Bloomington: Indiana University Press, 2010.

GA 22 = *Die Grundbegriffe der antiken Philosophie*. Ed. Franz-Karl Blust. 1993, 2004 (1926)./*Basic Concepts of Ancient Philosophy*. Tr. Richard Rojcewicz. Bloomington: Indiana University Press, 1997.

GA 24 = *Die Grundprobleme der Phänomenologie*. Ed. Friedrich-Wilhelm von Herrmann. 1975, 1997 (1927)./*The Basic Problems of Phenomenology*. Tr. Albert Hofstadter. Bloomington: Indiana University Press, 1982.

GA 26 = *Metaphysische Anfangsgründe der Logik im Ausgang von Leibniz*. Ed. Klaus Held. 1978, 1990, 2007 (1928)./*The Metaphysical Foundations of Logic*. Tr. Michael Heim. Bloomington: Indiana University Press, 1984.

GA 27 = *Einleitung in die Philosophie*. Ed. Otto Saame and Ina Saame-Speidel. 1996, 2001 (1928–1929).

GA 29/30 = *Die Grundbegriffe der Metaphysik. Welt—Endlichkeit—Einsamkeit*. Ed. Friedrich-Wilhelm von Herrmann. 1983, 2004 (1929–1930)./*The Fundamental Concepts of Metaphysics: World, Finitude, Solitude*. Tr. William McNeill and Nicholas Walker. Bloomington: Indiana University Press, 1995.

GA 34 = *Vom Wesen der Wahrheit. Zu Platons Höhlengleichnis und Theätet*. Ed. Hermann Mörchen. 1988, 1997 (1931–1932)./*The Essence of Truth: On Plato's Cave Allegory and "Theaetetus."* Tr. Ted Sadler. London: Continuum, 2002.

GA 36/37 = *Sein und Wahrheit*. Ed. Hartmut Tietjen. 2001 (1933–1934)./*Being and Truth*. Tr. Gregory Fried and Richard Polt. Bloomington: Indiana University Press, 2010.

GA 39 = *Hölderlins Hymnen "Germanien" und "Der Rhein."* Ed. Susanne Ziegler. 1980, 1989, 1999 (1934–1935)./*Hölderlin's Hymns "Germania" and "The Rhine."* Tr. William McNeill and Julia Ireland. Bloomington: Indiana University Press, 2014.

GA 40 = *Einführung in die Metaphysik*. Ed. Petra Jaeger. 1983 (1935)./*Introduction to Metaphysics*. Tr. Gregory Fried and Richard Polt. Revised and expanded ed. New Haven: Yale University Press, 2014.

GA 45 = *Grundfragen der Philosophie. Ausgewählte "Probleme" der "Logik."* Ed. Friedrich-Wilhelm von Herrmann. 1984 (1937–38). / *Basic Questions of Philosophy: Selected "Problems" of "Logic."* Tr. Richard Rojcewicz and André Schuwer. Bloomington: Indiana University Press, 1994.

GA 46 = *Zur Auslegung von Nietzsches II. Unzeitgemäßer Betrachtung "Vom Nutzen und Nachteil der Historie für das Leben."* Ed. Hans-Joachim Friedrich. 2003 (1938–1939)./*Interpretation of Nietzsche's Second Untimely Meditation*. Tr. Ullrich Haase and Mark Sinclair. Bloomington: Indiana University Press, 2016.

GA 53 = *Hölderlins Hymne "Der Ister."* Ed. Walter Biemel. 1984 (1942)./*Hölderlin's Hymn "The Ister."* Tr. William McNeill and Julia Davis. Bloomington: Indiana University Press, 1996.

GA 55 = *Heraklit*. Ed. Manfred S. Frings. 1979, 1987, 1994 (1943–1944).

GA 56/57 = *Zur Bestimmung der Philosophie*. Ed. Bernd Heimbüchel. 1987, 1999 (1919)./*Towards the Definition of Philosophy*. Tr. Ted Sadler. New York: Continuum, 2000.

GA 58 = *Grundprobleme der Phänomenologie*. Ed. Hans-Helmuth Gander. 1992, 2010 (1919–1920)./*Basic Problems of Phenomenology: Winter Semester 1919/1920*. Tr. Scott M. Campbell. London: Continuum, 2013.

GA 59 = *Phänomenologie der Anschauung und des Ausdrucks. Theorie der philosophischen Begriffsbildung*. Ed. Claudius Strube. 1993, 2007 (1920)./*Phenomenology of Intuition and Expression*. Tr. Tracy Colony. London: Continuum, 2010.

GA 60 = *Phänomenologie des religiösen Lebens*. Ed. Matthias Jung, Thomas Regehly, and Claudius Strube. 1995, 2011 (1918–1921)./*The Phenomenology of Religious Life*. Tr. Matthias Fritsch and Jennifer Anna Gosetti-Ferencei. Bloomington: Indiana University Press, 2004.

GA 61 = *Phänomenologische Interpretationen zu Aristoteles. Einführung in die phänomenologische Forschung*. Ed. Walter Bröcker and Käte Bröcker-Oltmanns. 1985, 1994 (1921–1922)./*Phenomenological Interpretations of Aristotle: Initiation into Phenomenological Research*. Tr. Richard Rojcewicz. Bloomington: Indiana University Press, 2008.

GA 62 = *Phänomenologische Interpretationen ausgewählter Abhandlungen des Aristoteles zu Ontologie und Logik*. Ed. Günther Neumann. 2005 (1922).

GA 63 = *Ontologie. Hermeneutik der Faktizität*. Ed. Käte Bröcker-Oltmanns. 1988, 1995 (1923)./*Ontology—The Hermeneutics of Facticity*. Tr. John Van Buren. Bloomington: Indiana University Press, 1999.

GA 64 = *Der Begriff der Zeit*. Ed. Friedrich-Wilhelm von Herrmann. 2004 (1924)./Partial translations: *The Concept of Time: The First Draft of "Being and Time."* Tr. Ingo Farin. London: Continuum, 2011. *The Concept of Time* (bilingual edition). Tr. William McNeill. Oxford: Blackwell, 1992.

GA 65 = *Beiträge zur Philosophie (Vom Ereignis)*. Ed. Friedrich-Wilhelm von Herrmann. 1989, 1994, 2003 (1936–1938)./*Contributions to Philosophy (Of the Event)*. Tr. Richard Rojcewicz and Daniela Vallega-Neu. Bloomington: Indiana University Press, 2012.

GA 66 = *Besinnung*. Ed. Friedrich-Wilhelm von Herrmann. 1997 (1938–1939)./*Mindfulness*. Tr. Parvis Emad and Thomas Kalary. London: Continuum, 2006.

GA 69 = *Die Geschichte des Seyns*. Ed. Peter Trawny. 1998, 2012 (1938–1940)./*The History of Beyng*. Tr. William McNeill and Jeffrey Powell. Bloomington: Indiana University Press, 2015.

GA 70 = *Über den Anfang*. Ed. Paola-Ludovika Coriando. 2005 (1941).

GA 71 = *Das Ereignis*. Ed. Friedrich-Wilhelm von Herrmann. 2009 (1941–1942)./*The Event*. Tr. Richard Rojcewicz. Bloomington: Indiana University Press, 2013.

GA 73 (2 vols., 73.1 and 73.2) = *Zum Ereignis-Denken*. Ed. Peter Trawny. 2013 (1932–1970s).

GA 75 = *Zu Hölderlin—Griechenlandreisen*. Ed. Curd Ochwadt. 2000 (1939–1970)./Partial translation: *Sojourns: The Journey to Greece*. Tr. John P. Manoussakis. Albany: State University of New York Press, 2005.

GA 77 = *Feldweg-Gespräche*. Ed. Ingrid Schüßler, 1995, 2007 (1944–1945)./*Country Path Conversations*. Tr. Bret Davis. Bloomington: Indiana University Press, 2010.

GA 79 = *Bremer und Freiburger Vorträge*. Ed. Petra Jaeger, 1994, 2005 (1949, 1957)./*Bremen and Freiburg Lectures: Insight Into That Which Is and Basic Principles of Thinking*. Tr. Andrew Mitchell. Bloomington: Indiana University Press, 2012.

GA 80.1 = *Vorträge. Teil 1: 1915–1932*. Ed. Günther Neumann. 2016 (1915–1932).

GA 89 = *Zollikoner Seminare*. Ed. Claudius Strube. 1987 (1959–1969)./*Zollikon Seminars: Protocols—Conversations—Letters*. Tr. Franz Mayr and Richard Askay. Evanston: Northwestern University Press, 2001.

GA 94 = *Überlegungen II-VI (Schwarze Hefte 1931–1938)*. Ed. Peter Trawny. 2014./*Ponderings II-VI: Black Notebooks 1931–1938*. Tr. Richard Rojcewicz. Bloomington: Indiana University Press, 2016.

GA 95 = *Überlegungen VII-XI (Schwarze Hefte 1938–1939)*. Ed. Peter Trawny. 2014./*Ponderings VII-XI: Black Notebooks 1938–1939*. Tr. Richard Rojcewicz. Bloomington: Indiana University Press, 2017.

GA 96 = *Überlegungen XII-XV (Schwarze Hefte 1939–1941)*. Ed. Peter Trawny. 2014./*Ponderings XII-XV: Black Notebooks 1939–1941*. Tr. Richard Rojcewicz. Bloomington: Indiana University Press, 2017.

GA 97 = *Anmerkungen I-V (Schwarze Hefte 1942–1948)*. Ed. Peter Trawny. 2015.

OTHER EDITIONS

BH = *Becoming Heidegger: On the Trail of His Early Occasional Writings, 1910–1927*. Ed. Theodore Kisiel and Thomas Sheehan. Evanston: Northwestern University Press, 2007.

BW = *Basic Writings*. Ed. David F. Krell. 2nd ed. New York: HarperCollins, 1993.

EGT = *Early Greek Thinking*. Tr. David F. Krell and Frank A. Capuzzi. New York: Harper & Row, 1975.

ET = *The Essence of Truth: On Plato's Cave Allegory and "Theaetetus."* Tr. Ted Sadler. London: Continuum, 2002.

MFL = *The Metaphysical Foundations of Logic*. Tr. Michael Heim. Bloomington: Indiana University Press, 1984.

OWL = *On the Way to Language*. Tr. Peter D. Hertz and Joan Stambaugh. New York: Harper & Row, 1971.

PLT = *Poetry, Language, Thought*. Tr. Albert Hofstadter. New York: Harper & Row, 1971.

QCT = *The Question Concerning Technology and Other Essays*. Tr. William Lovitt. New York: Harper & Row, 1977.

TK = *Die Technik und die Kehre*. Pfullingen: Neske, 1962./*The Question Concerning Technology and Other Essays*. Tr. William Lovitt. New York: Harper & Row, 1977.

UK = *Der Ursprung des Kunstwerkes*. Stuttgart: Reclam, 1960./"The Origin of the Work of Art." Tr. Albert Hofstadter. In BW.

WCT = *What Is Called Thinking?* Tr. J. Glenn Gray. New York: Harper & Row, 1968.

WP = *What Is Philosophy?* Tr. Jean T. Wilde and William Kluback. New Haven: College & University Press, 1958.

ZS = *Zollikon Seminars: Protocols—Conversations—Letters*. Ed. Medard Boss, tr. Franz Mayr and Richard Askay. Evanston: Northwestern University Press, 2001.

Editors' Introduction

Gregory Fried and Richard Polt

The premise of the New Heidegger Research series is that Martin Heidegger's thought remains thought-provoking. His voluminous and varied writings are, and will continue to be, philosophically relevant. Philosophy today takes place "after Heidegger" in that his views should not be accepted naively, and there are new issues and events that he did not directly address; but it also unfolds "after Heidegger" in that philosophers continue to think in the wake of important and legitimate questions that he raised.

However, this premise needs to be tested and explored. It is incumbent on Heidegger's readers to explain why his thought remains worthy of consideration, to articulate and develop the questions that his work raises, and thus to take up those questions in their own way rather than only elucidating Heidegger's way. This is why our title ends with a question mark.

The responsibility of questioning is especially pressing at a time when the publication of Heidegger's so-called *Black Notebooks* has exposed some disturbing anti-Jewish views and has made it clear that, even after developing extensive critiques of Nazi ideology on the metaphysical level, he continued for years to affirm the necessity of the National Socialist movement as he understood it (GA 95: 408). Given this evidence, most readers would agree more than ever that Heidegger must not be the object of a "Heideggerian" cult. A mature reception of his work must guard against the temptation to take any of his positions as dogma. His writings continue to invite analysis and development—but, especially in light of his political affiliations, they must also be critiqued. To the extent that the questions he raised remain worthy of thought, then, this situation makes it all the more incumbent upon those inspired by Heidegger to make those questions their own, in their own idiom.

With this state of affairs in mind, as the editors of the New Heidegger Research series, we invited the members of our editorial board to write brief essays on what remains philosophically relevant and provocative in Heidegger's work now. We challenged contributors to reflect on the most and least promising elements of Heidegger's legacy and on where his thought leaves philosophy today, over forty years after his death.

Most members of the board were able to accept our invitation, and we were also able to include a few other voices from the diverse world of Heidegger research. The results will allow readers to discover a wealth of interpretive issues and lines of thought that a variety of successful scholars consider important. Our topic has brought out a spectrum of positions, some of which are quite critical of Heidegger even though the authors still see his work as philosophically significant. While some contributors have focused on the *Black Notebooks*, or on political or ethical issues more generally, others have taken the opportunity to look elsewhere for what they consider of lasting importance in Heidegger's thought. All the authors reflect, to some extent, on the significance of Heidegger's work in general, but they have chosen different emphases that allow us to group their chapters into seven categories.

I. Overviews: What are the key ideas and problems in Heidegger's work as a whole? Drew A. Hyland praises Heidegger's insistence on open questioning, while asking why nothing held him back from supporting a supremely "diabolic political regime." Gregory Fried confronts Heidegger's challenge, in the name of temporal finitude, to the Platonic legacy of the West. Daniel O. Dahlstrom and Peter E. Gordon sum up what they see as Heidegger's greatest philosophical achievements and bluntly identify what they consider his greatest failings. As a propaedeutic to an "after Heidegger" Thomas Sheehan argues that Heidegger's own thought, from beginning to end, was a phenomenology of meaningful presence and of appropriated "ex-sistence" as what makes meaningful presence possible.

II. After the *Black Notebooks*: Where do these unique and often troubling texts leave us? Donatella Di Cesare assembles the disquieting discoveries about what she calls Heidegger's "metaphysical anti-Semitism" and explains why, in the view of many readers, they force us to rethink his work as a whole. Peter Trawny reflects on how "we"—the inevitably politicized academic establishment—have been shocked by Heidegger's transformative yet compromised thinking in the *Black Notebooks*. Julia A. Ireland rejects any effort to get Heidegger off the hook, but she also wants to get "us" ourselves "on the hook" by way of closely examining the affinities and discrepancies between Heidegger's thought and Nazi ideology. Babette Babich asks whether and how, in the "aftermath" of the *Notebooks* and in the "wake" of Heidegger's problematic texts, life, and thought, we readers ourselves are thinking.

III. Politics and ethics: What is the root of Heidegger's political and ethical errors? John McCumber points to the concept of the "history of being," which he sees as a remnant of metaphysics; he finds more promise in Heidegger's thoughts on mortality and temporality. Lawrence J. Hatab argues that, to a large extent, Heidegger's analyses of existence and his approach to unconcealment are irreducible to any specific political ideology. Arun Iyer reminds us of the revolutionary impetus in Heidegger's thought, which is not necessarily exhausted by his own failed attempts to participate in a profoundly misguided political revolution. Dennis J. Schmidt finds that Heidegger, despite his flaws, can help us appreciate the entwined phenomena of living philosophically and living ethically.

IV. Life and existence: What calls for attention in Heidegger's thoughts on human life and finite existence? Robert C. Scharff proposes to renew Heidegger's Dilthey-inspired "hermeneutic" challenge to modern philosophy and Husserlian phenomenology, only with "our" surroundings in mind more than his. Eric S. Nelson explains Heidegger's early call to "concreteness," but while he appreciates that call, he doubts that Heidegger does justice to actual life. Charles Guignon and Kevin Aho speak to the impact of Heidegger's account of being-in-the-world and his vision of anxiety and authenticity. Richard Polt focuses on the thought that Dasein's own being is at issue for it; he proposes to extend this insight by applying it to political philosophy and developing a "traumatic ontology." Lee Braver admires Heidegger for fleshing out philosophical abstractions and helping readers become more aware of the traditions that they inhabit. Theodore Kisiel explores the interpretation of existing in Heidegger's early work and connects it to his later concept of *Ereignis*.

V. Phenomenology and ontology: What is worth emulating in Heidegger's styles of phenomenology and his approach to the question of being? Steven Crowell rejects what he sees as the non-phenomenological, objectionably esoteric aspects of Heidegger's thought in order to take up a Heideggerian phenomenology of themes such as reason. Katherine Withy argues that, for Heidegger, meaningful presencing takes place in light of questionable norms. Simon Critchley takes up Heideggerian phenomenology as a call to notice and articulate what is already showing itself. In contrast, François Raffoul proposes that phenomenology must try to think of what can never be shown—the inapparent event of being.

VI. Thinking with late Heidegger: What calls for thought in Heidegger's work after *Being and Time*? William McNeill focuses on the crucial word *Ereignis* and argues that it is rightly translated as "event," although it is no ordinary, "actual" event. David Kleinberg-Levin explores Heidegger's understanding of sight as an event of appropriation. Miguel de Beistegui reflects on the event of thought and argues that, although it is involuntary, as Heidegger claims, its conditions are not of the order of the gift, but of a provocation or shock, which warrants a new thinking of the aesthetic. Günter

Figal adopts Heidegger's phenomenology of the "clearing"—which is not as foreign to the philosophical tradition as Heidegger would have it—in order to think about space. Daniela Vallega-Neu points to Heidegger's "poietic" and "middle-voiced" thought, and calls for a kind of thinking that is attuned to bodily time-spaces. Andrew J. Mitchell draws attention to Heidegger's relational thinking of "things" and the "fourfold," with its potential for a non-anthropocentric ethics. Richard Capobianco argues, through a close reading of a lesser-known lecture from the 1960s, that the late Heidegger leaves phenomenology behind him in order to affirm the independence of being as "*Alētheia*" in relation to the human being.

VII. Openings to others: Can Heidegger's thought help us envision a postmodern, post-Eurocentric, or post-patriarchal future? Iain Thomson explains how Heidegger challenges all "ontotheological" systems and opens the door to postmodern pluralism. Bret Davis discusses an important form of such pluralism in which Heidegger took interest: the dialogue between Eastern and Western thinking. Trish Glazebrook closes our volume by exploring an issue to which Heidegger paid little attention, but where his thought can be drawn upon creatively: gendered ontology in a globalized and technologized world.

Readers who make connections across these chapters will find substantive disagreements about central messages in Heidegger's thought. Does Heidegger succeed in returning to concrete life, or does he just succumb to a new kind of abstraction? Does he teach us to pay attention to the surface, to what appears, or does he challenge us to think about what can never appear directly? Was he always focused on the human, or does the greatest value of his work lie in helping us see past the human world? Is *Ereignis* a distinctive event, or not an event at all?

There are also differences in our authors' hermeneutic approaches. After the publication of the *Black Notebooks*, has it become impossible to separate Heidegger's politics from his philosophy? Should one always read his writings as a whole? Or is it perfectly legitimate to "cherry-pick" his most promising insights?

Are philosophers still trying to catch up to Heidegger, running "after" his far-seeing thought? Or are those who come "after" him able to appropriate the emancipatory and illuminating trends in his thought while avoiding his dead ends? What remains "unthought" in Heidegger's thinking? What are the insights that he himself could not see?

As long as these questions are debated with both passion and thought, Heidegger is continuing to provoke reflection. It is our hope that this volume will help to keep his thinking alive—not as a system or school, but as a wide range of contestations and conversations.

Part I

OVERVIEWS

Chapter 1

Heidegger: Enduring Questions

Drew A. Hyland

I want to begin this short chapter by reaffirming the guiding assumption articulated by our two editors, that despite Heidegger's deplorable political history, there is much, very much, philosophic work that remains to be done in response to his work. As I shall argue, the question of the relation between a philosopher's political life (in the broadest sense of that phrase) and his or her philosophical writing is itself a *philosophical* issue, and certainly one not adequately addressed by rejecting Heidegger as a philosopher or relegating his work to the section of our libraries on the history of Nazism.

The editors have asked what are some of the most pressing and challenging issues for philosophy after—that is, in the philosophical wake of—Heidegger. I want to briefly discuss three issues: first, the centrality of *the question* as the core philosophical stance and speech act in Heidegger; second, and related, Heidegger's development of the distinction between "calculative" and "meditative" thinking and his call to preserve meditative thinking under the threat of the total dominance of calculative thinking; and third, as mentioned earlier, the question of the relation between a philosopher's thinking and the life lived, particularly if that philosophical thinking includes an affirmation of thinking as "beyond good and evil." I turn first to the question of the question.

Book after book of Heidegger's is titled as a question, and as if to underline the importance of this, Heidegger presses the limits of syntax to find alternative ways to formulate the question asked in his titles. Thus we find *Die Frage nach dem Ding* (The Question of the Thing), "Zur Seinsfrage" (On the Question of Being), *Was heißt Denken?* (What Is Called Thinking?), *Was ist das, die Philosophie?* (What Is Philosophy?), *Was ist Metaphysik?* (What Is Metaphysics?), among others. Even *Sein und Zeit* (Being and Time), though not titled as a question, makes it clear from the beginning that the whole purpose of this groundbreaking book is to raise *the question* of the meaning of Being.

And of course, none of Heidegger's texts ask the question of the title and then *answer* it in the book! The point of Heidegger's thinking, that is, is not to "answer" this or that question but rather to *deepen the question-worthiness* of the issue at hand. One might say that the questions Heidegger asks call not for answers but for *responses*, where the difference would be that answers seek for a kind of closure on a given issue, whereas responses seek rather to *open up* that issue, to deepen our sensitivity to its nuances of meaning. In a world increasingly dominated by the kind of thinking that demands answers (more on this presently), Heidegger's thought-path tries to keep alive a kind of thinking that attempts to dwell—and it will demand a dwelling—in what we might call the *open of the question*. That phrase hints at an even larger issue: for the call for questioning as the fundamental speech act of philosophy occurs as a response to an *open*, and an open which, if Heidegger is right, will ever remain open (even if always also partially hidden), not one that will be "closed" or "solved" by any future thinker. Throughout his career, Heidegger names this open with various provocative words: Being, event of appropriation (*Ereignis*), that-which-regions (*das Gegnet*), clearing (*die Lichtung*), and the Open. But for me, what remains "the same" through these various pathways is what Heidegger sees as the appropriate response to them, which remains, always, questioning. One might say that whereas for almost all of philosophy since Descartes, the fundamental philosophic speech act has been the *assertion*—the assertion of "truths," of theories, of proofs, of conclusions, of refutations—Heidegger, by contrast, is trying to preserve for philosophy the fundamentality of that speech act which is questioning.

In this, it strikes me that there is a deep kinship with a thinker that Heidegger himself might be uncomfortable acknowledging as akin: the Platonic Socrates, and in particular, Socrates's sustaining of *aporia* as his very stance of philosophy. In Plato's *Apology*, at the very end of his life, Socrates characterizes his "human wisdom" precisely as his *aporia*, his recognition that he is not wise, a recognition whose appropriate response is always that of questioning. To be sure, in many dialogues, read superficially, Socrates *seems* to be seeking closure, to want a "definition" of courage, or friendship, or *sophrosynē*, or beauty, or knowledge itself. But we must note—and surely Plato wanted us to note this—that these attempted definitions, these apparent attempts at the closure of full knowledge, *always fail*. Do the dialogues therefore fail? Not at all! The dialogues succeed, succeed in opening up for us the question-worthiness of the issue at hand, help us to deepen our understanding of the *call of the question* concerning courage, or friendship, or knowledge. Socrates succeeds, moreover, not in *reducing* his interlocutors and us, Plato's readers, to *aporia*, but in *raising them up* to the *achievement* of *aporia*. In this affirmation of *aporia* and its questioning, Heidegger will always be a Socratic. And in a world that increasingly demands answers, a world that increasingly understands questions as a kind of weakness to be overcome, Heidegger seeks to sustain for us a recognition of the power of the question and of the open that gives us the question. One task for philosophy after Heidegger, surely, is to continue cultivating this openness, to sustain the priority of the question for philosophy and for human living.

Second, and intimately related to this, is the preservation of what Heidegger calls in his "Memorial Address" to the citizens of Messkirch "meditative thinking," or, in his "Conversation on a Country Path," "releasement," or sometimes simply "thinking." The general point is this: Heidegger distinguishes between two basic kinds of thinking. The first is the one we use all the time in our "pragmatic" activities of life. In the "Memorial Address" he calls it "calculative thinking" (*rechnendes Denken*). It is characterized by being goal oriented, by its emphasis on order, system, and problem solving. Logic and mathematics are perhaps the paradigms of calculative thinking, though one gets the impression that almost all goal-oriented or problem-solving thinking counts as calculative. The second kind of thinking, "meditative" thinking, "releasement," or just "thinking," is quite different. Understandably, it is less precisely defined, since it is characterized not by logic, an urge to system, or a goal-oriented striving for closure on a given issue, but on an openness, yet not an openness to a specific, pre-calculated end. In the "Memorial Address" Heidegger calls this "openness to the mystery." In the "Conversation on a Country Path" he speaks of it as "releasement" (*Gelassenheit*), a kind of "waiting" but not an "awaiting," where the difference is that "awaiting" is an expectation of some specific happening, whereas "waiting" remains open to what may eventuate. It is in this openness that the kinship with questioning becomes clear. Both the questioning he espouses and the "releasement" he commends are characterized by a certain openness, not a predetermining of outcomes or even expecting certain outcomes. The English phrase "to hold open to question," taken in its full sense, captures something of what Heidegger intends by this mode of thinking.

It must be emphasized that there is nothing in principle *wrong* with calculative thinking. To the contrary, it is imperative for "getting along" in the world, and the last thing that Heidegger would ask is that we do without it. The problem he sees is that particularly and increasingly in our epoch, calculative thinking threatens to become *the only* acceptable mode of thinking, indeed to be regarded as thinking itself. Meditative thinking, releasement, may be lost as a human possibility as the emphasis on technology, on calculation, on statistical analysis, takes over our lives more and more. The point of Heidegger's drawing the distinction is to keep alive the very possibility of this other thinking, this thinking that, Heidegger seems to hold, in the end is what makes us human, for one fine day we shall learn that machines are much better than we are at calculative thinking.

I think that in this distinction Heidegger identifies a very important issue in the modern epoch. The dominance of technology, what might be regarded as the triumph of calculative thinking, is all around us. Even in the intellectual world in which we academics live, we see its dominance everywhere. We must all "document" our teaching ability through "measures" often called "learning assessment." The legitimacy of traditional "liberal arts" education is being increasingly questioned precisely because its "practical" value is not obvious to all. In the "discipline" (itself a calculative word) of philosophy, the dominant understanding of philosophy today is called "analytic" philosophy, a movement whose explicit aim is to "solve philosophical problems." Heidegger's challenge in this regard is therefore ever more important and ever more difficult: how do we preserve that manifestly less "practical," less goal-oriented, less closure-achieving thinking in an age where those very values are increasingly dominant? One "calculative" issue much discussed today has to do with the fact that machines—computers in particular—are increasingly capable of doing all the calculative thinking that we humans do, only more accurately and faster. Is Heidegger then perhaps right that it is this "other" thinking that would make and keep us human?

I turn to the third issue I want to address by noting that so far as I can see, not a thing I have discussed so far could be plausibly associated with a particular political standpoint, much less with the specific political standpoint which Heidegger himself took at least in the early 1930s, that of Nazism. Even less would questioning and meditative thinking have anything to do with anti-Semitism, a vice in which Heidegger also indulged. Yet questioning and this "released" mode of thinking are important and sustained themes in Heidegger's thought-path. They both therefore stand as manifest refutations of any claim that Heidegger's thinking is "through and through" Nazistic or anti-Semitic. Such a claim is nonsense.

Nevertheless, Heidegger *was* a Nazi, at least for a while, and an anti-Semite, and therefore the question must be raised: what are we to make of the fact that one of the greatest philosophers of the twentieth century was an enthusiastic advocate of what was surely the most diabolic political regime of that century? And we must also note that to ask this very question is to raise a *philosophical* issue.

As indicated earlier, the issue here should *not* be something like "Was Heidegger *really* a Nazi and anti-Semite, is his published thinking Nazistic and anti-Semitic, and therefore should we stop taking him seriously as a philosopher?" The answers to these questions are too easy: yes, he was, at least for a while, a Nazi and anti-Semite. No, his philosophic thinking is neither Nazistic nor anti-Semitic, at least not in any comprehensive sense. So, no, his work remains genuinely and profoundly philosophic and should continue to be taken seriously by serious philosophers. We can and should still wonder and be troubled by the few now notorious references to the "inner truth and greatness" of Nazism and the "Jewification" of culture, but doing so, I think, should not allow us to miss the genuinely philosophical issue at stake in this sorry situation.

The real issue for me has always been not "was Heidegger a Nazi or anti-Semite?" or "is his philosophy Nazistic or anti-Semitic?" both of which have been easily answered earlier, but rather this: why was there apparently nothing in his philosophy, nothing in his thinking, that enabled him, no, that demanded of him, to say "No!" to anything like the Nazis or anti-Semitism? To raise this question is to raise a most serious issue about the efficacy of Heidegger's thought-project as a whole. But, as I shall argue, it raises that issue not just about Heidegger but about much of twentieth-century philosophy.

Considerations such as these lead me to suggest a different and in a way more demanding formulation of the question of Heidegger's involvement with Nazism: was there anything in his philosophy that should have led Heidegger to *reject* National Socialism and its accompanying anti-Semitism, even though we know that it did not? And if not, what are we to make of a philosophic view that contains nothing within it that might call for the rejection of a political position as diabolical as Nazism?

I suggest that there is nothing in Heidegger's thought that would have forbidden the affirmation of Nazism because from at least the time of *Being and Time* (1927), Heidegger claimed that all questions of ethics and politics were "ontic" questions of "everydayness," whereas his thought, concerned always with the question of *Being*, was "ontological" and therefore prior to and independent of questions of ethics and politics. In *Being and Time*, developing the thesis that values are "ontic" and even "present-at-hand," that is, treated as objective or quasi-objective "things" in the world, Heidegger argues that "these value characters themselves are rather just ontical characteristics of those entities which have the kind of Being possessed by things" (MR 132). Much later in the work, in the development of his notion of ontological "guilt," and insisting that we must not think of guilt within the usual, "ontic" parameters of evil or good, he adds that "Just as the *bonum* and its *privatio* have the same ontological origin in the ontology of the *present-at-hand*, this ontology also applies to the idea of 'value,' which has been abstracted from these."[1]

In a somewhat later work, the *Letter on Humanism*, Heidegger preserves the theme that the fundamental thinking of the sort that he pursues, the thinking of Being, is prior to and therefore independent of any thinking of values, that "here, as always, thinking in values is the greatest blasphemy imaginable against Being" (BW 251), and later adds that "such thinking [his thinking of Being] has no result. It has no effect. It satisfies its essence in that it is."[2] Given convictions such as these, it is hardly surprising that Heidegger's thought would contain no teachings that would forbid—or affirm—a given ethical or political standpoint. Put differently, Heidegger's thinking of Being, precisely when he is being consistent, is ethically and politically *vacuous*. It would seem to follow from Heidegger's position, given the radical separation of this "thinking of Being" from all questions of value or the good, that, when faced with "ontic" questions of political commitment or moral choice, this greatest of fundamental ontologists has no more philosophic foundation for his ethical and political commitments than any other "good old boy," whether from the Black Forest or elsewhere.[3] His own philosophic position allows and even implicitly warrants his being dictated in such choices by local prejudice. After all, on his view, what else is there?

To repeat, in my view the problem with Heidegger's position is not that it is inherently wicked but that it is ethically and politically vacuous. That is, the fault of his position is not that it *led* him to Nazism, or that it is implicitly or explicitly a *defense* of Nazism, but rather that there was nothing there to *prevent* it, to say no to it. Heidegger's situation teaches us that the "space" opened up by a philosophy "beyond good and evil," a philosophy which claims to excuse itself from questions of political and ethical commitment, is all too likely to be filled by unreflective local prejudice.

However, having said this of Heidegger, it must immediately be added that he is hardly alone in this predicament among twentieth-century philosophers. From the positivists' call for "no value judgments" to the "pure description" of phenomenology, from analytic philosophy to structuralism and deconstruction, it would not be an exaggeration to say that the separation of ethical and political commitment from "genuine," "deep," "fundamental," or "authentic" philosophic thought, and therefore almost inevitably the reduction of such commitments to convention or prejudice, has been characteristic of much—although happily not all—of twentieth-century philosophy. How we arrived at this point would take a long, complicated study of the history of philosophy. Nevertheless, having criticized Heidegger for this predicament, I hasten to add that he is just one particularly painful and troubling instantiation of a problem of twentieth-century philosophy itself.

To return our focus to Heidegger, I want to acknowledge that the position I am espousing puts me in a complicated situation. On the one hand, I want to insist that despite Heidegger's deplorable ethical and political conduct in his own life, particularly his affirmation of Nazism and his rather vulgar anti-Semitism, there is much in his philosophy that is nevertheless profound and provocative in the best sense. But on the other hand, I would not want this to be interpreted as *excusing* Heidegger—or any other thinker—from the demand of the Platonic Socrates that one's philosophy should surely have something to do with the quality of a life lived by the lights of that philosophy. Something was clearly missing from Heidegger's thinking, something that would have, should have, enabled him to reject the deplorable politics and prejudice that he nevertheless affirmed, something like, again to return to Socrates, a concern with the good. Surely it is vital for those of us moved by the power of Heidegger's thinking to rethink his own work with an eye to either finding hidden in it or by adding to it, an affirmation of the concern with the good.[4]

It is crucial to note that I say a *concern* with the good. The Platonic Socrates, to return to him briefly, fully appreciated the issue here. When, in Plato's *Republic*, Socrates raises the issue of what he calls at first "the idea of the good," and then more often simply "the good," he does so by acknowledging both the absolute fundamentality of the issue of the good, yet the enduring instability of our access to it. In his very first introduction of the good, at *Republic* 505a, he first states how fundamental it is, that "it is by availing oneself of it along with just things and the rest that they become useful and beneficial," and even more strongly that "this is what every soul pursues and for the sake of which it does everything," but then immediately follows it with a second acknowledgment, that "we don't have sufficient knowledge of it." This coupling of two great insights, of the affirmation of the fundamental inescapability of the issue of the good, yet of our sustained and inevitable *aporia* concerning it, gets repeated virtually at every subsequent mention of it. On the one hand, against Heidegger (and all too much of modern philosophy), Socrates would insist that there is nothing "merely ontic" about the good. On the contrary, it is an unavoidable issue of our very *being*, indeed of the being of the whole. That is to say, using Heideggerian language, the good is *ontological* through and through.[5] The thinking of Being *cannot avoid* the issue of the good if it wants to be comprehensive, for nothing, Socrates says, is *more* comprehensive to our being—indeed to the being of the whole—than the good. On the other hand, and here Heidegger would have the thought-space to acknowledge this, our *access* to the good, always and in every situation, is *open to question*. We do not and cannot *know* the good, yet we cannot avoid its issue and its power.

The Platonic Socrates, in my judgment, has his own complicated response to this predicament.[6] Heidegger, by contrast, seeks to avoid it altogether, by jettisoning the very issue of the good from the realm of "fundamental" thinking. I close by urging us all to reconsider the power, the urgency, and the necessity of the Platonic response, which is to say, to reconsider whether we can avoid including in our philosophical thinking, at the deepest level, the *question* of the good.

NOTES

1. MR 332 (Heidegger's emphasis). For other indications of the ontic status of value, see MR 37, 91, 133, 190, 191, 264, and 265.

2. BW 259; see also pp. 261–69. For a view which does not cite passages such as these but otherwise plausibly develops the basis in Heidegger's philosophy both for his early involvement with National Socialism and for his later "withdrawal" from it, see Karsten Harries, "Heidegger As Political Thinker," *Review of Metaphysics* 29:4 (June 1976): 642–69.

3. For a study that argues, in effect, that this absence is precisely its virtue, that there *can* be no "foundational principles" for our political commitments, see Reiner Schürmann, *Heidegger on Being and Acting: From Principles to Anarchy* (Bloomington: Indiana University Press, 1987). For the best account that certain ethical principles are at least *implicit* in Heidegger's work, see Lawrence Hatab, *Ethics and Finitude: Heideggerian Contributions to Moral Philosophy* (New York: Rowman and Littlefield, 2000).

4. The first of these challenges has been best responded to by Lawrence Hatab in his *Ethics and Finitude*.

5. Or even "supraontological," since Socrates insists at *Republic* 509b that the good is "beyond being."

6. I have attempted to support this claim at some length in my "*Aporia*, the Longer Road, and the Good," *Graduate Faculty Philosophy Journal* 32:1 (2011): 145–75, and in my "Philosophy, Political Ideology, and the Good: The Case of Martin Heidegger," presented at Suffolk University, April 2016.

Chapter 2

On Beyond Heidegger

Gregory Fried

In considering what it might mean to think "after Heidegger," it is well to remember Heidegger's motto to his Collected Writings: we should read these texts as "*Wege, nicht Werke*," "Ways, not works" (GA 1: 437). This fits with his wish not to have "Heideggerians" as his followers. At his most generous, then, Heidegger did not want those who read him to become overly entangled in the claims and terminology of his published work (e.g., GA 14: 30/24), but rather that we find our way into the questions that animate that work and make them our own, in our own way. This has always been a serious challenge, because of the mesmerizing power of Heidegger's ideas and the hermetic difficulty of his conceptual vocabulary, both of which require a great deal of patience and devotion to understand well enough to engage on one's own terms—and by then it may be too late for independent thinking. And so, if what is most important is entering into the way of thinking, we need to say more about what those most significant pathways are and what can continue to motivate our own inquiring.

The first signpost for a path on beyond Heidegger is his daring. Daring is an explicit theme in Heidegger's work, beginning with his interpretation in *Introduction to Metaphysics* (1935) of Sophocles's so-called Ode to Man in *Antigone*, where Heidegger attributes daring—in Greek, *tolma*, in German, *Wagnis*—to the one who ventures forth beyond the given strictures of the city (GA 40: 170). *Tolma* also governs at least the initial spirit of the *Black Notebooks*: in 1932, Heidegger quotes Plato's *Theaetetus* as the epigram to the first volume: *panta gar tolmēteon*—"we must dare [or risk, wager] everything" (GA 94: 3). The German verb *wagen* and noun *Wagnis* echo the English "wager," as both verb and noun. Heidegger's *Wagen* echoes Pascal's Wager, which lays all of being and all of time on the line. There is something to the idea that philosophy must embody the spirit of daring: if thinking is not willing to venture past accepted opinion, it can never be free. The "I am" of Heidegger's letter to Löwith points to that spirit: he discerns a scholasticism in the practice of academic philosophy that prevents it from engaging with life as it is lived.[1] That daring is also present in *Being and Time*, where Heidegger calls for a *gigantomachia peri tēs ousias* (SZ 2), a battle of the gods against the giants over "the question of the meaning of Being" (SZ 1). It was the giants who stormed Mount Olympus, and by suggesting that the question of Being has not been asked, at least not properly, since before Plato, Heidegger is mounting a frontal assault against the Olympians of the Western tradition. In the years after *Being and Time*, Heidegger makes it only more clear that he holds Plato responsible for the West's decline into metaphysics and nihilism, and he is bold enough, or megalomaniacal enough, to believe that through himself, thinking might find a way past the West's crisis.

While there may be grandeur to such philosophical daring, there is also danger, and not just the personal risk of suffering from delusions of grandeur. Heidegger's assault on the entire Western tradition, especially upon the Platonism he sees as underlying it, "risks everything" in more than an obscure philosophical dispute about ontology; it also attacks the entire edifice of liberal democracy erected from the Enlightenment, a world-structure that Heidegger traces back to Platonism: "The entire spiritual Dasein of the West is determined to this day by this doctrine of [Plato's] ideas" (GA 36/37: 151). Heidegger wants to refute an understanding of Being he attributes to a Platonism pervading the entire Western history, including its science, politics, and social life. This means that his critique of Western thought—that it is a metaphysics that proceeds from Plato's ascription of world-transcendence, universality, permanence, and placelessness to Being—also applies to the universalism of post-Enlightenment liberalism that ascribes metaphysical properties, such as rights, to human beings, on the basis of timeless principles, regardless of history and place. A passage from a late-1933 lecture course epitomizes this understanding:

> If we talk of [Plato's] doctrine of ideas, then we are displacing the fundamental question [about truth and Being] into the framework of ideas. If one interprets ideas as representations and thoughts that contain a value, a norm, a law, a rule, such that ideas then become conceived of as norms, then the one subject to these norms is the human being—not the historical human being, but rather the human being in general, the human being in itself, or humanity. Here [that is, in Platonism in all its forms], the conception of the human being is one of a *rational being in general*. In the Enlightenment and in liberalism, this conception achieves a definite form. Here all of the powers against which we must struggle today have their root. Opposed to this conception are the *finitude*, *temporality*, and *historicity* of human beings.
>
> (GA 36/37: 166)

When, in *Being and Time*, Heidegger interprets Being on the horizon of time, he understands that what is essential, to use that word guardedly, about human existence is that as Dasein, we are always already located in a space of meaning that we ever and again must interpret and reinterpret; we are radically finite, embedded in history as a fundamental feature of our temporality. To recuperate *this* sense of Being is not merely about abstruse ontology: it dares to reject the notion that what it means *to be* properly human is to respect universal norms, from Platonism's *eidos* as the transcendent essence of ethics and justice, through to the secular liberal Enlightenment and the notion of human rights. Slavoj Žižek has understood that Heidegger's project involves such risks when he says that "Heidegger took the right step, but in the wrong direction" in 1933 by siding with the Nazis.[2] What Žižek intends, of course, is to affirm Heidegger's daring to rupture the Western historical tradition in revolution, to take a leap, but he wishes that leap had been to the Left rather than the Right.

This break from the West's Platonism links daring, the first signpost, to a second one: Heidegger's history of Being, his *Seinsgeschichte*. The appeal of Heidegger's wager is that, given some hard work and an open mind, it offers a powerful and plausible alternative to the Western tradition's trajectory, which Heidegger describes as resulting in the crisis of nihilism in a modernity that has exhausted its own history. That crisis is itself a plausible diagnosis of modernity, and not only because the accomplishments of science and technology are, to any candid observer, Janus-faced:[3] modernity promises the conquest of nature, disease, and want, on the one hand, and, on the other, threatens the cataclysms of global climate change, drug-resistant pandemics, and nuclear war, if not the outright obsolescence of the human species in the face of radically transformative genetic engineering or digital-robotic cybernetics. Heidegger always insisted that such ontic catastrophes were only the epiphenomena of a deeper crisis, what he called the oblivion or the abandonment of Being. The "of" here is crucial, because it is not merely his claim that we have forgotten Being, but also that Being has forsaken us. What does this hieratic pronouncement mean? What does Being have to do with the crises we face?

Everything depends on how seriously we take Heidegger's history of Being and whether, if we do take it seriously, we agree with his account of its trajectory. At the core of that story is the idea that not even Plato is responsible, as Plato, for that trajectory, but rather that every thinker is a conduit for thinking, that what Being means to historical humanity happens *to* us through the thinkers of the tradition we share. To take Heidegger's history seriously, one must confront his narrative: that through Plato, Being gets interpreted as a trans-temporal domain of universal ideas, that this gets taken up into the Judeo-Christian conception of an eternal creator God as the ultimate source of reality, that Cartesian subjectivity takes over God's relationship to the world in modernity, and that Nietzsche's will to power represents the final exhaustion of this metaphysics. For Heidegger, the catastrophes of nuclear war, climate change, industrialized genocide, the pending cybernetic replacement of human thought and labor, and so on, spring from a refusal or simply an inability to think Being in a way that is not metaphysical, that is, as a Supreme Being or an Ultimate Reality, some imputed universal essence of the real, be it mathematical physics or the will to power, that might serve as final foundation for submitting the entire world to domination and control.

This is why Heidegger's question of the meaning of Being is decisive. It is very difficult to try to express what is at issue in this question without lapsing into Heideggerian jargon, but I think that Thomas Sheehan does very well by explaining this as a question about how meaning is possible for us, as occupants of a world that is already intelligible to us, and about how meaning itself happens.[4] Anything "is" for us only *as* meaningful, *as* what we take it to be, even when we are mistaken. As a landmark in the domain of philosophy, the question of Being is about as fundamental as it gets: it seems to ask about the nature of everything, of reality itself, the whole of what is. But Heidegger insists that asking what something is, or indeed what is as a whole, presumes we know already what it means *to be*, which is in fact profoundly obscure, not obvious. Because he holds that the question of Being is a question about how things can *mean* to us, and how meaning itself happens, Heidegger argues that Being is *temporal*: meaning happens; it is given, it unfolds and lingers, and shifts and fades over time—or, to use Heidegger's locution, Being *presences* and *absences*. That presencing and absencing of the world of historical meaning is nothing that we can ever get behind and control—or, if we do, it means that human beings will cease to be human, for there will no longer be any more genuine questions, only problems in bringing the world, including ourselves, to heel.

Of course, one need not have read Heidegger to see that we are poised on the brink of disaster. One can also recognize that a prime element of that disaster is the hubris of human reason, proclaiming that science and technology, as well as the organizational efficacy of reason itself, will be our salvation, as promised by Bacon and Descartes.[5] There will be no technical or technological solution to this crisis because at bottom it is a crisis in how we think—about the world and what it means for us or for anything *to be*. Is the world a collection of things, ourselves included, to be understood as a domain of facts and natural laws abstracted from historical meaning, and therefore ultimately subject to codification and manipulation as information, materiel, and quantums of power—what Heidegger called the *Ge-stell*, the framework, the enframing, or the im-position, in which all of nature is contained and arranged as a pool of resources, including human resources, for the sake of power? Or is the world truly only a world as an historical world, sustained by the stories we tell about it, that requires constant reinterpretation so that the stories don't go stale? If it is the latter, then if we treat it as the former, as the framework, we are bound for disaster, because we fail to accept our finitude and our fallibility. Like the magician's apprentice, we will never get behind "reality" far enough to dominate it in the way our arrogance aspires. Our own finitude will finally get the better of us. Ask yourself, what are the odds that humanity will make it through this twenty-first century without some world-historical catastrophe, and if those odds strike you as alarmingly bad, then we have much thinking to do.

What help is Heidegger in all this? Isn't the warning about human arrogance as old as the legend of Icarus? But if read seriously, Heidegger forces us to confront the meaning of the arc of Western history, which has now merged with planetary history in the modern age, and to reevaluate its most salient thinkers through a conceptual lens that is capable of jarring us out of our complacency about the implications of history's trajectory. This by no means requires that we agree with Heidegger about the meaning of that history, only that there are questions worth asking about it. For me, the most decisive point in this tale lies with Plato, because I agree with Heidegger that Plato is responsible for much of our history's trajectory.

And here is the third pathmark beyond Heidegger: to think, and genuinely to think for ourselves, after Heidegger, requires that we question the monolithic, mono-directional story he tells about that history as the history of metaphysics and the forgetting of Being, including the accusation against Plato as the onset of metaphysics. As brilliant as Heidegger's many readings of figures in the history of philosophy may be, thinking after him calls upon us to rethink those figures in dialogue with his readings, because his interpretation of the history of Being goes too far in locking them all into the story of metaphysics, with only the thinkers before Socrates, and perhaps some scattered figures such as Eckhart and Hölderlin after him, escaping this straightjacketed account. The effect of this too often is to close us off from thinking again with these thinkers, and thereby from unlocking possibilities that have gone unnoticed in the larger stream of history and which might point to possibilities other than the apocalyptic ones Heidegger augurs. This should begin with Plato himself, as Stanley Rosen and Drew Hyland have argued. Without going into great detail here, my own hunch for thinking after Heidegger involves asking to what extent what he calls metaphysics, the Platonic postulating of ideas and ideals beyond history, is an inevitable feature of the human condition. Rather than being a betrayal of thinking, a qualified Platonic idealism is necessary for thinking's orientation and for ethical action, so long as we live up to our call to questioning, one that may counterbalance the nihilism of human hubris.

Heidegger said that "questioning is the piety of thinking" (GA 7: 36). This is not so much a statement as an invitation to find the balance between hubris and resignation. Thinking after Heidegger must be temporal in this sense, because finding the balance is a matter of *phronēsis* that never comes to rest. Heidegger's invitation is paradoxical, because "piety" ordinarily signals the recognition of limits, the boundaries of respect beyond which thought and deed must not transgress. Yet questioning is a form of *tolma*, a daring and dangerous transgression beyond the expectations of our finitude in received opinion. To think, then, is to question the given in its very givenness, but if questioning is how thinking is pious, because thinking cannot be what it is without running against such limits of understanding, what boundaries does it recognize in this piety?

How does this questioning-as-thinking not careen off into hubris and impiety? Perhaps by learning that thinking not only questions the given in its givenness, but also the very giving of the given, what Heidegger called the *Es gibt*. What gives? If the given is the world of meaning into which we are thrown which forms the horizons, and so the limits, of our understanding, and if givenness is the brute facticity of this rather than that world of historical meaning we inhabit, then the giving of the given, what Heidegger called the "event" (*Ereignis*) that makes human beings and a world of historical meaning belong as proper to one another, is something that we can never get behind. Yet, we only run up against that limit and genuinely experience it by questioning, and as questioning, which is what makes it the piety of thinking. That limit is also where the hubris of thinking, its daring, encounters its own finitude and therefore can strike a balance—but only if daring accepts this limit with gratitude rather than rage.

Such talk may seem abstruse in the extreme, but at stake is Being in the sense of meaning, how things and a world are meaningful to and for us. Plato captured this dynamic in the allegory of the cave, where the prisoners inhabit a realm of meaning as given, but some manage to push at its limits and escape beyond; yet even when they do, they run up against a further limit, and so they return to the bounded world of the cave. Now, some might argue that Plato's escaped cave dweller precisely does not reach a limit but rather attains the end in the sense of the fulfillment of all wisdom out in the light of the sun. I cannot rehearse here my analysis in "Back to the Cave,"[6] but this fulfillment interpretation assumes that Socrates's *myth* about philosophers attaining and retaining the Idea of the Good is Plato's last word on philosophy; instead, not even Socrates pretends to such final fulfillment of wisdom; philosophy for him is always a striving for the truth, not its possession, a striving, led forth by the projection of the ideas as beacons, not dogma.

In the allegory, Socrates says that the founders cannot permit the freed prisoners "what is now permitted . . . To remain up there [out in the sun] . . . and not be willing to go down again" into the cave (519d). This makes sense in the context of the parable: presumably the escapee could survive and indeed thrive out in the light, but *we* cannot simply leave our bodies behind and live entirely in the life of the mind. Even the bookish scholar and the recluse monk depend on the polity that supports their contemplation, directly or indirectly. We are always already compelled to engage in the cycle of daring rupture from and reconstructive return to the embodied and historically situated world of givens that we share with others. In Plato's account, the returning escapees, the putative philosophers, do not merely do nothing but contemplate back in the cave; their prior transgression of limits allows them to lead, presumably by reconfiguring more justly how the dwellers understand their world. But they do so only to a degree. The released prisoners who return to govern do not attempt to transform the cave entirely or to lead everyone out, because their ambition has been tempered by the realization that dwelling in a world always requires and cannot entirely escape the given. The world may be nudged and coaxed and bent toward transformed meanings, but the balance between hubris and modesty recognizes that total transformation would imply that human thinking could reconstitute meaning in its totality and ex nihilo. Were this possible, it would be the ultimate in impiety, for it would mean the end of human-Being as a questioning that runs up against the limit and returns to its dwelling with a balanced understanding of what must be accepted and what transformed in one's historical situatedness.

Heidegger's mistake about Plato was a failure to see that Plato also understood the piety of thinking; Plato saw that without projecting the ideas and ideals about the world we share as the *zōon politikon*, questioning can gain no foothold in its struggle, its *polemos*, with the limits of given meaning. Heidegger misses this projecting as a fundamental feature of lived experience as a phenomenon, both in how we encounter what we call the natural world and how we encounter the ethical life of the social world, if we take them seriously as question-worthy. The projecting of hypotheses, of ideas and ideals, need not be the static, metaphysical dogma Heidegger takes it to be, but precisely the way we can find our balance in the historical dialectic between hubristic daring against and resigned acceptance of the given. To experience the given as a gift, then, is the prelude to what Heidegger called *Denken* as *Danken*, thinking as thanking (GA 8: 142–47). To be thankful for the gift of a meaningful world is to dare to test its limits. This requires struggling with questions of truth and justice in the world we inhabit, while recognizing that the most we can do is reinterpret and reconstruct that world's meaning, not recreate it all in our own image, as if meaning as a totality were something we could create rather than always already inhabit.

To think "after" Heidegger is therefore not to follow in his wake by mimicking his terminology, nor is it to blindly agree with him that philosophy is at an end in the dusk of metaphysics and therefore to embrace the spreading darkness, nor is it to recognize that Heidegger offered us only blind alleys and that we must simply get out of them to get past him. Rather, thinking after Heidegger demands that we recognize that we inhabit a world in crisis, but a crisis in the Greek sense of *krisis*, a moment of decision where what the world is and means is at stake. To take up this challenge means questioning what it means to think, what thinking is about, and how the currents of the history of philosophy may underlie the impending catastrophes of the natural and human worlds—so that the catastrophe in thinking may be the worst one of all.

Far from mimicking Heidegger in thinking after him, we must bring our own traditions back alive, rediscovering in the phenomena of our own experience, in our own idioms, and in our traditions, a renewed language for expressing what is at issue in the question of the meaning of Being, on beyond Heidegger.

NOTES

1. Martin Heidegger, letter to Karl Löwith, August 19, 1921, in Karl Löwith, *Martin Heidegger and European Nihilism*, ed. Richard Wolin, tr. Gary Steiner (New York: Columbia University Press, 1995), 236.
2. See Slavoj Žižek, "Why Heidegger Made the Right Step in 1933" and Gregory Fried, "Where's the Point? Slavoj Žižek and the Broken Sword," both in *International Journal of Žižek Studies* 1:4 (2007), http://zizekstudies.org/index.php/IJZS/issue/view/3.
3. I am grateful to Robert Scharff for this insight.
4. See Thomas Sheehan, *Making Sense of Heidegger: A Paradigm Shift* (London: Rowman & Littlefield International, 2015).
5. The most pithy expression of this ambition comes from Descartes, who argued in *Discourse on Method* that "it is possible to find a practical philosophy, by means of which, knowing the force and the actions of fire, water, air, the stars the heavens, and all the other bodies that surround us, just as distinctly as we know the various skills of our craftsmen, we might be able, in the same way, to use them for all the purposes for which they are appropriate, and thus render ourselves, as it were, masters and possessors of nature": *Discourse on Method and Meditations on First Philosophy*, 4th ed., tr. Donald A. Cress (Indianapolis, IN: Hackett, 1998), 35.
6. See Gregory Fried, "Back to the Cave: A Platonic Rejoinder to Heidegger," in *Heidegger and the Greeks*, ed. Drew Hyland and John P. Manoussakis (Bloomington: Indiana University Press, 2006).

Chapter 3

In Heidegger's Wake

Daniel O. Dahlstrom

It ain't over till it's over.

—Yogi Berra

This volume's title can be taken as a question of what philosophical tasks remain in the wake of what Heidegger's philosophy did and did not accomplish. Or it may be waggishly questioning whether Heidegger's thinking is a legitimate marker of any philosophical tasks at all. But the title can also be probing whether we have Heidegger's philosophy in our rear view mirrors. Perhaps we have no clearer idea of what it means to be "over" his philosophy than he, in his more sober moments, admitted having of what "getting over" and "winding back" metaphysics means.

The following remarks are made in the spirit of all three questions. In the first part I sketch five aspects of Heidegger's thinking that continue to point the way for thinking in the present. In the second part I review shortcomings and missteps in his style of writing and thinking.

FIVE MAJOR CONTRIBUTIONS

With no evaluative intent, the following sketch of Heidegger's contributions sets aside his invaluable discussions of such themes as language and freedom, moods and tools, humanism and religious life, things and dwelling (to name only a few) as well as his innovative, if also frequently iconoclastic interpretations of past philosophers.

1.1 Being and existence. According to Heidegger, the tradition of Western metaphysics (the science of being) suffers from being a kind of super-physics, drawing its categories for everything from only a part of reality, the part that is not distinctively human. His fundamental ontology reverses this approach by taking its cues from an analysis of what is distinctively human (existential analysis). Setting forth this fundamental thesis about being and existence—namely, the inseparability of the traditional question of what it means to be from the question of the meaning of human existence—is among Heidegger's central contributions to philosophy. Through his insistence on this fundamental thesis, he challenges a recurrent tendency of Western thinking from antiquity to the present, while showing, by example, that philosophical analysis should not be confined to scientific theories, but firmly grounded in considerations of the sorts of concrete situations and decisions that make up a human life.

The problem that remains pressing is how to sustain these existentially grounded considerations without deadening them into a system or an objectifying scientific treatment. The problem, in other words, is the nature of the very enterprise we call "philosophy." In his own development Heidegger faced this problem (for more discussion of this development, see Robert Scharff's contribution to the present volume). Shortly after the publication of *Sein und Zeit* he comes to eschew the very idea that philosophy can take the form of a science (an "objectification of being," as he once labeled his early project). Instead of pursuing ontology and metaphysics in a revolutionary way, he increasingly criticizes them. In his mature writings, he heralds the task of thinking and the end of philosophy (though in writings from the same period he also equates thinking and philosophy). To his credit, Heidegger's thinking is never merely a critical philosophy, a criticism from an explicitly assumed perspective (in Kant's case, e.g., formal logic and its forms of judgments, the foundation of categories). Instead, even if he wavers at times, his thinking predominantly exemplifies a hermeneutic phenomenology: returning to how things manage, to some degree, to manifest themselves to us, while all the while listening to how language makes sense of their disclosure.

1.2 Truth, *alētheia*, and the eventful hiddenness of being. Heidegger's fundamental thesis motivated the many analyses in SZ that account for its lasting appeal. Underlying all these analyses is Heidegger's innovative interpretation of what principally distinguishes human beings, namely, truth as disclosedness (*alētheia*). For much of the Western philosophical tradition, there is a long-standing, logical prejudice that truth is solely a property of a proposition or judgment. But what makes a proposition true (correct) is the manifestness of the thing it is about; propositional truth presupposes ontic truth. But ontic truth (the manifestness of something to someone, its uncovering) presupposes the ontological truth, the disclosedness of its being (*genitivus appositivus*), that is its presence and absence. To exist is for us to be here in the sense of being the site of the disclosedness (the clearing). Like the Greek *alētheia* that is its inspiration, this conception of truth as a thing's presence (disclosedness, openness) presupposes its absence (its being closed off, hidden from us). As much as we are in the truth, we are also in the un-truth (not to be confused with error). In other words, as much as we are in one way exposed to the presence of things (including ourselves), those same things are also in one way or another hidden from us. (The uses of "nothing" and cognates for negation derive from synchronic and diachronic forms of this hiddenness, above all, the way things relentlessly "slip away.")

There is, moreover, a history to this dynamic interplay of hiddenness and unhiddenness (or better, the interplay is "the original history"), though it is less clear from the largely nonhistorical, systematic style of the published sections of SZ. Heidegger later flags that history as the human beings' eventful appropriation (*Ereignis*) of and by being. In the distinctive way that being withdraws or holds itself back from human concerns (even as the presence—overlooked or forgotten, to be sure—of things to them), it appropriates human beings. (Its withdrawal accounts, at least in part, for the all-too-human tendency to overlook or forget it.) Humanity in turn (*kehrig*) makes this peculiar appropriation its own through a respective, epochal understanding of beings as a whole, an understanding that is all the while fraught by the withdrawal (or, as Heidegger also puts it, the self-concealing-of-being that is characteristic of the epochal appropriation).

Heidegger's accomplishment in conceiving truth as this eventful *alētheia* is nonpareil. His conception explains how truth can have a fundamental, determinative role in thinking, without falling prey to the many pitfalls of correspondence and deflationary theories of truth. Yet his account also leaves the relationship between the levels of truth underdetermined, and the issue of this underdetermination is particularly acute, given the fact that he articulates these levels through propositions that he puts forward as true. The problem is not simply that truth as disclosedness is necessary but insufficient for other truths, but precisely how it is. Particularly given the diminishing status of truth in various quarters (from postmodern dismissals to analytic treatments of truth as superfluous), elaboration of the concrete distinctiveness and trenchancy of truth as the eventful *alētheia* is sorely needed.

1.3 The timeliness and historicality of human existence and the history of being. Heidegger takes over Husserl's insight that time in some sense is the fundamental constitutive condition of intentionality. Yet just as Heidegger sees that intentionality presupposes being-in-the-world, so, too, he sees that time and the traditional conception of being as presence are bedfellows. Hence, inquiry into the meaning of being via existential analysis entails the monumental task of elaborating a conception of time more fundamental than the traditional views of time (e.g., a now-sequence, clock time, the time of the world). Taking his cues from what is necessary for existing authentically, he argues for the primacy of the future, since it is only by anticipating death (the authentic future of resolutely projecting one's impossibility) that we retrieve the mortal condition (the authentic, inherent past-ness—*Gewesenheit*, not *Vergangenheit*—coinciding with our thrownness) and open ourselves to the situation and the moment (*Augenblick*) of decision (the authentic present) that our situation entails. Concretely, these decisions take the form of being-historical, that is, authentically being-with others in retrieving/repeating a heritage, in defiance of a mindless preoccupation with the present and the next new thing.

As the center of gravity of Heidegger's thinking shifts from being-here (*Da-sein*) to the eventful appropriation (*Ereignis*, "the original history itself") by and of being in its epochal self-concealing (i.e., truth as the eventful *alētheia*), Heidegger continues to affirm the future's primacy. However, this eschatological dimension is not so much what we project as it is what is coming to us (*uns zu-kommt*, *Zukunft*)—the culmination of a process that began with the first responses of human thinkers to the mystery of being, at once disclosing and concealing itself. All the while, to be sure, the existential dimension of resoluteness (*Entschlossenheit*) persists in the form of corresponding or not—opening ourselves up (*sich erschliessen*) or not—to this truth, that is, the truth of being's historical character (albeit in this idiosyncratic sense of "the original history").

In an effort to deflect any appearance of yet another form of transcendental subjectivity (anthropomorphic exceptionalism), Heidegger contends that our relation to historical being (*Seyn*) belongs to its essential unfolding, which is also to say that it needs us insofar as we are being-here and not simply being human. Sometimes Heidegger depicts this unfolding as inexorable; other times as something yet to be decided (albeit no less inexorably). In any case, he frequently strikes an eschatological tone: the truth of historical being grounds being-here by transforming future human beings into beings who are truly here (*da*) and not away (*weg*). This process is a struggle (*polemos*), that of the human being's appropriation by historical being, and it is nothing less, he submits, than "the genuine history." The appropriation entails a particular stance (*Haltung*) that coincides with knowing through thinking (*denkerisches Wissen*) the truth of history as the history of being—and that means, above all, coming to terms with its intrinsic self-concealment in our appropriation of and by it. The acknowledgment of this self-concealing marks the final unwinding/rewinding of Western metaphysics' tendency to equate the being of beings with what we can make present by producing it or placing it before us.

Again, there is nothing comparable to this thinking among twentieth-century philosophers. Yet an analogue to the problem plaguing Heidegger's analysis of truth is patent: that of relating different, allegedly subordinate levels—traditional views of time (ontic, ordinary, world time) and history (chronological, recorded)—to what Heidegger (circa 1927) deems the fundamental timeliness and historicality of existence and (circa 1937) the history of being. So, too, particularly given allusions to the promising rhetoric of our transformation into truly *being-here*, he leaves woefully under-determined the relation between what is allegedly coming to us and that transformation (analogously, between the thrownness and the projection of the *entworfenen Entwurf*).

1.4 The experience of truth in art and poetry. *Ars gratia artis* (the MGM logo) epitomizes a tradition of understanding art aesthetically, that is, via its impression on viewers, listeners, or readers. In a powerful reflection on the truth of the conflict of world (the unhidden) and earth (the hidden) that great art beautifully produces, Heidegger challenges this aesthetic tradition. Art is not simply for the sake of art but, together with its creators and preservers, it grounds history.

While Heidegger's account of art restores to it a classical dignity, it does so by tying the account, by Heidegger's own admission, to the question of being. As such, his analysis can appear to be a paradigmatic example of a philosophical disenfranchisement of art. The challenge here is similar to the one voiced in his discussion of the relation of poetry and thinking, such that genuine thinking is poetic, even as poetry and thinking dwell on the most separate mountains. Yet, insofar as the thinker, not the poet, is making this claim, the challenge is patent. To the extent that art is truthful, Heidegger's thinking presents us with the challenge of thinking its truthfulness poetically.

1.5 The essential challenge of modern technology. Heidegger recognized that the rise of modern technology to the point that it increasingly dominates every aspect of life is tied to a conception of being, an understanding of things generally. He showed, moreover, that this understanding is rooted in the Western metaphysical tradition of construing beings as presence in three complementary senses. To be is to be presently$_1$ present$_2$ to us$_3$; that is to say, it is to be currently$_1$ in a position$_2$ before us$_3$. On this conception of being, it is restricted to what is potentially present in this threefold sense. The Greek understanding of being as what is or can be present (*ousia* as a domicile) gives way to understanding beings as what are or can be placed before us (*uns vor-gestellt*) and, if need be, produced by us (*von uns her-gestellt*), that is, the setup or imposition (*Ge-stell*) essential to modern technology. In other words, it is of the essence of modern technology to understand being as the presence of what can—in principle—be put at our disposal or produced by us. Accordingly, whatever is not yet at our disposal or produced by us becomes a goal of research. It is not inevitable that we buy into this paradigm, succumbing to the tendency to regard everything, not least ourselves, as inherently disposable or producible. What is needed is not a Luddite destruction of technology, but a free, noninstrumental relationship to it, the sort of relationship to technology that is capable of not letting technology overplay its hand in our lives precisely because the relationship springs from the knowledge that the essence of modern technology is, in the final analysis, not in technology's grip.

SIX PRESSING PROBLEMS

Critical examination of the contributions flagged earlier—and they only scratch the surface—remains a pressing but largely neglected task of contemporary philosophy across the globe. Yet any attempt to appropriate Heidegger's contributions responsibly cannot fail to address several pressing problems, six of which are sketched below. The first five concern his seemingly cowering refusal (1) to engage in public debate with his contemporaries, (2) to reflect critically on the metaphysical import of his concepts and alternative approaches to them, (3) to disambiguate his metaphorical terminology, (4) to deflect the reverberations of a kind of ontological animism, or (5) to face issues of value and causation. One final problem concerns (6) a view of the history of philosophy that is part myopia, part delusion of grandeur.

2.1 An irresponsible aloofness. Heidegger's provincial upbringing and graduate studies within the Catholic philosophical establishment in Freiburg may have left him with a sense of insecurity, as he endeavored to demonstrate his abilities to the more urbane, Protestant environment of mainstream German philosophy. Whether or not this insecurity accounts for his awkward behavior toward colleagues (e.g., Nicolai Hartmann) and his distrust of contemporaries' liberal political views, there is an aloofness in his work that verges on being irresponsible, when it comes to engaging contemporary philosophers in print. He is, to be sure, a frequent interlocutor of Husserl, Scheler, and Jaspers (i.e., there is ample evidence of their conversations during the 1920s). Yet he refrains from addressing even their views directly or taking them up explicitly in any critical fashion in publications from the 1920s through the early 1930s. (Admittedly, his publications during this time—in contrast to lectures to students—provide a small sample, but that sample is all we have.) By avoiding public philosophical debate, he saved himself the trouble of constructing arguments in the face of alternative, contemporary treatments of issues.

2.2 A parochial, uncritical metaphysics. Corresponding to this aloofness is an ironically parochial, uncritical view of metaphysics. I say "ironically parochial" because his conception of metaphysics is at the same time broad in the traditionally Aristotelian sense of including an understanding of beings as a whole (ontology) that relies upon a conception of some preeminent particular being (theology). His own fundamental ontology can be construed as an attempt to approach metaphysics differently. Nonetheless, in his heady pursuit of fundamental ontology, he relies uncritically upon concepts and structures (e.g., relations, properties, parts and wholes, dispositions) that (1) rely, for their meaning, upon traditional metaphysics; and (2) have nonetheless been interpreted in many different ways by metaphysicians. In addition to closing the door to fruitful dialogue, his failure to specify the meaning of these concepts/structures threatens to undermine the project itself insofar as they potentially draw upon (get their traction from) a limited conception of being. There are, for example, multiple ways of conceiving wholes (*Ganzheit*) and dispositions (*Seinkönnen*), but Heidegger's analyses proceed with only a few, unquestioned conceptions in mind. (By the same token, Heidegger's analyses in this regard provide unexplored, fertile soil for plying contemporary analytic metaphysics.) Similarly, one searches in vain for an explanation of why, for example, the structure of primordial time is or is not timeless, and that of historicality is or is not nonhistorical. Every period of his thinking raises similar sorts of recursive questions, *mutatis mutandis*.

But there is no more blatant instance of this lack of critical reflection than the expansiveness and trenchancy that he attributes to being's self-concealing. Such claims have the ring of the universality and necessity proper to metaphysical claims (synthetic a priori claims). Heidegger owes us a better explanation of why such claims are not just another form of metaphysics (or, if you will, a meta-metaphysics, given his claims about traditional metaphysics). Finally, given being's allegedly inherent hiddenness, its self-concealing, on what basis do we know it at all, let alone with the structure, content, and relation to presence that Heidegger attaches to it? Or if there are telling clues (*Winke*) or reverberations (*Anklänge*), how do we recognize them, that is, distinguish them from wishful thinking? To be sure, things are constantly coming to an end, and our finitude is such that things invariably escape our perceptual purview and reach. But the experience of nothingness in the form of such absence (things passing from view or their demise) is one thing; the self-concealing of being—or so it would seem—quite another.

2.3 Metaphors amok. Heidegger has an uncanny knack of drawing upon and drawing out meanings of terms widely used (e.g., *das Man*, *Bewandtnis*, *Ent-schlossenheit*, *vor-stellen*, *Ereignis*, *Verwindung*) as well as generating illuminating neologisms from them (e.g., *Ge-stell*, *Zuhandensein*, *Gewesenheit*). Yet even his most basic philosophical concepts are metaphors, terms that have an ordinary meaning and/or etymology upon which the intelligibility of his analysis relies, even as he transports those concepts to different contexts (e.g., fundamental ontology, thinking being-historically, the fourfold). He relies upon some of the native meanings of his terms even as he indulges selectively in metaphorical uses of them. In short, his terms are words of art that trade on their meanings before being introduced as technical terms. Take the term *Da-sein*. In addition to reserving it—at least in the late 1920s—for what is equivalent (not identical) to human being, he calls attention to the fact that it is composed of *da*, an adverb of place ("here" or "there"). But while telling us that he does not intend *da* in these ordinary spatial senses, he describes *Dasein* as a site! *Dasein* is the clearing, the site of the disclosedness of being, and his many references to *da zu sein* trade on that spatial connotation. When Heidegger further informs us that terms like *Dasein* and *Ereignis* cannot be translated, he is overlooking his own glosses to fix their metaphorical (systematic) senses and his own dependency upon the ordinary use of these terms to do so. (Moreover, who is Heidegger—someone who must rely upon a translation of Mill to lecture on him—to tell us what can and cannot be translated into English?) Nor is it unproblematic that a metaphorical use of a term is used to characterize the ground of the nonmetaphorical use (ordinary uses of *Dasein* and *Ereignis* allegedly presuppose their extraordinary, philosophically elaborated uses).

2.4 Ontological animism. Heidegger reifies being insofar as he nominalizes *Sein* and places the term in sentences that have the effect of personifying or, at least, attributing an agency to what is designated, even as he denies that *Sein* is anything like a thing or being itself. The same applies, mutatis mutandis, to terms like *Seyn*, *Ereignis*, *Wesen*, and more. Heidegger wrestles with this problem, to be sure. His use of such phrases as *Welt weltet* (*Sprache spricht*, *Wesen west*, *Grund gründet*), as well as his apparently changing view as to whether *ist* should be predicated of *Sein* (saying at one point that it should not, at another point that it should only be predicated of *Sein*), indicate his awareness of the difficulty. Still, these linguistic maneuvers are less than successful in overriding the effect of nominalization and personification. I am reminded of the "duck test" argument made by a senator, complaining about his colleagues' contention that the revenue-raising provisions in a bill did not amount to a tax. The senator said something to the effect: "If it walks like a duck and it quacks like a duck, I call it a duck, and the same holds for a tax." His protests to the contrary, Heidegger's personifying accounts repeatedly fail a comparable duck test, giving rise to an ontological or, better, post-ontological animism, ridden with binaries that call for deconstruction.

Animism is a strong term, suggesting, as it does, belief in invisible, spiritual beings governing things' behavior and mutual relations. Yet, insofar as being or being as *Ereignis* conceals itself, it is not something given. Consequently, claims about it seem to ride less on any phenomenological access to it than on quasi-transcendental considerations, the *thought* that between being-here and being (including the respective epochal meanings of things) there just *must be* an eventful, reciprocal relation.

2.5 A world without values and causes. Little perhaps need be said about this glaring deficiency in Heidegger's analysis, due perhaps to the lasting influence of phenomenology. He insists that his analyses treat themes that do not invoke questions of causation and value (including value in the sense of moral principles), largely because addressing those questions allegedly supposes the separate treatment of those themes. But there are at least two difficulties with this insistence. First, Heidegger does not present a compelling argument that his basic themes (e.g., being, being-here, the eventful appropriation, the truth of being, and the like) can be characterized without invoking values or causes. (In fact, he seems to concede as much in SZ when he acknowledges that his account of authenticity in terms of anticipatory resoluteness presupposes a factical ideal. So, too, his account of the reciprocal U-turn in *Ereignis* sounds like a gloss on an Aristotelian view of the causal structure of living substances.) Second, even if there is a sense in which discussion of these themes articulates what is neither a value nor part of a causal chain, Heidegger owes us an account of how it can be valued or causally determined or, short of that, how it relates to what can be valued or causally determined.

2.6 History of philosophy myopia and philosophical grandstanding. Heidegger's view of the history of philosophy is problematic in at least two fundamental ways. His highly select view of what counts as part of the history demonstrates a remarkable myopia, not only with regard to non-Western traditions (a bias he eventually concedes; for more on this topic, see Bret Davis's contribution to the present volume) but also with regard to the Western (albeit non-German) tradition itself. Heidegger ignores, for example, late antiquity (Stoics, Epicureans, Neo-Platonists), Jewish thinkers (Maimonides, Spinoza, Mendelssohn), and the Scottish Enlightenment. These oversights are problematic for someone who makes such claims for the epochal account of the history of philosophy as metaphysics, not least because they present perspectives (think of skepticism) that do not fit neatly into his narrative.

Even more egregiously problematic is Heidegger's view of philosophy's role in history. He contends that the history of Western metaphysics, initiated by the pre-Socratics, is the ground of our own history and future decisions. In this regard, Heidegger betrays a Teutonic proclivity (reminiscent of Hegel and Nietzsche) to make philosophy itself the engine of history. Maybe it is, but there are powerful arguments to the contrary, though they obviously presuppose alternative conceptions of history and its relation to thought.

We are unthankful if we ignore the gift of Heidegger's thinking, the wave upon wave of powerful insights he left in his wake. There are ample reasons to endure its turbulence. But the criticisms voiced earlier suggest the necessity, too, of verging out from the choppy waters of his wake and making our own.

Sometimes we ask too much of the thought of a great thinker. Heidegger's silence about so many issues is maddening and deafening and even arguably venal, as many have charged. But maybe, too, there was a little Yogi Berra buried somewhere in his Teutonic soul, telling us by his silence, as Yogi put it, "if you ask me anything I don't know, I'm not going to answer."

Chapter 4

The Critical Appropriation of Heidegger's Philosophy

Five Motifs

Peter E. Gordon

For all readers who remain sensitive to the deepest and most enduring values of humanity, the scandal of Martin Heidegger's political affiliation with the Third Reich calls for an ongoing reassessment of his philosophical legacy. But a truly critical appropriation of an intellectual inheritance must also allow for at least the possibility of validity-claims that transcend the moment of its original articulation. This principle applies not only to the inheritance of Heidegger's work; it belongs to the very meaning of philosophical interpretation itself. Its violation would abolish the very distinction between insight and ideology, dispensing with the baby alongside the bathwater. We should not forget Adorno's remarks concerning the risks of an aggressively political hermeneutic, which would "extirpate, with the false, all that was true also." To read philosophy *only* as ideology would be to annul the very sense of philosophical reading itself.[1]

Although Heidegger himself may have (too frequently) collapsed the distinction between philosophy and political ideology, his own transgression gives us no license to repeat the error. The shadow that will forever darken the legacy of Martin Heidegger does not rule out of bounds the possibility of a thoughtful and critically responsible appropriation of certain philosophical motifs that are associated with his work. To consider these motifs, however, cannot absolve us of the task of understanding how they may also bear within themselves a certain danger of philosophical and ideological exaggeration. In what follows I discuss five such themes, distinguishing in each case between the conceptual content that continues to merit philosophical consideration and the hyperbolic, ideological *distortion* of that content that must now strike most readers as philosophically indefensible.

1. *The critique of the disembedded Cartesian subject.* Surely among the greatest themes of Heidegger's philosophy is its attempted rebellion against the "disembedded" model of consciousness. Drawing its legitimacy from Cartesian epistemology and the conventional distinction between mind and world (which borrowed its metaphysical underpinnings in turn from the older, Christian distinction between soul and body), the disembedded model of the subject served as a kind of default for both epistemology and metaphysics in the modern era. Its key feature is the conception of the subject as a *solus ipse*, a consciousness or *cogito* metaphysically distinct from the empirical-material world. Such a subject does not experience any of its essential characteristics as derivative of or dependent on its surroundings.[2] Against this model of the disembedded subject, Heidegger argued that human being should be conceived as (in Charles Taylor's phrase) "engaged agency."[3] The human being is best understood not as a subject as opposed to a metaphysically distinct object but rather as a situated and practical being-in-the-world.

It would be misleading, of course, to credit Heidegger alone for this rebellion; it is already anticipated in Hegel's *Phenomenology of Spirit* and in the young Marx, especially in the *Economic and Philosophic Manuscripts* which radicalizes the Hegelian model of self-expressive realization through worldly labor. It also resonates with familiar themes of North American pragmatism. But it would be hard to deny Heidegger's uniquely powerful role in dismantling the Cartesian idol of the subject-as-consciousness.

This achievement, however, was too easily radicalized into a philosophically indefensible syncretism that grafted a cultural-political protest against the cosmopolitan mind onto an ontological protest against subjectivism. Already in the existential work of the 1920s, Heidegger's preference for engaged rather than disengaged agency harmonized too easily with the artisanal pathos of a provincial thinker who romanticized skills of the hand and looked with suspicion on the fruitless affairs of the deracinated intellect. It should hardly surprise us that the same philosopher who aimed to destroy the priority of consciousness over artisanal labor could also sympathize in the 1930s with an ideological assault on "Semitic nomads" and rootless intellectualism.[4]

In *Being and Time*, this turn toward the "practical" had not yet fully severed its original bond to modern epistemology. Ironically, it retained from Husserlian phenomenology a strong element of subjectivism. According to Heidegger's own statements of phenomenological method, Dasein enjoys a first-person or proprietary relation to itself: it is always characterized by *Jemeinigkeit* ("mineness"). In relation to the world, Dasein comes burdened with the unique pathos of a being for whom its own being is "at issue" and who struggles to recall the "sense of being" (*Sinn des Seins*) that underlies its own practice. This capacity for understanding remains a distinguishing mark of Dasein; it signals the early Heidegger's continued allegiance to idealism and the "philosophy of consciousness."[5] (That Heidegger acknowledged this element of idealism in *Being and Time* has not deterred some of his most prominent interpreters from extolling his philosophy as a variant of realism.[6])

After the so-called "turning," these subjectivistic elements in Heidegger's philosophy were obscured, only because he adopted the Delphic voice of an oracle who pronounces on the self-revelation of an anonymous "event" (*Ereignis*). Heidegger could never explain how this shift to a post-theological narrative of revelation was supposed to immunize him from the supposedly discredited dualism of subject and object. For such a disclosure would be possible only if it revealed itself to a subject gifted with a special endowment of receptivity. After all, only within the "clearing" of human understanding could the history of Being become intelligible. This double bind of a subjectivistic anti-subjectivism could not be undone by turning from the rationalistic and technological paradigm of production to the ostensibly non-technological revelations of art and *poiēsis*. For Heidegger could never really own up to the fact that *poiēsis* itself bears witness to a human capacity for symbolic expression, the very same power which Marx alongside his German Idealist predecessors called *Entäußerung*, or self-externalization.

To be sure, the new rhetoric of *Gelassenheit* (or "letting-be") displaced the resolute decisionism of the early system and enwreathed the late work with an aura of pious simplicity. But this passive model of the human subject only enhanced the paradox of a philosophy that wished to surpass humanism by retreating into yet another variant of humanism. The self who gazes with gratitude upon the self-revelation of Being is still essentially Cartesian, since Dasein bears within itself the *Seinsverständnis* that serves as the condition for the possibility of world-disclosure; this disclosive thesis reflects a continued investment in the theory of constitutive subjectivity.[7] Heidegger's supposed démarche "beyond" humanism thus remains caught in the double bind, regressing halfway into an archaic notion of thought-without-mind while still relying on a disavowed philosophy of the subject.

2. *The existential analytic of the lifeworld.* Although he borrowed more than is commonly acknowledged from Husserlian phenomenology (especially from the late studies), Heidegger should nonetheless be credited for his role in overcoming the transcendental bias that, via bracketing (or *epoché*), was supposed to leave out of play the rudimentary facts of "human immanence."[8] Husserl felt that the prestige of philosophy as a "rigorous science" could be secured only through a phenomenological method that withdraws from the "natural attitude." By contrast, much of Heidegger's philosophical work might be characterized as a phenomenology *of* and *within* the natural attitude itself. The greatest achievement of *Being and Time* is just this attempt to

develop a philosophy of existence *from the inside*. Heidegger eschews the transcendental standpoint of a consciousness that remains somehow immune to the world it describes: this entanglement of philosophy with its surroundings justifies Heidegger's self-characterization of his work as an exercise in "hermeneutics." In seizing upon the structures of lived experience as themes for philosophical analysis, Heidegger dignified the realm of everyday meaning that the modern natural sciences, in their search for law-like regularities, had largely abandoned. In his work the lifeworld is reclaimed from the debased status of merely subjective experience and it is elevated into a legitimate realm of philosophical inquiry: a transsubjective and historically transmitted horizon whose meanings and normative investments are maintained through the largely anonymous repair-work of the collective.

This phenomenology of the lifeworld was taken up with fruitful consequences in the discipline of social phenomenology, first by Alfred Schütz and, much later, by Peter Berger and Thomas Luckmann in *The Social Construction of Reality* (1966). Heidegger's own ideological commitments may have constrained, but they did not wholly obstruct, the inheritance of this motif even among politically progressive and neo-Marxist social theorists. The analysis of the lifeworld left a deep imprint on the phenomenological analysis of symbolically transmitted social power as developed by Pierre Bourdieu, especially in his attempt to coordinate the phenomena of "field" and "habitus," for example, in *Outline of a Theory of Practice* (1977). And (via Schütz and anthropologists such as Peter Winch) even the critical theorist Jürgen Habermas drew upon the phenomenological theory of the lifeworld, especially in *The Theory of Communicative Action* (1981), though in Habermas's analysis the hermeneutic and intersubjective technique for understanding the lifeworld is counterbalanced by a sociologically realistic analysis of the "system." Habermas was thus able to introduce a sober appreciation for objective economic and institutional structures that Heidegger ignored.

The existential analysis of the lifeworld represents one of Heidegger's most enduring contributions to late-modern philosophy and social theory. To his great discredit, however, Heidegger interlaced his phenomenology of everyday meaning with a strong element of anti-modernist *ressentiment* against the cognitive and practical achievements of the modern natural sciences. Running through much of his philosophical work is an implausible and polemically overdramatized contrast: between the fragile space of cultural-historical meaning on the one hand, and the coldly objectivistic, ahistorical realm of nonhuman nature as theorized by mathematical-physical science on the other. In this contrast one might detect an unacknowledged remnant of Windelband's neo-Kantian distinction between the *idiographic* and the *nomothetic* sciences (cf. GA 56/57: 166–68): Heidegger inflates the former at the expense of the latter; the hermeneutic understanding of unique meaning-formations assumes an unwarranted priority and diminishes the status of logical and law-like explanation. Despite his own antipathies to the neo-Kantian epistemologies and sociologies of the early twentieth century, Heidegger apparently agreed with Max Weber's declaration that with the rise of the natural sciences, the belief in anything like a "meaning" to the universe threatens to die out at its very roots.[9]

Enhanced by a typically Weimar-era *Kulturpessimismus*, this Weberian view of nomothetic and mathematical-logical reason overdetermined Heidegger's faulty characterization of modern natural-scientific understanding as a neutralization or "deworlding" (*Entweltlichung*) of Dasein's existentially meaningful world.[10] It is hardly surprising that in *History of the Concept of Time* Heidegger called nature "the unintelligible pure and simple." It is the "deworlded world, if we take nature in this extreme sense as entities as they are uncovered in physics" (GA 20: 298). Altogether absent from this account is any appreciation for natural science as a meaningful and normatively rich practice, one that occupies its own legitimate place within the lifeworld alongside the cultural-historical (artistic, poetic, linguistic) practices on which the later Heidegger lavished philosophical attention. This fundamental misunderstanding of the natural sciences helps to explain, but does not excuse, the passage in *What is Called Thinking?* where he blithely declared that "science does not think" (WCT 8).

Heidegger's analysis of the modern natural sciences (*and* modern technology, since he typically addressed them together) reflects the ideology of a twentieth-century political and cultural conservative who could not overcome his nostalgia for the provinces and who saw in modern civilization an array of dissolvent forces that threatened to break up the fragile and holistic textures of inherited cultural tradition. The phenomenology of the lifeworld will nonetheless remain a fruitful avenue for philosophical and social-theoretical exploration, though it must be rescued from the hyperbolic and ideologically distorted contest (between culture and science) that informed so much of Heidegger's own work.

3. *History as an* a priori *horizon of understanding*. Among Heidegger's most significant legacies for modern philosophy is the attempt to thematize history itself as the ground of Being. Much of this attempt is pursued through historical criticism: notwithstanding its opening homage to the *Sophist*, Heidegger's first major work of philosophy unfolds as a radical dismantling of Platonic metaphysics. With a largely unacknowledged debt to Nietzsche, Heidegger follows the path laid down by his predecessor in *Twilight of the Idols*, in which the philosophical abandonment of the real world is narrated in successive steps as "the history of an error."[11] *Being and Time*, too, is animated by a similar belief that philosophy must abandon its search for an intelligible

realm of pure form beyond the bounds of temporality. In his determination to expose this ideal as a metaphysical error, Heidegger called for (though he did not in fact carry through) a so-called "destruction" of the history of ontology in multiple stages. Much like the genealogist of morals who came before him, Heidegger pursued his work of a genealogical destruction of ontology as an exercise in interpretative unmasking: the reader would confront at last the unsettling fact of time as the ultimate horizon of Being.

Although the negative project of destruction was never fully realized, *Being and Time* and associated lectures from the 1920s offer a compelling account of the temporal constitution of being-in-the-world. Heidegger deepens and ontologizes the Kantian transcendental doctrine that time serves as a "pure form of intuition" and is therefore the condition for objects to appear at all. But he presses much further than transcendental idealism in arguing that the temporal character of entities does not derive merely from the mind but is rather grounded in a deeper temporality that serves as the common horizon for Dasein together with its world. This temporality is thus "primordial," an ineluctable mode of being-in-the-world. To be human is to find oneself thrown into an already established horizon of past significations that can be retrieved as one's heritage and then reclaimed in resolution for one's own projected future. This is Dasein's "historicality," the analysis of which serves as the preparatory step for thematizing the temporality of Being as such. In Heidegger's later work it is Being and not merely Dasein that becomes the self-concealing and self-revealing site of historically variable horizons: "Metaphysics grounds an age in that, through a specific interpretation of what is . . ., it gives the age the ground of its essential form" (QCT 115). Humanity is not the origin but merely the passive recipient of an anonymous *Ereignis* or event.

Heidegger's historical ontology historicized the Kantian theme of transcendental conditions: all phenomena obey the "historical a priori" that is given to them as the governing dispensation of the age. This historical-transcendental theme drew upon many antecedent doctrines (notably those of Hegel, Dilthey, Nietzsche, Rickert, and Count Yorck von Wartenburg). But in its articulation and depth it surpassed all of these influences and bequeathed to modern philosophy a repertoire of themes that have not yet been exhausted. Here too, however, Heidegger unfortunately interlaced insight with ideology. First, the doctrine of Dasein's historicality slackens one's confidence in the possibility of historical criticism. Although we should acknowledge that we are shaped by our heritage, this shaping power stops short of thoroughgoing determinism: we retain the possibility of withholding our consent from the pressures that are exerted upon our present by the past. Second, such dissent is possible in part because the historical ontology of any given epoch is less totalizing than Heidegger implied. No unique and all-encompassing regime of metaphysics can be said to govern the whole spectrum of reality within a given historical epoch; by discerning the fragmentation within historical reality one gains points of leverage for criticism and resistance. Third, and most implausible of all, was Heidegger's readiness to promote his ontology with the quasi-mythological doctrine of the "sending of Being" (*Seinsgeschick*). With this notion of a post-theistic revelation Heidegger abandoned the terrain of philosophical argument and adopted a language of windy mysticism that resists rational scrutiny. The very notion of an "epoch" that obeys its own intrinsic logic or *Zeitgeist* has always carried the whiff of mythological thinking. According to Heidegger, the metaphysical grounding of an age serves as the "basis" which "*holds complete dominion over all the phenomena that distinguish the age*" (QCT 115, em). Under the wrong conditions, the totalizing tendency in historical ontology becomes a license for totalitarian submission: one bows to a given authority because it is imagined to be the irresistible truth of one's age.[12] To be sure, Heidegger must have believed there could be some room for critical distance on the dominant metaphysical frameworks of a given age—his own philosophy enacts that distance—but without some plausible story as to how this was possible he risked a performative contradiction.

Enchanted by his own appeals to historical-contextual conditioning, Heidegger's conservative ideology underplayed the critical-emancipatory gesture by which heritage can be not just selectively appropriated but also subjected to critical revision or even dissolved when its authoritarian power grows too pronounced. On the one hand, contextual determinism is *anti-historical*, since it inhibits us from imagining how change can occur between one context and another. On the other hand, radical historicism *vitiates possibility*: it permits the past wholly to control the present, as if all meaning were merely recapitulation or an eternal repetition of the same. To be sure, Heidegger acknowledged that historical repetition can effect *some* species of second-order reflection: in the *Wiederholung* of the past one "hands down" the past to oneself, but not necessarily *as* tradition (SZ 386), but on this crucial point, Heidegger's argumentation remained frustratingly vague. Nor can philosophy accept the strong thesis of discontinuity between epochs: Radicalized into a crudely deflationary historicism, historical ontology abolishes not only the fact but also the regulative idea of a context-transcending appeal to truth.

4. *Language and world-disclosure*. Following upon previous insights by Herder and von Humboldt (among others), Heidegger succeeded in elevating language into a central theme for philosophical inquiry. In *Being and Time* (§§31–34) the propositional structure of "assertion" is made contingent upon prior and sedimented acts of interpretation. Any "is" depends on a prior "as." The result is a powerful theory of hermeneutic understanding that challenges the epistemological model of disengaged knowledge at its very heart.

Because one first encounters the world from *within* the horizon of interpretation, the Cartesian model of reality as an objective state of affairs loses its prestige. What Bernard Williams called "the absolute conception of reality" no longer lies at the foundation of knowledge; it becomes instead the anomalous instance of a breakdown in interpretation. It follows that language for Heidegger is more than a mere vehicle for information; it is an *existentiale*, that is, a fundamental condition for the disclosure of phenomena at all. In his later work, Heidegger transforms this thesis into the memorable maxim: "Language is the house of Being" (GA 9: 313/239).

In philosophy, a focus on language is hardly new. The Socratic elenchus makes language into an intersubjective medium for the discursive revelation of thought; neo-Platonism went even further, viewing *logos* not just as a vehicle for revelation but as its metaphysical substance. The thesis of divine emanation through language was carried forward historically not least by the Kabbalah, whose influence via Schelling could still be detected in Heidegger even though it remains an "unthought" debt.[13]

Well before Wittgenstein, such doctrines confronted the intuitionist doctrine of Ideas with a pragmatic challenge: What rules could possibly govern the language of mere thought if such a language remains wholly private? With Heidegger the argument against private language prepares the ground for a linguistic ontology: it is only in the common medium of language that the world reveals itself at all. In his early work, however, this devotion to language as the world-disclosive horizon was compromised by Heidegger's fear that public speech could detach itself from genuine phenomena and thus degrade into mere "chatter" (*Gerede*). In *Being and Time* the promise of a linguistic ontology thus remained conflicted: with one hand it gestured toward the idea of language as the shared medium of publicity, but with the other hand it condemned public discourse as a falling-away from authentic disclosure. In the later work this moralism disappears: especially in his writings on language and poetry, Heidegger deepens our understanding of Hölderlin's phrase *dichterisch, wohnet der Mensch auf dieser Erde*.[14]

Heidegger's theory of language has enjoyed considerable prestige; it served, for example, as a crucial inspiration for French post-structuralism. But a purely linguistic ontology also exhibits notable weaknesses. A theory that ascribes to language an a priori role in the constitution of the world runs into serious difficulty when we have to explain how reality can also impinge upon our interpretations *from the outside*. For our language is not always right about the way things are. Interpretations may be linguistic, but they remain open to a nonlinguistic reality. Language, we might say, is not only *constitutive of* the world; it is also *responsive* to it. Among the deepest ironies of the Heidegger reception is that his work was often characterized as a form of "anti-humanism" when in fact its linguistic ontology inflates the human capacity for "world-making" beyond the bounds of plausibility.[15] To be sure, Heidegger disavowed the theme of humanist agency: he insisted that language is not something we wield, its constitutive-hermeneutic horizon is deeper than any humanist claims to expression or mastery; *die Sprache spricht*. But the thesis that language serves as the "house of Being" is nonetheless a remnant of a disavowed humanism: it retains a hidden bond to the idealist theory of constitutive subjectivity. This theory can be retained in a less extravagant form if and only if one dispenses with its crypto-idealist attitude toward the plenitude of a nonlinguistic reality. We cannot permit culture to dominate nature, but this is precisely what the hyperbolic thesis of linguistic constructivism promotes. Nor can we build a responsible environmentalism merely on the basis of the mythopoetic distinction between "world" and "earth." Only a deflationary version of Heidegger's philosophy of language can allow for the possibility of our encounter with a nature whose plenitude always exceeds the force of a merely human *poiēsis*.

5. *A revival of the pathos of human finitude*. The version of modern philosophy that developed in academic research universities in Western Europe became highly restrictive; it not only withdrew in embarrassment from its theological interests, it also developed a certain professional hostility to the ancient Stoic conception of "philosophy as a way of life."[16] *Weltanschauung* became a term of abuse. Since Hegel, it became a commonplace of academic philosophy that the first-person perspective should be sublated into the differentiated omniscience of third-person objectivity, or "absolute knowing," while the finitude of the solitary individual was redescribed with the pathologizing label of the "unhappy consciousness." It was left to Kierkegaard to contest this verdict by declaring the incommensurable truth of subjective interiority as the privileged space of the believer. Heidegger inherited from Kierkegaard the pathos of finitude but stripped it of its religious aura. Dasein lacks the bond with divinity that still nourished Kierkegaard's confidence in the power of the subject. But even if Dasein lacks all metaphysical security, it is still distinguished as the being for whom its own being is "at issue." Its unshakable investment in the unfolding event of its own existence retains just enough of its disavowed piety to wrap itself in a new aura of *Sorge*, or care.

In *Being and Time* this pathos of finitude retains a strongly individualist character. Heidegger acknowledged the constitutive power of social normativity through the neutral agency of *das Man* (the "One"), but he could not escape his Kierkegaardian distrust of the crowd as a realm of inauthenticity and mindless comformism. The unjustified focus on being-toward-death as the inverted *telos* for life-meaning may have made sense for a religious believer—a confrontation with mortality opened up the possibility of repentance—but without the comforts of theism, it simply looks like a last-ditch attempt to rescue metaphysics in a post-metaphysical age. The "nothing" reoccupies the space evacuated by God. In the moment of resolve the act of decision permits Dasein to seize upon that which is one's "ownmost," even if the meanings that are available for reappropriation are merely the ones given by one's own historical community. The proprietary theme remains strong. But the unapologetic individualism of this doctrine may also help to explain why Heidegger's early work struck so many of his own students as ethically impoverished. Because the "One" supplies the answer to the "who" of Dasein, Heidegger worried that authentic selfhood would be lost: "Everyone is the other," he wrote, "and nobody is himself" (SZ 128). The thought did not occur to Heidegger (as it did to his student Lévinas) that an ethical obligation to the other might be the very condition for being a self at all.

Even if one does not go so far as to endorse the immoderate and metaphysical appeal to alterity that Lévinas proposed, one should admit that Heidegger had great difficulty in recognizing a genuinely *intersubjective* relation between self and other. His theory of social being emphasizes solidarity over intersubjectivity, exaggerating the holism of the community and suppressing the possibility of social fragmentation. Just as for Heidegger the authentic individual discovers through finitude the possibility of "being-a-whole," so too the authentic community or nation becomes a seamless totality. Heidegger had much to say about the historical maintenance of one's heritage (via "appropriation"). But he had little to say about an ethically motivated, active resistance to that heritage. *Being and Time* offers a phenomenology of fate rather than dissent.

Heidegger should nonetheless be credited for reintroducing into philosophy a pathos of care and finitude that was largely abandoned with the rise of secular and scientific paradigms in European philosophy. But he did a disservice to his own philosophical legacy by enveloping the themes of nation (*Volk*) and historical civilization with the same aura of authenticity that he also applied to individual Dasein. Enchanted by his own philosophy of history, he overdramatized the holism of ethno-national cultures—hence his grandiose allusions to "the Germans" and "the Greeks"—and he fetishized the surviving linguistic fragments of past civilizations on the specious premise that language is not a medium of communication but instead a preserve for redemptive meanings otherwise lost to the world.

This elevated tone came at a high price. It is one thing to reestablish the significance of such long-neglected themes through the rigors of careful argumentation; it is quite another thing to secure their importance by means of a mystified jargon that disallows critical scrutiny. In much of his later work Heidegger donned the garments of a sage rather than a philosopher, with the unfortunate consequence that, even today, his intellectual legacy seems to impose upon the reader a stark choice: either one assents to the holy script as a faithful disciple or one is branded as an uncomprehending heretic. A philosophical discourse that abandons the field of critical-rational argumentation for poetic allusion may be edifying and inspiring, and it may even change one's life. But it is no longer philosophy.

NOTES

1. Theodor Adorno, "Baby with the Bathwater," in *Minima Moralia: Reflections from Damaged Life*, tr. E. F. N. Jephcott (London: Verso, 1974), 43–45.

2. On "disembedding," see Charles Taylor, *A Secular Age* (Cambridge, MA: Harvard University Press, 2007), ch. 3, 146ff.

3. Charles Taylor, "Engaged Agency and Background in Heidegger," in *The Cambridge Companion to Heidegger*, ed. Charles Guignon (Cambridge: Cambridge University Press, 1993), 317–36.

4. See Peter E. Gordon, "Heidegger in Purgatory," in Martin Heidegger et al., *Nature, History, State: 1933–1934*, tr. and ed. Gregory Fried and Richard Polt (London: Bloomsbury, 2013).

5. Jürgen Habermas, *The Philosophical Discourse of Modernity: Twelve Lectures*, tr. Frederick Lawrence (Cambridge: MIT Press, 1985).

6. For Heidegger's stated alliance with idealism, see, for example, SZ 207. On this theme see Peter E. Gordon, "Realism, Science, and the Deworlding of the World," in *A Companion to Phenomenology and Existentialism*, ed. Hubert Dreyfus and Mark Wrathall (Oxford: Blackwell, 2006), 425–44. For the reading of Heidegger as a realist, see Hubert Dreyfus and Charles Taylor, *Retrieving Realism* (Cambridge, MA: Harvard University Press, 2015).

7. On constitutive subjectivity, see, for example, Theodor Adorno, *Gesammelte Schriften* VI: *Negative Dialektik: Jargon der Eigentlichkeit* (Frankfurt: Suhrkamp, 2003), 10. See also Peter E. Gordon, "Heidegger, Metaphysics, and the Problem of Self-Knowledge," in *Hermeneutical Heidegger*, ed. Michael Bowler and Ingo Farin (Evanston, IL: Northwestern University Press, 2016), 173–200.

8. The phrase comes from Husserl's student Eugen Fink. See Ronald Bruzina, *Edmund Husserl and Eugen Fink: Beginnings and Ends in Phenomenology, 1928–1938* (New Haven, CT: Yale University Press, 2004). On Heidegger and the late Husserl, see Dan Zahavi, *Husserl's Phenomenology* (Stanford, CA: Stanford University Press, 2003).

9. Max Weber, "Science as a Vocation," in *From Max Weber: Essays in Sociology*, ed. H. H. Gerth and C. Wright Mills (New York: Oxford University Press, 1958), 129–58; quoted from 142.

10. Gordon, "Realism, Science, and the Deworlding of the World."

11. Nietzsche, "How the 'True World' Finally Became a Fiction: History of an Error," in *Twilight of the Idols*, tr. Richard Polt (Indianapolis: Hackett, 1997), 23–24.

12. Iain D. Thomson calls this Heidegger's "ontological holism": *Heidegger, Art, and Postmodernity* (Cambridge: Cambridge University Press, 2011), 7.

13. Marlène Zarader, *The Unthought Debt: Heidegger and the Hebraic Heritage*, tr. Bettina Bergo (Stanford, CA: Stanford University Press, 2006).

14. Heidegger, "Poetically Man Dwells . . .," in PLT.

15. See, for example, the debate about Nelson Goodman and "worldmaking" in *Starmaking: Realism, Anti-Realism, and Irrealism*, ed. Peter J. McCormick (Cambridge: MIT Press, 1996).

16. Pierre Hadot, *Philosophy as a Way of Life*, ed. Arnold Davidson (Oxford: Blackwell, 1995).

Chapter 5

But What Comes *Before* the "After"?

Thomas Sheehan

A fruitful discussion of what comes *after* Heidegger would seem to presume a coherent idea of what came *before*, that is, what Heidegger himself was about. But in the Heidegger guild there's nothing more controversial than the question of what his central topic was.

Some think the answer is obvious: Heidegger was all about "Being"—or perhaps "*Ereignis* as just another name for Being"—even though he said he wasn't. When it comes to the core of his thought, he noted, "there is no longer room for *even the word* 'Being'" (GA 15: 365.17–18; numbers after the period indicate lines on the page).

Others think "the thing itself" was ἀλήθεια—but which ἀλήθεια? The term has at least five distinct meanings in Heidegger.

Still others think that even *attempting* an answer is a fool's errand. Who could possibly fathom the vast treasure that is the *Gesamtausgabe*, much less distill its 15 million words into a comprehensive summary of Heidegger's thought?—this despite his insistence that his work was about a single simple issue.

Heidegger didn't make it easy to discover what that single issue was, or how he got there. Consider the esoteric language, the arcane dicta, the almost misological take-it-or-leave-it refusal to provide arguments. Heidegger seemed content to just tell a story (μῦθόν τινα διηγεῖσθαι) about a Mysterious Something That Hides and Reveals Itself, without bothering to give a plausible account (λόγον διδόναι) of why that is so. Does an occasional Swabian or Greek etymology constitute a philosophical argument? Is even *asking* for a discursive account a sign that one has lapsed into "calculative thinking"?

Socrates suggested that serious questioning begins with knowing where you're starting from and where you want to go, the ὅθεν and the ὅποι. How, then, are we to discuss a possible "*after* Heidegger" when there's so little agreement about the *terminus a quo*, the Heidegger who came *before* any such "after"?

The following theses are an effort to run the fool's errand mentioned earlier, that is, to cross the *pons asinorum* of Heidegger scholarship into the disputed territory of what Heidegger was about. I touch on only the more salient elements of his work, and in doing so I follow Heidegger's suggestion that spending some time with Aristotle can be of help (GA 8: 78.9). I'll also invoke the aid of my seventh-grade teacher, Sister Constantia (cf. *Continental Philosophy Review*, 34: 187–89), who years ago, in the spirit of Episode 17 of Joyce's *Ulysses*, summarized in catechetical form what Heidegger was about.

Sister Constantia's Catechism
(1954, all rights reserved)

Q. What does Heidegger mean when he says that something "is"?
A. "Is" means "is meaningfully present as" (*sein* = *bedeutsam sein*), not just "is out there in the universe."

Q. Why are things necessarily meaningful?
A. Because a priori we are the field of possible meaning. Whatever shows up within that field necessarily is meaningful.

Q. Why didn't metaphysics ever notice that fact?
A. Because the field of possible meaning is intrinsically hidden: it is the ultimate presupposition of everything we do, and we cannot give an account of it without begging the question.

Q. How do we even know the field of possible meaning is a fact?
A. Because in moments of dread we can experience it and its source in our mortal finitude.

Q. What's the takeaway from all this?
A. "Become what you already are." Embrace your mortality and live your life accordingly.

Given Sister Constantia's conciseness, let me flesh out some of her catechesis in the following seven points:

- Heidegger's basic question concerned

  the meaning of "being" (*Sein*) as "meaningfulness" (*Bedeutsamkeit*) and why there is meaningfulness at all (i.e., why *es gibt Sein*).

- Heidegger's work is made up of two moments, the analytic and the protreptic, which we may articulate with Pindar's γένοι' οἷος ἐσσὶ μαθών (Pythian II, 72): "Learn and become what you already are."

- The *protreptic* moment (γένοι') is the exhortation to personally *become* one's ex-sistence and to authentically enact what it makes possible. Apart from SZ, the protreptic moment often lies in the background, even though it is the final goal of all Heidegger's work.
- The *analytic* moment (μαθών) aims at showing

  how ex-sistence is the Open (cf. SZ I.1–2)
  what ex-sistence *as* the Open does (cf. SZ I.3).

Some major elements of the analytic moment concern:

1. *Existenz*: thrown ahead and open
2. *Lichtung*: the Open, the clearing, the world-of-meaning
3. ἀλήθεια-prime/λόγος-prime: the source of all meaning and language
4. *Sorge*: concern-for-meaning
5. *Differenz*: the ontological difference
6. *Verborgenheit*: the Open as intrinsically hidden
7. *Zeitlichkeit*: the existential movement of aheadness-and-return
8. *Eignung*: movement as bringing-*ad-proprium*
9. *Ereignis*: ex-sistence as a priori brought-*ad-proprium* as the finite, mortal Open
10. *Phänomenologie*: existential correlativity with whatever one encounters
11. *Seinsvergessenheit*: overlooking the intrinsically hidden Open
12. *Kehre*: from *Da-sein* to *Da-sein* in their oscillating sameness.

- SZ I.3 was to complete the analytic moment by showing how the Open (aka "time"), sustained as it is by thrown-openness (aka "temporality"), determines the meaning (aka "being") of whatever we encounter.
- Heidegger didn't publish SZ I.3 in 1927, but he spent the next half century trying to articulate it in a different form, which he later entitled "The Open and Meaningful Presence" (*Lichtung und Anwesenheit*, GA 14: 90.2). In 1962, he summarized the outcome of that project as: The Open makes possible (*erbringt*) meaningful presence (GA 11: 151.27–28).
- To the further question "What 'gives' the Open?" (GA 14: 90.3) Heidegger's answer was: ex-sistence. In turn, the world-of-possible-meaning, which ex-sistence itself is, makes possible ("gives") all forms of meaning.

  Welt "gibt" Sein; das Dasein ist das je vereinzelte "es," das gibt; das ermöglicht und ist das 'es gibt.'" (GA 73.1: 642.28–29)

The following theses address the question "What was Heidegger about?" by spelling out the twelve topics listed earlier. I propose these theses as a propaedeutic that might guide and contribute to an "after Heidegger."

1. EX-SISTENCE

1.1 Heidegger distinguishes between
- *Existenz*, aka *Da-sein*: the structure (existenti*al*) of human being; and
- the persons and activities (existenti*el*) that this structure makes possible.

1.2 Following Heidegger's lead (GA 80.1: 71.22), I translate *Existenz/Da-sein* as ex-sistence, intentionally misspelled and hyphenated in order to emphasize its etymology (ἔξ—ἵστημι). Ex-sistence is made-to-stand-out-and-beyond. There is no "inside" to ex-sistence (SZ 162.27).

1.3 Heidegger never got beyond *Existenz/Da-sein*, nor did he need to, nor could he have gotten any farther had he wanted to.

1.3.1 Heidegger sought only human wisdom (ἀνθρωπίνη σοφία, *Apol.* 20d8), and throughout his career he remained focused solely on the human (τὸ ἀνθρώπινον, *N.E.*1094b6–7). In doing so, he completed the program he had projected in SZ.

2. EX-SISTENCE IS THE WORLD-OF-MEANING

2.1 Ex-sistence is transcendent, thrown ahead as the field of possible meaning—what Heidegger called the Open, the clearing, the social and linguistic meaning-giving-world, the nothing, the *Urphänomen* (GA 14: 81.13), and sometimes *Seyn*.

2.2 As the Open, ex-sistence is ἀλήθεια-prime or λόγος-prime, the realm of possible intelligibility that SZ called *Rede* (SZ 349.32). This existential structure makes us existentielly able to

2.2.1 "open things up," that is, make sense of them (ἀλήθεια-2 or λόγος-2); and

2.2.2 "open them up *correctly*," that is, make true statements about them (ἀλήθεια-3 or λόγος-3).

2.3 The technical term "being-*in*-the world" could be misread as meaning that ex-sistence is merely "in" space and time "within" the material universe. But for Heidegger, "in" indicates familiarity with, and "world" denotes meaningfulness (SZ 87.19–20). As ex-sistent we are structurally familiar with meaningfulness as such (*Bedeutsamkeit*) as well as a range of possible meanings (*Bedeutungen*) that might apply to what we encounter.

2.4 For Heidegger, meaning comes in wholes, that is, contexts or "worlds" (SZ 65.5–6, 68.24–25) that are (1) existenti*ally* made possible by ex-sistence's thrown-openness, (2) existenti*elly* shaped by one's interests and concerns which in turn (3) existenti*elly* shape the meanings of things within that context. For example, depending on the context, a stone might become a handy paperweight, an ersatz mallet, or a lethal weapon.

2.5 One's worlds-of-meaning usually go unnoticed, but they can *become* thematic when a purpose is thwarted or a tool breaks down, and they can be *made* thematic by reflection, for example, in a phenomenological reduction.

2.6 Since ex-sistence *is* the world-of-meaning (SZ 364.34; GA 9: 154.18–19) and since the world-of-meaning is the Open (GA 9: 326.15–16), there is no need of a "relation" that would span a "gap" between ex-sistence on the one side and the Open on the other. The so-called "relation" is the Open itself; and ex-sistence is this very "relation."

> Der Bezug ist jedoch nicht zwischen das Seyn und den Menschen eingespannt . . . . Der Bezug ist das Seyn selbst, und das Menschenwesen ist der selbe Bezug. (GA 73.1: 790.5–8)

3. EX-SISTENCE HOLDS OPEN THE WORLD-OF-MEANING

3.1 As "thrown ahead," ex-sistence holds open (*aussteht*) the world-of-meaning.

3.1.1 "Thrownness" bespeaks *Befindlichkeit*, the a priori fact that we are *affectively attuned* to the world-of-meaning and whatever we encounter within it.

3.1.2 "Aheadness" bespeaks *Verstehen*—not "understanding" as an existentiel act but the a priori fact that we are "beyond" the persons and things we encounter, that is, familiar with various meanings that can be connected with them.

3.2 *Befindlichkeit* and *Verstehen* are inseparable aspects of the same existential structure, and they express Heidegger's overcoming of the disastrous mind–body split. At one and the same time ex-sistence is an *affective minding* of meaning and a *mindful attunement* to meaning.

4. EX-SISTENCE IS CONCERN-FOR-MEANING

4.1 As "thrown-ahead," ex-sistence is simultaneously "present-to."

4.1.1 The "thrown-aheadness" indicates that ex-sistence's actuality is *possibility*.

4.1.2 The "presence-to" indicates that, *as* possibility, ex-sistence is able to make sense of itself and of whatever it encounters.

4.2 This bivalent structure of *immer schon vorweg* and *sein bei* (SZ 192.36–37) constitutes ex-sistence as "concern-for-meaning" (*Sorge*). Ex-sistence is simultaneously

4.2.1 a priori ahead *as* meaningful possibility (existenti*al*) *among* meaningful possibilities (existenti*el*); and

4.2.2 a priori present to—able to make sense of—whatever it encounters. It does so by "returning from" its aheadness to link a possible meaning with whatever is currently present, including oneself (GA 21: 147.24; SZ 366.17).

4.3 This concern-for-meaning (existential) enables us to make sense (existentielly) of whatever we meet, by *taking-it-as* having this or that meaning, or in Heidegger's jargon, by "projecting the thing towards" a possible meaning. As existentially *already pro-jected* (thrown ahead) we can existentielly pro-ject what we encounter "towards" a meaning.

4.4 Such taking-as or projecting-toward (*entwerfen auf*) results in *meaning* but not necessarily *truth* in the sense of *correctness*.

5. DISCURSIVE MEANING AND THE ONTOLOGICAL DIFFERENCE

5.1 Unlike God, ex-sistence is condemned to being ontological (GA 3: 280.30–31). We have to make sense of things by interpreting them (λέγειν τὰ ὄντα) rather than intellectually intuiting what they are.

5.2 Our knowledge is discursive: we have to "run back and forth" (*dis-currere*) between possible meanings and whatever is present, as we work out the fit between them.

5.2.1 In practical knowledge we look ahead to the task, estimate the tool's suitability for it, and then either use the tool or discard it.

5.2.2 In theoretical knowledge we are already "ahead," that is, familiar with a range of possible meanings (predicates), from which we "return" to what is present (the subject) to combine one of those predicates with it.

5.3 We always do so fallibly, but in each case the outcome is *meaning*, even when it's the *wrong* meaning. (Saying "Socrates was a Theban" is meaningful, even though it is incorrect.)

5.3.1 To put this in metaphysical language: we propose what we think is the current "being" (the whatness and howness) of something: *das jeweilige Sein des Seienden.*

5.3.2 But such "being" is always changeable and not necessarily true, as is evident when we correct ourselves and say "Socrates was an Athenian."

5.4 Hence there is no such thing as "*the*" being (single and unchanging) of anything. Each thing has many possible "beings" (where "being" means "being meaningful"), some of which on occasion are even correct.

5.5 Ex-sistence is the site of composition-and-distinction (σύνθεσις and διαίρεσις, *compositio et divisio*), and therefore only of *mediated* meaning (GA 21: 135–42). As such, ex-sistence is the site of the distinction that defines classical metaphysics: the onto-logical distinction between an *ens* and its *esse*, a thing and what we take it to be.

6. THE OPEN IS INTRINSICALLY HIDDEN

6.1 By 1930, Heidegger had reached his decisive insight that the Open is intrinsically "hidden" (GA 80.1: 371.29–30; cf. GA 9: 193.24–27). This is often misread as if a Super-Something called "Being" chose to "hide itself" from us. Heidegger meant something quite different.

6.2 All human knowledge is a matter of synthesizing-and-distinguishing a thing and its possible meaning. To relate those two relata to each other, we must (in Heidegger's metaphor) "traverse an open space"—the Open—within which the synthesizing-and-distinguishing can take place (GA 15: 380.6).

6.3 The Open is the ultimate presupposition of all human activity. Therefore, to ask what accounts for the Open, we have to presuppose the very Open that we are questioning, thereby falling into the error of "circular reasoning" or "begging the question" (*Prior Analytics* 57b and 64b).

6.4 Our inability to give an account of the Open (τὴν αἰτίαν γιγνώσκειν, ibid., 71b10–11; GA 15: 398.21) is what Heidegger means when he speaks of it as "intrinsically hidden." (His use of the faux reflexive *sich verbergen* does not mean the Open "hides *itself*" as if it exercised some kind of agency.)

6.4.1 Heidegger calls this state of affairs "the hidden mystery of ex-sistence" (GA 9: 195.23, 197.26).

6.5 Although the intrinsically hidden Open cannot be explained, it can be directly experienced in rare moments of personal attunement to our groundless ground (SZ 136.1–5).

6.5.1 In SZ such an awareness is called dread (*Angst*): existentielly realizing the finitude that is concretized in our mortality. Dread is a foretaste of the possibility that ends all possibilities.

6.5.2 Personally embracing one's mortality and living one's life in terms of that is what Heidegger means by "authenticity."

7. EX-SISTENCE IS EXISTENTIAL MOVEMENT, AKA "TEMPORALITY"

7.1 As "ahead" and "present-to," ex-sistence is structured as a unique existential movement (GA 21: 147.24) that SZ termed, with almost inevitable confusion, "temporality."

7.2 In 1928, Heidegger diagrammed this movement of simultaneous aheadness-and-return as follows (GA 26: 256.15):

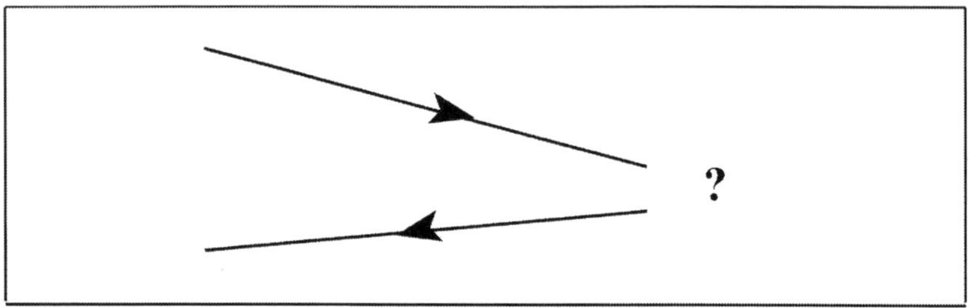

7.3 We may equally represent that as:

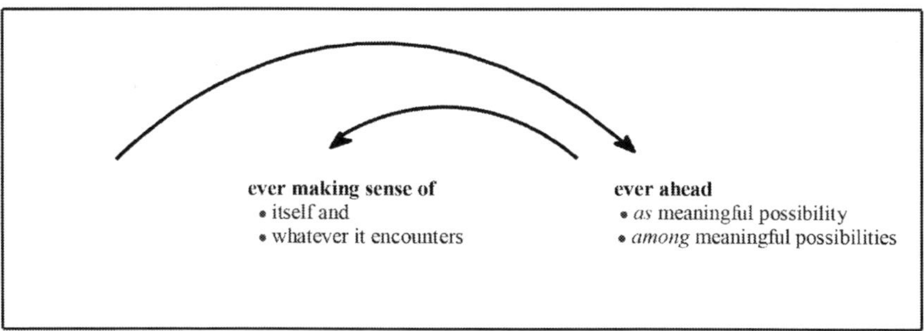

8. MOVEMENT AND *EIGNUNG*

8.1 In describing ex-sistence's actuality as *possibility*, Heidegger was modeling ex-sistence on Aristotle's notion of movement: κίνησις as ἐνέργεια ἀτελής.

8.2 Κίνησις is a thing's ontological condition of being real (ἐν ἔργῳ) but not yet fully (ἀ-τελές), that is, actual *to a degree*, yet still coming into its own:

8.2.1 ἐνέργεια is a thing's essential activity (*Im-Werk-stehen*), its functioning
- either as fully within its τέλος (if its movement is already complete)
- or as still underway to its τέλος (if its movement is not yet complete).

8.2.2 δύναμις is a moving thing's *Eignung* (GA 9: 285.25; GA 19: 265.14; etc.), its condition of
- coming-into-its-own/*eigen*, coming-*ad-proprium*, that is:
- being ap-*propri*-ated by and unto its τέλος.

8.3 Two examples, one from nature (φύσις), the other from human know-how (τέχνη):

8.3.1 An acorn has the δύναμις/*Eignung* of being an oak tree. It is "drawn" into its proper wholeness by its τέλος ("oak tree"). This τέλος lies *within* the acorn; it is the origin and ordering (ἀρχή) of its movement. Put otherwise, the acorn already has itself *in* its τέλος (ἐν τέλει ἔχει), but not fully. The realness (actuality) of the acorn has the form of ἐν-τελ-έχεια ἀ-τελής.

8.3.2 Guiding the construction of a cabinet is the carpenter's know-how (τέχνη), beginning with the prior projection of an idea of the outcome, the εἶδος προαιρετόν that will function as the τέλος of the activity. The wood that has been selected as appropriate (*geeignet*) for the task then undergoes a process of appropriation (*Eignung*) to being a cabinet. In this case the process is guided not by an internal τέλος, as with the acorn, but by the external τέλος residing in the mind of the carpenter who first projected the outcome (GA 9: 191–93; *Marx Engels Gesamtausgabe* II 5, 129.31–36).

8.4 In short, *Eignung* names the reality of a something that is in the process of being brought-*ad-proprium*, still coming into its proper status as complete and whole.

9. *EREIGNIS*

9.1 What *Eignung* is to artifacts and acorns, *Ereignis* is to ex-sistence—but with an important twist.

9.2 *Ereignis* does have to do with κίνησις, and κίνησις does have to do with incompleteness. However, *Ereignis* applies exclusively to *existential* κίνησις.

9.2.1 Ex-sistence is unique in being already "complete" in its incompleteness, already "whole" as never being whole. Ex-sistence is perfectly "perfect" in its imperfection, its inability to achieve complete self-coincidence.

9.3 In SZ, what accounted for ex-sistence's finitude (its open-ended-ness versus full self-presence) was called "thrownness." But in 1936 Heidegger began calling thrownness *Er-eignis* ("ap-propri-ation"), a term modeled on *Eignung*.

9.4 Appropriation names the fact that ex-sistence has been *er-eignet*, a priori brought into its proper ownness as the finite, mortal Open (GA 73.1: 226.26; GA 12: 128.29–30; 248.16; 249.5–6).

9.4.1 The word *Ereignis* simply reinscribes the basic structure of ex-sistence that SZ had called thrownness. (GA 65: 34.8–9; 239.5; 252.23–25; 322.7–8 with SZ 325.37; GA 9: 377, note d; GA 73, 1: 642.28–29; etc.)

9.4.2 Appropriated ex-sistence is *Zu-sein*: as possibility, ex-sistence is in the condition of ever-becoming.

9.4.3 To name this asymptotic condition of ex-sistence, Heidegger adopted Heraclitus' hapax legomenon Ἀγχιβασίη, "ever approaching" (fragment 122).

9.5 Appropriation is not an "event" in any sense of that term (GA 14: 25.33; GA 11: 45.19–20; GA 70.17–19). It is an existential *fact*, the very facticity of ex-sistence.

10. PHENOMENOLOGY

10.1 Heidegger made it clear that all his work, from 1919 until his death, was phenomenological (cf. GA 14: 54.2–14 and 147.16).

10.2 Phenomenology is correlation-research. As such it is about meaning, and specifically about the meaningful presence (*Anwesen*) of what one encounters (GA 64: 23–25).

10.3 In the natural attitude we mostly look "through" (i.e., ignore) the meaning-constituting correlation. Thematizing the correlation entails shifting the philosophical gaze *away from* an exclusive focus on the object and redirecting it *onto* the correlation itself.

10.3.1 The difference between Husserl's phenomenology and Heidegger's begins at this point. For Husserl the correlation is between the meaning-constituting subject and the meaningfully constituted object. For Heidegger, on the other hand, the correction is between the meaning-constituting *eject* and whatever it encounters (GA 14: 131.16–17). The two diagrams below illustrate that radical difference.

10.4 For Husserl human being is subjectivity, whether psychological or (ultimately) transcendental, and the phenomenological correlation is between the meaning-conferring subject and its object. In Husserl, therefore, the phenomenological refocusing of the gaze is a *re*-duction

(*Zurück-führung*: ἐπαν-αγωγή): leading the gaze *back* to the subject's relation to the object.

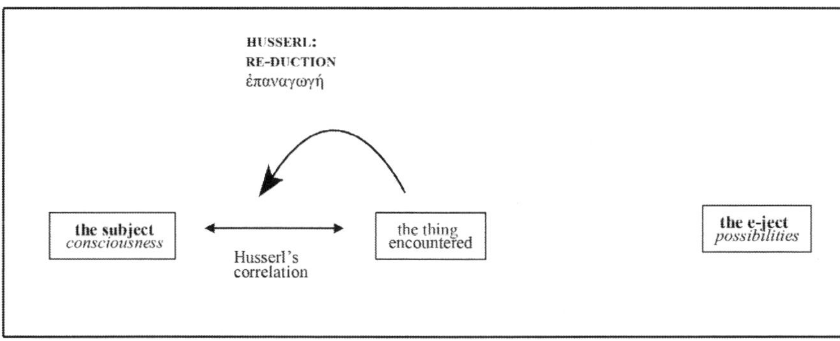

10.5 For Heidegger the essence of human being is not sub-jectivity but e-jectivity: ex-sistence, thrown ahead *as* possibility *into* possibilities. Existentielly, those possibilities are a matter of our own purposes, interests, desiderata, etc., which open up a meaning-giving context, a social and linguistic world-of-meaning. For Heidegger the phenomenological correlation *is* the world-of-meaning, the meaning-giving context that lies "between" what we encounter and the meaningful purposes and possibilities we are living into. Heidegger's refocusing of the phenomenological gaze, therefore, is not a *re*-duction (ἐπαν-αγωγή) but an *in*-duction (ἐπ-αγωγή), a redirecting of the gaze *forward* to the correlation between what we encounter and our concerns (GA 62: 131–32, 191–92; GA 22: 250.29; GA 9: 244.12–35).

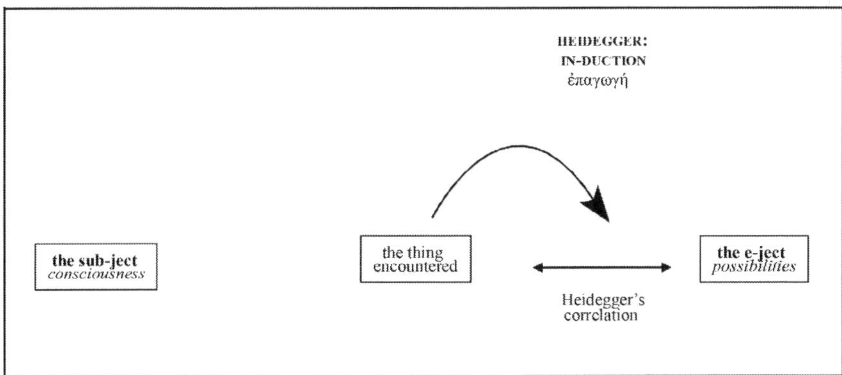

10.6 We could call Heidegger's refocusing of the gaze a phenomenological *re*-duction, as he himself did (GA 24: 29.15), so long as we remember that leading the gaze "back" means leading it *back to where we already are*: a priori ahead as possibility among possibilities.

10.7 Objections raised against Heidegger as a phenomenologist include such claims as:

- Interpreting Heidegger as a phenomenologist means relapsing into Husserlian transcendental subjectivity.
- Heidegger never employed a phenomenological reduction in the sense just adduced.
- Heidegger eventually abandoned phenomenology for the "thinking of Being."

10.8 These objections neglect Heidegger's own statements about phenomenology, subjectivity, and ex-sistence, not to mention his own understanding—which he never abandoned—of "transcendence" and "the transcendental" (GA 11: 150.10–12; GA 12: 91.3–6, 114.25–27; GA 89: 238.21–24; 286.2–14; etc.).

11. *SEINSVERGESSENHEIT*: OVERLOOKING THE OPEN

11.1 Heidegger's basic question was: How does meaningfulness (*Bedeutsamkeit*; or in metaphysical language, *Sein*) come about at all?

11.1.1 In Heidegger's early work, meaning is made possible by the *thrown-openness* of ex-sistence, whereas in his middle and later work, he expressed that as the *appropriation* of ex-sistence.

11.1.2 Heidegger's *seinsgeschichtliches Denken* (usually mistranslated as "being-historical thinking") is about how appropriated ex-sistence

- is overlooked both in everyday life and in the history of metaphysics
- even as it makes possible ("sends") various configurations of the Open.

11.3 Thrown-open ex-sistence cannot be accounted for: it remains "intrinsically hidden," or in Heidegger's language, "bracketed out" (= in ἐποχή).

11.3.1 As a result, one focuses on *things* (in the everyday) or on the current "*being*" of things (in metaphysics) and ignores the thrown-openness that makes things and their current "being" possible.

11.4 Focusing on "being" in whatever form—εἶδος, ἐνέργεια, *esse*, etc.—while overlooking the appropriated Open is what Heidegger called a metaphysical "epoch" (cf. ἐποχή).

11.4.1 An "epoch" is not a period of time but a bracketing out of the Open. Metaphysical "epochs" (e.g., Plato's, Aristotle's) can overlap, and the entire history of metaphysics can be considered a single "epoch."

11.5 Strictly speaking one can never "get out of" metaphysics because, as thrown "beyond things" (μετὰ τὰ φυσικά) into their possible meanings, ex-sistence itself *is* metaphysics (cf. GA 9: 122.12–13; GA 80.1: 345.13–15). But one can get free of being *restricted* to metaphysics as an "epoch," by embracing one's appropriation and living out of it (*die Einkehr in das Ereignis*: GA 14: 51.33).

12. *KEHRE*: "THE TURN"

12.1 Heidegger was clear on what "the turn" did *not* mean, but he was never crystal clear what that term *did* mean.

12.2 Toward the end of his career, Heidegger indicated what the turn was *not*. Contrary to what many Heideggerians believe, the turn was

- not something Heidegger carried out in the 1930s, beginning with GA 65, *Beiträge zur Philosophie* (GA 13: 149.29–30);
- not the change in how he thought through his fundamental question beginning in the 1930s; that was what he called not the *Kehre* but the *Wendung* or *Wandel im Denken* (GA 13: 149.21–22);
- not a change in the standpoint of SZ (GA 13: 149.23);
- not a change in his fundamental question: "What accounts for the fact that there is significance at all?" (GA 9: 201.30–32);
- not a change in his *answer* to that fundamental question: ex-sistence as appropriated to being the Open (GA 9: 202.5–9);
- and therefore not a matter of "demoting" ex-sistence in relation to the Open (aka "Being Itself").

12.3 There are two major candidates for what the turn *was*. The first: The turn was the shift of emphasis that was already programmed into the original plan of SZ and that Heidegger carried out over the next fifty years of his career: the shift from *Da-<u>sein</u>* (SZ I.1–2): how ex-sistence is and holds open the Open; to *<u>Da</u>-sein* (SZ I.3): how ex-sistence, as the Open, determines the meaning of whatever we encounter (SZ 17.32–33; 18.32–34). In both instances, of course, *Da-sein* is meant existentially, not existentielly.

12.4 The second candidate, which is not hard to conjugate with the first, is: The turn is the oscillating sameness (*Gegenschwung*) of *Da-<u>sein</u>* and

Da-sein (cf. GA 65: 29.15 et passim; GA 70: 126.18; GA 75: 59.15; etc.; cf. GA 26: 270.4–5).

12.5 It is probable that the issue of how the turn is to be decided was not of major importance to Heidegger and shouldn't be of great concern to Heideggerians. In 1962, Heidegger remarked:

> Instead of the groundless, endless prattle about the "turn," it would be more advisable and fruitful if people would simply engage themselves with the aforementioned issue [i.e., the Open and meaningful presence]. (GA 11: 150.3–5)

CODA: AFTER HEIDEGGER

Today Heidegger scholarship is in acute crisis. *Ab extra* it is under fierce attack from the philosophically challenged clique of Rockmore-Wolin-Fritsche-and-Faye. *Ab intra* it is caught in an embarrassing uncertainty about what Heidegger meant, how to express it, and how much of it to hold on to.

The attacks *ab extra*, motivated by Heidegger's toxic social and political convictions, are grounded in demonstrable ignorance of his philosophy. But they have had notable success not only in shaping the popular narrative but also in chipping away at the prospect of academic jobs in Heidegger scholarship.

But the uncertainty *ab intra* may end up having a more devastating effect on the future of Heidegger research. Almost fifty years after his death and nearly a century since his major work was published, experts on Heidegger still seem unable to reach a consensus on two basic issues: how he approached his work, and what the core of that work was. Regarding the first: Did he do all his work as phenomenology, and if so, of what kind? Or was his work a version of ontological realism focused on something called "Being"? As regards the second (and as only one example): Is it the case, as some scholars hold, that Parmenides and Heraclitus were already familiar with *die Sache selbst*, as evidenced by their discussions of ἀλήθεια and φύσις? Or, as Heidegger himself claims, did they miss the very core of "the thing itself" (GA 15: 366.31–32)? And if the latter is the case, what *is* "the thing itself"?

A further sign of that uncertainty is the difficulty Heideggerians have in expressing the substance of his thought in straightforward English—that is, without parroting Heidegger's statements in his own jargon or employing untranslated terms like *Dasein*, *Ereignis*, *Gestell*, and *Geschick*. Given this difficulty, some scholars pursue the "safe" path of echoing his idiosyncratic lexicon and babbling his esoteric mantras as if to prove that *l'érudition est moutonnière*. Such "scholarship" is painting itself into a corner of self-congratulatory irrelevance, where only the initiated understand what each other is talking about. This may be a harsh judgment, but as Husserl said, "One is never more severe than against errors he himself has recently abandoned."

It may be too early to speak of an "after Heidegger" as long as there is such confusion regarding what Heidegger's own work was about. Yes, Heidegger was a complex and difficult thinker—but so were Kant and Hegel. And yes, the work of every great philosopher is subject to endless interpretations, reinterpretations, and major shifts in understandings. But none of that justifies the scandalous state of Heidegger scholarship today.

What, then, does one do? Or as Socrates might ask: What is the ὅθεν we push off from in moving toward an "after Heidegger"?

Part II

AFTER THE BLACK NOTEBOOKS

Chapter 6

What Is Left of Heidegger

On the Future of a Philosopher

Donatella Di Cesare

It is not difficult to imagine that Heidegger and his oeuvre are destined to remain in our future. Contrary to what some foretold, the *Black Notebooks* did not mark the end of his thought. The opposite turned out to be true: Heidegger has been the protagonist of a debate that has gone beyond the borders of academia and gained access to the world of culture, so much so that it is involving an ever-greater public. The *Schwarze Hefte* already represent a relevant component of the *Wirkungsgeschichte*, the history of effects produced by Heidegger's thinking.

Very few and isolated are the voices that intend to support the campaign to banish Heidegger once and for all. This is the case with moralists who claim to be able to distinguish between the good and the bad, between white and black, as if philosophy did not just dwell in the complexity of the *chiaroscuro*. After a debate of almost three years we can say that the position of ideological anti-Heideggerism has not had any effect.

No less sterile proved to be the opposite position, that of the "resentful orphans." This is what in my book *Heidegger & Sons*[1]—which is a book about legacy, about necessarily unfaithful faithfulness, and about Heidegger's (very political) future—I called those who reacted with nostalgic vehemence to the shock suffered by the world of philosophy after the publication of the *Black Notebooks*. The resentful orphans represent a way to inherit—that of reaction, the reactionary way both from a philosophical viewpoint and a political one. "How do you dare jeopardize Heidegger because of a few anti-Semitic junctures?" Their claim culminates in such a rhetorical question, sometimes articulated outspokenly, but most of the time just hinted at. Immersed in the dogmatic sleep of Heideggerian axiomatics, of which they believed themselves to be the gatekeepers, the resentful orphans have closeted themselves in the archive, that legacy almost taken to be a property; they are entrenched in the idolatrous cult of the lost Big Father.

These two extreme positions have so far hindered the debate. Despite this, there have been international meetings and workshops in which philosophers from different continents have had the opportunity to discuss Heidegger's anti-Semitism, but also, more generally, the *Black Notebooks*, the topics tackled therein, and their status within the ambit of the *Gesamtausgabe*.

What emerges with clarity is the close link that ties the *Schwarze Hefte* to the rest of Heidegger's work. This debunks the hypothesis meant to legitimize a selective reading, one that allows us, with little caution, to pick out some texts rather than others—and that would also have the advantage of doing away with the so-called "mistake" of his political involvement. Yes to *Being and Time*—no to the *Black Notebooks*. Such a grotesque either-or, which might come in handy to a certain traditional phenomenology, appears to be utterly arbitrary.

That it is impossible to sever *Being and Time* from the *Black Notebooks*, as well as from his posthumous work in general, is attested by Heidegger himself. The *Anmerkungen I-V* (1942–1948), in GA 97, contain a great deal of pages entirely devoted to *Sein und Zeit*. This rethinking initially takes the appearance of a self-defense, but then emerges as a certainty that his work will have a future (GA 97: 166). Heidegger reclaims that which he thought and wrote. He lays emphasis on the importance that he attaches to his own work: "1807: *Phenomenology of Spirit*. 1867: *Capital*. 1927: *Being and Time*" (GA 97: 131).

While exactly on the basis of the last *Anmerkungen* it seems meaningless to separate *Being and Time* from the *Black Notebooks*, the question reemerges once more of the threads that can be traced to that first work and that can philosophically motivate his successive political choices. In the postwar period Heidegger straightforwardly writes that his mistake was not only political—*der Irrtum war nicht bloß "politischer"*—and, moreover, from an onto-historical vantage point it was not a mistake; on the contrary, it was a mistake from a philosophical perspective, as he was ahead of his time and had believed he was faced with the overcoming of metaphysics, whereas this overcoming was not there yet (GA 97: 148).

We do not know what the fortune of this author will be after the *Black Notebooks*, but for sure the reception of his writings will change, that is to say, the way we interpret his reflections, concepts, and insights. Our reading of the essays "The Question Concerning Technology" or "Letter on 'Humanism'" cannot be the same on account of what Heidegger says in the *Notebooks* about technique and uprooting.

Therefore it is worth asking what the new topical themes are, and what the open questions are. Here I can offer a provisional answer. Certainly the

Black Notebooks unsettle the schemes through which Heidegger has been interpreted thus far.

The truly genuine novelties of the *Black Notebooks*, as was clear from the very beginning, are his anti-Semitism and the conception of the Shoah which derives from it. Eventually the *topos* of Heidegger's silence on Auschwitz vanishes.

The issue "Heidegger and Nazism," on the contrary, is not a novelty. This does not mean that it is not relevant. However, the pages of the notebooks show that the core does not lie in the relationship between politics and philosophy. Heidegger embraced Nazism committedly. Hence, it was not a "mistake," for it was a long and deep relationship. After the *Black Notebooks* we can discuss the way in which Heidegger understands Nazism, the way in which he pinned Germany's hopes on it and how he tasked it with a mission in the history of Being.

After the *Black Notebooks* it will be difficult to contend that Heidegger was indifferent to or scarcely interested in historical events. Such a commonplace is to be revised. The pages of the notebooks are also most of all a commentary on what was happening in those years, often supported by specific references. In much the same way, the stereotype of the philosopher who indulges in an apolitical conformism proves to be totally unjustified. Heidegger was by no means a "conformist" and in the *Black Notebooks* he comes across as a politically radical philosopher. It is therefore necessary to rewrite the chapter "Heidegger and politics" in a way that promises to be much more complex than we have so far believed. Unprecedented are the reflections on globalization.

Strictly connected to the issue of politics is that of theology, which is made even more complicated by the anti-Judaism that, especially in the notebooks of the late 1930s and 1940s, takes acute forms. On the other hand, it is impossible not to recognize that the eschatology of Being makes Heidegger scratch his head over the question of God and the relationship between God and Being.

Two particularly critical topics are ethics, to which he does not return in the postwar period, and metaphysics, or better, the critique of metaphysics, which certainly has to be discussed anew.

In my book *Heidegger and the Jews*,[2] I address the subject of anti-Semitism in the *Black Notebooks* between 1931 and 1948. Reflecting on the relationship between the "Jewish question" (*Judenfrage*) and the "question of Being" (*Seinsfrage*) does not in any way mean that this is the only theme of the work. Of course, anti-Semitism is the biggest news of the *Black Notebooks*. But beyond that, Heidegger's *Reflections* and *Annotations* on the Jews, Judaism, and the Shoah are not marginal, but rather have a profound importance. Why do I speak of metaphysical anti-Semitism? The adjective "metaphysical" does not mitigate the anti-Semitism. Rather, it indicates its gravity and extent. Metaphysical anti-Semitism in my discourse has at least three meanings:

1. "Metaphysical" indicates, first, the continuity of Heidegger's anti-Semitism. I was convinced of this continuity even before the issuance of the volume GA 97, which contains the pages dating to the postwar period and which confirms this continuity. However, anti-Semitism is not a feeling that comes and goes and that can be limited to just one period. It cannot be reduced to personal hatred toward the Jews. Whoever understands it as such makes it a biographical detail, lacking theoretical relevance. The Enlightenment prejudice that considers it a form of hatred that has escaped from reason but can be remedied by reason is, after Auschwitz, not only ethically problematic but philosophically unacceptable.
2. "Metaphysical" indicates the continuity of anti-Semitism in the metaphysical tradition and thus refers to the connection that, in the context of anti-Semitism, ties Heidegger unwillingly to that tradition. This anti-Semitism boasts of a long history that has only partly been written. In his metaphysical anti-Semitism, Heidegger is not alone: he follows a long line of philosophers from Kant to Hegel to Nietzsche. Emphasizing the continuity of an entire tradition that, to be precise, dates back to the anti-Judaism of the Church Fathers does not mean reducing the seriousness of Heidegger's anti-Semitism. Rather, the intent is to show that if the many stereotypes (and more than a few concepts) that emerge in the pages of the *Black Notebooks* recall, on one hand, the National Socialist outlook of those years, they arise, on the other, from philosophy and the way in which philosophers from Kant to Fichte to Hegel, particularly in modern times, have addressed the "Jewish question." Like it or not, there exists a "Jewish question" in philosophy.
3. "Metaphysical" qualifies Heidegger's anti-Semitism. That is, it indicates the way in which he gives in to the pressure of defining the Jew that was dominant in the years of the Nuremberg Laws. I thus use the term "metaphysical" in the sense understood by Heidegger. It is paradoxical that, while he ties the Jews to metaphysics with a Gordian knot (and I will return to this point) in defining the essence of the Jew, Heidegger falls, in turn, into metaphysics. I speak of metaphysical anti-Semitism because, in taking up an old theme in the Western tradition, the relationship between Being and the Jew, Heidegger delineates a *metaphysics of the Jew* reduced to an abstract figure, a figural Jew, and in order to define him, he makes use of the old binary oppositions of metaphysics that he himself had placed into question. In his history of Being, Heidegger runs into the Jew. He feels that the Jew is not the "enemy" but rather, the

Other who, in his otherness, could represent the passage he is looking for beyond metaphysics. But Heidegger steps back.

However, because of the strong connection that exists in the *Black Notebooks* between the question of Being and the Jewish question (e.g., GA 96: 243), the Jew appears inscribed in the heart of Heidegger's thought, at the center of philosophy's question *par excellence*.

The pages of the *Black Notebooks* that cover 1942 to 1945, immediately preceding the defeat of Germany, are filled with a weak expectation that gives way to gloomy resignation. The moment approaches, unstoppably, in which "the Germans will be put to the test of universal history" (GA 97: 18).

The word that recurs in the *Anmerkungen I* is *Vernichtung*, annihilation. As the worldwide character of the war emerges, however, the term *Selbstvernichtung*, "self-annihilation," surfaces. What does this disturbing composite mean?

In "planetarianism," the end will not be a simple one, the result of a finishing. Rather, it will be an apocalyptic translation into nothingness even of the end itself. Only in this way will a new beginning be able to arise. In the global war, there will no longer be fronts; the danger is annihilation of self. This is because the "supreme act of politics" consists of pushing the adversary "into a condition in which *he is forced to proceed to his own self-annihilation*" (GA 97: 260). But for Heidegger, the "form in which one achieves self-annihilation" is technology (GA 97: 188). "Technology reaches the highest level when, being consumption [*Verzehr*], it no longer has anything to consume—except itself" (GA 97: 18). Technology consumes itself, wears itself out, destroys itself. It is simultaneously the paradigm and place of self-consumption—another way of saying, on the worldwide horizon, the recovery from metaphysics.

In this context, Heidegger returns to speaking of the Jews in a passage that contains the onto-historical interpretation that Heidegger gives to the Shoah—while the Shoah is being carried out. With this passage, the big *topos* of twentieth-century philosophy, Heidegger's silence about Auschwitz, ends: "Only when what is essentially 'Jewish,' in the metaphysical sense, struggles against what is Jewish, is the peak of self-annihilation in history reached" (GA 97: 20).

If the "Jewish question" is a metaphysical one, the solution would be similarly metaphysical. The *Endlösung*, the "final solution," if read within the history of Being, turns out to be "self-annihilation." Heidegger interprets the extermination as a "self-annihilation": the Jews would self-annihilate. Agents of modernity, complicit in metaphysics, the Jews follow the destiny of technology, which is summed up in the word *Verzehr*: the usurers cheat themselves, the consumers consume, the destroyers end by destroying themselves. The link between technology and extermination must not be missed here. Also not to be missed, however, is the way in which that ontological massacre should have passed into history: No one, in fact, could have been involved—if not the Jews themselves. The Shoah would be the "summit of self-annihilation in history," the apocalyptic moment in which the end that does not want to end would finally be translated into nothing. But the "summit of self-annihilation" was not reached.

After 1945, Heidegger speaks not so much of Jews, but of "foreigners," of "emigrants." As appears evident in the so-called "note for jackasses" (GA 97: 159) against Jewish prophecy, he withdraws the open anti-Semitism. The reason for this choice is his embarrassment. But Heidegger had not changed position. The passages addressed against the God of the Jews or against Judeo-Christian monotheism become more numerous. Just as anti-Semitism had developed in the wake of anti-Judaism, so too within the margins of that wake does it provisionally make its return. Metaphysical anti-Semitism becomes suspended, so to speak, in an anti-Judaism that, in the tradition of Nietzsche, takes aim at Christianity too, understood as Judaism for the peoples.

In 1948, he speaks of *Geist der Rache*, the spirit of revenge. The theological themes spill over into the political ones. He writes, *Ein alter Geist der Rache geht um die Erde*, "an old spirit of revenge roams the earth" (GA 97: 445). This phrase echoes the opening of the *Manifesto* of Marx and Engels, 100 years after its publication. Here again, then, is that old Jewish spirit that returns, that ghost of which Europe did not free itself.

Just two observations at the end. The *Black Notebooks* open a new scenario on Heidegger's political thought, which reveals itself to be well-organized, compound, and often rich in ideas. Heidegger comments on historical events, develops a politics within the horizon of a philosophy of history in which—as Peter Sloterdijk has observed—he looks toward the end. I would like to speak, for instance, of his concept of revolution, of his ideas on planetarianism. If the dominant tone in the *Black Notebooks* is apocalyptic, Heidegger is not, however, like Schmitt, an "apocalyptician of counterrevolution"—to use the words of Jacob Taubes. Heidegger does not want to hold back the revolutionary drive that runs through history. But neither is he an apocalyptician of revolution. Rather, he finds himself at an impasse between apocalypticism and revolution. This is the result of his ambivalent attitude toward messianism. His apocalypticism is missing the messianic "however" of an anarchical interruption. Thus, there is neither redemption nor liberation.

The ambivalence toward messianism also reemerges—at closer glance—in Heidegger's overall relationship with Judaism, in which there are not a few affinities and points of convergence.

In my book *Heidegger & Sons*, I have given a lot of space to the daughters. And I asked myself about the encounter between Heidegger and Arendt that, after the *Black Notebooks*, seems symbolic. *Hannah*—which means "grace" in Hebrew—is the name of the event that breaks Heidegger's *ordo amoris*. And it leaves him at an impasse that is not only existential, but also philosophical. Hannah is the missed chance, the escaped *kairos*, the refuge of a rejected *Heimat*, perhaps, because it is too disturbingly foreign. In the kaleidoscope of his love story with Arendt, the obstacles of his "political theology" can already be seen. The messianic character of love does not move Heidegger, who chooses the safety of distance.

What would Arendt have said, reading the pages of the *Black Notebooks* where Heidegger tries to define the Jew and the Jewish, where he speaks of the *Weltjudentum*, of "world Judaism, instigated by emigrants allowed to leave Germany" (GA 96: 262), and in which he imputes to Judaism a *Weltlosigkeit*, an "absence of world" (GA 95: 97)? For here, he seems to be explicitly referring to Jews such as her.

We cannot know. Arendt's is one of those voices that today are missing. But the battle of love between Heidegger and Arendt becomes an indispensable key to understanding the reflection on the figure of the Jew in the *Black Notebooks*, while the latter opens a new retrospective view on that relationship.

The Jew, for Heidegger, must respond to the most serious fault, the oblivion of Being. Behind the oblivion of Being, one perceives the echo of an older fault, that of deicide. Precisely because the most serious fault—the metaphysical one—is imputed to the Jew, he remains inscribed in the heart of Heidegger's thinking. Because of this, it is impossible, as perhaps some would hope, to easily dismiss the Jew and the passages in which he appears in the *Black Notebooks*.

In the attempt to grasp the essence of the Jew, Heidegger falls, in turn, into metaphysics, delineating a *metaphysics of the Jew* reduced to an abstract figure, a figural Jew.

In my interpretation, Heidegger's encounter with the Jew is crucial. For it is an encounter that could express a new "turn" in his philosophy, but which fails to seize this opportunity. While he goes through the night of the world, searching for the other beginning, a foreign figure bursts into his path. Hannah? No. Heidegger encounters the shadow, the ghost, the *figural Jew*, burdened by a metaphysical weight. He senses that the Jew is not the limit, but is the Other that, in his otherness, can open the beyond to him. And yet he steps back. He chooses Being; he lets the Jew fall away.

When I speak of metaphysical anti-Semitism, while I worsen Heidegger's position—and I believe that my interpretation is the most severe—at the same time I indicate, in the metaphysics of the Jew, an impasse in Heidegger's thinking, a relapse into metaphysics, from which it is possible, indeed indispensable, to start again.

NOTES

1. Donatella Di Cesare, *Heidegger & Sons: Eredità e futuro di un filosofo* (Turin: Bollati Boringhieri, 2015).

2. Donatella Di Cesare, *Heidegger e gli ebrei: I "Quaderni neri"* (Turin: Bollati Boringhieri, 2014) = *Heidegger, die Juden, die Shoah* (Frankfurt am Main: Vittorio Klostermann, 2015).

Chapter 7

Thinking-Time

Or, Why Do "We" Ask About the Future of Heidegger's Thinking?

Peter Trawny

Why do "we" ask about the future of Heidegger's thinking? I am posing the question in the plural—a decision that I make quite rarely, because this plural is deceptive. How can I claim a community which does not exist? Or do I identify this plural with universal reason? This would be most deceptive. I do not want to demand it. It is not the case that I would doubt the argumentative and therefore rational character of philosophy, but I don't want to appeal to it as if it would be the highest court. Philosophy is an event of freedom, and we do not know its conditions.

Nevertheless, I am speaking in the plural, for obviously the international network of Heidegger researchers poses—"we" are posing—the question of how or even whether there will be a future for Heidegger's thinking. This question can be modified in many ways. One can ask, what do "we" want to do with Heidegger's thinking (*que faire?*). Or: how will "we" continue with it? Can "we" still read Heidegger? What remains? Can his thinking still be taught at the university? But considered more closely, all these questions are so vague that a reformulation is necessary.

Certainly, the publication of the first series of *Black Notebooks* with its (sometimes) anti-Semitic content has caused a shock that is not easy to overcome, at least not for scholars both philosophically open to Heidegger and also willing to subject him to critique. The reactions of the feuilletons were—as on the occasion of the publication of the letters written by Martin Heidegger and his brother Fritz[1]—fierce, and not without reason. Many authors are dedicating themselves to intricate and divisive problems such as these emerging from the "*Black Notebooks*."

It is not often that a community of researchers—a community which is not a community, or which is only a community like every other "community," organizing itself on the basis of an unjust regimen of inclusion and exclusion—is faced with such pressures as it has been by that publication. The community's center and its periphery had to be rebuilt anew. Fronts and divisions appeared, sometimes through slander and other means of defamation.

*

Ever since Jürgen Habermas responded in the *Frankfurter Allgemeine Zeitung* to Heidegger's publication of *Introduction to Metaphysics* in 1953, Heidegger research has had to cope with the suspicion that it is dedicated to a philosophy contaminated by National Socialism and anti-Semitism. The climax of this suspicion was Emmanuel Faye's idea, formulated in 2005, that Heidegger's thinking serves as an "introduction of National Socialism into philosophy."

On the question of what could be the future of Heidegger's thinking, it is also Faye who has claimed the most extreme position. For him, Heidegger's philosophy appears as a weapon in a "battle where the future of mankind is at stake."[2] By spreading National Socialist and anti-Semitic ideas, Heidegger's supposedly profound thinking serves as a Trojan horse of inhumanity. There is no reason not to think that Faye and his disciples would prefer a total collapse of Heidegger scholarship, at least in the realm of philosophy. Then Heidegger's writings would serve only as monuments of a barbarous, despicable evil.

In contrast to this, "we" find the view that all critique of Heidegger is justified only concerning his concrete engagement with the National Socialist German Workers' Party (NSDAP; the Nazi party). But this engagement lasted only for a year (1933–1934). Later, Heidegger himself confessed that it was the "biggest stupidity of his life" (according to Heinrich Petzet). According to this view, every interpretation that finds anti-Semitic statements in the "*Black Notebooks*" is simply wrong, if not outright slanderous. Thus Friedrich-Wilhelm von Herrmann and Francesco Alfieri claim to explain to "us" "The Truth of the '*Black Notebooks*.' "[3] For von Herrmann or François Fédier[4] Heidegger's thinking remains totally unaffected by the anti-Semitic propositions in the notebooks—if such propositions exist at all.

*

"We" cannot ignore that the discussion about the future of Heidegger's thinking—however this formulation should be understood—has inscribed itself within a confrontational realignment of politics that is being realized across the world. This realignment may perhaps be best understood as a conflict between fundamentalist-nationalist and globalist-universalist conceptions of politics. Thus, in recent years, concepts which were successfully pushed aside for decades have returned to political discourse; prominent among these concepts, for instance, is that of "people" (*Volk*, folk, *peuple*, *popolo*).

In this emerging political discourse, Heidegger's thinking is—whether correctly or not—used by right-wing positions. In Germany, the Alternative für Deutschland, and in Austria, the so-called Identitären make use of Heidegger's ideas. Ibrahim Kalin, a political advisor of the Turkish president Recep Tayyip Erdoğan, has been quoting Heidegger in his lectures. Perhaps the most prominent right-wing Heideggerian is the Russian ideologue Alexander Dugin, who advocates for a virulent anti-liberalism grounded in his interpretation of Heidegger.

This political use of Heideggerian terminology and ideas has an effect on the institutional conditions for Heidegger research. If, in the face of the critiques made by Adorno and Habermas in the 1950s and 1960s, this research was forced to act defensively, at least in Germany, then the presence of Heidegger in right-wing discourse now seems to confirm the suspicions of his most violent critics. The latent aversion of academic philosophy to Heidegger's thinking appears confirmed. Now more conventional philosophy can refer to Heidegger's anti-Semitism in order to dismiss his thinking as a whole, as if academic business were intrinsically humane in itself.

This response of academic philosophy is relevant. For one may suspect that this reaction to Heidegger shows that we should understand philosophy as principally defined by political contexts. In such a view, the institutional discourses of legitimation are never free from political and social presuppositions. The presumptuous claim of an apolitical institutional practice of philosophy as a neutral field of academic research betrays itself by hypocritically excluding philosophies with problematic political backgrounds. This institutional practice even treats as illegitimately political any philosophy that critiques the dominance of scientism and the sciences in academic philosophy and in society more generally; such a philosophy is seen as something that disturbs the apparently nonpolitical, neutral sphere of the sciences and sober research in the humanities.

The deceptive condition of the academic "we" is connected with this sociopolitical context of philosophy, where philosophy is the subject as well as the object of political strategies. The community of "researchers" organizes the question of what stands inside or outside of legitimate academic discourse. It would be naive to believe that these strategies would not be important in Heidegger research in times of its reformulation in a period of intense controversy, such as now.[5] The fact that "we" ask what remains of Heidegger, what Heidegger's remains are, what "we" can do with them, is related to these strategies.

*

Philosophy as the source of political (and metapolitical) strategies seems to entangle itself in struggles for positions and discourse allotments. One could emphasize that, with his engagement with the NSDAP, Heidegger provides a paradigmatic model for this entanglement. Also, on the basis of his political presuppositions, Heidegger drew conclusions relevant to his university as an institution.[6] It would be wrong to separate Heidegger's philosophical interests during the time of his most intense engagement with National Socialism (1933–1934) from his academic decisions as rector of his university.

This Heideggerian integration of philosophy with a political event, Heidegger's vision of a "*metapolitics of 'the' historical* [*geschichtlich*] *people*" (GA 94: 124/91) opens up a specific perspective on the relation of philosophy and politics in general. It was Marx who introduced, in his third thesis on Feuerbach, the concept of a "revolutionary praxis." At stake is not (merely) theory, the precise observation of the world, but *changing* the world; and the necessity of this "change" emerges as a recognition of this observation.

Marx radicalizes a philosophical thought that ever since Plato has occupied and obsessed philosophy as well as religion, and not only in Europe. Plato, in the allegory of the cave, subjects the soul to a turning-around of perspective (*periagōgē tēs psychēs*) in order for the soul to achieve enlightenment: the human being is introduced to an understanding of education which, in its exemplary form, is revolutionary, a turning in a paradigmatic sense. Philosophy (and religion) transform a human being who tries to lose himself or herself in everyday life, and who then attempts to resist this philosophical transformation. From Plato to Heidegger, philosophy was—even in its theoretical intentions—nothing other than a strategy of transformation.

From Plato to Heidegger. Indeed, every ambitious philosophy claimed that the introduction to philosophy is intertwined with an alteration or transformation of the human being. Philosophizing means entering a transformation, a turning, that can only lead to a higher and better condition of the human being. Performing philosophy means transforming the subject of this performance.

*

In Heidegger's thinking we can find the following transformations: the collapse of the "inauthentic Dasein" through "anxiety" as realization of the "factical ideal" (SZ 310/MR 358) of "authentic Dasein"; the "turning" from a thinking of the "being of beings" to one of "beyng": "Yes—for here the *turning* announces itself—such that humans, if they *are* actually and steadfastly seekers, appertain to the turning, which means they are appropriated by the *event* as the essential occurrence of beyng itself" (GA 94: 343–44/250). We find the "leap" from the "first" to "the other beginning" (GA 94: 246/180); the "transformation" (*Verwandlung*) of the "*animal rationale*" to "Da-sein" (GA 95: 239; GA 65: 294/232); the "twisting free [*Verwindung*] from metaphysics" (GA 97: 381); the "decline into the distinction [*Unter-Schied*]" (GA 97: 375); and later the "awakening [*Entwachen*] into the event of appropriation" (GA 14: 63).

It seems that these transformative shifts of significations in the sphere of written and oral, esoteric and exoteric thinking were always understood as "real" transformations—and that from the beginning they should have been understood in this way. Heidegger's engagement for the NSDAP demanded the realization of the transformative moment of thinking, both his own and that of the Western tradition as a whole. Transformation is revolution. But soon Heidegger realized that *this* revolution, the National Socialist one, was no transformation in his sense, and no genuine transformation at all, but rather a further intensification of the West's nihilism. His response to this was to transform "revolution" itself, its meaning, into a "being-historical" signification. Heidegger's thinking is therefore the revolution of the "revolution."[7]

Both his critics and his apologists acknowledge that in this political engagement there appears a political-ethical problem in Heidegger's thinking. But whereas the critics think that in the transformative character of Heidegger's thinking, nothing other than the National-Socialist-anti-Semitic dogma (whatever this is in particular) calls for its realization, the apologists claim that there is no real connection between the transformative element in Heidegger's philosophy and the National-Socialist-anti-Semitic dogma.

It would not be difficult to show how the critics insist too unilaterally on the entanglement of the transformative character of Heidegger's thinking and the National-Socialist-anti-Semitic dogma (an entanglement which certainly existed), particularly in order to degrade and to disqualify his thinking from a moral perspective. And it would also not be difficult to indicate the moral belittlement in the strategies of the apologists, who are not willing to recognize a problem in the transformative challenge of Heidegger's philosophy. The question of what "we" still want to do with Heidegger, or even what "we" *should* do with him, is located in this alternative between moral disqualification and moral belittlement.

Both positions fail to recognize that Heidegger's transformative thinking inscribes itself in the National-Socialist-anti-Semitic dogma by at the same time destroying it, as I will try to show in what follows. The destruction does not withdraw the inscription; the inscription does not hinder the destruction.

In fact, in Heidegger's philosophy, both happen at the same time: radical revolutionary thought confirms and transforms political revolution in one move.

*

The transformative character of Heidegger's thinking finds its achievement in the concept of the "event of appropriation" (*Ereignis*). With this, Heidegger presented the ideal word for what he wanted to say since *Being and Time*. "Being" is historical in its temporality, it is "beyng-historical." It is inscribed into history as "beings" in their "beingness" (*Seiendheit*), from Plato's *idea* to Nietzsche's "will to power." In this inscription, philosophy thinks one and the same "being," and comes in modern times to the endmost and outermost, in which quite literally every-thing will be decided.

The concept of the event of appropriation underlines this movement of Heidegger's thinking, especially in its tension with the event of disappropriation, *Enteignis*. Nothing is itself, all is "disappropriated," only in order to become tautologically itself at some time, that is to be "appropriated." This step, this *metabolē*, establishes the matrix of the transformative character of Heidegger's philosophy. The event of appropriation gathers all possible transformations in its unity, which is differentiated in itself.

But there is still another feature emphasizing the importance of the concept: the "event of appropriation" gathers all the transformations of Heidegger's thinking—by structuring actuality (*Wirklichkeit*). With this, Heidegger's whole thinking arrives at its ownmost character. This is because the concept of the "event of appropriation" implies that such an event has more than a merely conceptual status. An event takes place, it happens, but it does this not only in a concept or in a text. Of course, there are also events in narratives, in movies, fictional moments of highest intensity, but they do not unfold the ontological possibilities of the concept. If somebody says that he has witnessed an event, I will not think that he is referring to a fictional event. On the contrary, I will think that something important has happened in the world we inhabit together.

By gathering the transformative character of his thinking in the concept of the "event of appropriation," Heidegger's philosophy comes to its ultimate transformation, namely to that of its text, of its writing. In Heidegger's writings, philosophy leaves the framework of a mere text. This does not mean that the concept of the "event of appropriation" *really* describes actuality. It opens up an in-between of actuality and fiction; Heidegger's thinking becomes something like a myth, a narrative oscillating between actuality and fiction (therefore, some have emphasized that Heidegger's thinking is neither an idealism nor a materialism). Thus, is Heidegger's "history of beyng" perhaps *the* myth of the twentieth century? It inscribes itself in what is called "event of appropriation," by being written by this "event" itself—or so Heidegger says, at least.

*

Heidegger often emphasized that his thinking is a "movement,"[8] using an archaic and hyphenated form of the German word *Bewegen*. He employs *Be-wëgen* to indicate a thinking that gives ways and marks ways in the landscape of thinking as a questioning that does not presume to arrive at definitive propositional answers. Heidegger's work, at its best, generates pathways on which thinking can unfold its attempts. This possibility can be realized only by destroying the dogmatic tendency which emerges sometimes, but not necessarily, in Heidegger's transformative thinking. Propositions which appear to have a prophetic character always have a preliminary and performative essence arising from the movement of thinking as *Be-wëgung*. In this sense, one can read Heidegger as a prophet, but at the price that one no longer recognizes in this philosophy the destruction of all prophecy as authoritative pronouncement about the future.

Heidegger's thinking gets its restlessness from a permanent destabilization of its significations. Its dogmatic tendency, appearing necessarily in its transformative character (one has to know the goal of the transformation), calls for destruction. All these movements are not only inherent in Heidegger's thinking. They show the paradigm of philosophizing as such—its ownmost temporality. Not only Heidegger's thinking is a "movement"; philosophy in general "moves" (*be-wëgt*), so long as we allow that further questioning along unexpected pathways is always possible.

In this context, the *Black Notebooks* can be interpreted as the most performative texts that Heidegger ever wrote. In these writings, the thinker makes his performance in gestures which dramatize the movement of thinking itself. As in Nietzsche's later texts, philosophizing itself becomes thematic by barely having any other topic. All apparent things and affairs retreat into groundlessness. They do not count as specific problems. What remains is thinking as such, which says and shows: "Look, here thinking is happening! And this is what all philosophy is about: Think!"

Temporality of thinking: *thinking-time*[9]—it develops within the progressive steps of particular thoughts, or of the significations that are formed in these thoughts. These significations emerge by continually referring to different, further significations. This means that in this flow, significations always have to be passing by, they are already in the past, just in order to give space, to render possible further and different significations. Derrida characterized this event as *différance*.

To interrupt this movement understood as *Be-wëgung* means that thinking arrives at another status. Now it becomes thinking *about* thinking, *about* thoughts. It is to this interruption of thinking that we owe what "we" view as the various philosophies across the various periods of the long Western tradition. It is obvious that this objectification of philosophy by historians is a thinking of the second order. It is an appropriation of an "object" that withdraws itself from the genuine movement of thinking.

"Here thinking is happening!" This is a claim emphasized not only by Heidegger's work. Every ambitious philosophy offers this appeal: "Participate in philosophy, philosophize, do not merely reduce questions and thought to their historical context!" Philosophy is the ultimate challenge to philosophize for yourself. Although Heidegger's philosophy sometimes seems to determine a specific idea, although it does have its own dogmatic aspect despite itself, its authentic meaning is the experience of continuing philosophy by philosophizing.

*

The terrible inability to address the factual crimes in the extermination camps as what they were: a mass murder industrially organized by the Germans; anti-Semitic propositions sounding like crude echoes of official Nazi propaganda; attempting to excuse the German crimes of the Nazi period by playing them off in a false equivalency with the Allied occupation of Germany after the war; keeping silent about the Shoah—these are all entirely plausible reasons to break off every interest in Heidegger's philosophy.

Morality promises a rigor in which a decision stipulates the attitude to a certain affair. I mark it or even cross it out: "Enough!" Moreover, one can be resolved to enjoin one's decision on the others, because one suspects that Heidegger's thinking endangers ethical standards in general. Faye and his followers represent this resolution. The professional norms inherent in academic institutions and methodologies tend to it as well.

Here ethics is understood as the God of philosophy. This is without a doubt a familiar apotheosis. Descartes, Kant, and Levinas agree that the practical dimension of philosophy should claim primacy. The good human being and the good world are more important than the philosophizing human being and the world comprehended through questioning—most of all, because the philosophizing human being can be an organizer of a mass murder, and the world as comprehended can become a concentration camp. Moral judgment—which always and only can be made by me (not by "us")—brings the movement of philosophy to a halt. It craves an end to it.

But this is impossible. Moral judgment cannot finish the movement of philosophizing, in the sense of completing it or just being done with it, because in the relation to this movement, to its temporality, moral judgment cannot define a limit. Moral judgment wants to freeze what is judged, so to speak; it wants to establish its signification once and for all. Maybe this succeeds when it faces a specific deed, a murder, for example. But the movement of thinking withdraws from the moral judgment simply because it continues. If I judge morally, the judged person, institution, act, or event does not disappear; they linger on by immediately provoking further judgments. Moral judgments are, of course, neither impossible nor pointless, but in thinking they cannot realize their inherent will to unmake deeds or ideas by putting an end to thinking about them.

Perhaps, therefore, it is inherently difficult to judge philosophers morally. Considered more specifically, those judgments work only by drawing a connection between propositions and real crimes. One presupposes that there must be a relation. But how, and what?

Certainly a philosophical thinking itself could judge crimes according to moral standards. It could also take care not to come close to the affirmation of these crimes. This is exactly what can be claimed about the failure of the *Black Notebooks* of 1931 to 1948: The philosopher missed the opportunity to distance himself from the German crimes. How could this horrible default happen? The omission is painful. But already the question about this Heideggerian failure to make a clear statement against the extermination of the Jews bears witness to the fact that thinking is "moving," that it is always most properly a *Be-wëgen.*

*

The question of the future of Heidegger's thinking, the question of what will remain of it, what "we" still can do with it, is simply wrong. The question objectifies this thinking, reducing it to *one* proposition or at least to a manageable number of propositions. Such a discursive situation has its own legitimation in its ethical orientation, but as regards the questions mentioned earlier, it must be characterized as un-philosophical.

Hence "we" could ask why the institutionalized form of philosophy has such a significant interest in neglecting the genuine character of philosophy in its temporal unfolding as *Be-wëgen.* Why do "we" not philosophize anymore in the institutions of so-called higher learning? Why do "we" objectify philosophy into a traditional canon? Why did it become a *possession* of a specific "we" who alone are authorized to legitimate what counts as philosophical work?

The event of philosophy consists in philosophizing. It presupposes a liberation from the objectifications of its institutionalized forms. It is such a liberation. Philosophy is never a possession, it cannot be appropriated. Perhaps the

Black Notebooks are especially a scandal because they withdraw Heidegger from "us," showing us that "we" do not possess Heidegger. This scandal would then be a possibility, a *productive* possibility. Because in philosophy, every disappropriation is better than all the ephemeral appropriations, which flee from that liberation. Heidegger took the *Black Notebooks* seriously. "We" should be grateful.

NOTES

The author of this chapter intended to include a line from the song "Imagine" by John Lennon as an epigraph. The line challenges us to imagine that there could be a life without possessions. The author obviously doubts that we can. But because of copyright law, we cannot reproduce the line in this chapter.

1. *Heidegger und der Antisemitismus: Positionen im Widerstreit: Mit Briefen von Martin und Fritz Heidegger*, ed. Walter Homolka and Arnulf Heidegger (Freiburg im Breisgau: Herder Verlag, 2016).
2. Emmanuel Faye, *Heidegger: The Introduction of Nazism into Philosophy in Light of the Unpublished Seminars of 1933–1935*, tr. Michael B. Smith (New Haven, CT: Yale University Press, 2011), 11.
3. "We" can still study these arguments only in the Italian version: Friedrich-Wilhelm von Herrmann and Francesco Alfieri, *Martin Heidegger: La verità sui Quaderni neri* (Brescia: Morcelliana, 2016).
4. Cf. François Fédier, "Martin Heidegger et le monde juif," *La règle du jeu* 58/59 (2015): 201–32—a massive and barely fair attack on my book *Heidegger and the Myth of a Jewish World Conspiracy*, tr. Andrew J. Mitchell (Chicago, IL: University of Chicago Press, 2015).
5. Cf. Dieter Thomä, "Heidegger als Philosoph des Ausrufezeichens," in *Heideggers Weg in die Moderne: Eine Verortung der "Schwarzen Hefte,"* ed. Hans-Helmuth Gander and Magnus Striet (Frankfurt am Main: Vittorio Klostermann, 2017), 244: "In these times there is a fight for the supremacy of interpretation, and especially in Freiburg there are researchers who are sitting like proud guards on Heidegger and defend their fortress compulsively."
6. Cf. the "judgment" about Richard Hoenigswald in GA 16: 132–33.
7. "'Revolution'—but finally we have to understand its essence in a revolutionary sense, i.e. in the meaning of the word as rolling the essence back into the inceptual" (GA 97: 19).
8. This translation by Peter D. Hertz in OWL is, of course, insufficient.
9. The German *Denk-Zeit* is a neologism. But in German there is the formulation *sich Bedenkzeit ausbitten* (to ask for time to think a decision over). Philosophy is finally nothing else but the time in which you philosophize.

Chapter 8

Getting Ourselves on the Hook

Julia A. Ireland

In the concluding chapter of *Heidegger: The Introduction of Nazism into Philosophy*, Emmanuel Faye writes that Heidegger's *Gesamtausgabe* "cannot continue to be placed in the philosophy series of libraries; its place is rather the historical archives of Nazism and Hitlerism."[1] The censure expressed in this "cannot continue" attempts a philosophical quarantine just as ideological as what it would seek to contain, and is not without historical irony given the Nazis' cataloguing of "phenomenology" under "the schools of the Jewish-liberalist dissolution," which was similarly intended as an archival designation.[2] Faye's is the most heavy-handed interpretation of the phrase "after Heidegger," up there with trigger warnings peremptorily aimed at the unsuspecting, well, who? One can't help but wonder about the imaginative construction of a reader in need of saving from the act of reading itself and the terrible submission undertaken on her behalf.

What does it mean to contribute to a volume entitled *After Heidegger?* at this particular moment? Prior to the revelations of the *Black Notebooks*, the phrase "[fill in the blank] after Heidegger" was used to express the idea of a bequest and provocation, itself the acknowledgment of a living philosophical legacy. "After" as "pursuit," "after" as "in appropriative imitation of" (here meant as "contestation" in the Heideggerian spirit of *Auseinandersetzung*), "after" as "to follow" and "follow from." But not "after" in the "Before" and "After" of the rigid chronology announced at a recent conference on Heidegger's politics in a strange and entirely serious debate over whether "we" "can keep" *Being and Time*, as though something had been decided and the only thing remaining was to sift through the ruins. Nothing has been decided. At the same time, it is disingenuous to pretend that the word "after" implies a continuity and not a trauma. Which is to express my concern that the title of this volume contributes to a shift in meaning that is a variation on Faye's fantasy library in its temptation toward the production of a philosophical good conscience that gets us off the hook rather than on it.

I want to stay with the discontinuity opened by the traumatic "after" in addressing what remains most striking for me about the *Black Notebooks*, which is how the trenchancy of Heidegger's metaphysical critique of racial biologism can live together with his anti-Judaic statements. Let me clarify that in adopting the term "anti-Judaic" in place of "anti-Semitic" I accept the argument put forward by historian David Nirenberg in *Anti-Judaism: The Western Tradition.*[3] The degree to which Jews, Jesuits, Bolsheviks, Americans, the English, Modernity, the Gigantic, Calculability, and even the Nazis themselves can substitute for each other in Heidegger's text indicates that his references to "Jews" and "Jewry" function as something more than a run-of-the-mill, conventional anti-Semitism. Indeed, there is every suggestion that with respect to this logic of substitution "Heidegger" may well name the apotheosis of anti-Judaism within a tradition that is alternate to the "history of Being" and over which Heidegger—despite his pose of polemical exaggeration—has no rhetorical control. In contrast to the thesis advanced by Peter Trawny concerning a *seynsgeschichtlicher Antisemitismus*, which remains parasitic on Heidegger's own gesture, Nirenberg suggests that what is called for is an investigation into how the entire Western "discourse" of anti-Judaism is absorbed into Heidegger's statements. At the center of this alternate *Historie* would be Heidegger's conversion of traditional anti-Judaizers into Jews themselves, the final perversity of which elides the distinction between persecutor and victim as Nazis become Jews due to their supposedly shared conception of a people as the blood-belonging of race.

My desire to focus on racial biologism also picks up a statement by Giorgio Agamben about "modern democracy's decadence and gradual convergence with totalitarian states in post-war democratic spectacular society," for which the election of Donald Trump serves as evidence.[4] Certainly one of the more uncomfortable aspects of the *Black Notebooks* for contemporary theory is the way Heidegger's analyses of "life" (*Leben*), Nietzschean becoming, modernity, and the will to power prefigure what Foucault designated "bio-power," without Heidegger's dismantling of the subject allowing him to advance a political alternative (preferably some version of leftism) that was itself not the seeming equivalent of fascism. This situation animates nostalgia for a pre-Heideggerian universal rationality unable to be coherently rehabilitated after Heidegger, as though Kant could save us now. Where for Agamben, modern democracy's "convergence" with totalitarianism lies in the relationship between politics and "bare life" as a constitutive exclusion, my claim is that Heidegger's politics is situated by an ambiguity between *physis* ("Nature" as the totality of beings) and *zōē* (life) announced in two competing conceptions of growth, and from growth, two competing conceptions of how becoming, possibility, and destiny are conceived. The difference here is between the "biology is destiny" of a polluted Darwinism and the Nietzschean-Pindaric imperative, "Become what you are," intoned in §31 of *Being and Time* that we may or may not get to keep. Heidegger's interpretation of *physis* supplies a necessary access for understanding the crucial term *Bodenständigkeit* in the *Notebooks*, whose "rootedness" points toward a natality that is not the mechanistic "expression" (*Ausdruck*) of a vitalistic biologism but a reserve of possibility—a "nativity," if we can hear this word—whose "blessing" (*Segen*) is quite capable of betrayal.

According to the interpretations Heidegger advances throughout the 1930s and 1940s, the biologistic conception of life thinks growth as "process" (*Vorgehen*) and "increase" (*größer werden*) or, more accurately in including the innovation he understands to have taken place in the convergence of modern experimental science with the mathematical, as change of position calculable over time. Within the self-promulgated National Socialist "worldview" (a concept Heidegger never stopped deriding), the metaphysics of life is not just mapped onto "the political" through race, which takes the place of the abstract, universal, and therefore spatially and temporally rootless "citizen." Rather, it is in the "scientificity" or *Wissenschaftlichkeit* with which National Socialist ideology produces the racial subject that National Socialism produces "the political" in an entirely *new* way, reflective of an entirely *new* order on earth. It is as biological that Hitler's vision was theological. ("The restriction to a certain small surface of soil as conditioned by domestic colonization, and the same final result which is achieved by limitation of propagation, lead to an extremely unfavorable military political situation of the nation involved. . . . The acquisition of the new land and soil for the settling of the overflowing population has no end of advantages, especially when turning away from the present towards the future."[5]) To miss this is to miss how racial biologism implicates an understanding of time that constrains the future into being a function of process, modifying the projective structure of possibility into the ever-expanding movement of life administered as a planned program of repopulation.

To lay out my claim, I want to take Faye seriously by "shelving" Heidegger next to Alfred Baeumler's 1934 essay "Der politische Volksbegriff" ("The Political Concept of the *Volk*"), which first appeared in the Nazi organ *Jugend und Recht*. The piece's opening, which owes no small debt to Marx, begins with the statement, "A Giant has stepped onto the stage of world-history"—this "Giant" is *das Volk*. By the end, it turns out that Baeumler's task was to distinguish the "dynamic" *Volksbegriff* from its "static" and essentialist competitor, "so-called '*Volkstheorie*,'" which fails the test of being active, since "political concepts are action-concepts," and "action-concepts" are about the "future." This is a metaphysical statement. What makes the piece rhetorically interesting is the way it enacts the definition of "political science" it promotes through the establishment of the concept of the *Volk* it requires in order to secure itself as "political" and therefore a "science." Methodologically, this is all vitalistic biology, so let us grant that there is an important (and readable) difference between a hermeneutical circle and an ideological self-justification. What is known in 1934? That Hitler's pronouncements on race are politically foundational.

The importance of Baeumler's essay lies in its entirely original conception of "biological legislation" developed through the loaded use of the words "dynamic" and "living" in relation to, precisely, the future. After addressing how the *Volk* has been considered "unpolitical" over and against the "political" state (he writes that this "false dualism" is "the final position of conservative liberalism"), Baeumler asserts that the *Volk* is just as political as the state but "*only in a different way*."[6] A key question is how he would define the word "political" to overcome this "dualism" while maintaining *Volk* and state as conceptually distinct. Yet Baeumler provides no such definition but instead offers an explanation through action—one that inverts cause and effect. As Nietzsche so effectively diagnosed, such linguistic sleights of hand operate by way of a reduplication whose temporal transposition generates conceptual difference by masking what is in actuality a metaphysical grounding. Baeumler's effort to change the conventional meaning of the word *Volk* does not merely redefine its concept; it produces "the political" as the effect of the act of redefinition in order to retroactively conceptualize the *Volk* in terms of it. Here is Baeumler: "The National Socialist state-leadership [Hitler] has, by contrast [to the absolute princely state and Weimar], already established [*schon zugrunde gelegt*] the political concept of the *Volk* in its first legislative actions."[7] The problem with this statement lies in the "already," since the state cannot confer political status on the *Volk* if what was so revolutionary about 1933 was the *Volk*'s self-discovery as independently "political." How is it possible to split this hair on which the philosophical legitimation of the *Führerstaat* resides and from which the authorization of Hitler's pronouncements is understood to follow?

Surprisingly—or perhaps not for a man whose first iteration as a philosopher was as a Kantian—the answer to this question is "legislation" (*Gesetzgebung*). Roughly one year prior to the 1935 Nuremberg Laws, which revoked citizenship for Jews and prohibited Germans from marrying Jews, those with "hereditary illnesses," blacks and Roma, Baeumler expounds: "The soul of this concept of the *Volk* is the knowledge that the *Volk* is, in its innermost kernel [*Kern*], *life* and has to obey the eternal laws of Nature and of life. *This biological legislation is the first emanation of the political concept of the* Volk. The political concept of the *Volk* cannot be achieved without the *race*-concept [Rasse*begriff*]."[8] It is philosophically and historically distracting to pretend that Heidegger could have written these particular sentences. In contrast to the false "antithesis" of the (apolitical) *Volk* and the (political) state, what Baeumler next refers to as "Hitler's biological legislation" collapses the state into the *Volk* as obedience to "the eternal laws of Nature and life." Put simply, *race* is *the expression of life as political*. This act of redefinition supplanted natural law's traditional foundation in rationality as central to the concept of citizen and state with blood-lineage (*Ahnen*, *Stamm*). Biological legislation thus contributed to "legally" undoing the notion of a national border as well as that of a right, and paved the way for annexation and denaturalization. Yet philosophically revolutionary it is not—a point Heidegger repeatedly makes, even prior to 1934, in charging the Nazis not with a "conservative liberalism" but with a "reactive" one that merely reinstalled the racial subject into the place vacated by the modern subject. Here, our contemporary interpretations of racial biologism as narrowly "essentialist" and bound up with conceptions of personal identity are compelled to misread the expressive dynamism fundamental for Hitler in the equation life = race = the dynastically political (*Reich*), the destinally political. Baeumler makes this point when he writes, "The *political* concept of the *Volk*, as it is manifest in biological legislation, is *dynamic* because it reaches out beyond into the *future*."[9] In its political "emanation" as race, biological legislation—and this is now bad Nietzsche—becomes the expression of the transcendence of life, and what life most needs in order to express itself *as life* is room to move, to grow, and to expand.

Which of Heidegger's writings is likely to be on the shelf next to Baeumler? In the 1934–1935 lecture course, *Hölderlin's Hymns "Germania" and "The Rhine*," Heidegger offers the following interpretation of Hölderlin's naming of "Nature" as *Innigkeit*, or "intimacy," which Heidegger asserts goes beyond the Greek *physis* and toward the "future of the Germans" (GA 39: 255/231). Indeed, it is in the different ways that the Greeks and the Germans are disposed toward the "origin" that the Greeks are a *stammverwandtes Volk*, that is, a *Volk* of "shared lineage." This is not a metaphysical statement but a statement about the very capacity for metaphysics. Yet what makes this passage striking are its veiled references to Baeumler's "heroic science" and to the specific terminology of "The Political Concept of the *Volk*," which are found nowhere else in Heidegger's corpus. Heidegger writes:

> This saying [about Nature as intimacy] is not something merely at hand in the *Volk*'s libraries . . . but is right in the innermost midst of their language . . . and can be such only because it is the kernel [*Kern*] of historical Dasein—that language which each day in the depth of its flowing can splash over . . . its own saying because, in what is concealed, it remains a river in which and as which beyng founds itself.

> Poetizing as the founding of beyng is original legislation [*ursprüngliche Gesetzgebung*], in such a way that laws as such do not emerge at all, and yet everything enjoins itself to such dispensation [*Fug*]. (GA 39: 256–58/232–33)

Given the linguistic volatility of the emergent propaganda state of 1934–1935, how would a student sitting in a lecture hall in Freiburg have heard these lines about the *Volk*'s relationship to the splashing of a river?—and is the best we can do today to hear them as a metaphor, which Heidegger insists they are not? What critical shift does this passage invite, a shift captured in Heidegger's statement that "Nature as the 'universal' . . . is not the primal soup or primal swamp and bubbling over with which the biological-organic worldview begins and ends" (GA 39: 257/232)?—So read the "historical archives" after Heidegger.

By way of illuminating juxtaposition, I want to transition from Baeumler's bad metaphysics to Judith Butler's post-9/11 work on "precarious life" by means of a remark Heidegger makes in the Fall 1931 "black notebook": "The philosopher as the one who goes alone [*Alleingänger*]; but alone not with his 'small self'—but rather with the world, and this *prior* to all 'with one another' " (GA 94, 56/42). The entry serves as a clarification about the place from where the future is to be thought in its exertion of a temporal backpressure whose resistance or "storm" Heidegger understood to configure the "not yet" of Germany's revolutionary "mission" (*Auftrag*). Here, it must be stated that although this future has nothing to do with the ever-expanding dynamism of life and a subject that biologically expresses itself as race, it too bears the title *das deutsche Schicksal*. Can we read Heidegger's critique of the Nazi metaphysics of life from out of his thinking the future as German destiny, or does this act of reading make itself complicit with a contaminated alternative? In §18 of *Being and Time*, Heidegger characterized the priority of world as the "ontological or transcendental perfect" of the worldhood of world, whose "previous freeing" grants access to the being of others as constitutive of the disclosure of Dasein's "there." The *Notebooks* entry is problematic not because "going alone" introduces a solipsism (it introduces the solitariness of the "creative ones"), but because the philosopher's singularizing being ahead "with the world" projects the relevant "with one another" into a future community whose event it thinks and, in thinking, anticipatorily prepares. That Heidegger felt compelled to write this statement as the declaration of philosophical vocation—and then return to it as the definition of "leadership" (*Führerschaft*) taken up in the "Rectoral Address"—reveals the extent to which worldly others announced themselves as a temptation against greatness.

It was Levinas who first identified a problem with the priority Heidegger accorded the Other in relation to Dasein's transcendence, and Butler seeks to extend his analysis of "precariousness" in her effort to theorize a "Jewish ethics of non-violence." However, what Butler adds (and what she struggles against in seeking to avoid the bloodless universality of intrinsic value or "dignity") is a concern for life that brings forward what going "with the world" prior to all others necessarily eclipses—namely, bodily vulnerability as the articulation of the human being's exposure, what Heidegger terms *Ausgesetztheit*. Heidegger is no less a thinker of exposure than Levinas. Yet Heidegger's privileging of poetic language as "the manifesting of beings in their totality"—and this designates "'universal' Nature" as the inceptive event of world—cuts him off from Dasein's exposure not just *as* world but *within* the world. The ecstatic opening up of the "as" takes place in the factical embodiment of Dasein's delivery over to the receptivity to touch, which occurs with the irruption into language. For Heidegger, the disclosivity of Dasein's exposure already implies its "transposure" (*Versetztheit*) into the "with one another," whose address is "taken over" and extended as care through which the inaugural promise of world is realized in the becoming of a *Volk*. Getting ourselves on the hook requires we be clear that the Heideggerian a priori is just as devastatingly efficacious as Baeumler's "eternal laws of Nature and life," even though it lacks the propaganda power of ideological conformity and its simplified intelligibility. To return to the *"Germania" and "The Rhine"* course, the way "dispensation" binds the disclosure of Dasein's "there" into language's manifesting beings means that Heidegger does not need laws, rights, or the conception of subjectivity and the state to which they adhere. But he does need earth, whose abyssal relation to concealment and possibility is not reducible to "territory" or the Hitlerian "surface of the planet." And he does need a geography mapped by Hölderlin's rivers, whose imperial surge and "pure" "origin" in Germany destines them to the having-been of Greece, but not to expansion into "Bolshevik" Russia through the astounding conflation of space and time that derives from the interpretation of life as growth. Poetic dwelling is not *Lebensraum*.

Butler comes to her concern with embodied life by way of Sophocles's *Antigone* and the question, "Whose life is grievable?"—a textual inheritance she shares with Heidegger. While Butler's understanding of life is not biological in Baeumler's sense, it is nonetheless materially "conditioned" through "a primary vulnerability." In contrast to Dasein's thrownness, whose absorption in the world results in a compensating overemphasis on structures relating to Dasein's "mineness," vulnerability for Butler is disclosed in the newborn's need for bodily sustenance through which she is delivered over into the hands of others "even *prior* to individuation itself." As Butler continues, "this conception [of life] means that we are . . . also vulnerable to another range of touch, a range that includes the eradication of our being at the one end, and the physical support for our lives at the other."[10] Exposure occurs in our receptivity to touch beyond—or, more accurately, *before*—the constitution of the self in its irreducible dependency on others. This ex-appropriation of the body takes place as the movement of an exposure/transposure that converts matter into mattering by way of our vulnerability to touch. Butler develops this by borrowing on Freud's notion of "attachment," which is further taken up in her use of the suffix "-able" through which she attempts to circumvent traditional notions of transcendence. But it is here that she runs into difficulty: Butler wants the immediacy of physical, even biological, life to make a universal claim predicated on our shared condition of vulnerability, yet she is postmodernist enough to be compelled to acknowledge that the body *qua* body is constituted through language.

I want to return to Butler's posing the question of the precariousness of life from out of Antigone's burial of Polyneikes, juxtaposing it with Hölderlin's line, "Life is death, and death is also a life" ("In beautiful blue . . .," l. 99), which is central to Heidegger's recuperation of Antigone in the 1942 *"Ister"* course. While the delivering over of the newborn into the hands of others is necessary for sustaining life, the same cannot be said of the corpse, whom Heidegger refers to as "the deceased" in *Being and Time* (SZ 238/MR 282). Where Butler's insight into our vulnerability to touch reveals life as more than biological, she reduces embodiment to physical need at the expense of the exposed corpse, which points beyond the physical in prompting the question "Whose life is grievable?" What does the dead body's being beyond all help *need* that calls for burial? How is the deceased's provocative "change-over" (*Umschlag*) from being-in-the-world to an innerworldly being—but still not "Being-present-at-hand-and-no-more"—an excess, one that for the Greeks linked the exposed corpse to the *ob-skene* and thus to obscenity? How does that excess become the invitation for carrying through on the relationship between embodiment and life not as a physical event but as a world-event in implicating our being with others?

Heidegger answers these questions in his paraphrase of the line, "Life is death, and death is also a life," when he writes: "Death and human being, human being and embodied life (blood) in each case belong together. 'Death' and 'blood' in each case name the different and extreme realms of human being, and such being is neither fulfilled in the one nor exhausted in the other" (GA 53: 147/117–18). In addition to signaling the complete incompatibility of his analysis of the *Antigone* with that of Hegel, Heidegger's interpretation challenges understanding Hölderlin's line as dialectical—or even symmetrical—in traversing so as to transpose the "belonging together" of life and death. While the line requires being read as the unfolding of a progression (that "life is death" sounds like a biological statement of fact), Heidegger's paraphrase shows that its second half folds back onto the first in order to recontextualize that linear progression from out of the insight into embodied life yielded by the dead body. The second half of the line thus comes first, and the excess of the "and . . . also" allows the progression, "life is death," in a manner that goes beyond physical demise to the revelation of life as a world-event. Whence Heidegger's insistence that in their extremity life and death do not "fulfill" or "exhaust" one another, but traverse one another in the excess of their belonging as embodiment—a belonging factically articulated as Dasein's being-in-the-world with others.

Heidegger's comments about the dead body in *Being and Time* are important here, for dying does not ex-appropriate the human being of its individuation prior to its being with others, but individuates her to the terminal exclusion of others. (In the uncanny plasticity of its being "no longer Da-sein," the *Gestorbene* ["the dead one"] threatens to replace the *Verstorbene* ["the one dead"] with sheer likeness.) Death ex-appropriates the human being of the "Being with" that constitutes the disclosure of Dasein's "there" and that Heidegger characterizes as its "being with one another in the *same* world" (SZ 238/MR 282, em). This "*same* world" is the "with-world" of the living as embodied—vulnerable to touch, vulnerable to wounding, vulnerable to words, vulnerable to a finitude different in kind from political errancy and machination, and yet nonetheless the privileged site of its articulation by way of the body's exposure. It is this definition of life that Heidegger excludes in the relentless invulnerability of his "going alone," and it costs him the world.

Undoubtedly, the most startling aspect of Heidegger's parsing of Hölderlin's line is his equation of embodied life with "blood." As I have indicated through my interpretation of Baeumler, within Nazi ideology blood meant the vitalistic biologism of life as race that constituted the *Volk* as political. Yet according to Heidegger's interpretation, Antigone's burial of Polyneikes shows the recontextualization of the meaning of blood from out of embodiment, which has to be understood as a world-event. And *this* is the important point for what comes next, the equivocal question mark that follows "After Heidegger?"—because Heidegger doesn't develop any of it. The transformation of the meaning of blood has always been a sticky business. To my knowledge, St. Paul is the only one who succeeded in rethinking it through the question, "Who gets to inherit?" as adoption, which became the basis for a universality. However, the significance of Antigone's action for Heidegger lies in the way she makes visible the question of belonging per se from out of blood as embodiment and as ontologically prior to all clannish notions of kinship and political community. What Butler wants is exactly such belonging per se as the basis for a politics of life, whose universal (which means nonviolent) claim resides in the irreducible vulnerability of the physical body. Yet I fear this too eclipses world as the context for the bindingness of such a claim in its articulation of belonging per se. Can we think world's coming first as the basis for a right and in a manner that carries through on our exposed being with one another as embodied? I believe the answer is yes.

My question is this: What is life after Heidegger? How does getting ourselves on the hook require our thinking *this question* for the sake of our politics, not his?

NOTES

1. Emmanuel Faye, *Heidegger: The Introduction of Nazism into Philosophy in Light of the Unpublished Seminars of 1933–1935*, tr. Michael B. Smith (New Haven, CT: Yale University Press, 2009), 319.

2. Karl Löwith, *My Life in Germany Before and After 1933: A Report*, tr. Elizabeth King (Chicago: University of Illinois Press, 1994), 153n21.

3. David Nirenberg, *Anti-Judaism: The Western Tradition* (New York: W.W. Norton, 2013).

4. Giorgio Agamben, *Homo Sacer: Sovereign Power and Bare Life*, tr. Daniel Heller-Roazen (Stanford, CA: Stanford University Press, 1998), 10.

5. Adolf Hitler, *Mein Kampf*, Chapter IV. See http://www.anatomyofthethirdreich.com/index.php/national-socialist-ideology/the-nazi-years/mein-kampf-chapter-iv

6. Alfred Baeumler, *Politik und Erziehung: Reden und Aufsätze* (Berlin: Junker und Dünnhaupt, 1937), 47.

7. Ibid.

8. Ibid.

9. Ibid., 47–48.

10. Judith Butler, *Precarious Life: The Powers of Mourning and Violence* (London: Verso, 2004), 31–32, em.

Chapter 9

Aftermath

Babette Babich

The question after any disaster is the question of *what remains* and that, to the extent that there is still something that remains, is the question of life. It is life that is the question after Auschwitz—how go on, how write poetry, how philosophize? What is called thinking after Heidegger? Are we still inclined to thinking, after Heidegger? And what of logic? What of history? And what of science? In addition, we may ask after ethical implications, including questions bearing on anti-Semitism, but also issues of misogyny, as well as Heidegger's critical questions concerning technology and concerning animal life and death.

PHILOSOPHIZING IN THE WAKE OF HEIDEGGER

We modern, postmodern, ideally even *transhuman* human beings want to go further. Not only with Heidegger but generally. And we want to overcome, if not exactly ourselves (as Nietzsche's Zarathustra had recommended), at least those restrictions we find constraining, traditions that seem obscure or outdated. As an aid to getting all of this behind us, we academics find ourselves seeking to define a center that will not hold: writing handbooks and encyclopedias as if their entries alone could make their contents certainties. We are especially minded to do this in these days of truths contested, "alt-facts," "post-truth." Certainty seems essential, yet where shall we find it? And what to do about Heidegger? Indeed, what to do after Heidegger?—a question to be asked given all the things we have learned of his person. Nor can we but imagine that new publications will bring ever more detail, ever more dirt, to light.

But even apart from the moraline cottage industry whose self-appointed role it is and has been to denounce Heidegger, there is another problem. There is the analytic-continental divide which we are anxious to dispense with: analytic philosophers do not like to be called analytic philosophers and viciously resist the idea that there might be any kind of divide. Things are compounded in various departments of philosophy by the triumph of analytic philosophy, pushing out philosophers who had been named continental, dominating appointments made, and changing the curriculum in the process just to secure the change.[1] Thus these days we no longer teach traditional texts, having dusted them from the philosophical canon as all so very much "history of philosophy," "old philosophy" by contrast with new. Thus analytic philosophy maintains its death grip on the field.

After denying the divide, we are encouraged to do "good work," as opposed to the "bad work" we might otherwise do. (What is "good work"? What does it look like? Who decides?) Those of us interested in thinkers like Heidegger or Nietzsche or Empedocles morph into so many historians of philosophy, as the analytic philosophers describe scholars with such interests. But are we historians? Did we study history? Or is specializing in some figure from an era not the contemporary sufficient to make us historians?

What is certain is that the publishing world has never seen so many introductions, all written as if leagues of new philosophers stood in need of these. In addition to encyclopedias and handbooks, one can find a range of "companion" type volumes. One can almost imagine a volume on "the compleat" phenomenologist, perhaps as part of a matching set, with another on hermeneutics, encased in a steampunk cassette, just to lock in all the bells and whistles. And there are such volumes (less the slipcase), together with histories of analytic philosophy and classifications of philosophical kinds—one analytic historian of philosophy counts six of these.[2]

PHILOSOPHY AND PHILOLOGY

Assemblages of this kind, as Borges noted, as Foucault notes in another spirit, as Nietzsche also writes for his own part, are signs of decay. The point is also one Nietzsche spent some time reflecting upon: for what, for *whom* do we collate such handbooks? Nietzsche might have been an even more central part of this culture of decay than he already is. For Nietzsche was slated to prepare, with Hermann Diels, what would become *Die Fragmente der Vorsokratiker*.[3] And had he done so, as he factually did not, we scholars might be invoking not DK—Diels-Kranz—when we cite the pre-Socratic fragments but ND—Nietzsche-Diels. Diels, some four years Nietzsche's junior, and privileging Aristotle and the doxographic tradition (where Nietzsche, by contrast, specialized in Diogenes Laertius), would not publish *Die Fragmente der Vorsokratiker: Griechisch und Deutsch* until 1903. The resultant standard work in classical or ancient philology and ancient philosophy makes modern scholarship possible, distinguishing it from the nineteenth-century disciplines of philology and philosophy. Indeed: Diels's edition meant that, as of the first years of the twentieth century, scholars could read the ancient Greeks without being able to read ancient Greek.

Heidegger, who invokes Anaximander's fragment in 1946, cites it following not Diogenes Laertius but Simplicius, but he proceeds to cite Nietzsche's rendering from his *Philosophy in the Tragic Age of the Greeks*. Here Heidegger also refers to Nietzsche's Basel lecture courses, on the *Preplatonic Philosophers*. And:

> In the same year, 1903, that Nietzsche's essay on the Preplatonic philosophers first became known, Hermann Diels' *Fragments of the Presocratics* appeared. It contained texts critically selected according to the methods of modern classical philology, along with a translation. (EGT 13)

Adding that the work is dedicated to Wilhelm Dilthey, Heidegger then quotes Diels's translation. Some seventy years on, Heidegger seems to have had a point: Anaximander's terms are difficult to translate to everyone's satisfaction.

On the matter of translation, Heidegger's 1942 lecture course on Hölderlin's "Ister" reflected on the meaning of *deinon* (GA 53: 74/61). Here we read (in translation) an explicit reflection on translation as such, just because Heidegger's translation, following on Hölderlin's own rendering of Sophocles, had been criticized: Was it accurate? Heidegger reflects on the inevitable conventionality and thus the very circularity of reproof, both in his own respect and with regard to the poet:

> who decides and how does one decide, concerning the correctness of a "translation"? We "get" our knowledge from a dictionary or "wordbook" [*Wörterbuch*]. Yet we too readily forget that the information in a dictionary must be based upon a preceding interpretation of linguistic contents from which particular words and word usages are taken. In most cases a dictionary provides the correct information about the meaning of a word, yet this correctness does not guarantee us any insights into the truth of what the word means and can mean given that we are talking about the essential realm named in the word. (GA 53: 74–75/61–62)

Heidegger's own reading/rendering of *alētheia* had similarly been called into question. But, as Heidegger goes on to say, the precision of *le mot juste*, the ideal of an accurate lexical definition, a one-to-one correspondence, word to word, as it were, drawn from a given "wordbook," attests to what Nietzsche for his own part would name a "lack of philology." For Heidegger:

> every translation must necessarily accomplish the transition from the spirit of one language into that of another. There is no such thing as translation if we mean that a word from one language could or even should be made to substitute as the equivalent of a word from another language. (GA 53: 75/62)

There have been many reflections on the challenge this poses for us, even as we continue to stipulate Heidegger's translations as idiosyncratic (at best) and perhaps misleading (at worst).

Nietzsche's philological reflection on philology goes beyond the question of veridicality to consider just who we might be thinking of when it comes to the *readers* of our compendia, our handbooks, our critical editions—including, as just this is a contested matter today, a *critical* edition of Heidegger. Many scholars find employment in the production of such editorial ventures—think only of the production of Heidegger's own *Gesamtausgabe*, or the varied commentaries produced, again and again, on Nietzsche's own texts, or think of Kant or Hegel or Hölderlin and so on. Here it is useful to recall Nietzsche's meditation on his own discipline in *The Gay Science* (§109):

> *A remark for philologists*. That some books are so valuable and so royal that whole generations are well employed in their labors to produce these books in a state that is pure and intelligible—philology exists in order to fortify this faith again and again. It presupposes that there is no lack of those rare human beings (even if one does not see them) who really know how to use such valuable books—presumably those who write or could write, books of the same type.[4]

There is a lot to unpack here, and Nietzsche offers as much challenge as clue to the "few and rare," as Heidegger describes those for whom *he* writes, borrowing this designation from Nietzsche. Nietzsche, a little less loftily in this locus, characterizes such "rare human beings" as effectively *invisible* readers ("even if one does not see them"), "who always 'will come' but are never there."[5]

Who are the readers for our current reflections after Heidegger?

We know at least this: the revelations of Heidegger's Nazism, Heidegger's anti-Semitism,[6] tell us unpleasant truths about a man whose work we might otherwise admire, once we are done truth-checking his translations and his reflections on ancient words for truth. Indeed, Heidegger has always been "a bit 'post truth,' "[7] and we are gaining, thanks to the current US political regime under Trump, vastly more insight than we had perhaps wished to gain into the fluidity of truth and metaphor. And yet—and I remark on current politics for this reason—it turns out that one can do terrible things, from swindling—as this is the essence of the "art" of the (real estate) deal—and calumniating others, including misogynistic attacks (quite patently serial ones, as most misogynists are systematically repetitive about it), and still be elected to office. We do not mind misogyny in politics—heck, we practice it in philosophy, we denounce it and talk about it, and go on practicing it. Ditto racism. Ditto anti-Semitism. But for me it matters that we are prepared to tolerate Heidegger's misogyny (he gets a free pass: think of Arendt, not that we actually do) but not his anti-Semitism.

And when we are done, given that Aristotle was a massive misogynist—Aristotle wrote the book, as it were—we may come to understand why Heidegger thought that we could say of Nietzsche, another massive misogynist, as it was thought appropriate to say of Aristotle, that he was born, he worked, he died (GA 18: 5/4). Still: the "new" Nietzsche introduced for Anglophone readers in the 1970s, making them "continental" in the process, was ushered in under a specifically Heideggerian flag, because without Heidegger, no French Nietzsche.[8] Still we have learned to do philosophy hermeneutically, hermeneutico-phenomenologically.

And Heidegger is hoist on his own petard.

To quote the title of Thomas Sheehan's 1981 book collection, *Heidegger: The Man and The Thinker*, Heidegger is henceforth not to be read apart from his Nazism, his anti-Semitism. But that said, how is one to read *Being and Time*? Are we to read it as a Nazi volume, *unterwegs*, *avant la lettre*? Oh, yes: Richard Wolin and Emmanuel Faye tell us, Tom Rockmore tells us, and another generation likewise. But are those readings useful? Surely. It is another question to ask whether those readings translate the work of 1927 into our times. Do they, to use Heidegger's query with respect to translation, "accomplish the transition from the spirit of one language into that of another?" I have argued that to do so would require a *Heidegger philology* we have yet to develop. Hence, I am not sure that knowing Heidegger's misogyny, however smarmily egregious it happened to have been, helps. So: should we just bracket it? Heidegger, like Aristotle, lived, worked, died, "and there's an end on't"? Surely it matters that Heidegger, anti-Semitic in a world-historical sense and convinced Nazi devotee (*avant la lettre* to be sure), wrote *Being and Time*. Here the question might be, did he also happen to write *Being and Time*, or was being a world-historical anti-Semite/Nazi-devotee-to-be/inveterate misogynist or any part of the preceding a necessary or even contributing condition? Most scholars will take the lesser charge, so Heidegger gets a plea bargain. We add this to our thinking about *Being and Time* as about his other works. And many of us, troubled as we should be, wonder if we might save ourselves some trouble (and some reading) by fixing on the later Heidegger (or as the move is a similar one, the early Heidegger). It goes without saying that this is a surface remedy at best; convicted Nazis remain so, and so too anti-Semites, and so too ladies'-man-style misogynists.

The "decadence," to use Nietzsche's language and to which decadence I began by referring—pointing to our obsession with companion volumes, dictionaries, encyclopedias, introductions—comes with a death certificate issued by the famous, public-intellectual-type scientist Stephen Hawking, who some years ago made the pronouncement: "philosophy is dead."[9] Hawking's declaration was tailor-made for the trans-generation, the humanity 2.0 scholars, the transhumanists, surfing the cutting edge. And yet, as with Nietzsche's reflections on decadence, Hawking's certification of philosophy's death is not new, and an appeal to the crowd, the popular voice that is the voice of the public intellectual, has been with us since antiquity. How else was Socrates able to corrupt the youth in his old age? Or why would acolytes flock to sit at the feet of various Stoics, or Plotinus have his own cult following? Make no mistake: we academics, we scholars, are keen on recognition. Hegel made it the cornerstone of his dialectic of consciousness, Kojève enshrined it for all of Paris: the locked key to Lacan's master's discourse. And we want to be up on the latest thing, which latest thing, we are convinced, simply must be better than anything past. And that is understandable, as scholars tend to have a reputation for being fuddy-duddy types, nose-in-a-book types. Writing on the "new" Heidegger, post the devastating publication of the *Black Notebooks* and the pronouncement of Heidegger's anti-Semitism to match his well-known Nazism, we write "after" Heidegger.

It's a wake, forty years late.

And we will not be distracted by efforts to take the question too much back to Heidegger himself, reflecting, as we do, that perhaps this language, given the current constellation that impels us to raise questions once again, might yet shed light on Heidegger's thinking on questioning, on raising or posing the question concerning technology, not to mention "Being."

Heidegger is hardly alone in being subject to this, if his circumstances do outclass other scholarly scandals. Philosophy is thus just what every textbook about philosophy suggests: a list of names for popular consumption. The great philosopher is identifiable by a Google or Twitter ranking. Maybe just, more soberly, by citation frequency. Nietzsche's new *Zarathustra* might have to be rewritten as "A Book for All and Everybody."

I began by noting our passion for drawing lines, and there seems little that is not post-or anti- or "Afterphilosophy." Yet this does not seem to be like a *vernissage*, a celebratory after-party. Indeed, "Afterphilosophy" bears comparison to "Afterphilology," and considering the constellation introduces Nietzschean reflections.[10] If the science in question for Nietzsche—ancient philology, ancient linguistics, ancient comparative literature, ancient history—hasn't in the interim managed to pose the question of its own discipline, what does that tell us? Thus, what Classics has not done is to pose the question of its own foundations, as Nietzsche argued that it should, namely to raise the question of its own discipline, which Nietzsche himself called the question of science qua science. Nietzsche claimed he was the first to do this, and, having written on Nietzsche and science for these many years, I am fairly sure that apart from Heidegger and in ways no Heideggerian has taken up, no one has sought to raise this question as a question since—not in the sense that Nietzsche meant by speaking of "the *problem of science itself*, science considered for the first time as problematic, as questionable" in the second edition of *The Birth of Tragedy*.[11]

There is a parallel failure to pose the problem of philosophy itself. If this benumbed circumstance does not mean that philosophy is "dead," as Hawking contends, it is spellbound. The becalmed circumstance is not Hawking's doing and has nothing to do with the *Black Notebooks* scandal: we are adrift, and have been for quite some time.

Still, and as my passing remark on the problem of science suggests, the larger question or unframed theme is the absence of a thinker of the rank of a Nietzsche or a Heidegger today.

That would be the elephant in the room.

Asking after Heidegger, it matters that Heidegger could be utterly misogynistic and still write *Being and Time*. So too for his anti-Semitism, we must suppose. Perhaps the question should be what just what it is that we expect of philosophy, before, during, or above all, *after* Heidegger?[12]

LOGICAL REFLECTIONS

May we go on reading Heidegger? Is this not a finished endeavor, of a limited term? This question as such takes its cue from Emmanuel Faye and Richard Wolin and already had its best expression in pithiness in Gilbert Ryle's "wasn't a good man" apothegm.[13] But as Richard Rorty pointed out in good American pragmatist fashion in response to Farías, we do read "Gottlob Frege, a vicious anti-Semite and proto-Nazi" without being hindered by his anti-Semitism.[14] Sitting in my office in New York is Michael Beaney's collection *The Frege Reader*.[15] In my office I also have a book by Andrea Nye, *Words of Power: A Feminist Reading of the History of Logic*.[16] Nye reads from Parmenides through to Frege with an indispensable chapter, *A Thought Like A Hammer*.

In the current context, after Heidegger, at stake is the logical point of view as such. Every detail concerning human beings—whether we name them Preplatonic (Nietzsche) or Presocratic (Diels), or whether we read Nietzsche from Heidegger's perspective or from the point of view of the Nazi hegemony in university courses then offered on Nietzsche,[17] or else with respect to our current concern, thinking after Heidegger—from the logical point of view, all these details are distractions, which means that they shift our focus.

Indeed all of our ethical discussions on the advantages and disadvantages of tossing or not tossing a fat man onto the tracks in the path of a passing trolley, in the so-called trolley problem, depend on this *irrelevance*. In fact, no one is throwing anyone, regardless of girth, anywhere: it is the conception that counts in ethical thinking.

And yet perhaps philosophy, the doing of, the reading of, is not an inherently edifying enterprise. How many outstanding philosophers are outstanding human beings? And of these exemplary beings, how many are outstanding *because* they are philosophers? Philosophy may not, as Nietzsche argued, referring to the educational institutions of Basel (and the rest of Europe), make us better citizens. Nietzsche had in mind the Swiss requirement that all citizens have a classical education, meaning an education in ancient philology and ancient philosophy. But what philosophy was for the ancients (and that is why the gods are involved in every case) had to do with preserving one's mind or "soul" in the transition from one life to another, saving one's place in the transition that is part of metempsychosis. If one has abandoned that metaphysical notion of the soul along with the Christian version, it would seem that philosophy's value for life (or life eternal) might also be abandoned.

SCIENCE AND CRITICAL HISTORY

Perhaps, after Heidegger, we might work to be relentlessly critical in our reading of Heidegger, highlighting the negative. This would be scientific, and yet Heidegger emphasized "science" as a question. In the spirit of both Kant and Nietzsche, Heidegger had supposed that we might attend to the prerequisites for putting philosophy on the path of a science. This reflection was still with him, as it might be given the death of Husserl in the Spring of 1938. To this extent, Heidegger offers a sustained reflection on understanding the significance of Nietzsche's meditations on history as a science, invoking standard references, but also seeking to explore the relevance of Nietzsche's own conjunction of use (calculation) and value for life (GA 46: 106–14/88–94).

Here I note only that few scholars have taken up the issue of "Heidegger and Science" and that those who have done so are inclined not to notice the work done by others in the same field. For my part, I elsewhere argue that philosophers get over their allergies to citing one another, as if noticing the work of others somehow diminished one's own originality.[18] The problem of non-citation (obliviousness) is an endemic one in philosophy; it crosses the analytic-continental divide, Heidegger and Nietzsche studies, and much else besides. And to those meaning to invoke Heidegger's reservations concerning "the literature" to defend their ongoing philosophical autism, I would respond by observing that the topic of *Heidegger and Science*, like *Heidegger and Theology*, or *Heidegger and Anti-Semitism*, is nothing but literature.

We can, as we have seen and as has been done for years now, read Heidegger for the dirt: we can stand around and lament his anti-Semitism, as we might and should. And yet it is instructive (and we should think about this) that we, as philosophers, do not lament his deep and thoroughgoing misogyny. And there is a lot of dirt there, even more than we can guess at, when it comes to the woman question that we could add to the Jewish question, or the American question, or the question of Heidegger's unrelentingly critical take on the same techno-science that we deeply believe will save us (all we need for that is to declare our "belief" in climate change and then, with a little help from science, we will be saved).

ON THE DEATH ANIMALS DO NOT DIE

Elsewhere, I advert to the difficult question of Heidegger in conjunction with the animal question, which is, so I argue, less a matter of the animal's putative world-indigence—though this is part of it, just insofar as this poverty is engendered—a matter of our obliviousness to the lives of animals. This was true for Heidegger too, despite his attention to Karl von Frisch, who was no friend to animals (quite in spite of his observations and as attested by the same). In Heidegger's sense, the same indigence is manufactured by way of the systematic breeding of animals that deprives them of their lives as much as it deprives them of their own deaths. Animals are manufactured, as Heidegger says in the purest of metonymic connections, as so many corpses-to-be, as the standing reserve of industrial agribusiness, and quite as such, they do not die. Specifically, they do not die their own deaths in mass slaughter but are instead challenged forth into technological reserves and by-products, for the production of food and—in addition to clothing and shoes, cosmetics and paint, soap and ink—their organs, destined to be used for the sake of human life extension and preservation.[19]

We might think about that.

NOTES

1. See Babette Babich, "Good for Nothing: On Philosophy and Its Discontents," in *Why Philosophy*, ed. Diego Bubbio and Jeff Malpas (New York: Davis Publishers, 2017).

2. Justin Smith, *The Philosopher: A History in Six Types* (Princeton, NJ: Princeton University Press, 2016).

3. Wolfgang Roßler, "Hermann Diels und die Fragmente der Vorsokratiker," in *Die modernen Vater der Antike: Die Entwicklung der Altertumswissenschaften an Akademie und Universität in Berlin des 19. Jahrhunderts*, ed. Annette M. Bertschi and Colin G. King (Berlin: de Gruyter, 2009), 369–96, particularly 374–75. See Jaap Mansfeld and David T. Runia, *Aietiana: The Method and Intellectual Context of a Doxographer: The Sources. Volume I* (Leiden: Brill, 1997), 93ff. for a discussion of Nietzsche as a contemporary of Hermann Diels in the circle established around Ritschl.

4. Friedrich Nietzsche, *The Gay Science: With a Prelude in Rhymes and an Appendix of Songs*, tr. Walter Kaufmann (New York: Vintage, 1974), 157.

5. Ibid., 158.

6. Among others, Tracy B. Strong urges that we make a politico-historical distinction between Heidegger's anti-Judaism and his anti-Semitism. See Strong, "On Relevant Events, Then and Now," in *Reading Heidegger's Black Notebooks 1931–1941*, ed. Ingo Farin and Jeff Malpas (Cambridge: MIT Press, 2016).

7. Steve Fuller, "Science Has Always Been a Bit 'Post-Truth,'" *The Guardian*, December 15, 2016.

8. Cf. Dominique Janicaud, *Heidegger in France*, tr. François Raffoul and David Pettigrew (Bloomington: Indiana University Press, 2015) and Ethan Kleinmann, *Generation Existential: Heidegger's Philosophy in France, 1927–1961* (Ithaca, NY: Cornell University Press, 2006).

9. Matt Warman, "Stephen Hawking Tells Google 'Philosophy Is Dead,'" *Telegraph*, May 17, 2011.

10. The term refers to the title of a defense written by Erwin Rohde on Nietzsche's behalf but addressed to Wagner in response to Wilamowitz-Möllendorff's "Future-Philology." See further: Christian Benne, *Nietzsche und die historisch-kritische Philologie* (Berlin: Walter de Gruyter, 2005).

11. Nietzsche, "Attempt at an Auto-Critique, §2," in *The Birth of Tragedy or Hellenism and Pessimism*, tr. Walter Kaufmann (New York: Vintage, 1967).

12. I address additional elements in "The 'New' Heidegger," in *Heidegger in the 21st Century*, ed. Tziovannis Georgakis and Paul Ennis (Frankfurt am Main: Springer, 2015).

13. "Heidegger. Can't be a good philosopher. Wasn't a good man": Gilbert Ryle as quoted by James Thrower, letter to the editor, *The Times Higher Education Supplement* 850 (February 17, 1989), 12.

14. Richard Rorty, "Taking Philosophy Seriously: Victor Farias' *Heidegger and Nazism*," *The New Republic*, April 11, 1988, 32.

15. Gottlob Frege, *The Frege Reader*, ed. Michael Beaney (Oxford: Blackwell, 1997).

16. Andrea Nye, *Words of Power: A Feminist Reading of the History of Logic* (London: Routledge, 1990).

17. For a discussion of Nazi readers, focusing on the "biologism" of Rosenberg and Krieck, see Christopher Rickey, *Revolutionary Saints: Heidegger, National*

Socialism, and Antinomian Politics (State College, PA: Penn State University Press, 2001), 220, in addition to Hans Sluga, *Heidegger's Crisis: Philosophy and Politics in Nazi Germany* (Cambridge, MA: Harvard University Press, 1993). I would add, as fundamental to Heidegger's invocation of Nietzsche as a "life philosopher," less Jaspers or Löwith than Ernst Krieck's *Leben als Prinzip der Weltanschauung und Problem der Wissenschaft* (Leipzig: Armanen Verlag, 1938).

18. See Babette Babich, "Are They Good? Are They Bad? Double Hermeneutics and Citation in Philosophy, Asphodel and Alan Rickman, Bruno Latour and the 'Science Wars,'" in *Das Interpretative Universum*, ed. Paula Angelova, Jaassen Andreev, and Emil Lessky (Würzburg: Königshausen & Neumann, 2017).

19. See the discussion of Paul Virilio on the pitiless in contemporary art in Babette Babich, "On the Aesthetic Edge: Futures of the Contemporary in Agamben, Virilio, Nancy," in *Futures of the Contemporary: Music and Performance*, ed. Paulo de Assis et al. (Louvain: University of Louvain Press, 2018).

Part III

POLITICS AND ETHICS

Chapter 10

Heidegger: Beyond Anti-Semitism and *Seinsgeschichte*

John McCumber

There will be much to come "after Heidegger," of course; thinking did not end with him, even if he thought the history of philosophy had. But will future thought be after *Heidegger*? Is he, in other words, destined to have any lasting influence at all? Or will the future of thought unroll as if he had never lived or worked?

Prediction, if possible at all, is always dangerous (as we will see in a moment). Asking whether Heidegger will have an influence on future thought brings the specific danger that we will be ensnared in other, more fraught issues. First and foremost, can anything in Heidegger's thinking be rescued from his lifelong anti-Semitism? This question is close to one which receives much attention, that of whether Heidegger was ever a full-blown racist Nazi. That issue, while important, is in some respects a red herring. Whether or not Heidegger's undoubted anti-Semitism sank to Nazi depths, if any form of anti-Semitism inextricably infects his thought, it will fully suffice to discredit it. And if that proves to be the case, the future will correctly "appropriate" Heidegger's thought by forgetting it entirely. So if Heidegger is to have influence on future thought (whether or not we call that thought "philosophy"), then the current "Heidegger Controversy" must not only have been definitively resolved—an outcome which itself is currently something of a pipe dream, even on a purely factual level—but resolved, to some degree, in Heidegger's favor.

The question of the role of anti-Semitism in Heidegger's thought brings yet another question, indeed a whole set of them. For it presumes that the nature and principles of that thought are settled matters. Such a situation seems barely conceivable today, when the potential of the works Heidegger published during his lifetime, to which I will largely restrict myself here, is far from exhausted—to say nothing of the enormous *Gesamtausgabe*.

The issue of unrealized potential, however, extends far beyond Heidegger's thought. As he himself showed, the future is predictable only around the edges, for its core is shaped by the ultimate mystery—our death. Death is the "possibility of no more possibilities," and though its eventual arrival is entirely predictable, we do not know when it is coming or what it will be like. Because death is the final event in our future, and because understanding is futural for Heidegger (to understand something is to grasp its possibilities for us), its unknowability infects everything that comes before, leaving a "reservoir of the unthought"[1] in everything. But if everything harbors such a reservoir, not only is Heidegger's future unpredictable—everyone's is, including philosophy's.

The question of what will come "after Heidegger" thus places the askers of it in a complex situation. On the one hand, the question cannot be asked from within a Heideggerean perspective, because it requires a prediction and the future for him is radically unpredictable. On the other hand, it also cannot be asked from a perspective entirely outside Heideggerean thought, which would simply forget about him.

Asking about Heidegger's anti-Semitism enables us to find a way among these unanswerable questions to another, more tractable one. Unlike the issue of his Nazism, that of his anti-Semitism has been definitively answered, in the affirmative, by the publication of the *Black Notebooks*. Any vindication of Heidegger will therefore have to show that the anti-Semitism infects at most a part of his thought, rather than the whole. And if that is the case, we learn something about the nature and principles of that thought—viz., that it is not a systematic whole, but contains mutually independent strands. We will thus find and occupy a position that is both inside and outside of Heidegger's philosophy—outside the part infected by his anti-Semitism, but inside other parts of it.

The infected part of Heidegger's thought, I will argue, is an undigested Aristotelianism that structures his view of *Seinsgeschichte*, of the history of being (the German term is more economical and I will use it here). I will then argue that when Heidegger's version of *Seinsgeschichte* is excised from his thought, important insights remain, and I will briefly adduce a few of those. Finally, my efforts will not be predictive: I will claim, not that future philosophy will be somehow indebted to "good" strands in Heidegger's thought, but merely that certain of its components strands are not infected by his anti-Semitism. If they come to be forgotten or rejected, as they may, it will not be because they are anti-Semitic.

This enterprise requires a couple of informal observations concerning the current state of the "Heidegger Controversy."

THE STATE OF THE CONTROVERSY

First, no one now dismisses Heidegger's anti-Semitism as a mere "escapade," as Hannah Arendt tried to do.[2] Whatever the fate of his Nazi dreams after 1933, the *Black Notebooks* show that anti-Semitism was tied permanently to him.

This means that anyone who wants to defend Heidegger's thought *in toto* from his anti-Semitism must claim that the latter is a merely personal flaw, and so must draw a sharp line between Heidegger the thinker and Heidegger the man. Such lines are always problematic, and this one is especially suspect. I have elsewhere argued that here is no "Heidegger the man," no coherent personality to be found among his many contradictory actions.[3] Thus, for example, in spite of his anti-Semitism, he was personally kind to many Jewish students.[4] This does not count against Heidegger's anti-Semitism, for as Himmler told the camp guards at Poznan in 1941, "every Nazi had his favorite Jew."[5] But it does mean that anti-Semitism cannot have been a basic trait of Heidegger's personality, for he had no single personality. Anti-Semitism was, however, recurrently in the mix; and that, of course, suffices.

But whether Heidegger the man was anti-Semitic or not is irrelevant here, for at least part of his thought, his account of *Seinsgeschichte*, is clearly infected with his anti-Semitism. To give only a few examples:[6]

- "Jewry" is the "greater groundlessness" that "is bound to nothing and makes everything serviceable to itself." (GA 95: 96–97)
- "Jewry" is the machinating principle behind "the historical process that is now playing out to its end within Americanism and Bolshevism, and this at the same time means within world Jewry. The question of the role of world Jewry is not a racial question, but the metaphysical question about the kind of humanity that, without any restraints, can take over the uprooting of all beings from being as its world-historical 'task.'" (GA 96: 243)
- We should suppose that "the 'Jewish' has everywhere completely seized mastery, so that even the fight against 'the Jewish,' and it above all, becomes subject to it." (GA 97: 20)

If, in *Introduction to Metaphysics*, America and Russia incarnate the overarching historical forces that threaten humanity (GA 40: 40–41/41), "world Jewry" encompasses them both. Even the (Nazi) fight against Judaism is subject to it. Anti-Semitism thus belongs not only to the congeries of contradictory traits that constituted Heidegger the man, but to his thought itself, and so is on both sides of whatever line we may try to draw between them.

Second, the controversy has an obvious subtext in contemporary European politics. The "democracy deficit" of the European Union means that the people actually making decisions for that community are unelected; their legitimacy relies wholly on their expertise, which in turn is a function of the "enlightened" caliber of their discourse. However we understand the Enlightenment, to question it is to undermine the legitimacy of Brussels, and since so much questioning of the Enlightenment today traces back to Heidegger, it becomes extremely important—indeed urgent—to demonize him. Hence, I suspect, the hasty excesses that Thomas Sheehan has so carefully documented among Heidegger's detractors.[7]

Heidegger the man, I have suggested, was fundamentally disunified. I would like here to make a similar argument concerning his philosophy. If anti-Semitism, as I have mentioned, has been found in his project of *Seinsgeschichte*, and if he was a systematic philosopher, this would give us warrant at least to suspect that the rest of his philosophy—his theories of things like language, poetry, death, and the future—are infected with it. But what if his thought had a number of components that have little to do with each other? What if Heidegger was, in Isaiah Berlin's terms, more of a fox than a hedgehog?

The question of just how systematic Heidegger's thought is can only be answered by either finding some unified set of ur-doctrines that determine what Heidegger says on any issue that he discusses philosophically, or showing that such a set is impossible. If we want to claim that philosophy's future should be one of complete rejection of Heidegger's thought because of its anti-Semitism, that set of ur-doctrines not only exists but has components that are anti-Semitic in character. Thus, we have two fundamental possibilities: (1) Heidegger's thought could be just a series of disconnected meditations; (2) it could be systematically interconnected in that it all follows from, or is conditioned by, a single set of premises of some sort. In the case of (2), it is also possible that (3) that fundamental set of premises contains anti-Semitic views. Only (3) permits us to conclude, with for example Emmanuel Faye, that Heidegger's works should be removed from philosophical libraries altogether.[8]

WHAT IS SEINSGESCHICHTE?

We must therefore begin with one part of Heidegger's philosophy where he unequivocally espouses anti-Semitic views: with *Seinsgeschichte*. If we want to know whether that anti-Semitism extends to the rest of his thought, we need also to know the status of *Seinsgeschichte* in that thought; and before we can know that, we have to know what *Seinsgeschichte* is. For that I will turn to Heidegger's characterization in "The Age of the World Picture":

> In metaphysics, meditation on the essence of beings and a decision concerning the nature of truth are brought to completion. Metaphysics grounds an age in that it gives it the ground of the *form of its essence* via a determinate interpretation of beings and a determinate comprehension of truth. This ground *thoroughly dominates* [*durchherrscht*] all the phenomena that distinguish the age. (GA 5: 75/QCT 115, em)

Seinsgeschichte is thus the history, not only of being, but of everything else as well—at least, of everything that distinguishes one historical period from others. The claim is that all the manifold characteristics that distinguish one age from others derive from a single interpretation of beings and comprehension of truth. *Seinsgeschichte*, then, views each historical epoch as closed off from others and "thoroughly dominated" by its own essential form. I have examined this kind of structure, in which one thing grounds and explains a plurality of other things, at length elsewhere,[9] and have argued that its philosophical deployment derives from Aristotle. The Aristotelian derivation is not stated explicitly here, but is indicated by three key words Heidegger uses to expound it: "form" (*eidos*), inherited from Plato, is crucial to Aristotle's metaphysics, while "essence" (*to ti ēn einai*) is his own distinctive contribution. "Dominates" echoes the *kratein* by which a biological form "dominates" matter (and, when it fails to do so, produces things like women).[10] Here, of course, the domination is complete, or "thorough": *durchherrschen*. *Seinsgeschichte* is Aristotelian ontology (minus the teleology, to be sure) applied to history.

So understood, *Seinsgeschichte* is not only implausible but also:

(1) *Circular*: which phenomena in an age are "distinctive" of it? Those grounded by its essential form, we are told; and which are those? Surely, the ones "distinctive" of it.
(2) *Vague*: what does it mean to "ground" something? What precisely is the "thorough domination" of which Heidegger speaks, and how does it work? How, for example, is the European Cup (distinctive of the postwar epoch) "grounded" in the essence of postwar Being, and how does this differ from the way the rise of ISIS (also distinctive) is "grounded"?
(3) *Unempirical*: actually tracing "all" the concrete phenomena distinctive of an age back to metaphysical "decisions," even if the phenomena and their grounding in the decision were spelled out, would take many more volumes than even Heidegger could write (when would he get to the European Cup? to the iPhone?). Absent that, we have nothing more than

appeals to his conceptual authority, as if he were to say "I've seen enough to make a judgment that nothing escapes the paradigm. The onus is now on you to provide counterexamples!"

(4) *Potentially anti-Semitic*: the unifying form of an age does not have to take effect through a set of people, but it may, and if those people constitute "Jewry," *Seinsgeschichte* is certainly open to the anti-Semitic twist Heidegger gives it. Whether *Seinsgeschichte* can be freed from Heidegger's anti-Semitism need not detain us however, for characteristics 1–3 have finished it off. We can suspect that it is not via *Seinsgeschichte* that Heidegger's thought will influence future philosophy.

But other aspects of Heidegger's thought are more promising. I will adduce three of them here and ask whether they can be connected with *Seinsgeschichte* through anti-Semitic ur-premises. I will argue that they cannot, because they cannot be connected with *Seinsgeschichte* at all: they contradict it.

THE FINITE FUTURE

When we look at the history of continental philosophy, at least at the strand of it that I reconstruct in my *Time and Philosophy*,[11] we see that as the nineteenth century ended it was at an aporia. The key issue had to do with knowledge and time. Hume had shown that we can have no knowledge of timeless entities *outside* our minds (such as God and the soul), and Kant's effort to show that we can know timeless structures *inside* our minds (such as the categories of the understanding) had ended in failure. So Hegel took the fateful step of writing a book—the *Phenomenology of Spirit*—that did not appeal to the timelessness of anything. In so doing he opened up a way to talk about the past without making it into a sort of virtual present—that is, to talk about it without just saying true things about it; by his own admission, he rearranges the facts of history into his own story.[12] But he had not made any such progress with the future, and Marx's early attempt to predict it ended in failure.[13] Kierkegaard and Nietzsche then took the step of seeing the future as intrinsically unknowable, as a mystery ever coming at us and only a nanosecond away. Traditional philosophical methods could not cope with this, so Kierkegaard took refuge in his religious tradition, while Nietzsche turned to riddles, stories, jokes, poems, and various other "nonphilosophical" gestures.

It was Heidegger, working from a phenomenological basis, who solved the problem. For phenomenologically, the future as such, in the sense of all the events that will ever happen, can never appear: there is no rational way in which, say, the mathematics of 40,000 CE, which will likely look very different from today's mathematics, can be said to make a phenomenal difference in contemporary experience.

What does make such a difference is an *individual's* future—the "finite future" of concrete possibilities that shapes one's life as she lives it. And this future can, at least to an extent, be dealt with rationally, that is, in a way that has standards. The technique for such dealing, which Heidegger calls *Destruktion* in *Being and Time* and pursues, for example, in his many later discussions of Hölderlin, is to find the lacunae and interstices in what has been thought and done, the questions still open, which leads in turn to an appreciation of what remains to be thought (the "reservoir of the unthought"). These procedures predict nothing: they merely prepare the genuine questions. They stand to be of use to philosophers dealing with many issues, and in particular to those attempting, in the wake of Hegel and many others, to develop a fully temporal account of reason.

THE FINITE FUTURE AND THE PHENOMENALITY OF DEATH

What finitizes the future of an individual is her death, which means that there are some things one's future will not contain: some possibilities must be allowed to go by *definitively*. The standard name for this is "commitment," which in terms of the finite future is not merely the wholehearted adoption of a course of action, but always also the definitive forsaking of its alternatives. This is predicated on mortality, for if one were going to live forever, all decisions could be revisited: one could never be certain that, 5,000 or 6,000 years into the future, one would not revisit one's current decision—be it that of a profession, a life partner, a domicile, or whatever. Someone who is immortal would, therefore, be unable to make commitments; they would be able to adopt certain courses of action in the here and now, even wholeheartedly, but they would not be able to forsake their alternatives definitively. Philosophers interested in this aspect of ethical decision may make ongoing use of Heidegger's rooting of it in the temporality of the phenomenological, or finite, future.

THE TEMPORALITY OF MEANING

One characteristic of contemporary accounts of meaning, as I have noted elsewhere, is their presentism: the "meaning" of an utterance or sentence must be contemporaneous with it, so that one can look, as it were, from one to the other.[14] One problem with this lies in determining just where it is that the meaning is present. It is not given sensorily, that is, together with the experience of the utterance or sign whose meaning it is, so it must exist in some other realm. The questions of what such a non-sensory realm could be, and of how it could relate to the sensory realm, have tormented philosophers for millennia. Since Aristotle, meanings have been considered to reside in the mind,[15] but the relation of mind to sensory reality remains a mystery.

Heidegger's account of "reference" (*Verweisung*) in *Being and Time* §17, which can be expanded into an account of meaning as such, avoids this problem. Reference is what moves Dasein along its path. The context of significance (*Bewandtnisganzheit*) within which a tool is used thus opens itself in stages and functions step by step, as a sort of "script" which guides Dasein through the various situations into which it is thrown. The "meaning" of any given step in such a script is simply what we call the remainder of the steps. What a shout of "fire" means in this sense is: make sure you are safe; if you are not, move to where you are safe. Then make sure other people are safe. Then locate the fire. Then look for materials to put it out safely; and so forth. This temporalized account of meaning avoids the mystification noted earlier in the traditional account: the meaning of a sign is not given as part of the sign, not because it resides in some ontologically contrasting realm, but because it is in the future, that is, in the finite future of the individual: it is the remaining part of an uncompleted script.

CONCLUSION

None of these three areas of Heidegger's thought has anything obvious to do with anti-Semitism. *Seinsgeschichtliche* anti-Semitism is predicated for Heidegger, we saw, on the view that "Jewry" is part of the "form of the essence" of the contemporary world, and thus helps to determine everything that is distinctive about that world. Since individuals count as distinctive components of their world, this is a case of the "thorough domination" of the individuals in a world by the form of its essence. In the case of Heideggerean *Seinsgeschichte*, this yields the anti-Semitic idea, conveyed in the quotes mentioned earlier, that everyone in the contemporary world is "thoroughly dominated" by world Jewry—even the Nazis.

The sections of Heidegger I have adduced here present a rather different, and more promising, picture. On this view, a "world" is just a totality of scripts; in the case of the modern world this totality is enormously large, encompassing everything from flying particular types of aircraft to performing caesarian sections to voting to eating fast food. Tracing all of them back to some single metaphysical "decision" is, I have noted, preposterous on several counts. But the simple fact that I, as an individual, will never be able to master all of them means I am able to adopt (or commit to) only a small subset of them; the rest must be forsaken. This selectivity means that an individual does not live in the large world of an historical epoch, but in a small subset of it—a personal world that she has, to some degree, chosen. She has, we may say, had to forsake many aspects of her epoch in order to live in that personal world—the one that will end at her death. This necessary distance on her larger historical epoch is then a condition of her freedom within that epoch.

This concern with individual finitude in the face of death, and so with individual freedom, is ongoing with Heidegger to the extent that throughout his later thought he calls us "mortals." Because of its emphasis on individual finitude, this concern with individuals denies the possibility that any one thing—be it a definition of Being or anything else—can "thoroughly dominate" an individual life (unless, to be sure the individual herself makes a commitment to, for example, a cause). It is thus incompatible with the "thorough domination" postulated by *Seinsgeschichte*, and so with Heidegger's anti-Semitic formulation of it.

But this incompatibility must be wrested from Heidegger's texts. Already in *Being and Time*, the unconditional inherence of Dasein in its world is presupposed and underwritten by the view, unstated but clearly implied, that language itself—the privileged, but not the only medium of scripts—is inauthentic.[16] Later on, only German—and then only when written with due etymological attention—can escape this. The later Heidegger, though referring to us as "mortals," continually looks beyond the individuality that mortality brings to the supra-individual, and supposedly primordial, dimension of being. The mortality of the individual is replaced by the mortality of the epochs of being, which inevitably die and are left behind.

Thus, though Heidegger's thought has insights which are free of *Seinsgeschichte* and can be of great benefit to all those who seek to understand the "human condition"—who seek to philosophize—they are constantly imbricated in his texts with the *seinsgeschichtliche*, and ultimately anti-Semitic, side of that thought. Unearthing and preserving Heidegger's promising insights regarding temporality, meaning, and the ethics of mortality (and there are doubtless others) thus requires painstaking, sentence-by-sentence examination of his texts, instead of overall condemnations or defenses of a mythical being called "Martin Heidegger"—and another mythical being called "Heidegger's thought."

NOTES

1. ". . . die Herkunftsbereich des noch-nicht (des Un-) Entborgenen im Sinne einer Verbergung": Martin Heidegger, *Der Ursprung des Kunstwerkes* (Stuttgart: Reclam, 1960), 67.

2. Quoted in Adam Kirsch, "The Jewish Question: Martin Heidegger," *New York Times*, May 7, 2010.

3. John McCumber, *Metaphysics and Oppression* (Bloomington: Indiana University Press, 1999), 5–13.

4. One of them, Hans Jonas, insisted on this personally to me.

5. On Himmler's statement see Frederick C. Tobach (with Sally Paterson Tobach), *German Voices: Memories of Life During Hitler's Third Reich* (Berkeley and Los Angeles: University of California Press, 2011), 61.

6. I am indebted to Richard Polt for providing me with a list of the anti-Semitic statements in the *Black Notebooks*.

7. Thomas Sheehan, "L'Affaire Faye: Faut-il Brûler Heidegger? A Response to Fritsche, Pégny, and Rastier," *Philosophy Today* 60:2 (Spring 2016): 481–535.

8. Emmanuel Faye, *Heidegger: The Introduction of Nazism into Philosophy in Light of the Unpublished Seminars of 1933–1935*, tr. Michael B. Smith (New Haven, CT: Yale University Press, 2011).

9. See McCumber, *Metaphysics and Oppression*, passim.

10. See McCumber, *Metaphysics and Oppression*, 56–60.

11. John McCumber, *Time and Philosophy* (Durham: Acumen, 2011).

12. See John McCumber, "The Baffling 'Nature' of Time," *Parrhesia* 15 (2012): 14–23.

13. For Hegel's denial that his account of history is "true to the facts" see McCumber, *Time and Philosophy*, 72–75.

14. John McCumber, *Reshaping Reason: Toward a New Philosophy* (Bloomington: Indiana University Press, 2005), 14–22.

15. Aristotle, *On Interpretation*, 16a.

16. John McCumber, *Poetic Interaction: Language, Freedom, Reason* (Chicago, IL: University of Chicago Press, 1989), 124–28.

Chapter 11

Ecce Homo/Ecce Cogitatio

On Heidegger's Politics and His Philosophy

Lawrence J. Hatab

Heidegger research faces a significant threat. Graduate students are commonly warned against concentrating on Heidegger's thought. Beyond the postwar "Heidegger case"—where his affiliation with National Socialism chastened many followers and diminished his high stature in many philosophical circles—the current climate runs from calls to ban Heidegger's writings from the domain of philosophy, to expectations that Heidegger will recede to the background of minor figures, to Heidegger scholars trying to ward off such things while acknowledging his failures and shortcomings. The problem goes further than Heidegger's political decisions and the growing evidence that the "Official Story" minimizing his Nazi involvement cannot be sustained. Heidegger's so-called *Black Notebooks* (GA 94–97) exhibit anti-Semitic remarks and pro-Nazi sentiments, which has added fuel to Emmanuel Faye's charge that Heidegger's political choices were not simply a personal failing separable from his thought because his philosophy, already in *Being and Time*, was itself intrinsically fascist and racist.[1]

I oppose such an extreme attack because I believe that Heidegger ranks among the greatest figures in Western philosophy, that he should remain so, and that his thought is not coextensive with National Socialism. The common reception of Heidegger's writings after the war in Europe and America was not at all in the spirit of something like fascism or anti-Semitism. What does this say about Heidegger's philosophy? Either we have missed the Nazi code in *Being and Time* or something different can and does emerge from his thinking. And yet Heidegger's political decisions cannot be separated or isolated from his thought. How can I say this? Focusing on *Being and Time*, I will argue that Heidegger's political venture indeed followed the contours of his formal phenomenological account of being-in-the-world, but so would something like Zionism or the American Revolution. The greatness of a philosophical work can be measured by the comprehensiveness of its conceptual scheme and how it addresses the basic questions facing human thought. *Being and Time* is remarkable because it articulates almost every main issue that might arise in philosophical inquiry: cognition, affect, practical life, temporality, history, individuation, socialization, freedom, constraint, decision, commitment, and principally the question of meaning, in everything from semantics to matters of life and death.

The following is a venture to reflect on Heidegger's early philosophy and his politics *together*—but in a discriminating manner contrary to bogus attempts to conflate them. Heidegger scholars must not flinch from addressing the current climate, because anti-Heideggerian forces are having a field day with his anti-Semitism, and I remain dismayed at the effectiveness of Faye's book, which is long on polemics but very short on philosophical competence. We try to do better, and I hope to contribute to that effort.[2]

First I present a very brief sketch of Heidegger's early phenomenology, as I read it, which might not fit everyone's taste. It is important to get right the radical nature of *Being and Time*. The being-question has always been a staple in Western philosophy, but the concept usually is limited to notions of presence, extant objects, universality, generality, or a vacuous grammatical function. In advancing a phenomenological ontology, Heidegger begins with how being is disclosed in everyday involvement with the world, therewith showing itself as meaning-laden, concrete, practical, temporal, and finite. The "argument" of *Being and Time* has two pillars: (1) immanence and (2) comprehensiveness. Immanence means that phenomenology cannot begin with advanced philosophical concepts like matter, cognition, objectivity, consciousness, or intentionality, but rather with the immediate lived world into which we are born and find ourselves before reflective attention. All philosophical systems have acknowledged such a "first" world, but commonly find it lacking and needful of philosophical re-formation. Immanence simply rejects this remedial posture. Philosophy must first simply describe, clarify, and sort out immediate existence—in such a way that any human being or culture could recognize its features. Any further philosophical development must pass through this first world and be grounded in its primal evidence. Immanence here is not simply counterposed to some transcendent or otherworldly reality, but also to any initial assumption that the first world exhibits intrinsic shortcomings or barriers blocking the discovery of truth (for instance, embodiment in Platonism, the Fall in Christianity, or common sense in modern rationalism).

The preliminary phenomenological concepts of *Being and Time* indicate the following ontology of immanent factical existence: being-in-the-world shows that we are carnal beings engaged with natural and cultural environments; we have needs, concerns, and interests driven by the assignments of life; we possess habits, abilities, and skills that enable dealings with things and other people; the world is opened up by a host of feelings, moods, perceptions, and comprehensions; individual existence is intrinsically engaged with and furthered by social relations; everyone is born into a world not of their choosing and shaped by inherited customs and traditions; finally, factical life is finite in being temporal, ever-changing, and contingent, also in pressing limits on knowledge, agency, achievement, and well-being—all consummated by the ultimate limit of death. In summation, the being-question must begin with a world that is embodied, environed, meaningful, active, capacious, felt, understood, social, inherited, temporal, and finite.

Heidegger's phenomenology does not reject notions of objectivity, thinghood, presence, and such, only their ontological priority, because they emerge out of, and are derived from, the immanent factical world. This is why the *zuhanden-vorhanden* dynamic is so important, but not always well understood. It is not simply a matter of practical usage and objective presence because it entails the full span of engaged immersion—which is to say, meaningful dealings with the world in a spontaneous, automatic manner that does not involve reflective attention to a "self" staging inferential relations to separate, external conditions.[3] Specific attention to objective properties emerges *out of* engaged immersion by way of interferences, or contraventions to pre-reflective experience (SZ 72–76).[4] Contrary to the modern subject–object divide, we are first ecstatically immersed in life, and contraventions make tacit meanings explicit and *then* draw awareness to features of self and world with respect to these meanings. In other words, finite limits figure in meaningfulness (SZ 82), in everything from practical tasks, to solving scientific problems, to the significance of life itself.

The comprehensiveness of Heidegger's phenomenology is such that all elements of human existence, from hammering to physics, can be accounted for and grounded in the lived world. Scientific objectivity is a sophisticated extension of the *vorhanden* perspective (SZ 360–62), but since it is derived from *zuhanden* conditions, it cannot pretend to adjudicate all philosophical questions. Science itself is a meaningful endeavor grounded in the factical life of scientists. In addition, finitude is a check on extending any notion that might arise in human understanding to some pure space of perfection, universality, or permanence. The priority of finite immanence shows that traditional philosophy, while acknowledging the lived world, was driven to overcome its temporal, variable, unreflective, unruly character. Heidegger's phenomenology simply brings philosophy back to its factical, finite base.

The inauthenticity–authenticity dynamic in *Being and Time* is also crucial because it addresses the tension between socialization and individuation, between common patterns of enculturation and individual appropriation of, or divergence from, these patterns. Authenticity involves the way in which individuals come to terms with, and decide for, particular pathways of finite existence—as opposed to thoughtless, commonplace routines. The decisional character of authenticity shows that human enterprises cannot be grounded in some secure warrant, because even if one has a warrant in mind, one must decide to follow it.

Everydayness and inauthenticity are not deficient modes that must be overcome; this would simply fit the remedial posture of traditional philosophy (see SZ 44, 130, 179). The phenomenology of *Being and Time* moves not *from* these conditions *to* some other standpoint, but *through* them to a deepened and more perspicacious disclosure of the meaning of being. For instance, disturbance over the malfunction of a tool shows the temporal meaning of the practice (as a planned aim), and this structure is deepened and brought to a "whole" by the disturbance of anxiety in the face of death, which opens up the meaning of life itself.[5]

We have come to know, or should know, that *Being and Time* has a formal-indicative character with three main components: (1) philosophy should provide a formal conceptual analysis of factical life, namely an existent*ial* account of its basic features, structures, and implications; (2) the formal account is indicative of its existent*iel*, concrete environment, which is both its source and destination (GA 60: 8/6–7, 62–63/43); (3) owing to its factical base, philosophy should be geared toward a "transformation of human Dasein" (GA 29/30: 423/292), toward opening up the authentic tasks and possibilities facing those who philosophize. Authenticity in *Being and Time* is both philosophical, as responsive attention to a factical ontology, and personal, as a call to engage one's own time and circumstances.

As expressed in section 74, Dasein has both an individual and a collective sense, in that Dasein's essential *Mitsein* is concretely embodied in the historical tasks of a community, of a people (*der Gemeinschaft, des Volkes*). Contrary to individualistic biases in liberalism, Heidegger insists that individual existence cannot be understood apart from its coexistence with others and its historical situation. From the beginning we are shaped by, and always in the midst of, larger cultural forces and narratives. Accordingly, *Being and Time*'s call to facticity should include social/political attention and decision (see SZ 383). Philosophy, therefore, is intrinsically open to, and geared toward, whatever specific questions and contraventions one's time and culture might face.[6]

This is how Heidegger's commitment to National Socialism was indeed consistent with *Being and Time*, as his own factical-existentiel engagement with his time—and Germany in the 1930s was certainly facing deep crises and wide-ranging volatile conditions. He, like many others, saw National Socialism as a viable path for the German people. Yet the notion that *Being and Time* as a philosophical text is nothing more than a recipe for fascism is erroneous because it stems from a conflation of the formal and the factical (see SZ 383). The power and cogency of *Being and Time* as a philosophical work, in my view, is that its formal structure can be indicative of any factical culture.[7] Indeed, I see nothing in *Being and Time* that could not fit something like Zionism or the American Revolution. Both involve meaningful endeavors in the midst of contravening forces, with individual and collective significance, with a temporal/historical scope, with both cognitive and affective comprehensions, requiring a host of practical tasks and capabilities, and calling for decisions in the midst of finite risks and an open future.

At the same time, I do not take *Being and Time* as simply validating any conceivable social-political movement. Space constraints permit me only the following stipulation: the *finite* ontology of *Being and Time* harbors certain checks on belief systems based on metaphysical closure—that is, fixed conceptions presumed to be secure, certain, inviolable, and universal—which cannot square with *Being and Time*'s picture of chosen *possibilities* (not finished actualities) out of the abyssal anxiety of being-toward-death. Extant National Socialism was possessed of many metaphysical postures that cannot pass the test of finitude. Such a normative take on *Being and Time* is not something pursued by Heidegger, but I think it is implicit and there for the taking.[8]

I maintain that the formal pertinence of *Being and Time* to any factical culture implies the possibility of cultural interrogation in the following way, taking the American Revolution as an example. The existential structures of finite being-in-the-world do not pertain to any metaphysical warrants that were operating in the inception of American democracy (say, natural rights endowed by a Creator) but rather to the existentiel engagement with, commitment to, and risking of, political possibilities in the uncertain course of historical action. In the language of the Declaration, it is the *holding* of truths, not their self-evidence, that counts in a phenomenological analysis. Moreover, after the revolution, the actual crafting of the American system was nothing like metaphysical construction or deductive inference but a complex and conflicted negotiation. Indeed, metaphysical and foundational warrants have generally become more and more questionable over time. Can American democracy be sustained without such warrants? I believe that Heidegger's hermeneutic phenomenology can apply here by redescribing political life in finite existential terms.[9] For instance, constitutional provisions can be understood as formal indications setting boundaries for the performance of legislation and jurisprudence.

National Socialism too was a factical political movement, but it was animated by many exclusionary assumptions, and its execution was driven by secure conceptions that were not open for interrogation or challenge. Heidegger himself in his early enthusiasm seemed to subordinate the individual to the state in a startling manner. For instance: "The individual . . . counts for nothing; the destiny of our people in its state counts for everything."[10] Such talk seems to cancel out the individuated force of authenticity in *Being and Time*, wherein social-political cohesion could not be the first and last word.

Dasein's finitude, for Heidegger, includes the limits of human agency, in that it is *thrown* into its world, "always already" shaped by its social environment and an historical inheritance not of its own making. Dasein's thrownness is thus counterposed to intimations of sovereignty and mastery in the modern conception of a self-grounding, autonomous subject. Yet Dasein's thrownness cannot be reified into any kind of social or historical determinism, because its world too is finite in being unstable and changeable. Dasein's "historicality" (SZ §74) refers not simply to its past but also to its open future (which is why history involves a set of changes in the first place). Dasein's world is always susceptible to disruptions and alterations, and this is where the "individuated" elements of authenticity come into play. I said earlier that authenticity involves a tension between individuation and socialization, but it is also a tension between Dasein and its heritage (SZ 383). I have argued in another work that authentic individuation can be understood as the fourfold possibility of *owning*, *unmasking*, *innovating*, and *interrogating* one's culture and heritage.[11] I culled various remarks in *Being and Time* to organize this set of possibilities: (1) One can freely appropriate as one's "own" (*eigen*) a tradition that has been handed down, but no longer simply *as* handed down (SZ 383). (2) One can unmask the disguises, superficialities, and other concealments that block a richer and deeper understanding of cultural phenomena (SZ 129, 391). (3) One can discover or initiate new possibilities that are normally impeded by inauthentic immersion in the commonplace (SZ 194–95). (4) One can challenge normalization and its tendency to suppress "new inquiry" and "disputation" (SZ 169). The individuating elements of authenticity do not bring a severance from the cultural world because Dasein always remains "situated." But authenticity is also a situated *openness* in not being reducible to any closed form of actuality—an openness that is the precondition for any change or innovation in Dasein's world. The fixed, secure assumptions of extant National Socialism and its hyper-communal/authoritarian dictates seem to be antithetical to the individuated force of authenticity.

In general terms, *Being and Time* and the surrounding lecture courses offer a rich, compelling ontology that applies to any significant philosophical question (not always worked through thoroughly or adequately, but there in germ), grounded in an existential/existentiel base—for instance, not simply the nature and possibility of science, but why science matters and gets off the ground in the first place. Yet Heidegger's subsequent writings, in my opinion, show that the early phenomenology really was simply preliminary to a larger philosophical aim: getting to some fundamental essence that can ground thinking and that might be taken as something unto itself (being as such or

Ereignis, understood as independent of beings). Although Heidegger was surely attentive to factical life—early lecture courses exhibit some beautiful descriptions of things like his kitchen table and his lecture room—its details did not matter as much to him as the deeper goal. The consequences of his own political decisions likely pushed him even further away from factical situations. Indeed, I would like to think that his myopic philosophical interest in some essential *an sich* made him a very poor political agent—too prone to see National Socialism in grand epochal terms, at the expense of careful attention to its actual practices and implications.

It is in this vein that I take the damning remarks about "world Jewry" in the *Black Notebooks*.[12] Aside from being repugnant, they are embarrassing in their presumed explanatory function. Even if we temper them by granting Heidegger a "metaphysical" anti-Semitism, it is no less tendentious. Like all racism, it swims in a sea of vacuous generality and abstraction. I am not interested in some subtle account of why Heidegger may have tied Jewry to modern calculative technicity. It doesn't matter. If we take that association out, nothing of Heidegger's diagnosis of technology will be lost. What his thinking opens up has nothing to do with such a chimerical cause.

To conclude this chapter, I engage two essential elements in Heidegger's philosophy. The first is truth conceived as unconcealment, where concealment and disclosure are reciprocally related, where errancy is not the opposite of truth but intrinsic to it. From an ontological standpoint, errancy names the concealment of concealment in unconcealment—how the mystery of concealment gets lost in the compelling force of disclosure.[13] But we can notice an important ontical register as well. With finite unconcealment, any disclosure will be selective and thereby conceal, omit, or suppress other possibilities. Such selectivity in disclosive truth calls for caution and reserve when advancing any standpoint, because what is "other" can be unduly covered up, or worse. This is especially true with regard to politics. In this respect, to paraphrase Foucault, all political views are dangerous. The errancy of National Socialism is clear, but those who castigate Heidegger on behalf of Enlightenment ideals forget or cannot fathom the errancy of modern political reason—something that Heidegger's thought can help uncover—especially how rational "universality" was in practice a disguised bias against different cultures, where a lack of, or discomfort with, being lifted up to universal rational standards were judged as backward, or worse. Such is the root of colonialistic rhetoric: the paternalistic control of peoples for their own good (and their resources).

On the matter of Heidegger and the German *Volk*, there is nothing intrinsically wrong with Folk-thinking, in the sense of affirming cultural particularity. Behind current movements of multiculturalism and identity politics lies the notion that group identifications of all sorts are part of human existence and that ethnic traditions enhance and enrich human lives. But within particularism lies the danger of tribalism, where a myopic fixation on one's own group can obscure or cancel out the dignity and humanity of other groups. Heidegger's sincere commitment to National Socialism came from his interest in freeing a Folk for their authentic culture. In a time of crisis, Heidegger's idealized vision of National Socialism can be understood as a response to four supposed threats: American materialism, Russian communism, Enlightenment universalism, and rational individualism, all posing interrelated threats to what Heidegger took to be genuine German culture and a proper engagement with being. Chief among Heidegger's concerns were: that being would be reduced to economic resources and technological controls (Americanism and communism); that the social order and high culture would be ruined by consumerism and the celebration of private experience (Americanism and individualism); and that a particular culture and heritage would be overcome by a rationalized, global construct (communism and universalism). In any case, the Nazis were tribalists, whose primary aim went beyond the affirmation of the German folk to the domination and annihilation of *other* Folk.[14]

In addition to the danger of tribalism in Folk-thinking, the danger in rational cosmopolitanism is a washed out horizon that cannot abide ethnic particularity, which must be silenced, secluded, or overcome in the name of rational progress. How can both dangers be avoided? No epochal thinking or traditional philosophical theory can easily resolve this intrinsic tension between particularity and commonality that we continue to face today; and no social or political viewpoint is immune from the hazard of exclusionary effects.[15] What was missing in Heidegger's early politics, and what is currently quite needful, is the difficult balance that affirms a cultural heritage as essential to one's world, but without a reductive attachment that takes one's culture as the full limit of one's world. In other words, a culture can be a finite presence that remains open to, and keeps open a space for, other cultures—along the lines of what the later Heidegger called *Seinlassen*.[16]

The second element of Heidegger's philosophy that I want to emphasize is the temporal structure of history.[17] Dasein's being-in-the-world is essentially temporal, which is a primary indication of finitude in the sense that we are stretched between birth and death, and experience is never a purely fixed condition. Here we confront one of the perennial conflicts between philosophical categories and the factical world: how general concepts relate to the changing, variable realm of concrete experience marked by temporal movement. The most prominent example is the concept of "being," which has been counterposed to time because the former designates something actual that *is* the case, rather than a state of becoming and something past or future. Traditional philosophy has analyzed time as a series of now-points, where the governing concept is the now-as-present, so that the past is no-longer-now and the future is not-yet-now. Since the course of time therefore seems to involve negation and nonbeing, the question of what time "is" has been an enduring puzzle. But lived temporality can be shown to sidestep this problem. We *dwell* in a temporal, narrative condition; we experience time as a looping intersection of time dimensions, as a coming to presence out of the future and shaped by the past. The "absences" of the future and past have a *presence* in anticipation and recollection. In this way human experience is *extended* into the future and past, as being presently engaged with future possibilities enabled and prompted by past orientations.

There is a certain priority of the future in lived time. We are always presently occupied with the coming-forth of life. Even the past comes forth in a way because memories are occurrences that arise and come to us. The meaning-laden character of human experience and activity is usually for the sake of some purpose or aim; what lies ahead in the future is animating current concerns. Thus life is continually occupied with a not-yet, something yet to come. But the future is not on that account nonexistent or separate from the present and past. Future possibilities are prepared by present capacities and concerns that are shaped in the past. And factical presence is never "the present," or the "now," because it is a movement, a circulation of the future and the past with a looping figure-eight structure; it is both retentive and protentive (as recollection and anticipation), laden with the past and pregnant with the future.

The existential content of temporality is history, which involves the specific narratives, concerns, and projects that animate living endeavors, in other words the course of meaningful events in time. History is not simply given in the past, because an interest in the past is not purely antiquarian but attention to its value for present life and its future aims. History therefore shares the figure-eight structure of temporality, which should be kept in mind when studying the past—to avoid the trap of interpreting a previous age in terms of what happened afterward and how it moved toward (now known) future developments. In a past time, the future was yet to be determined, and that indeterminacy was part of a past culture's own (then present) concerns.

Given the temporal structure of factical life and its finitude, a sense of history in a culture provides, either implicitly or explicitly, a stabilizing function in the face of temporal contingency. We continually encounter contraventions and chance disruptions of expectations and plans. The future is sheer expectation and possibility, which is engaged *as* something contingent, open, and thus infused with possible contraventions. Retention of a tradition reduces the stress of uncertainty. Yet tradition can provide varying degrees of stability: the past can be conceived as repeatable continuity (which tends to be conservative), or as a kind of telic process of development (more open but guided by presumed ends), or as a launch of possibilities with no presumed goal (more open to contingency but still guided by preparation and past cultural formats). That said, it seems that history should be understood as an inherited openness, with inheritance providing a stabilizing element and futurial openness providing a destabilizing element that undermines foundationalist urges for cultural security. History in this sense can support neither a strict conservatism nor a radicalism that moves to sever the present and future from the past.

Being historical means that one *is* responsible for one's choices, but as suggested earlier, the futurial openness of historicality should warn against a complete reduction of a past period to what happened afterward. Heidegger is surely responsible for supporting a despicable political regime. Yet if we exclude the racist and supremacist elements of Nazism from Heidegger's outlook, we see something distinguishable from the monstrosity he so blindly endorsed. To put it simply, Heidegger was an antidemocratic, conservative nationalist, which was very common among German intellectuals of his era.[18] If the war and the Holocaust had not happened, what would be thought of Heidegger's politics? Most people would still be critical, but the level of intensity would be greatly diminished. But the war and the Holocaust did happen, and so Heidegger's words and deeds become retrospectively more ominous in light of this terrible fact. Try this experiment: Take any American political speech you like, substitute German references, and see if the tone darkens ("Make Germany great again!"). I am not trying to sanitize Heidegger, or to deny his culpability and the dangers in his thought. I am only saying that the culpability and danger have been overstated.[19]

Some have argued that perhaps Heidegger's later historical-destinal-epochal thinking and its sweeping critique of modern technicity might provide resources for, or perhaps was deliberately advancing, an indictment of National Socialism as itself caught up in technological nihilism.[20] Heidegger's initial "error" accordingly was failing to see the complicity of existing Nazism with the modern oblivion of being. I do not share this kind of proposal, for the following reasons. Although the historical character of being is a major contribution of Heidegger's philosophy, it need not and should not be turned into epochal-destinal thinking, which gathers this and other ages into a metanarrative that defines their essence, ontological modality, effects, and prospects. National Socialism (not to mention communism) was itself driven by epochal-destinal thinking, and Heidegger's political statements in the 1930s reek of its overheated historical fantasies. The problem as I see it is not any particular mode of metanarrative like National Socialism that might be critiqued, but epochal-destinal thinking itself, no matter what form it takes, whether as National Socialism, communism, the oblivion of modern technology, secular humanism, democracy, or the fateful sending of being's grace. Heidegger's epochal drama cannot adequately speak to the evils of Nazism because it is part of the problem, in soaring above the contingencies of finite life in the name of some global dereliction and deliverance. Indeed, the lessons of facticity and finitude drawn from Heidegger's early phenomenology, at least as I read them, should inhibit the urge to discover in history any "essential" metanarrative, even with Heidegger's temporalized conception of *Wesen*. I have come to believe that despite the early Heidegger's presumed sensitivity to factical life, he always was and remained a typical philosopher aiming to unify and ground thinking with a quasi-Platonic source of illumination. Such a propensity likewise gave birth to the framework of epochal thinking. But metanarratives infect historical understanding with a determinate shape that belies its intrinsic openness and encourages myopic worldviews.

NOTES

1. Emmanuel Faye, *Heidegger: The Introduction of Nazism into Philosophy*, tr. Michael B. Smith (New Haven, CT: Yale University Press, 2009). It should be said that the notebooks also contain many critiques of mainstream Nazi ideology.

2. For a cogent critique of Faye's work, see Thomas Sheehan, "Emmanuel Faye: The Introduction of Fraud into Philosophy?" *Philosophy Today* 59:3 (Summer 2015): 367–400.

3. *Zuhandenheit* includes dwelling in one's house and yard, sunlight and heat (GA 24: 152–53/108); likewise in language usage (SZ 82, 161, 224).

4. Contravention includes such things as malfunction, obstacles, resistance, and lack.

5. As Heidegger puts it, "Just as every loss first really allows us to recognize and understand the value of something we possessed before, so too it is precisely death that illuminates the essence of life" (GA 29/30: 387/266).

6. As Theodore Kisiel points out in this volume, for Heidegger the facticity of one's own time and generation is the proper object of philosophical research (GA 62: 366).

7. Note Heidegger's occasional references to "primitive Dasein" in *Being and Time* as relevant to his research (SZ 51–52)—as opposed to Western rationalized cultures and their colonialistic assessment of New World peoples in the Age of Exploration and beyond. See my article "Heidegger and Myth: A Loop in the History of Being," *Journal of the British Society for Phenomenology* 22:2 (May 1991): 45–64.

8. I attempted such a project in my book *Ethics and Finitude: Heideggerian Contributions to Moral Philosophy* (Lanham, MD: Rowman & Littlefield, 2000). In effect I was addressing a legitimate question raised by thinkers such as Habermas: Does *Being and Time* have resources that could stand against something like Nazism? As Drew Hyland indicates in this volume, Heidegger's posture in *Being and Time* would take ethical and political questions as ontical concerns that cannot take precedence over ontological matters. The question for us is how one might think ethically and politically in light of Heidegger's ontology.

9. See my *Ethics and Finitude*, Ch. 7; also Leslie Paul Thiele, *Timely Meditations: Martin Heidegger and Postmodern Politics* (Princeton, NJ: Princeton University Press, 1995).

10. Cited by Hugo Ott in "Martin Heidegger als Rektor der Universität Freiburg i. Br. 1933/34," *Zeitschrift des Breisgau Geschichtsverein* 103 (1984): 117.

11. Hatab, *Ethics and Finitude*, 174.

12. There are comparable remarks about Communism, Americanism, and Christianity. For a collection of interpretive essays, see *Reading Heidegger's Black Notebooks 1931–41*, ed. Ingo Farin and Jeff Malpas (Cambridge: MIT Press, 2016).

13. See "On the Essence of Truth," in GA 9.

14. It should be noted that Heidegger did not support the Nazi regime's racialism, biologism, militarism, and supremacism. See Michael E. Zimmerman, *Heidegger's Confrontation With Modernity: Technology, Politics, Art* (Bloomington: Indiana University Press, 1990).

15. The great contribution of Levinas has been the ethical priority of the Other, in contradistinction to a reductive "sameness" supposedly indigenous to ontology. Yet in a 1982 radio interview, he rejected the idea that Palestinians are the ethical Other. See Judith Butler, *Parting Ways: Jewishness and the Critique of Zionism* (New York: Columbia University Press, 2013), Ch. 1. What bothers me is not the criticism of Heidegger but the hypocrisy in some of it. Americans are rightly proud of their democratic heritage, but we are usually quiet about how our nation was founded on conquest and enslavement. Although we have owned up to the evils of slavery and its aftermath, we are almost completely silent about the fate of Native Americans, which is arguably the worst sustained story of genocide in human history. And we should not ignore how some of the assumptions in our "enlightened" tradition made such atrocities possible, or at least easier to sanitize.

16. I appreciate Peter Gordon's point in this volume concerning the possible slippage in Heidegger attributing to a Folk or national culture the same kind of authenticity dynamic he gave to individual Dasein. But since authenticity for Heidegger is not individualistic, since it includes the broader range of Mitsein, perhaps we can say that any conception of an individual culture cannot be isolated from the wider world. It is evident that nationalism is a strong and growing current today, but modern mobility, emigration, and interpenetration are just as surely rendering such nationalistic fervor to be a myopic and nostalgic fantasy.

17. A full discussion is found in sections 67–75 of *Being and Time*. Some of what follows is drawn from the epilogue to my *Ethics and Finitude*, 201–8.

18. See Hans Sluga, *Heidegger's Crisis: Philosophy and Politics in Nazi Germany* (Cambridge, MA: Harvard University Press, 1993).

19. For a concise and evenhanded treatment of various critical perspectives and responses in the matter of Heidegger's politics, see Richard Polt, *Heidegger: An Introduction* (Ithaca, NY: Cornell University Press, 1999), 152–64.

20. See, for instance, Dominique Janicaud, *Heidegger in France*, tr. François Raffoul and David Pettigrew (Bloomington: Indiana University Press, 2015), Ch. 10.

Chapter 12

Thought, Action, and History

Rethinking Revolution After Heidegger

Arun Iyer

In volume two of his Nietzsche lectures, Heidegger writes, assessing Nietzsche's own account of the genesis of the thought of the eternal return:

> in a time of decline, a time when all is counterfeit and pointless activity, *thinking in the grand style* is genuine action, action in its most powerful—though most silent—form. Here the actual distinction between "mere theory" and "mere praxis" makes no sense. (GA 6.1: 230–31/10–11)

This passage will serve as the scaffolding for the ensuing reflections on what constitutes action for Heidegger, his attempt to radically transform our understanding of the relationship between thought and action, and the implications of his elevation of thought to the pinnacle of all action. These reflections aim to show that within the complex of Heidegger's thought, which did not remain static, there lies a vision of thinking as the most radically transformative action, the most revolutionary of all actions. Heidegger's attempt to reveal the praxiological essence of thinking, which cannot be extricated from his reflections on history as the history of be-ing (*Seynsgeschichte*), compels us to rethink the very notion of revolution, something that continues to remain significant for us today.

THINKING AS RADICALLY TRANSFORMATIVE ACTION

In his "Letter on Humanism," Heidegger laments the fact that we still have not come to a proper understanding of what it means to act, arguing that actions should not be understood as causes of effects. The true essence of an action lies in what it accomplishes (*vollbringt*). Marshaling the entire semantic force of the German *vollbringen*, Heidegger explicates action as that which brings something to the fore in the fullness of its essence. This does not make action a creation ex nihilo. Rather, to accomplish is to bring an entity's being, which always already encompasses the meaningful presence of any entity, into fullness, through words. Action is thus, fundamentally speaking, an articulation of being. Thinking, as the articulation of the relationship between being and the essence of the human being, is the highest action.

The essence of an action, according to Heidegger, cannot be captured at the level of cause and effect. The radicality of action cannot be assessed from the spectacularity of its effects. Ontic transformation alone cannot tell us anything about the radical nature of an action. An action is truly radical only when it is able to produce an ontological transformation. Even creation ex nihilo turns out, then, to be an ontic transformation. What is this ontological transformation that Heidegger here implies? Let us try to understand this through his account of thinking.

As an action, thinking accomplishes the relationship between being and the essence of human beings. This should not be understood as an ontic change, wherein a new conceptual understanding is gained through bringing together two concepts, that of being and the human being, into a relationship which is then expressed in the form of a proposition. Instead, the accomplishment of the relationship between being and the human being implicates the thinker, not merely at the level of understanding. Thinking is the accomplishment of the relationship of the thinker, who is also a human being, in his very essence, to being. Thinking involves listening to being and reciprocating the call of being. Thinking is thus a radical experience that permeates thinkers through and through and brings them face to face with their very finitude. That is the reason why thinking, for Heidegger, cannot be *theoria*. For in *theoria* the very being of the one who theorizes is not implicated in its finitude. In the modern conception of theory, the being of the theorizer as a concrete existence is bracketed out of the act of theorizing, as a merely subjective accretion. Even in the ancient conception of theoretical activity, as found in Aristotle's *Nicomachean Ethics*, for example, where the being of the theorizer is implicated, it is implicated not in its finitude as a historically existing being-in-the-world, but rather in its apparent infinitude and in its ability to imitate the divine by transcending history and the world itself. Rather, genuine thinking, for Heidegger, is an experience in which being is brought to word, in which the *radical* and fundamental experience of historicity and finitude is articulated. *Theoria*, whether in its modern or ancient form, does not take the finitude of the subject of theoretical understanding seriously. It is simply about the technique of making the object conform to the subject through the medium of concepts and their articulation in propositions, an articulation which, according to Heidegger, is not commensurate with the experience of being (GA 9: 314/240).

We must digress briefly to come to grips with the peculiar turn that Heidegger's discourse about being undergoes in the period from the 1930s to the early 1940s, when he explicitly links be-ing (*Seyn*) to history and starts speaking of *Seynsgeschichte*.[1] In order to do this, we have to follow Heidegger in translating into the language of metaphysics his discourse about be-ing (*Seyn*). Although Heidegger sometimes uses *Seyn* interchangeably with *Sein*,[2] some of his writings in the 1930s do reflect a clear distinction between the two terms. In the history of Western philosophy, which, for Heidegger, is also the history of metaphysics, being (*Sein*) is synonymous with the beingness (*Seiendheit*) of beings, which despite all caveats ends up being conceived in terms of another entity: the universal as some kind of general category under which beings stand. By using "be-ing" (*Seyn*), Heidegger wants to ensure that the word contains no trace of any sense of beingness (GA 65: 75). Now, metaphysics is a discourse in which the being of beings is understood as another being. Its highest manifestation is ontotheology, wherein the being of beings is interpreted as depending upon the highest being, the unmoved mover in Aristotle or God in Christian theology. How then do we get a sense of what Heidegger is trying to call "be-ing" by using the language of metaphysics? In the "Letter on Humanism," Heidegger himself gives us a hint in this direction when he argues for the understanding of be-ing as the possible. But being as possibility is to be confused neither with the transcendental conditions for the possibility of X nor with the logical possibility of X. What kind of possibility do we have here then?

One could argue that Heidegger is implying what can be called a concrete possibility. This interpretation allows us to achieve some much-needed clarity on the distinction between historiography (*Historie*) and history (*Geschichte*) and more importantly on the relationship between being/be-ing and history. What we see is Heidegger's attempt in the 1930s to understand history not in terms of actualities but rather in terms of events (*Ereignisse*). The starting point of all historiography, in Heidegger's understanding, is actuality. In stark contrast to this approach, thinking in terms of history (*Geschichte*) takes events as its starting point. History (*Geschichte*) is about beginnings and ends, indeed ruptures. An event is to be seen neither as the effect of an actuality nor as its cause. It has to be seen as the surging up or an emergence of concrete possibilities.[3]

If thinking is response to be-ing, if it can take place only within the history of be-ing, then thinkers are no longer on a trajectory toward absolute knowledge, taking as their vantage point some place out of the world looking down upon it, surveying the whole of what is from the position of a disinterested and disengaged spectator. The realization of the finitude of thought, that to be a thinker is to be in the world, in history, no longer allows for any such fancies. To think is to take a stand in the world in the midst of the things among which one finds oneself. It presupposes an engagement with the world that does not mean a harmony, a being at peace with the world and the things in it. It could very well amount to a being entirely out of joint with beings as a whole. Even further, to think is not to extricate oneself from the warp and woof of history, to look down upon history as the realm of the relativity of the particular. To think is rather to find oneself suffocated by the present so that it becomes necessary to break away from it, to radically transition oneself to the future.

Heidegger characterizes this suffocation as the experience of homelessness. But in this becoming at odds with beings, in this homelessness, we come to the realization that no specific beings or combinations of beings are going to help us a find a way out. Although Marx and Nietzsche were the only thinkers to have experienced this homelessness, according to Heidegger (GA 9: 339/258–59), they failed to articulate it in words that are commensurate with it. Hence neither of their theoretical proposals—communism or the reversal of Platonism—succeed. We can add all of the other political ideologies such as nationalism, internationalism, capitalism, socialism, and National Socialism to this mix. They all fail. Heidegger hints that only poesy (*Dichten*) is the way to get us out. This homelessness, not being a psychological, economic or sociopolitical phenomenon, is to be understood ontologically as the abandonment of beings by being. All of these ideologies and theoretical proposals, because they concern themselves exclusively with the ontic, disqualify themselves as answers to the homelessness of humanity. Most of these ideologies remain absolutely oblivious to this homelessness. They are incapable of experiencing it, incapable of thinking.

THINKING, POESY, AND HISTORY

In GA 71, composed in 1941–1942, Heidegger reflects on the essence of thinking in conjunction with poesy, and in so doing gives us the starkest rendition of the essence of thinking. Heidegger asks, with a very Leninist slant: What must thinking do? Heidegger claims that it could become necessary either to teach or to think inventively (*Erdenken*).

If teaching became necessary, it would involve "lecturing other human beings through historiographical concepts about what was thinkable and what has been thought in previous times" (GA 71: 285/248, tm). If inventive thinking became necessary, it could take two forms. The first form would be that of remembering the first beginning in Europe, its progression into metaphysics, and the subsequent completion and end of metaphysics. The second form would be that of thinking ahead—a transition from metaphysics to the knowledge of the history of be-ing. The thinking ahead could again take two forms: a preparation for the poesy appropriate to the history of be-ing in the moment of transition or a thoughtful, imageless articulation of the event.

Heidegger distinguishes thinking as an imageless experience (GA 71: 322/279), as the imageless word (GA 71: 330/286) of a question, from poesy, which articulates by naming, that is, communicates in the imagistic word. On the one hand, by putting everything, including be-ing itself, into question, thinking becomes the experience of homelessness, which pulls us out of our day-to-day dealings with beings, breaks with the existing foundations and is a "de-founding." Thinking renounces beings and renounces the holy, the divine, in its movement toward homelessness in being. Poesy, on the other hand, discovers the foundation, what cannot be questioned. It founds that which abides—the history of a humanity—by the act of naming what is holy. The poet can poetize neither about the event of be-ing nor about be-ing, but only about beings, in particular the holy (GA 71: 244/211). Poesy belongs to the realm of the ontic. Poesy embraces beings. It is always about beings. Poesy is the experience of being at home among beings. This would very well apply to Heidegger's own attempts at poetry.

Thinking cannot articulate the future, the world, the history that is to be founded. For this it needs poetry. In the same way, poetry needs thought to render everything questionable and hence to depart from the existing foundation, so that it becomes necessary to find another beginning, another world, another history.

Thoughtful action, which is the highest form of action, encompasses teaching the history of thought, listening to, questioning and articulating the event of being into which the thinker is transposed. Heidegger acknowledges that pedagogy requires the use of historiographical concepts, which are metaphysical by nature, even if the aim is to overcome metaphysics. Teaching the historiography of Western thought is always an attempt to destabilize our existing conceptions of history and communicate another sense of history: the history of events. This is a task which, for Heidegger, goes hand in hand with thinking the event itself.

It is now easy to see the radically transformative nature of both thinking and poesy, which are about transitioning to another beginning and founding that beginning, respectively. Heidegger takes care to distinguish his notions of overcoming and transition from the more conventional understandings of revolution, which he argues are not revolutionary enough (GA 69: 23), for they all imply, contrary to what they intend, the simple perpetuation of what is already there (GA 71: 269/233). By contrast, a genuine revolution is not to be understood as simply engendering a new situation ex nihilo. Rather it is to experience and actualize through thinking and poesy other concrete possibilities for radically different ways of relating to beings, possibilities that are not human creations, but in and through which both beings and beings acquire a different essence, so to speak.

THE REVOLUTIONARY URGENCY OF THINKING

In GA 65, Heidegger understands the abandonment of beings by being as the reduction of beings to objects of machination and lived experience. Beings are reduced to their capacity to be represented, to their conformity to human subjectivity, which subjugates them in an absolute manner. This subjugation is illustrated by machination, which is the absolute manipulability of beings for human purposes. Indeed, the only standard to measure the actuality of a being is its capacity to provide a lived experience. Lived experience (*Erlebnis*), for Heidegger, is founded on the unshakable substratum of the subjective certainty of the ego, which goes hand in hand with the objective anthropological certainty of human life (GA 65: 131). Lived experience is the enjoyment of the artifacts of human technological manipulation, which in our time encompasses all of our interactions with everything that is. In stark contrast, thinking is characterized as an experience (*Erfahrung*), wherein the certainties of the ego and human life are shattered and radically transformed. With the abandonment of beings by being, all of being is reduced to lived experience, brought about by the infinite manipulability of beings. For Heidegger, lived experience is the relationship between subject and object that the technological essence of science is able to bring about. We cannot diagnose this situation merely at the ontic level, as the perversion of values, as Nietzsche did. In GA 69, Heidegger understands the abandonment of beings by being as the reduction of being to power. Power exists through ensuring its own existence by overpowering everything that poses a danger to its existence. This is nothing but a situation of unmitigated, borderless war. All the contemporary political ideologies, be it nationalism or socialism, English liberalism or communism, are manifestations of the abandonment of beings by beings, where subjectivity comes to be equated with humanity and being with power.

Heidegger declares that in this scenario, be-ing loses its question-worthiness completely. The absence of questioning goes hand in hand with the absence of any distress and need. This absence of need is the highest need, the highest urgency. What is needed is to experience this lack of need as something unbearable. How? By beginning to think. Heidegger wonders whether there is anyone in the human species who can undertake this task of thinking. For to think is to experience this extreme distress, which Heidegger characterizes in different places as homelessness and as the abandonment of beings by being. To think, as we have seen, is not just to give oneself over to a radical experience of utter alienation, but also to question, teach, and articulate what is necessitated by the history of Being.

Let us now contrast this to how Marx envisages the revolutionary urgency of proletarian action in his work. Marx understands revolution broadly as the dissolution of a social order along with the overthrow of the existing political regime, whereby every revolution has to address the particular social conditions and the more universal political conditions under which the revolutionary class lives, be it the bourgeois or the proletariat.[4] When discussing the proletarian revolution in particular, Marx too speaks of distress when describing the world-historical role of the proletariat as an agent of socialist revolution. The urgency of revolutionary action comes from a proletariat that has been stripped of all, even the summary appearance, of its humanity, but which has, at the same time, arrived at a theoretical consciousness of the loss of its humanity. The urgency of the act of revolution comes from the intensity of the distress provoked by the absolutely inhuman conditions in which the proletariat finds itself, coupled with its theoretical consciousness of those conditions. In another place, Marx describes this distress as the distress of exclusion from the social life of the human being. Since the essence of the human being is nothing but social, this distress is ultimately the distress of alienation from one's own essence, the distress of dehumanization.[5] The intensity of the distress (*Not*) is the practical necessity (*Notwendigkeit*) of revolution. However, the proletariat can emancipate itself only when revolutionary action has acquired both a theoretical necessity through conscious understanding and a practical necessity through the intensity of the distress into which it is put.[6] What is this theoretical consciousness that Marx speaks of? It is the consciousness of the world-historical mission of the proletariat to end capitalism by ending the very phenomenon of class distinction engendered by capitalism. But this world-historical role needs to be clarified; it needs the aid of a thorough theoretical understanding of the structures of capital, which would necessarily include a degree of technological mastery that Heidegger would regard as machination. Once the structures of capital and its historical trajectory that intensify the dehumanization of labor are understood, the proletariat becomes aware of its own nature. It becomes aware of the actions to which it is compelled by world history. It is raised to the pinnacle of self-awareness. Revolutionary action is thus the perfect synthesis of theory and praxis.[7] An insight into the theoretical necessity of action alone is not enough; one must experience the practical necessary of action too. It is distress, sharpened to the extremes of human degradation, which takes the form of practical necessity.

The vantage point from which the revolutionary urgency of action is experienced, according to Marx, is at the crossroads of the universal (political) and the particular (social) as well as the theoretical and the practical. Indeed, the revolutionary act is not an act of choice. As the feeling of being forced by the very hand of world history, the revolutionary act in Marx is the individual person or class, here the proletariat, seizing its own destiny. But the knowledge of this destiny is possible only from the absolute standpoint that looks down at the contingent particularities of its own individual history, from the absolute standpoint of world history. This is a standpoint from which the past, the present, and the future can be absolutely synthesized under the continuity of a dynamic process that leads from feudalism to capitalism to communism. The revolutionary subject is thus split in Marx between the contingency of the feeling of the individual pain of dehumanization from within its own individual and social history and the universality of the knowledge of the dynamic of world history.

In contrast, the vantage point from which revolutionary urgency is experienced according to Heidegger is from within the history of be-ing. This is not a standpoint to which any absolute knowledge of world history is given. From this standpoint, all one can experience is the distress of the present at the very lack of distress in the way humanity goes about its day-to-day activities immersed in machination and lived experience. This Heideggerian vantage point on the revolutionary urgency of thinking is not on a teleological curve, on the cusp of a grand culmination of history. It is the point of an impasse, which is the exhaustion of all possibilities of acting and thinking, where the technological planning and management of things and human beings have gained a planet-wide dominance, where history seems to have indeed come to an end. All one can articulate from this vantage point is something very modest: not the theory of the process of world history, but rather the imageless word of the event of a rupture, of the surging open of completely different possibilities of relating to beings, indeed of the beginning of another history.

CONCLUDING REMARKS: REVOLUTION AFTER HEIDEGGER

First, Heidegger's account of the relation between thought, action and history, especially through the 1930s and early 1940s, shows him, without doubt, as a thinker of revolution. Thinking within the history of be-ing is a truly revolutionary action, in the sense that it seeks to herald a real future, which is not to be a mere continuation of a static present. It seeks to articulate the end of the first beginning, to undo the foundations of the first beginning, and signal the transition from the first to the other beginning. Poesy as an ontic activity complements the ontological activity of thinking by founding the other beginning.

Second, Heidegger disentangles the thinking of revolution from the thinking of world history. World history is not the only way of writing history for the revolutionary. Indeed, the writing and teaching of the history of be-ing itself becomes an act of revolution in Heidegger. Such a history of be-ing is no longer the description of a grand teleological process, what Lyotard calls the grand narrative, whose impending culmination fills the revolutionaries with the hope to fight for a better world. Rather, history is now about liberating the event from the confines of the process in order to show how one does not have to succumb to the grand process that pulverizes everything.[8]

Third, with Heidegger, the thought of revolution is now tied to the thought of the event. As a result, capitalism and socialism, the two ideologies that have defined the past century and continue to define the present, do not have to be seen as ideologies in conflict, as stages in a revolutionary history. These adversarial ideologies can be seen as kindred twins stemming from the same event, enmeshed in the same ontological impasse of the first beginning of history, the event that culminates in the reduction of the being of beings to technological machination and the related thrill of lived experience. The true revolution would then herald an event that would overcome the end of the first beginning, in which both capitalism and communism find themselves helplessly caught, and usher in another beginning.

Finally, to think revolution in Heidegger is to think the overcoming of the abandonment of beings by be-ing in its twin form: machination and lived experience. We have seen that they completely impoverish our relationships to the world around us, to each other and to ourselves, degrading the very essence of beings. How should we envisage such an overcoming? It is tempting to read into Heidegger's many writings one of the two alternatives: The first is the abandonment of all technology, technological progress, and urbanization, and a retreat into a less hectic, rural past or an imitation of the ways of the indigenous peoples around the world who have somehow escaped technological modernity. The second is a more gentle moderation of our technologically informed ways of dealing with things: driving our cars and using our computers a little less, reading some poetry on the side, and finding some time to go to the seaside and contemplating the setting sun, and more generally the grace of natural beauty. I would argue Heidegger's writings deny both these alternatives. We should eschew such temptations to extrapolate from Heidegger's writings something more concrete to act upon and live by. For they do his writings no justice. What his writings show us is the possibility of a different space of relations between human beings and the world, which is quite difficult to render concrete: They point toward the cultivation a different kind of relationship to the world around us, to others, and to ourselves. They look toward a recognition of the richness in the variety of possibilities for relating to the world. The late Heidegger's notion of the fourfold is precisely such an attempt to recognize this richness. Such a relationship would mean a complete transformation in our essence and that of all other beings in this world. It would mean an overcoming of the anthropological framework through which we have understood ourselves as a *zōon logon echon* or an *ego cogito*.

NOTES

1. For an excellent summation of the various interpretations of be-ing in the commentaries on Heidegger, see Pol Vandevelde, "Language as the House of Being: How to Bring Intelligibility to Heidegger While Keeping the Excitement," *Philosophical Compass* 9:4 (2014), 256.

2. Heidegger acknowledges the need to adopt the language of metaphysics in the "Letter on Humanism." He is also explicit about it in his reflections on thinking in *Das Ereignis* (GA 71: 285/248).

3. In GA 71, Heidegger argues that in the first beginning the being of beings is understood ontically as *phusis*, which is seen as a surging up or an emergence of beings in their becoming itself (GA 71: 25/18, 26/20, 28/46, 57/46, 127/108). But at the same time Heidegger also understands the emergence of concrete possibilities as be-ing (*Seyn*) in relation to the history of be-ing (GA 71: 137/117, 139/118, 147/127, 303/263). For a more detailed account of be-ing as concrete possibility, see Arun Iyer, *Towards an Epistemology of Ruptures: The Case of Heidegger and Foucault* (London: Bloomsbury, 2014).

4. Karl Marx and Friedrich Engels, *Werke* (Berlin: Dietz, 1962), I, 409; Marx, *Selected Writings in Sociology and Social Philosophy*, ed. T. B. Bottomore and M. Rubel, tr. T. B. Bottomore (New York: McGraw Hill, 1964), 238.

5. Marx and Engels, *Werke*, I, 407; Marx, *Selected Writings*, 237.

6. Marx and Engels, *Werke*, II, 38; Marx, *Selected Writings*, 232.

7. Marx and Engels, *Werke*, II, 38; Marx, *Selected Writings*, 233.

8. Here we see Heidegger's influence on Foucault, who describes his own histories of the event as "insurrection of subordinated knowledges" ("*Society Must Be Defended*," ed. Arnold Davidson, tr. David Macey [New York: Picador, 1997], 7) and on the theorists of the subaltern who follow in Foucault's wake, for example, Partha Chatterjee, *The Black Hole of Empire* (Princeton, NJ: Princeton University Press, 2012).

Chapter 13

Ethics After Heidegger

Dennis J. Schmidt

I took my first class in philosophy because a professor, who had asked me what I intended to do if I was drafted for the Vietnam War, told me about Plato's *Crito* and how Socrates spoke with the laws of Athens about resistance and law. That conversation led me to take two philosophy classes the next semester: one on Plato, the other on Heidegger and Sartre. (I was told, for reasons I no longer remember, that those were the courses that the "radical" students were taking, and I followed suit.) The Vietnam War and the Civil Rights movement were powerfully present events in my student life, and my own turn to philosophy was indelibly coupled with real questions of justice, of law, of the good, and of ethical life. The texts we read as students—especially Heidegger, Plato, Sartre, Hegel, and Nietzsche—never seemed abstract and always seemed to lead back to the passions of a young student in turbulent times. (I say "we" because another feature of this moment was its sense of being shared and a matter for discussion.) Chance conversations and contingent choices for silly reasons combined to form a decisive moment in my life, and the strange alchemy of history and facticity gave birth to a conviction that I still struggle to understand: from the beginning, my sense has always been that somehow reading Heidegger has helped me understand something of how to respond to the urgent questions of a life. Heidegger was never alone in having such a place and being so coupled with a concern with justice and ethical choice, but he always stood out. My youthful enthusiasms are much more tempered—whether I have been worn down by life and become jaded or understood more clearly and grown wiser is still to be determined—but my conviction that reading Heidegger can contribute to thinking about the difficulties of ethical life still remains.

Of course, Heidegger—the person and even his texts—has made holding onto this conviction exceedingly difficult, in some ways impossible, and quite often has brought me to question my own judgment. But I still believe that there is much to be gained from Heidegger's works for thinking about how we are to understand ethical life. To explain this conviction is a complicated project and moves far beyond the scope of these brief remarks, so for now I simply propose to lay out as clearly as possible some of what I take to be the shape of an ethical sense that is tenable after Heidegger, perhaps even thanks to thinking along with Heidegger. To be clear, and to fit the brevity of this format, I will simply assert six theses in a rather dogmatic—and hence not genuinely philosophical—form. These theses are not exhaustive of what I believe needs to be said about ethics after Heidegger, nor are they always fully commensurate with Heidegger's own claims. To be sure, I am sure that Heidegger would find the very idea of developing an ethical sense out of his work problematic—at best. I suspect as well that he would have argued that all talk of ethics is premature—at best. In short, I do not want to make the claim that what follows could be called something like a "Heideggerian ethics" even if it does take as one of its clues Heidegger's call for ethics to become "original"—that is, closer to the sources of life—again. Nonetheless, these theses are indications of some of the hints that I have found in Heidegger's work toward an understanding of how one is to think the challenges of ethical life. The list is in no particular order, but begins with a remark about how the task of philosophy belongs intimately to the task of finding an ethical sense. After laying out this list, I will conclude by returning to this first point that argues for a coupling of philosophy and life. It is, as I will suggest in the end, a point that is at the heart of what one needs to understand, but perhaps is unable to answer philosophically.

1. Being a philosopher is not a matter of a job or title, nor does it belong in any essential sense to the academic world; it is rather a way of life, a practice. One might say that the way of life of the philosopher is, in the end, nothing more than an *intensification* of the life of a human being, of the life we all live. Heidegger makes this point as well when he says in *Being and Time* that all philosophical questioning arises out of an "analytic of *existence*" and it is "*folded back*" into it (SZ 436/SS 413–14). In other words, philosophical inquiry *arises from* the point to which it needs to *return*. Importantly, this movement belongs to the structure of existence itself. It is not an option, but the way our being in the world constitutes itself. Understood in this way, it seems that one becomes a philosopher because one has made an existential choice not to live with abstractions, but to remain riveted to life and to deepen one's connection to being the factical being one is. Understood in this way, philosophy is an act of real affirmation of life; it is a commitment to and intensification of life itself.

2. This return to factical life is not at all the same as the claim that philosophical theory needs to be "applied" to life as if the region of theory were utterly distinct from—and the typical presumption is also that it is superior

to—the praxis of life. The "return" to "existence" is not a return from "elsewhere," from some metaphysical realm, but is rather a pivot in understanding. Unlike the image of an "exit" from the "cave" that one finds in Plato, this fold in existence begins with a transformation in existence, not an exit from it. The notion that philosophy opens a realm of ideas superior to the realm of understanding life is simply untenable.[1] Quite the contrary, such a view of the clear-sighted authority of philosophy is anathema to the humbling lesson that, if honest, philosophers must learn in this return to life. Indeed it is precisely in this return to life that a peculiar humbling occurs. One comes to see the deep limits on one's own understanding insofar as one struggles to reconcile oneself to the contingencies of life. In this return one learns that the long-standing metaphysical assumption of the superiority of philosophical knowledge for life is thoroughly unfounded. One learns that the idea of a philosopher king is a disaster and far from what the choice of the philosophic life entails. This, of course, is something that Heidegger clearly forgot in his decision to assume the Rectorship at the University of Freiburg.

3. In this return, this being always already folded into factical life, one is brought back to the singularity of factical life and the overwhelming character of its situatedness. Heidegger referred to this as the "mineness" of existence (SZ 41/SS 41). Without engaging his treatment of this complex yet crucial notion, let me suggest that Heidegger's analyses of death, anxiety, and being-toward-death in *Being and Time* point to this singularity of factical life in an important way. I am, one might say, an idiom—untranslatable, stubbornly wedded to being this singular being that I am. This life is mine to live and to answer for, and understanding myself to be mortal is at the heart of this self-understanding. It is not the *cogito sum* that exposes me to myself, but the *sum moribundus*. In this inescapable mineness of existence I learn that this existence is mine to bear, it is my burden, and that I will have been responsible for it. This is the point at which we can speak of something like the birth of responsibility: nothing, no one, can lift the burden of being answerable to life from me. Kant makes a similar point when he speaks of the need to understand oneself as an end, as what should not be subordinated to anything else. What Kant reminds us—and here Heidegger always seems to thin out this important point—is that I also come to know myself as living in a *kingdom* of such ends; that is, I live among others who bear the same responsibility, the same weight of mineness as me: there is, in other words, a strange sort of solidarity to be found in my radical solitude. I bear the burden of existence, but never of the whole of existence. This is what it means to say that I must understand myself as living in a *moral universe*: I know myself to be ineluctably responsible, even if I also know myself as living in a world beyond my control and understanding. This, in part, is the point at which something like the discussion of ethical life can begin anew.

4. Any discussion of ethical life will need to be cautious about maintaining some of the long-standing assumptions that have guided ethical discourse and come to be taken for granted. Among the first steps toward opening the possibility of an ethics, it is necessary to undertake a critique of *technē* and of the notion that thinking is a technique. Nothing could be further from the sense of original ethics than the suggestion that "application" of an idea is a problem for ethical reflections. The knowing that characterizes ethical consciousness is distinct both from the *technical* knowing and from *theoretical* knowing. One might do well to simply say that ethical knowing is closer to what Heidegger and, even more so, Gadamer mean when they speak of *understanding*, or the sense of judgment we find in Kant's third *Critique*, or the account of *phronesis* we find in Aristotle. In other words, ethics is first and foremost what Plutarch described as an ethopoietic matter, as a way of life. In contrast to the long-standing conviction that reason, the concept, or the idea—some thought that is elevated above and apart from the mess of factical life and brought into play by being "applied" and validated by the authority of "theory"—should be the orientation point for any ethics, Heidegger argues that ethics can only be thought as a matter of how one belongs to factical life and "such thinking is neither theoretical nor practical. It comes to pass before this distinction" (GA 9: 358/272). This, in part, is what Heidegger means when he says that "it is time to break the habit of overestimating philosophy and asking too much of it" (GA 9: 364/276). This is also what Heidegger meant when he said that "in philosophical knowing a transformation (metamorphosis) of the human being who understands takes place from the outset" (GA 65: 14).

5. Along with rethinking the relation of thinking and life, and recognizing that the questions of lived experience will not be resolved by an appeal to a realm of ideas independent of experience, it also needs to be recognized that the language proper to thinking ethical life is not confined to conceptual language. In other words, philosophizing has no corner on how it is that we are able to take up the enigma of ethical life. That enigma is lodged in a life lived and suffered in the singular. But this is what is muted by conceptual language. The arts and literature are much more adept at exposing the real weight of being an idiom. That is one reason Heidegger argues that "The tragedies of Sophocles—provided such a comparison is at all permissible—preserve the ethos in their sayings more primordially than Aristotle's lectures on 'ethics'" (GA 9: 354/269). The insistence on conceptual language in philosophical reflections upon ethics has led to the misplaced emphasis upon the idea of the imperative as the supreme ethical measure and law as its highest expression. This is because the concept, which is governed by the law of its own possible universalization, naturally opens up the possibility of the universality of law (Kant's moral thought is founded upon this trope). One important consequence of this recognition is the discovery that art is better suited for thinking

through the tasks and difficulties of ethical life than philosophy is because art asks us to suffer, to be gripped by what the concept is trying to grasp. This is not to say that art is an illustration of ethical problems, but rather that it can disclose and genuinely unfold the difficulties of ethical life in original ways.

6. The domain of the ethical is not solely defined by the orbit of the human, by that which we define and can know. This means that when we ask about the ethical, we cannot confine ourselves to the human, but must understand the significance of the nonhuman as well. Nature, animal life, the earth, even the monstrous and the divine, belong to and define the realm of ethical questioning. This is one reason Heidegger argues that ethics can never be simply a matter of a humanism. There are several important consequences of this move out of the hegemony of the human, but one in particular should be noted: the categories that have long defined human interaction and the practice of power, that is, the categories that articulate the law are no longer appropriate for articulating the deepest structures of how we are to think about ethical life. This means that juridical notions such as right, wrong, guilt, innocence, and pardon no longer have an original place in ethical discourse and enter the discussions at a later stage.[2] Such an original discourse about ethical life must, as Nietzsche remarked, be beyond good and evil—or, as Heidegger might contend, ethical concerns need to be understood as more original, or before, good and evil.

Those are some of the features of an ethical sense that can be forged drawing upon Heidegger's work. There is, of course, much more to be said about each of these claims and there are more claims to be made, but the contours of what I believe can open ethical concerns in more productive ways are there. It is only a start.

One final point remains to be made. I mentioned that Heidegger does not always make it easy to find his thought a resource for ethical concerns. This remark had two impulses: the first concerned his texts; the second concerned his person.

The first impulse was that Heidegger had such a clear allergy to ethical discussions that he seems, at times, to go to great lengths to strip other ethical texts of anything resembling ethical discussions. The word "ethics" seldom appears in his work and at times it seems that he is ready to ontologize every issue of suffering, of justice, of death, and of conflict even at those moments when the limits of ontology are being exposed. Despite this "allergy," I have suggested that his texts do offer real resources for ethical considerations. That is something that could only be decided with further work, but further work will likely come to realize that this will be a constant puzzle without clear resolution.

The second impulse for my suggestion that Heidegger makes it difficult to turn to him for thinking about ethical life is that his own life is—to say the least—problematic. Now the relation between thinking and life, between biography and works, has always been difficult to disentangle. The more abstract thinking was understood to be, the less biography and the individual mattered. But, even though he frequently remarked that the biography of a thinker was insignificant,[3] Heidegger always pressed hard on the situatedness of thinking, of the rootedness of thinking in life, and so his work seems to provide warrant for making the facts of his own life fair game. Furthermore, Heidegger's letters to family and friends, his notebooks, and many of his actions (as well as some of his published work and speeches) have drawn his personal actions and decisions into question and opened up questions that we need to put to his work that emerge out of his own biography. In other words, Heidegger has drawn much of his own biography, his own story, into his work by explicitly linking the two. This does not mean that Heidegger should have the final word about how his work is to be interpreted. It is not the case that a philosopher is her or his own best interpreter. Quite the contrary, I tend to believe that the most original minds often exceed any real self-understanding. Indeed, one could argue that it is a real mark of an original mind that it is able to think in advance of its own self-understanding (Kant, who is forever trying to resolve many of the same questions that his work has dissolved, is a prime example of this capacity). Nonetheless, because Heidegger so frequently inserted National Socialist tinged remarks into the vocabulary of his work, because he represented and understood himself to be promoting Nazi ideology, because he defended himself in tribunals and in interviews, and because he dodged questions put to him directly, one cannot avoid confronting these remarks, deeds, and silences if one reads Heidegger.

I do not intend to even begin to address the special hermeneutic problems of reading Heidegger in light of those words, actions, silences, and other host of problems that belong first, but not solely, to his biography. But I do believe that an important—indeed perhaps the most important—question for any ethical reflection becomes visible in thinking about this problem that we confront in thinking about Heidegger's Nazi and anti-Semitic remarks. What becomes visible is not specific to Heidegger's own case, but a profound philosophical problem; namely, how are we to understand the relation of thinking to life?

My own personal beginnings in philosophy echoed one of the first and most enduring philosophical claims: that philosophy, that peculiar form of reflection upon oneself and one's world, should not simply expand one's consciousness, but equally should improve one's conscience. In other words, it should help to make one "better." That, in highly modified form, is what Plato argued when he suggested in the *Meno* that no one ever did wrong voluntarily: doing wrong was a matter of not thinking well enough, of not having understood. The conception of philosophy as an art of living that is formulated by Socrates and advanced by the Stoics has never really abated.

It seems to be a constitutive appeal of the turn to philosophy as a discipline, and so, when I, as a young student, began to study philosophy in order to live better and be a better person, I was simply—even if unknowingly—repeating one of philosophy's first assumptions about itself. The assumption is that a life dedicated to philosophy belongs to the life that the Greeks described by speaking of *eudaimonia*.

Of course, the empirical evidence to the contrary is ample. Discovering that even great philosophers have feet of clay and are capable of stupidity and worse is discouraging—to say the least. But, in the end, one comes to the understanding that making judgments about others is not what matters. What matters is what one comes to understand about oneself. In the end, the most important questions that emerge from this struggle to think the special case of Heidegger bounce back upon oneself. But that is the work of a lifetime.

The history of philosophy is sadly full of such examples, and so sorting out one's relation to Heidegger will not suffice. Clay feet seem more common than courage and conscience in that history. And so the theoretical question remains: How are we to understand the relation of thinking and life? Does thinking change us, does it make a difference, or do we change for other reasons? Does, in the end, philosophy make a difference in life?

I have no intention of even trying to respond to this question now, but I do believe that one remark is needed. There is one suspicion that I have come to hold as more and more true: that this theoretical question about the relation of thinking and life does not permit a theoretical answer. Indeed, what one needs to think as one begins is the *constitutive resistance* of that theoretical question to a theoretical, a philosophical, response. In doing this, one begins to arrive at the point from which something like a sense of responsibility begins. Somehow, in ways that I have yet to understand fully, my long engagement with Heidegger has helped me to come to this beginning.

NOTES

1. While I would argue that this is not Plato's own view, it is the legacy of "Platonism." I will not further detail the important differences between how this movement that describes philosophical reflection is presented by Plato in the "Allegory of the Cave" and by Heidegger, but the differences between the metaphysical and hermeneutic understanding of this movement are ultimately the key to understanding what one can learn from Heidegger's analysis.

2. Here one would do well to consider "The Verdict of Anaximander" (in GA 5), a text that more explicitly than others confronts this move away from the juridical in an effort to understand the question of justice.

3. The celebrated and oft-repeated (by Arendt and Gadamer, among others) comment that Heidegger made about Aristotle's life, that one only needs to know that "he was born, worked, and died," is a case in point (cf. GA 18: 5/4).

Part IV

LIFE AND EXISTENCE

Chapter 14

Becoming Hermeneutical Before Being Philosophical

Starting Again After Heidegger

Robert C. Scharff

Like other philosophers, Heidegger appears to be joining the ranks of past thinkers who took positions, made claims, promoted theories, leaving us to wonder what they "really meant" by their technical terms, and so on. In other words, despite Heidegger's warnings about "external" interpretations, public attention is turning toward recapitulation of his supposed philosophy, or post-philosophy, or anti-philosophy. So be it. I'm interested in another, not quite so external an option. Its theme is implicit in Heidegger's characterization of *Being and Time* as a "preparatory" work for raising the Being-question, and still present in his saying "The Question Concerning Technology" intends to "prepare a free relation" to technology; but it is explicit everywhere in his early Freiburg lectures. We need to recognize, he says in Summer Semester 1923, that something comes before philosophy—before our "research" and our taking "positions"—namely, a hermeneutic of the "how" of our life-experience (i.e., our "facticity"), in which philosophy originates. Only by first "making factical Dasein accessible to itself" *and in ourselves*, he says, will our inquiries be informed by "an existential knowing" of the fact that philosophy always "speaks *out from* and for the sake of" our "being-there for a while at a particular time" (GA 63: 14–20/11–17). In other words, what must come before philosophy "is not philosophy at all, but . . . *something preliminary* that runs ahead of it and has its own reason for being" (GA 63: 20/16, my emphasis). This concern for "something preliminary" is the underappreciated topic I want to discuss.

This hermeneutics that is not philosophy, says Heidegger, is interested in "what goes on in philosophy before it becomes what it is" (GA 63: 46/59). Hence in pursuing this interest, no method or logic of inquiry can be helpful, because it would necessarily derive from philosophy as it is already going on. Of course, among the philosophies that were going on in Heidegger's day was Husserl's deeply method-bound phenomenology. So his insistence upon pre-philosophical preliminaries is, among other things, directed against Husserl. Heidegger's differences with Husserl are now usually assumed to be obvious. For Husserl, phenomenology is a philosophy of transcendental consciousness; for Heidegger, at least during this period, a hermeneutic phenomenology of Dasein. For Husserlians, Heidegger will always fall short of philosophy's transcendental ideals. For Heideggerians, Husserl will always remain too Cartesian to offer us a way past the ontotheology of the Western tradition.

But Heidegger's idea of a pre-philosophical hermeneutics offers a more instructive way to interpret these differences. The key is to stop interpreting Husserl "from the outside," that is, analyzing his claims, theories, and methodological advice, and "cleaning up" his approach or suggesting an alternative position. Make this approach as sophisticated as you like, its weakness *as philosophy* becomes obvious as soon as one asks: What guides its practice? Formal logic? Pragmatism? "Directives" from philosophy's traditional branches? In short, taken by themselves, analytical clean-ups and position-takings are really disguised refusals to "understand" anything that fails to conform to whatever "guidelines" one already has comfortably in place.[1]

Heidegger's analysis of Husserl has a very different intent. He wants to determine what "basic philosophical posture" his inquiries and methodological advice articulate. Following Dilthey, Heidegger treats Husserl's phenomenology, but also the naturalism and historicism Husserl opposes, as all equally "expressions of life" (*Lebensäußerungen*), so that he can understand what "motivates"—that is, what is "going on" in—each of them. Actually, he says, treating multiple views in this "understanding" way is potentially phenomenology's special strength. This is what Husserl's "principle of all principles" really calls for: Treat everything "originarily . . . offered to us in 'intuition' . . . simply as what it is presented as being." *As phenomena*, then, Husserlian phenomenology, naturalism, and historicism all manifest concerns that emerge "from out of life itself," and Heidegger is committed to considering them as such without immediately evaluating their claims in light of some pre-given (e.g., "scientific" or ethical) value (GA 58: 145/111; cf. GA 59: 154–68/119–29). "And then what?" . . . is for later.

Interpreted this way, says Heidegger, phenomenology becomes a widened and deepened phenomenological version of what Dilthey calls "understanding life in its own terms" (assuming, of course, that "life" is not reduced to something biological, contrasted with something purely physical). Husserl is wrong to assume that *Verstehen* is something practiced only by human scientists. For Heidegger, Dilthey's idea is "the expression of an ultimately *philosophical* motive" that Husserl simply does not share.[2] Dilthey's writings (if not always his self-conception) show clearly that he wants to interpret life "from out of itself" *no matter what concerns emerge from it*, and this means noticing that natural science, human science, and worldview theories all emerge from historical-human life-experience as separate enterprises, that is, as manifestations (or "intensifications") of its *different* concerns.[3] Husserl rejects this possibility. In the human scientific contextualizing of scientific practice, he sees nothing but the threat of relativism; in appeals to immediate experience, he sees nothing but confusion between empirical and phenomenological "psychology"; and as for worldview theory, it "teaches the way wisdom does"—by offering culture-bound "profundities" about "lofty practical interests" expressed by "noble personalities." Worldview theorists who claim allegiance to the scientific ideal are at best confused and at worst, dishonest.[4]

Heidegger's critique of Husserl's transcendental phenomenology is familiar, but how Dilthey inspires him to make it is not. Heidegger starts from Husserl's famous *Logos* article and laments its unfortunate "theoretical-scientific attitude."[5] Judged by what Husserl *asserts*, he appears hopelessly confused and Cartesian. He claims there are two current conceptions of philosophy, the scientific and the historicist or worldview-like, and he says he shares the "values" of the former (albeit not the naturalistic scientism some deduce from it). But how can one share the values of the sciences, and yet assert that phenomenology is a unique "ur-science of origins," fundamentally different from and philosophically more basic than any other science?[6] How can Husserl be at once friendly toward the special sciences, unfriendly toward philosophies of wisdom, and yet somehow ultimately in his own camp?

None of this, however, tells us what Husserl is really driving at. To understand him ("in his own terms"), we must do what he failed to do: make a *problem* of his assertions—not a logical puzzle, but a life-problem (GA 56/57: 23–25). When we do, his genuinely productive "tendency" is disclosed—albeit *through* and in terms of the conflicting, traditional-sounding things he says. For example, his analysis of "internal time-consciousness"—with its diagrams, its constitutive analyses of acts upon acts, and above all its unquestioned reliance on the imagery of intentional consciousness instead of existential understanding—is certainly too tradition-bound to stand as a fully phenomenological account of time as actually *lived-through*; but isn't he deeply right about the ontological priority of this "inner" timing over the idea of time as the measure of movement with respect to before and after?[7] Moreover, the "motivational basis" of Husserl's reaction to historicism is "intuitively" sound. As against those who would psychologize or historicize away the certainty of mathematical reasoning or the genuinely objectifying powers of cognition, Husserl's intentional analysis of "thing-apprehending experience" is a telling response. *As a reaction and measured strictly in terms of what he rightly defends*, this "philosophical posture [*Haltung*]" is adequate to the task. A problem arises only when Husserl assumes this posture in relation to all possible phenomena. The result is a philosophy that "deforms the basic experience of all phenomenology."[8]

The obvious question, then, is: What is this "basic experience of phenomenology," and how might it be more adequately expressed? What is remarkable is that by 1919, Heidegger's answer is already a *non*-Husserlian—not a *post*-Husserlian—answer. He brings something *from* Dilthey *to* Husserl's work, to further a promising tendency he finds *in* it. To practice phenomenology phenomenologically, he says, we must begin from an experience that is "motivated from within life itself" and sets the tone for an "engagement [*Einstellung*]" that allows us to "directly 'participate' in personal life-experience with the greatest vitality and inwardness."[9] Here is the root of Heidegger's many remarks about pre-philosophical preparation. He is concerned with how to "be" phenomenological, and he sees that a transcendental consciousness is inhibited by its training to be so only in the presence of thing-objects. But the kind of "experiencing of experience" that cultivates and "intensifies" an "absolute *sympathy with life* that is identical with living through it" (GA 56/57: 109–10) can provide us with a different sort of preparation. It opens us up to the possibility of a "participant" orientation—what Dilthey calls the "standpoint of life"—from which manifestations of life like physical and human science, but also nonscientific alternatives expressive in other ways of "the whole manifold of life's concerns," are disclosed and become understandable in the way that they "are."

Obviously, this Dilthey-like phenomenological "attitude" is not yet explicitly conceived as an "authentic" way of being-in-the-world, nor is it joined specifically with any *Seinsfragen*, let alone any of the later moves from the meaning, to the truth, to the clearing and arrival of Being as *Ereignis*. All of this will change over the following decades, of course, and in retrospect it is easy to understand why it had to, if Heidegger's original "motivation"—that is, making philosophy responsive again to the *manifold* (and not just object-like) ways "to be"—was ultimately to win out against the tradition-bound resistance that still resonates in his early attempts to express it. Yet there is also something more here—something concerning "who" philosophizes—that deserves to be rescued and rethought. From 1919 to the early 1920s, the very period when Heidegger is finding his way toward a path of thinking genuinely his own, it is Dilthey's conception of how to philosophize, not Husserl's, that resonates in his speech.[10] Husserl and Dilthey might both be described as eager to engage with "the things themselves." But Dilthey's idea of understanding phenomena "in their own terms" defines a more phenomenological posture than Husserl's conception of intentionally analyzing what appears to a transcendental consciousness. Granted, this generous construal of Dilthey's idea of *Verstehen* far outruns his own philosophical self-conception, which remains primarily that of an epistemologist of science. But for Heidegger, the implication that understanding is really our basic (if usually occluded) pre-philosophical condition—one that is only sometimes shaped and enlisted for human scientific research—is clearly "retrievable" from Dilthey's writings.

Moreover, as Heidegger interprets him, Dilthey's account of *how one comes to be* an understanding human scientist involves a distinctly nontraditional kind of reflectiveness that indicates a way for us to be attuned to the things themselves, whatever they are and however we are related to them. Traditional *Reflexion*, even its Husserlian variant, implies a methodological distancing of thinking from experience. But Dilthey calls instead for an "*immanent* reflection," an enhanced self-awareness (*Selbstbesinnung*) or self-interpretive (*Selbstauslegung*) acknowledgment of the immediate "having of life in experience." This possible orientation is being obscured by a Cartesian inheritance that has convinced us that all philosophizing must be performed by a methodologically distanced cognitive consciousness.[11] But as Dilthey famously puts it, "No real blood flows in the veins of the knowing subject constructed by Locke, Hume, and Kant, just the diluted extract of reason as a mere activity of thought." Unsurprisingly, then, modern philosophy fails to see that even "[natural] knowledge and its concepts" must ultimately be understood "in terms of the manifold powers of a being that wills, feels, and thinks"[12]—that is, as "intensifications" of a lived-through concern for the causal explanations of encounters with material events.

Heidegger's treatment of Dilthey's "descriptive and analytical" psychology is instructive here.[13] For all its flaws, Dilthey shows decisively that philosophers of science must start by "relating [themselves] back to the *conditions and context* of consciousness," not by considering how to train it. For " 'life' in its historical context . . . is [to be sure] a possible *object* of the human sciences, [but] *above all* it is the *root* of these sciences."[14] Moreover, we can always return to this experiential "root" precisely because we *already understand it to be* that "from out of which" life expresses itself in many ways (GA 56/57: 164–65/139–40; also GA 59: 166–68/128–29). Later, these features of Dilthey's *Ideas* will be said to make it the pioneering attempt to "understand 'life' philosophically and to hermeneutically ground this understanding in terms of 'life itself.' " My notion of "hermeneutics as [ontological] self-elucidation," says Heidegger, follows Dilthey's "tendency to bring the reality of the historical [*as lived*] into view and make clear from this the manner . . . of its interpretation" (SZ 398; GA 20: 19/17).

Understanding experienced life and its manifestations "in their own terms," then, is Heidegger's non-Husserlian reinterpretation of how to become philosophically open to "the things themselves." In spite of traditional denials,

Dilthey shows convincingly that it is possible—from within "factical life in its typically improminent [*unabgehoben*] condition"—to "live *unreflectively yet still mindfully* [*besinnlich*] and so stay thoughtfully aware of the full web of possible motivations" for thoughts and practices, and to do so prior to any specifically theoretical development of these motivations or any "reflection" *on* such developments (GA 58: 111/87–88, my emphasis). In 1920, Heidegger calls this mindfulness a taking notice of (*Kenntnisnahme*) and a "going along with" experience; and he describes it as a "modification of factical life experiencing"—one that "maintains itself in the style of factical experiencing" itself and thus amounts to a kind of "articulation that is not yet really an articulation, as long as it remains in this basic style" without moving on decisively in a definitely motivated direction (GA 58: 114–19/90–94).

Here, then, is an obvious sense in which phenomenology must remain "provisional." Precisely because its task is to do justice to "everything originarily offered to us in 'intuition,'" phenomenology can presuppose no "guidelines" or defined outlook.[15] Long before *Being and Time*'s formal account of temporal existence, Heidegger puts it this way: "*Philosophy* can progress only through an absolute sinking into life as such, for *phenomenology* is never concluded, only *preliminary*; it is always sinking itself into the preliminary" (GA 56/57: 220/188). Because life itself is ongoing, phenomenology must continually "prove itself only through itself"—without any Husserlian recourse to a secured system of concepts or principles. Anything less would be "a sin against [phenomenology's] ownmost spirit."[16]

Yet there is more to avoiding sin here than just performing a demethodologizing reversal of the traditional philosophical ordering of lived experience and its conceptualization. On this issue, Heidegger is critical of Dilthey as well as Husserl. There are two reasons why "intuitively staying open" to life-experience is an unfinished task, and Dilthey really focuses on only one, namely, that understanding life remains unfinished because life itself is unfinished. However, "s*taying* open" is itself a never-ending struggle. Phenomenology *would* always proceed, method-free and "from" experience, *if* it were possible to be always "mindful." For ontological and not just empirical reasons, however, the most that even the best-intentioned phenomenology can do is continually "work back toward" immediate experience and repeatedly "free itself gradually from the theoretical." At first, Heidegger attributes this problem primarily to the influential hegemony of inherited philosophies of consciousness, but slowly he begins to associate it more with a "troubling tendency toward falling" that characterizes living-through life itself (GA 62: 355–56; SZ, §38). We all have a "deeply ingrained and stubborn tendency [*Verranntheit*] to favor the theoretical" (GA 56/57: 88/74, tm); hence, phenomenology must continuously struggle to *become* phenomenological. It must always think of its point of departure as involving "a sinking *back* down

[*Versenkung*] into life as such"—that is, a *recapturing* of the mindfulness that allows "intuitions" to emerge out of an "empowering experiencing-of-living-experience that takes itself along as it understands" life's articulations (GA 56/57: 220/188, tm, 117/99).

Here is the way to go forward from Husserl's still too epistemological conception of "preparing" to be phenomenological. He is right that life-experience is not just given to us; it does indeed have to be won back (GA 58: 29/24). Yet for him, the *Umwelt* that phenomenology must sink back into remains a "merely cultural" site of worldviews and naïve naturalisms that threaten to derail transcendental phenomenology. Even someone as attuned to life as Dilthey continued to self-identify as an epistemologist of scientific distancing, long after his practice as a historian was moving him strongly in the direction of a philosophy of understanding. Here is why Heidegger distinguishes *philosophy* from (hermeneutic) *phenomenology*. Usually philosophers begin by simply enacting their confidently held self-conception, tackling well-known problems, treating them with well-known tools, and then defending their productions. But phenomenologists, so as to "be" phenomenologists, start by turning first in the opposite direction, and "trying to understand how life-experience in its actualization is [everywhere to be] characterized . . . not just in the form in which life merely cognizes itself as an object and stops with the having of knowledge . . . but in terms of how life takes itself vitally, has itself, and fulfills itself in this having."[17] *Being and Time*'s Daseinsanalysis is Heidegger's ultimate "intensification" of this concern for a "hermeneutic[ally grounded] phenomenology."

* * * *

Yet isn't there an obvious objection to this exclusive focus on Heidegger's early lecture courses—something un-Heideggerian about so much separate talk of his "preparations," with so little about their ultimate point? Indeed, should we even take this material seriously? After all, 1919–1923 is the period of Heidegger's juvenilia, when his language still staggers under the weight of traditional biases not yet fully sorted out or responded to. Actually, I see a path available "after" Heidegger that would take these questions as encouragements.

It is true that in Heidegger's early accounts, what stands in the way of *becoming* phenomenological is more in focus than the fundamental ontological inquiry that *being* phenomenological opens up. And for all its suggestiveness, the idea that phenomenology must "sink back down into" environmental life, "follow along with" life's own movement toward "conceptually intensified" articulations, and do so without "losing touch" with the experience that motivates these intensifications—this idea certainly falls far short of the full, careful, much more systematic account of how philosophical hermeneuts become truly phenomenological that awaits us in *Being and Time*. Moreover, I think it is probably true that only taking up something like Heidegger's Being-question and following it all the way through to the possibility of thinking "at the ending" of a dismantled ontotheological tradition can actually open us up to considering how "the world civilization just now beginning might someday overcome its technological-scientific-industrial character as the sole criterion for our journey through the world" (GA 14: 75/60; cf. 89–91/75–77). Yet for me there is a prior question: Hermeneutically speaking, is the *present* atmosphere in our "developed" world any more encouraging of a phenomenological philosophy of openness than the atmosphere Heidegger breathed in 1919?

Of course, it would be blockheaded and insensitive in the extreme to ignore the radical "factical" differences between our two "situations," as if a concern for "questioning" and "thinking" requires that we turn away from such "ontic" matters. Yet at the same time, is our present "site" any less populated with Cartesian versus anti-Cartesian philosophers than Heidegger's? Have most philosophers stopped regarding themselves primarily as knowing subjects who develop epistemologies for dealing with various objects? Do they now go into the future convinced that "the primacy of the theoretical must be broken, not in order to proclaim the primacy of the practical, nor to . . . display [traditional] problems from a new angle, but because the theoretical itself . . . refers back to something pre-theoretical?"[18] Not where I live! A central feature of Heidegger's early lectures is their emphasis on the fact that for a philosophy that wants to take seriously the pre-theoretical condition of being-historically-in-the-midst-of-things, the initial problem is *how to become attuned* to this condition. The trouble with *Being and Time* is that this problem, though central, tends to get buried under the sheer bulk of systematic analyses and a misleadingly "transcendental" structure. And now, in addition, every part of the book has since been widely appropriated by confident philosophers who already knew "who" they are long before they went looking in Heidegger merely for some good ideas to help them pursue other projects.

Becoming *besinnlich* in our world seems to me just as remote from mainstream philosophy as Heidegger described it as being a century ago. The Husserl of 1911 already summed up our North American mainstream spirit very nicely: The philosophical life requires "theoretical talent," not wisdom and profundity. Period. Nothing further to be said. And so today, the American Philosophical Association website identifies philosophy's many topics, questions, and critical skills, and it speaks of the diversity and pluralism it hopes for in its membership; but not a word about how philosophizing "attunes" itself to all these topics and questions, or how this might transform one's sense of how to "be" a philosopher, or about self-understanding and self-critique rather than useful knowledge and answers to skepticism. Today's Socrates does a lot of inquiring and arguing; but he is no lover of wisdom.[19]

"Experientially," then, I find myself in a philosophical atmosphere that most closely resembles the one reflected in the writings of the young Heidegger, not the Heidegger of *Being and Time*, let alone the Heidegger of the *Beiträge* or later. Moreover, from this side of the Atlantic, I find it difficult to identify with or even directly relate to a tradition that moves through Nietzsche and the press of an interwar European "crisis" of eighty years ago, let alone draw inspiration from a national poet. Nor does my battle against personal complicity in cultural, political, and historical bias and bigotry find much resonance in the *Black Notebooks*. Of course, we benefit from having Heidegger's thoughts about all this—especially, I believe, his thoughts about the ongoing arrival of a global technoscientific sense of everything that hides its origin and poisons every attempt to be phenomenological about anything but "objects" for "consciousness." Indeed, if anything, this "arrival" seems to be growing at once more attractive in its happy effects and occlusive about its ontological dangers than in Heidegger's day. Think, for example, of how cloud computing hides most of what *really* happens when you press the link and order a book from Amazon, while all you "experience" is the quick delivery of a desired object.

But returning today to the Freiburg lectures, I feel quite at home with the infelicities of Heidegger's early language—both in what it is attempting to do and in its unsatisfactoriness. It is indeed often awkward and overly dramatic—still trapped, like much of mine, between misleading traditionalisms (e.g., "attitudes," "postures," "intuitive understanding," an "*Urwissenschaft*") and the sort of language that might "formally indicate" phenomena instead of closing them off in representations that themselves become the center of attention instead of what they are designed to conceptualize. In these lectures as still today, even among "phenomenologists," there is a tendency to subjectify phenomenologically elusive things in excessive deference to an objectivist world. Why, for example, is it formal indication, not scientific jargon, that is called a "special" kind of conceptualization, when we use the former routinely to tell each other what we "really mean" and facility with the latter requires years of high-level instruction? Or consider: Is "thinking" really information processing, plus something? And is our deep "distress" regarding the lived-through condition of our current global surroundings fundamentally just a sign of the start of an Anthropocene Age defined in terms of some behavioral and cognitive "properties" of human nature?

Superb Heidegger scholarship, together with a long-needed airing of political concerns about the man "and" his work, we undoubtedly have. Even a proliferation of communities committed to phenomenological research. But philosophically? Our very idea of a "developed" world resonates with nineteenth-century positivism, as does the continuing default preference for a "reflective" standpoint that privileges mathematical reasoning, the idea that there is a technique (and a mechanical device) for everything, visual perception, the primary realness of the logical and the material, and the assumption that intelligibility is a function of fully explicit and comprehensive conceptualization.[20] Modern philosophy remains (in Nietzsche's sense) a "burdensome" inheritance shot through with cultural scientism. We are still under pressure to begin by taking an "informed" distance from lived experience that will make every further reference to it (and even every attempt to contextualize the distancing process itself) seem counterproductive—something that constitutes a kind of weak-minded refusal to go where truth is found. "Techniques" insure that everyone does the distance-taking the same way; "becoming" educated means learning techniques, and any further discussion of this "process" is just psychology or biography. Methods change, but not what they accomplish. Every method reaffirms the idea that to "be" educated is to be properly distanced from everything one has not made objectively present.

All of this still feels familiar to me, and therefore in need of something like Heidegger's appropriation of Dilthey—not the epistemological Dilthey of the two sciences, but the "restive" Dilthey who is always "*on the way* toward the question of life." As Heidegger says in *Being and Time*, we are always inclined to be "caught up in the world of ordinary affairs so that we fall into interpreting ourselves in its reflected light. And at the same time we fall in with a tradition that we have more or less explicitly embraced—a tradition that deprives us of providing our own guidance in asking questions and making choices" (SZ 21; cf. 398). I think that Heidegger's impurely phenomenological Dilthey can still help us develop a nontraditional account of "life understanding life"—one that starts from this initial condition of historical ordinariness, with a realization that we never entirely succeed in being "mindful" and are always tending to fall back into a "derivative" understanding that looks down on experience as the "merely subjective" origin of objective practices.[21] Our own need for a phenomenology that avoids technique-happiness, sometimes achieves a heightened awareness that takes no distance from life, and speaks in a language that is "not yet" representational—this possible phenomenology seems to me "retrievable" from the early lectures, all the more so because it appears there in a problematic and tradition-bound form. "Experiencing tradition-bound ideas *as they distort* phenomenologically promising practices": This strikes me as a pretty fair description of how, philosophically speaking, it still "is" with us. I sometimes wish I could have started here, instead of with *Being and Time*.

NOTES

1. GA 59: 30–34/21–24. The same imagery recurs in SS 1920, in Heidegger's critical juxtaposition of Natorp and Dilthey and his appropriation of the latter (GA 59: 153–54/118–19).

2. GA 59: 154/119. Indeed, Husserl is so far from sharing it that when he hears philosophers like Dilthey say they wish to "remain immersed in the historical," he assumes they must be "*forcing* [themselves] to stay *mired* in historico-critical activity" and thus, poor things, doomed to always fall hopelessly short of achieving the standpoint of philosophical science: "Philosophy as Rigorous Science," in *Husserl: Shorter Works,* ed. Peter McCormick and Frederick A. Elliston (Notre Dame: Notre Dame University Press, 1981), 166–97. Cf. Husserl, *The Crisis of the European Sciences and Transcendental Phenomenology*, tr. David Carr (Evanston, IL: Northwestern University Press, 1970), 196.

3. Heidegger sees naturalism and historicism, Husserl's polemic, and Dilthey's "philosophical" response to all of them as opening out toward the "decisive problem . . . [of] history and life" (GA 59: 144–46/111–12). See my "Natural vs. Human Science: Dilthey's 'Threat' to the Unity of the Sciences?" in *Interpreting Dilthey*, ed. Eric S. Nelson (Cambridge: Cambridge University Press, 2017); and *How History Matters to Philosophy: Reconsidering Philosophy's Past After Positivism* (New York: Routledge, 2015), 168–72.

4. "Philosophy as Rigorous Science," 194–96. Philosophically, Husserl told Alexander Pfänder (1931), "I have nothing to do with Heideggerian profundity, with this brilliant unscientific genius." Heidegger's interpretation of my phenomenology "is based upon a gross misunderstanding; [indeed] he may be involved in the formation of the kind of philosophical system that I have always considered my life's work to make forever impossible": *Psychological and Transcendental Phenomenology and the Confrontation with Heidegger (1927–1931),* tr. Thomas Sheehan and Richard E. Palmer (Dordrecht: Kluwer, 1997), 482.

5. "Philosophy as Rigorous Science," 193–97; here, 196. For Heidegger's analysis, see esp. GA 17: 61/45; §§7–9 and §§13–14, passim. Cf. GA 56/57: 109–10/92–93; GA 58: 13–14/10–11; and his 1958 retrospective in GA 14: 95–97/76–78.

6. GA 58: 149–50/115. Husserl complained that his *Logos* article is too much a period piece to provide a truly philosophical picture of his phenomenology; but Heidegger replies that its depiction of phenomenology is not a quick-and-dirty image produced for the occasion; rather, it "emerges from and against the background of ten years' philosophical labor" (GA 20: 128/93). As Heidegger remarks in various places, philosophers often reveal the most about what they basically understand when they are in the midst of opposing something.

7. Edmund Husserl, *Collected Works,* vol. 4: *On the Phenomenology of the Consciousness of Internal Time (1893–1917)*, tr. John Barnett Brough (Dordrecht: Kluwer, 1990).

8. GA 58: 142/109; cf. GA 58: 18–24/13–17. I ignore here the now problematically objectivistic view of natural science and mathematics upon which Husserl's line of reasoning rests. My point is that no matter how one distinguishes research

programs from each other, it is the "posture" from which Husserl always makes such distinctions that Heidegger problematizes.

9. For example, GA 58: 254/192 (*Mitmachen*, participation, is in scare quotes).

10. Indeed, it is quite typically in Dilthey's language that Heidegger interprets, criticizes, and redefines Husserl's key ideas; and in his extended critique of Husserlian phenomenology in SS 1925, he states flatly that it is Dilthey, not Husserl, who first understood phenomenology's true aim (GA 20: 163/118). See my "Becoming a Philosopher: What Heidegger Learned from Dilthey, 1919–25," *British Journal for the History of Philosophy* 21:1 (2013): 122–42; and "Heidegger's 'Appropriation' of Dilthey Before *Being and Time*," *Journal of the History of Philosophy* 35:1 (1997): 105–28.

11. GA 63: 14–20/11–16; also GA 58: 155–61/119–24. The implication, says Heidegger, is that phenomenological "intuition" is not about discerning intentional objects and their essences; it is a "hermeneutic" intuition that opens us up to "the factical inwardness of our living-through-of life" (*faktische innere Erlebnis*) and all its manifold expressions, such that only some phenomena are disclosed to us as "objects." This phrasing is from the KNS 1919 lectures (GA 56/57: 117/99) and WS 1919–1920 (GA 58: 250/189), but Dilthey's language is ubiquitous in this period.

12. Wilhelm Dilthey, *Introduction to the Human Sciences* (1883), in *Selected Works*, vol. 1 (Princeton, NJ: Princeton University Press, 1989), 50–51.

13. Wilhelm Dilthey, *Ideas for a Descriptive and Analytic Psychology* (1894), in *Selected Works*, vol. 2 (Princeton, NJ: Princeton University Press, 2010), 115–210.

14. Quoted from SZ 398, but the thought derives from much earlier work. Cf. "Wilhelm Diltheys Forschungsarbeit und der gegenwärtige Kampf um eine historische Weltanschauung," *Dilthey-Jahrbuch* 8 (1992–93): 154–58 = "Wilhelm Dilthey's Research and the Struggle for a Historical Worldview," tr. Charles Bambach, in Heidegger, *Supplements: From the Earliest Essays to "Being and Time" and Beyond*, ed. John van Buren (Albany: SUNY Press, 2002, 155–59); and GA 20: 17, 116–19/19, 161–64.

15. Hence, when Heidegger complains that "the fundamental *demand of phenomenology to bracket all standpoints is* [still] *everywhere overlooked*" (GA 56/57: 109/92), he means to include Husserl.

16. GA 56/57: 110/93; cf. GA 58: 220/188; GA 61: 39–40/31; GA 63: 46/37.

17. GA 58: 156/120; cf. GA 56/57: 117/99. Such passages should be remembered as one reads SZ's assertion that "phenomena must be treated phenomenologically" (27).

18. GA 56/57: 59/50. "Even unbiased seeing is a seeing. . . ." Hence, the very idea of a position defined as "'freedom from all standpoints'. . . is itself something historical . . . not a chimerical in-itself outside of time" (GA 63: 83/64).

19. See, for example, "Philosophy: A Brief Guide for Undergraduates," http://www.apaonline.org/?page=undergraduates, n.d., accessed March 10, 2017.

20. I have argued this in detail elsewhere, for example, *How History Matters to Philosophy*, esp. 147–54; and "Comte's Positivist Dream, Our Post-Positivist Problem," in *The Routledge Companion to Nineteenth Century Philosophy*, ed. Dean Moyar (New York and London: Routledge, 2010), 435–66.

21. GA 58: 110–20/87–94, 161/123–24. "[E]ven when theorizing, I myself originate in and come out from lived experiencing, *and something experienceable is brought along from this experiencing,* with which one now does not know what to do, and for which the convenient title of the irrational has been invented" (GA 56/57: 117/99, em).

Chapter 15

The Strangeness of Life in Heidegger's Philosophy

Eric S. Nelson

> One is always the index of a multiplicity: an event, a singularity, a life.
>
> —Deleuze[1]

INTRODUCTION: LIFE'S QUESTION

In this chapter, I propose taking a historical step back in order to reconsider neglected possibilities for contemporary thinking "after Heidegger." It is no doubt appropriate to interpret Martin Heidegger's early lecture courses and lectures from 1919 to 1925 in light of his relation to life-philosophy (*Lebensphilosophie*) and as unfolding a "philosophy of life." As the works of Theodore Kisiel, John van Buren, and Scott M. Campbell have shown, Heidegger appropriated life-philosophical tendencies during this crucial early phase of his thought in ways that remain pertinent to his later philosophy and our own contemporary hermeneutical situation.[2]

The young Heidegger described his own thinking as intending to directly and immediately touch and, adopting Wilhelm Dilthey's motto, "understand life from out of itself."[3] Yet a clear difference between Dilthey and Heidegger is evident in how this task of self-interpretation is to be pursued: Dilthey depicted the self-understanding of life, in which life explicates itself and has its own hermeneutical structure, as occurring through the mediations of life's expressions and objectifications in the social-political, historical-cultural world.[4] Heidegger is not directly concerned with Dilthey's sense of world and life-nexus (*Lebenszusammenhang*). The lived historical world, the lifeworld in Husserl's language, is analyzed through existential categories such as fallenness and idle talk. Even as Heidegger stressed the correlational character of the ontic and the ontological, the ontic is relegated to its own sphere of empirical inquiry into beings in contrast to the more essential sphere of the question of being.

Heidegger's revolution vis-à-vis Dilthey's hermeneutics is to radically pose the question of one's own existence and its categories and structures in light of the question of being. Kisiel notes how in the early 1920s this is a promise of intimacy of life with itself in the medium of philosophical reflection.[5] However, Heidegger introduces a distance to life as it is lived that has contributed to contemporary philosophy's distance from such concerns; that is, life as *a* life with all of the biographical, contingent, and ontic conditions that concerned Dilthey and his student and early Heidegger critic Georg Misch.[6] This detachment from life is intensified on the road to *Being and Time* and more so in his later thought. It is already at work in the strategy of formal indication and hermeneutical anticipation that would disclose the structures of concrete existential forms of life through abstraction and separation from a particular life—that is, the concrete life that is interconnected with biography, proper names, and historical events and contingencies.

HEIDEGGER AND LIFE-PHILOSOPHY

Heidegger's early philosophy of life, despite its stated intention of recovering life, is already an estrangement from life that indicates his abandonment of the language of life for the language of being. What then is "life-philosophy"? Although there are earlier uses of this expression, it was retroactively applied by Max Scheler to describe a philosophical movement to encompass a diverse group of thinkers that included Bergson, Nietzsche, James, and Dilthey. It is primarily Dilthey in this group who engages Heidegger's interest at this time. It would be Nietzsche after 1929 whose notion of life Heidegger interpreted and critiqued in opposition to life-philosophy and its "subjectivism." I would like to explore why this might be the case in order to consider how Heidegger's early thinking of life remains significant for contemporary reflection, while keeping in mind the significance of the Christian experience of facticity that is decisive for Heidegger's development and motivates his endorsement of Count Paul Yorck von Wartenburg's conservative formulation of the historicity of life over Dilthey's "culturally liberal" conception in *Being and Time*.[7]

Heidegger's philosophy of life presents itself in a paradoxical way: on the one hand, Heidegger's early project centers on approaching life in its immediacy and interpreting it from its own immediate givenness in contrast to imposing external conceptual categories upon life. Heidegger's early practice of "interpretive violence," formalized as the destructuring of the history of being in *Being and Time*, intends to liberate this dimension from sedimentation and estrangement. Heidegger noted in a letter to his rationalistic Neo-Kantian teacher Heinrich Rickert that abstract thinking and logic are a violation and violent abbreviation of living spirit. Phenomenology in Heidegger's early conception ought to abandon such violence and liberate by returning to the encounter with the things themselves, with life itself. This liberation demands its own form of violence.

Violence against life requires counterviolence for life that promises a liberation from violence. The justification of violence would become an important feature of his hermeneutics in the late 1920s and 1930s. His destructuring of the fallenness of the public sphere in the they (*das Man*), and his destructuring retrieval of thinking in confrontation with the history of metaphysics, require a certain kind of violence. Particularly in *Kant and the Problem of Metaphysics*, interpretive violence is necessary to elicit and liberate the unsaid and the genuine sense of a philosophical text (GA 3: 249/141). Subsequently, Heidegger advocated the intrinsic violence of interpretation. Its violence is construed to be a mark of its authenticity and power. Heidegger advocates in the lecture courses and speeches of the early 1930s the necessity of violence for both interpretation of the unspoken and what he calls "authentic liberation," which "demands not only violence but endurance" (GA 36/37: 144/114). Heidegger contends in the *Introduction to Metaphysics* in 1935 that "the authentic interpretation must show what does not stand there in the words and nevertheless is said. For this, the interpretation must necessarily use violence" (GA 40: 171/180). In this context, Heidegger uncannily links the strangeness and uncanniness of life with its violence.[8] It is the moment of the interconnection of violence and life in Heidegger's thought that led Emmanuel Levinas beginning in the mid-1930s to link the ontology of being with the "struggle for existence" of Social Darwinism and National Socialism.[9] Heidegger's justification of the necessity of hermeneutical violence, first in the name of life and then for the sake of being, slips into a valorization of social-political violence in works such as *Introduction to Metaphysics*. To this extent, the problematic of life is not overcome by Heidegger, even as he rejected all forms of life-philosophy as expressions of modern metaphysics—culminating in Nietzsche's will to power as overpowering will to will—throughout the National Socialist period.

What is wrong with life-philosophy in Heidegger's assessment? How is it a violence against life and, more importantly, against being, as he suggested in his lecture courses on Nietzsche in the 1930s? To contextualize this fear by returning to the early 1920s, it is already evident that Heidegger's embrace of the vitality and sensibility inherent in life during this period has a particular strangeness and distance to life. It is not "a life," a singular life, which Dilthey and Deleuze address from their distinct perspectives, but it is life as verbal and impersonal that brackets its personal drama and suffering: just as the world is worlding, "it worlds" (*es weltet*), life is understood as "it lives" (*es lebt*) and no longer as "*a*" life (GA 56/57: 66/56, 73/61).

In contrast to the life-philosophers, whether in their canonical philosophical or in their vulgar popular forms, Heidegger is not concerned with individual life in its milieu. He explicitly rejects considering the psychological, biographical, autobiographical, and anthropological dimensions of a unique individual life. Phenomenology is often described as description in the first-person perspective; yet Heidegger often neglected the social-historically embedded first person, the "I" with its lived experience (*Erlebnis*), expression, and understanding, which is formalized through the formal indication of the "each time my own" (*Jemeinigkeit*) of being-there.

It is appropriate to ask in this context: What is life without these personal dimensions, which do not require a substantial ahistorical notion of person or self (as is evident in Dilthey and Misch), and which Heidegger initially rejected in the name of anti-psychologism and later as part of his destructuring of the history of metaphysics, including its modern forms? Further, what happens then to "life" in Heidegger's analysis? Is it in contact with immediacy, articulating life from out of itself, or do Heidegger's unfolding concerns with the ontology of being and philosophy of language introduce a distance or strangeness in the self-understanding of life? Strangeness indicates in this context the growing depersonalization and formalization of life perceptible in the movement from life to being; that is, an understanding of life that is itself "uncanny" in neglecting fundamental dimensions of personal and interpersonal life. The strangeness of life in Heidegger's early hermeneutics does not only have a philosophical and hermeneutical import; it has, as his thinking is focused on depersonalized Dasein and the communal aspirations of the German people (*Volk*), significant ethical and political consequences.

BIOGRAPHICAL LIFE AND FACTICAL LIFE

Heidegger's hermeneutics of factical life simultaneously elucidates the ordinariness, the vitality, the fallenness, and the ruination (*Ruinanz*) of that life. Human existence is fundamentally thrown and uncanny. Facticity indicates in these early Freiburg lecture courses both openness and closure to the world. If Heidegger is a thinker concerned with existence in its actual concreteness, what then has occurred to the ordinary happenings that constituted concrete factical life in the earlier historicist tradition? Did Heidegger remain in essence a transcendental philosopher despite his adoption of the language of the philosophy of life and existence, or is there another strategy to explain his apparent hesitation with regard to life?

Heidegger's early conception of "facticity" was modified from the one commonly used in the works of Neo-Kantianism, Husserl, and Dilthey. Husserl and Neo-Kantian philosophers, such as his teacher Rickert, primarily used the term "facticity" (*Faktizität*) in contrast to "validity" (*Geltung*). "Facticity" referred to the accidental, the contingent, and the conditional; "validity" signified that which holds and holds universally across all discourses and all possible worlds as a transcendental condition. But the expression "factical life" adopted by the young Heidegger has a different lineage that that of his teachers.

The historians associated with the "historical school" (Görres, Mosen, von Stein, among others) used the expression "factical life" (*tatsächliches Leben*) in an unphilosophical manner to refer to the realities of unreflective ordinary life that it was the task of the historian to recover and bring to expression. It was the hermeneutical life-philosopher Dilthey, who plays a prominent role in the development of Heidegger's hermeneutics of facticial life, who used the words facticity and life together in a philosophically oriented manner.

Dilthey probably adopted the expression from the historical school that he sought to make philosophical in his early work *Introduction to the Human Sciences* (1883). Factical life is no longer the bare happenings and events of everyday historical life; it is informed by and adopts the pre-reflective "categories of life" and, as explained in Dilthey's major 1910 work *The Formation of the Historical World in the Human Sciences*, has an interpretive-hermeneutical character through the structure of lived experience, expression, and understanding. Factical life does not stand in opposition to validity and reason; it is already structured through the pre-reflective operation of understanding and the categories of life that enable higher forms of understanding and rationally valid discourses.[10] Dilthey's conception of factical life operated as a medium for a fuller sense of the different possibilities of human life and indicated a middle between the extremes of rationalism and irrationalism that dominated German cultural and intellectual life in the early twentieth century.

Kisiel and Campbell have clarified the significant role Dilthey's life-philosophical hermeneutics had for Heidegger in the first half of the 1920s. Kisiel described the unpublished article "The Concept of Time" (1924) as the first draft and "Dilthey draft" of *Being and Time*. To briefly summarize a complex transformation, distinguishing the phases of Heidegger's early thought allows one to interpret Heidegger's initial fascination with Dilthey's thought and his increasing abandonment of it as his discourse became more radically ontological in the context of his deepening encounter with Greek philosophy, his interpretations of ontology and language in Aristotle and Plato, and his revived interest in reinterpreting Kant's transcendental philosophy in opposition to the dominant Neo-Kantian paradigm of the era.

The temporal-historical constitution of a sense of the "whole of life" in Dilthey is redirected toward the being-question in Heidegger. The primary philosophical object of inquiry for Dilthey and the early Heidegger is life. They understood and fleshed out this "life" in different ways. Dilthey argued for the intimate connection between the emotional and intellectual life of the philosopher, the social-historical conditions of personal life, and the experience of multiple conflicting worldviews. Heidegger adopted in a noticeable way Dilthey's account of Augustine that stressed the interconnection of life and thought in the lecture course *The Phenomenology of Religious Life* (1920–1921, GA 60). It is here that Heidegger presents his own version of the categories of life and existential structures of human life. Heidegger would, however, abandon the close connection between philosophy and a life understood in a personal or biographical manner. Heidegger's way is characterized by multiple turns and reversals, including enthusiastically embracing and then dismissing the philosophy of life in less than a decade. Heidegger remarked in his 1925–1926 lecture course *Logic: The Question of Truth* that "the being of plants and animals . . . is 'life' in today's sense of 'the biological,' whereas for the Greeks βίος, taken in a quite extreme sense, means the same as human existence or personal being, as for instance the word 'biography' shows" (GA 21: 34/29). He introduces biography in this passage to stress how *bios* is fundamentally a possibility of existence—a move that indicates the formalization that is at work in Heidegger's thinking of life. His conception of Dasein formally indicates and anticipates a multiplicity of concrete forms of individual biographical life, while being detached from any given particular life. Early readers of Heidegger (such as Misch, Herbert Marcuse, and Günther Anders) were concerned about the contentlessness of Heidegger's discourse of authenticity, conscience, decision, and resoluteness. Heidegger's articulation of authenticity, for instance, is formal rather than personal, and is disconnected from issues of faithfulness, sincerity, and the dynamics of concrete singular life at the core of Kierkegaard's discourse of authenticity.

Heidegger remarked in his 1924 lecture course on Aristotle that we need only focus on the thinking of the philosopher. It is sufficient to know concerning Aristotle's biography that he "was born, worked, and died" (cf. GA 18: 5/4). There is insufficient reflection on the relation between—to adopt a distinction from Levinas—the ontological truth of thinking (the said) and the personal sincerity and expression of the one who thinks (the saying). Heidegger repeats and extends this anti-biographical stance in his works after *Being and Time*. He asks in a 1969 letter to Jean-Michel Palmier: "Is it not rather such that the work makes possible an interpretation of the biography?"[11] He suggests in response to his question that the work cannot be a by-product of life. Heidegger's conception of factical life, the biography of

Dasein, remains distinct from the factical life that is tied up with the life of a person.

The strangeness of Heidegger's life-philosophy is perhaps more evident after he stopped speaking of "life"—in his later self-interpretations of his own life, work, and thought: whether it is *Being and Time*, his subsequent reinterpretations of it, or the rectorate speech and his involvement with National Socialism, Heidegger interprets his life and work through his account of the history of being in a way that distances himself from himself. He interprets historical philosophers as conduits for thinking that thinks through them. Heidegger has moved away from the hermeneutical life-philosophy of Dilthey with its attention to the life of the individual in all of its complexity—which is dismissed as a merely historiographical interest—when he maintains, for instance, that Nietzsche's most autobiographical and intimate of writings should be read in light of the destiny of the West: "*Ecce Homo* is a matter neither of the biography of Nietzsche nor of the person of 'Herr Nietzsche.' In truth, it is a matter of a 'destiny,' the destiny not of an individual but of the history of the era of modern times."[12]

Heidegger's depersonalizing stance is maintained not only against other philosophers, but against his own life, particularly when it is connected to his political activities.[13] The ontological turn in hermeneutics not only introduced a significant form of inquiry, it simultaneously reduced the scope of hermeneutics in limiting its critical, individual-personal, and ontic dimensions that are still at work in Schleiermacher, Dilthey, and Misch. The prospect of a hermeneutics that thinks with, against, and beyond Heidegger's privileging of the ontological over the ontic and being over the social-historical and intersubjective formation of meaning should recover and transform these forgotten aspects of earlier hermeneutics.[14]

The early Heidegger insisted that the factical life of Dasein is thoroughly historical. However, "factical life" as it was understood by the historical school, which resonated in Dilthey's account, no longer has a role in Heidegger's discourse. Their concern with historical conditions is dismissed as merely ontic and historiological. How can there be "factical life" without those particular characteristics that belong to and determine a particular personal factical life? Misch raised this concern in one of the earliest published critiques of Heidegger, *Lebensphilosophie und Phänomenologie: Eine Auseinandersetzung der Diltheyschen Richtung mit Heidegger und Husserl* (1930): Does Heidegger's notion of Dasein presuppose, repress, and reify the lived experience entwined with conditional, personal, biographical life such that Heidegger's hermeneutics can no longer access or address life? Or, keeping in mind Heidegger's earlier contrasting discussions of the lives of Augustine and Aristotle, should reflexive awareness and a critical autobiographical and biographical reflection (in Dilthey's sense of *Besinnung*), which does not reduce a life to one identity or narrative, be intrinsic or extrinsic to philosophy and the originary life disclosed through what could be called the "biography of Dasein"?[15] These questions indicate problems not only for interpreting Heidegger but for contemporary philosophy insofar as it remains committed to the primacy of the impersonal over the personal.

According to Heidegger, the concrete issues of life are not addressed by remaining at that level of understanding; they require a radically ontological thinking achieved through strategies such as "formal indication" and hermeneutical anticipation that poses the question of one's own life (Dilthey) or existence (Heidegger) in relation to the question of the meaning of being and the hermeneutics of authentic and inauthentic speech, logos as revealing and as concealing, which Heidegger unfolded in confrontation with Aristotle's *Rhetoric* in the lecture courses on the *Basic Concepts of Aristotelian Philosophy* (1924) and *Plato's Sophist* (1925).[16]

Heidegger's "biography of Dasein" is not the biography of "*a* life" or a concrete individual person, just as Dasein does not refer to the human being ordinarily understood. Dasein is not a particular individual being bound to and confronted by a multiplicity of particular historical contexts, institutions, practices, and worldviews; Dasein is being-in-the-world, being-toward-death, ruination and fallenness; or a being facing formalized structures of everydayness rather than particular conditional structures or the worldly practical concerns that Heidegger analyzes through his conception of distraction, flight, and inauthenticity. Heidegger's seemingly odd relationship with life and historical concreteness led to charges of pseudo- or phony concreteness by critics such as Misch, Marcuse, and Anders who conceptualized concreteness in relation to the historical and social analyses of Dilthey and Marx.[17]

Heidegger's understanding of history as primarily the history of Western philosophy, interpreted as the history of the forgetting of being, loses the specificity of the historical nexus of life with its pedagogical, ethical, and social-political textures, structures, and intersections. It is here, after all, where *a* life is significant and its meaning and meaninglessness usually and for the most part transpire. The strangeness of Heidegger's conception of life, in which human existence is constitutively distanced and alienated from itself, is not his thought-provoking reflections on the uncanniness of being and Dasein's lack of bearing and being-at-home in the world. Dilthey himself reflected on the strangeness of a life shadowed by its own inevitable death, as the goodness of life is placed in question by life's cruelty and destruction in nature and society.[18] The strangeness consists rather in Heidegger's neglect of the concrete textures of *a* life and the intersections of biographical life with the event of thinking. Where then should hermeneutics proceed after Heidegger?

CONCLUSION: HERMENEUTICS BEFORE AND AFTER HEIDEGGER

The contexts and conditions in which truth is encountered and interpreted cannot be adequately conceived of purely as an ontological event of being and its epochal history, as if each epoch had one rather than multiple possibilities. Heidegger's way problematically overemphasizes unity and ignores the conflicts, differences, and tensions that constitute any epoch and form of life that Dilthey (no doubt inadequately) articulated through the philosophy of worldviews. Heidegger's approach is not problematic for lacking unity—as Heidegger contended against Dilthey through his conception of the unity of Dasein, world, and the ontological difference in the Winter Semester 1928–1929 lecture course *Introduction to Philosophy*, his last sustained discussion of Dilthey (GA 27: 349–54). It is rather insufficiently pluralistic, and its formalism is insufficient for addressing the plurality of forms of embodied life in their singularity and concreteness.

The focus on the impersonal disclosure of the truth of being and language in Heidegger and the dominant tendencies in twentieth-century hermeneutics is in part a justified response to the perception of overly subjective and individualistic interpretations of meaning and truth in the hermeneutics of Schleiermacher and Dilthey. Nonetheless, this response is an overreaction that led to the neglect of the critical tasks of judgment and reflection in the formation of meaning and the human encounter with truth, as Rudolf Makkreel has recently argued.[19]

A problematic aspect of twentieth-century hermeneutics, associated with Heidegger and—to a lesser degree—with Gadamer, is the separation of truth as an ontological event and structure from the processes of subjective and intersubjective meaning formation and critical self-reflection as well as ontic social-historical formations and regimes of truth described by thinkers such as Dilthey and Marx. Two primary ways of reading Heidegger privilege sense (*Sinn*) or being (*Sein*).[20] Both fail to address the lacunae in Heidegger's thinking that demand going beyond Heidegger for the sake of functioning interpretive practices of individual and social-historical life and a multidimensional and intercultural hermeneutics.[21] Heidegger is a primary interlocutor for such a project even as his thinking and its limits must be recurrently questioned for the sake of a more adequate elucidation of the ethics and hermeneutics of personal life. "After Heidegger," we might begin to recover and reimagine—in part by reconsidering earlier hermeneutical philosophers such as Schleiermacher, Dilthey, and Misch—what was lost in the ontological turn.

Heidegger's thinking of the originariness of life and language in the mid-1920s suggests his affinities with Dilthey and the "Dilthey-school" that endeavored to develop a hermeneutical logic. These concerns distinguished his project from conventional forms of transcendental philosophy that focused on the constitutive role of consciousness and the self. Heidegger would later argue that his early project and *Being and Time* are beholden to this paradigm. I wish to conclude by posing a question about understanding Heidegger's philosophy as a whole. Did Heidegger ever overcome transcendental philosophy? Heidegger's ambivalent and tense relationship with transcendental philosophy is evident from his early to mature works. It shapes his early and later efforts to transform and overcome it as well as the trajectory of the question concerning the significance of life and the question of being.[22]

NOTES

1. Gilles Deleuze, *Pure Immanence* (New York: Zone Books, 2001), 30.

2. John Van Buren, *The Young Heidegger: Rumor of the Hidden King* (Bloomington: Indiana University Press, 1994); Theodore Kisiel, *The Genesis of Heidegger's "Being and Time"* (Berkeley: University of California Press, 1995); Scott Campbell, *The Early Heidegger's Philosophy of Life: Facticity, Being, and Language* (New York: Fordham University Press, 2012).

3. Theodore J. Kisiel, *Heidegger's Way of Thought: Critical and Interpretative Signposts* (New York: Continuum, 2002), 92. Dilthey described this as the dominant tendency of his philosophical thought in 1911: "das Leben aus ihm selber verstehen zu wollen" (*Gesammelte Schriften* 5: 4).

4. Gadamer attributed this phrase to Dilthey which does not seem to appear in Dilthey's own writings: "Das Leben legt sich selbst aus. Es hat selbst hermeneutische Struktur." Hans-Georg Gadamer, *Wahrheit und Methode: Grundzüge einer philosophischen Hermeneutik* (Tübingen: Mohr, 1960), 230.

5. Kisiel, *Heidegger's Way of Thought*, 92.

6. Georg Misch, *Lebensphilosophie und Phänomenologie: Eine Auseinandersetzung der Diltheyschen Richtung mit Heidegger und Husserl* (Bonn: F. Cohen, 1930). Misch considered autobiography as a philosophical category, an insight that shaped his multivolume *Geschichte der Autobiographie* (Leipzig: Teubner, 1907–1955).

7. Heidegger vowed to "cultivate the spirit of Count Yorck in the service of Dilthey's work" (SZ 404/SS 383). His earlier discussion of Yorck and Dilthey shows that this can be understood in a few different ways: as emphasizing (1) the ontological-historical over the ontic-historiological, (2) existence understood through spirit and intuition rather than through research and inquiry (work), and (3) Yorck's conservative vision over Dilthey's social-cultural liberalism. Gadamer described how Heidegger "recognized the weakness of Dilthey's cultural liberalism and the strength of Count Yorck's religious and deeply rooted stature." See Hans-Georg Gadamer, *Hermeneutics between History and Philosophy: The Selected Writings of Hans-Georg Gadamer*, vol. 1, tr. and ed. Pol Vandevelde and Arun Iyer (London: Bloomsbury, 2016), 215.

8. On violence and uncanniness in Heidegger's *Introduction to Metaphysics*, see Eric S. Nelson, "Traumatic Life: Violence, Pain, and Responsiveness in Heidegger," in *The Trauma Controversy: Philosophical and Interdisciplinary Dialogues*, ed. Kristen Brown and Bettina Bergo (Albany: State University of New York Press, 2009), 189–204.

9. See Robert Bernasconi, "Levinas and the Struggle for Existence," in *Addressing Levinas*, ed. E. S. Nelson, Antje Kapust, and Kent Still (Evanston, IL: Northwestern University Press, 2005), 170–84.

10. Georg Misch, *Der Aufbau der Logik auf dem Boden der Philosophie des Lebens* (München/Freiburg: Karl Alber, 2002).

11. Martin Heidegger, "Lettre à J. M. Palmier" (1969), in *Martin Heidegger*, ed. Michel Haar (Paris: L'Herne, 1983), 117. Translation from Parvis Emad and Kenneth Maly, foreword to Martin Heidegger, *Hegel's Phenomenology of Spirit* (Bloomington: Indiana University Press, 1994), xi. Palmier had published a work on Heidegger's political thinking the previous year: Jean-Michel Palmier, *Les écrits politiques de Heidegger* (Paris: L'Herne, 1968).

12. Martin Heidegger, *Nietzsche: The Will to Power as Knowledge*, vol. 3 (San Francisco, CA: Harper & Row, 1979), 3.

13. Heidegger wrote about his own life through his conception of the history of metaphysics in order to elucidate the significance of *Being and Time* and his troubled involvement in National Socialism, as well as his changing stances toward both. See Eric S. Nelson, "What Is Missing? The Incompleteness and Failure of Heidegger's *Being and Time*," in *Division III of "Being and Time": Heidegger's Unanswered Question of Being*, ed. Lee Braver (Cambridge: MIT Press, 2015); Eric S. Nelson, "Heidegger's *Black Notebooks*: National Socialism, Antisemitism, and the History of Being," in *The Bloomsbury Companion to Heidegger*, ed. François Raffoul and Eric S. Nelson, expanded ed. (London: Bloomsbury, 2016).

14. On the prospects for such a hermeneutics, see Rudolf A. Makkreel, *Orientation and Judgment in Hermeneutics* (Chicago, IL: University of Chicago Press, 2015).

15. On Heidegger's early project as a "biography of Dasein," see Campbell, *The Early Heidegger's Philosophy of Life,* xii, 5.

16. Cf. Ibid., 159.

17. Compare Misch, *Lebensphilosophie und Phänomenologie*, 228; Guenther Stern (Anders), "On the Pseudo-Concreteness of Heidegger's Philosophy," *Philosophy and Phenomenological Research* 8:3 (March 1948): 337–71; Herbert Marcuse, *Heideggerian Marxism*, ed. Richard Wolin and John Abromeit (Lincoln: University of Nebraska Press, 2005), 166.

18. Wilhelm Dilthey, *Gesammelte Schriften* 8: *Weltanschauungslehre: Abhandlungen zur Philosophie der Philosophie* (Göttingen: Vandenhoeck & Ruprecht, 1931), 80–81, cf. 144.

19. Makkreel, *Orientation and Judgment in Hermeneutics*.

20. Richard Capobianco has maintained the impersonal event character of the disclosure of being that is independent of human sense-creating activities and meaning-formation. Thomas Sheehan has elucidated the—often implicit—priority of human meaning-creation and sense in Heidegger's understanding of being. See

Richard Capobianco, *Heidegger's Way of Being* (Toronto: University of Toronto Press, 2014); Thomas Sheehan, *Making Sense of Heidegger: A Paradigm Shift* (London: Rowman & Littlefield International, 2015).

21. The intercultural character of hermeneutics is already part of the Western tradition of hermeneutics itself; on the need to overcome Heidegger's art of interpretation for a more adequately intercultural one, see Chapter 5 of Eric S. Nelson, *Chinese and Buddhist Philosophy in Early Twentieth-Century German Thought* (London: Bloomsbury, 2017).

22. On Heidegger's ambiguous relationship with transcendental philosophy, see Eric S. Nelson, "Heidegger's Failure to Overcome Transcendental Philosophy," in *Transcendental Inquiry: Its History, Methods and Critiques*, ed. Halla Kim and Steven Hoeltzel (Basingstoke: Palgrave Macmillan, 2016).

Chapter 16

Alienation and Belongingness

Charles Guignon and Kevin Aho

KINDRED SPIRITS

We decided to collaborate on this chapter because of our years of teaching and writing about Heidegger together. Trying to see the basis for our deep respect for Heidegger, we have found that one crucial aspect of his thought, in our minds, is his strong sense of *Heimat* (or "home-ness"). Heidegger's early years, and their relation to his life's work, are fairly well known. He grew up in a small town in the southern region of Germany. Even after he left the area to teach at larger universities, he continued to show a nostalgic connection to his rural place of origins. This enduring concern with belongingness is evident in the Bavarian peasant garb he occasionally wore to classes, in the mountain hut where he wrote books with titles such as *Holzwege* ("forest paths") and *Wegmarken* ("trail markers"), or in his decision to remain in the provinces despite the offer of a chair at a prestigious university in Berlin. In his writings, he intimates that choices of this sort were motivated by his deep love of the land and the quiet wooded places nearby.

Although we both have backgrounds quite different from Heidegger's, we have had experiences that seem to echo some themes in Heidegger's life. We both see ourselves, to some extent, as "loners," content with reading books and thinking apart from the crowd. We also grew up in exurban or semirural communities some distance away from big cities, and we both preferred activities that involved closeness to the wilds of nature: Charles hiked the Appalachian Trail and combed the Los Padres National Forest at Big Sur, while Kevin skied the pristine slopes of the Rocky Mountains.

Having grown up in exurban areas, we both initially went to big-city universities, Kevin at The New School for Social Research in New York City and Charles at the University of Pittsburgh. We both recall feeling a strong sense of alienation in these places. In New York, Kevin felt uprooted and torn away from his native ground in Idaho, and Charles felt anxiety and disconnectedness at a school where not even one course in existentialism, his primary interest, was taught. In the next few years, both of us moved to schools located in more bucolic settings—Kevin first to Salt Lake City, then to Tampa, Florida, and Charles first to Berkeley, then Vermont, and finally Tampa. Located in what we experienced as more congenial environments, we discovered and came to admire more deeply Heidegger's thought.

Interestingly, both of us found that our first encounter with Heidegger's magnum opus *Being and Time* brought about a transformation in our lives. Whereas mainstream American philosophy departments in the second half of the twentieth century focused mainly on developing skills of puzzle-solving and argumentation, Heidegger suggests that philosophers adopt the method of *phenomenology*, influenced by Husserl and Aristotle, aimed at describing what shows up in ordinary living, independent of theory-laden distinctions and concepts. The goal of such a method is to capture how things (in the widest sense of this word) appear for ordinary people in the course of their day-to-day activities. Starting with some very mundane examples—a lectern adjusted too high, or an office desk encountered as a center of gravity for pens, inkstand, paper, and so forth—Heidegger draws our attention to the intelligibility and arrangement things have in the context of our workaday lives. Especially vivid is his picture of a carpenter hammering in a workshop. These ordinary practical settings convey a sense of the kinds of "dwelling" in which familiar activities go on—work such as repairing a bookcase, lecturing, or writing a paper.

The concreteness of these examples stands in stark contrast to what we saw as the sterility and abstractness of standard Anglophone philosophy at the time. Even Heidegger's jargon can seem commonplace and homey—focusing, as he does, on what is "handy" (*zuhanden*) in the workshop. On this account, the being of things—roughly, their significance—is found not in the ways we theorize about them, but in the ways we use and handle them in everyday situations. We both felt at ease with these Heideggerian descriptions. There was nothing contrived about the idea of being at home with what is handy. The pervasive sense of alienation that had accompanied mainstream philosophy seemed to fade away, replaced by something familiar, something tried and true.

We originally met when Charles moved from the University of Vermont to the University of South Florida in 2000. The age difference between us was striking—Charles is almost exactly the same age as Kevin's father. That difference notwithstanding, we found that we had a great deal in common. We had both passed through a "dark night of the soul" of alienation and isolation, and had found consolation in Heidegger's unique approach to philosophy, one that offered an alternative to the dry logic chopping of "the schools." We spent hours together in discussions touching on literary works (especially those of Dostoevsky) and new developments in psychology and psychiatry. Previously we had immersed ourselves in the works of Camus and Sartre and were struck by the similarities and differences in Heidegger's texts. Above all, we were impressed by Heidegger's early focus on human existence in its concrete ways of being with others and with the world. Friends and coauthors to this day, we share the conviction that Heidegger's thought has, and will continue to have, enduring significance for philosophy.

BEING-IN

Division One of *Being and Time* is devoted to a phenomenological description of human being (or *Dasein*) as "being-in-the-world."[1] This is the way things show up when we catch a glimpse of what is going on in the midst of practical affairs. Heidegger's suggestion is that people are typically—that is, "proximally and for the most part"—enmeshed in a practical life-world, up to our elbows in the midst of things, as we handle what needs to be done. Under ordinary conditions, according to Heidegger, we do not experience any gap between our "selves" and what we are dealing with. Instead, in Heidegger's view, our most common mode of being is *dwelling* in the swirl of a life-world, responding with no special awareness to the solicitations of what surrounds us. We are "in the world," not in the sense in which a knife is in a sheath, but in the sense of involvement, of "being in trouble," "being in love," or "being into video games." As a rule, we are so caught up in the flow of what is unfolding that it takes a special, wrenching effort to try to disengage ourselves from this holistic involvement in order to adopt the standpoint of detached observation extolled by more traditional philosophers. Far from it being the case that the stance of detached objectivity gives us a superior "view from nowhere," Heidegger holds that detachment and disengaged inspection is a distorting lens that conceals what is "primordial" in our lives.

"Worldhood" is the general name that Heidegger gives for the all-encompassing background of intelligibility that provides the arena in which we act. We know our way around this context because we have mastered worlds of this sort. And our mode of involvement is called *dealings*—"the kind of concern which manipulates things and puts them to use" (SZ 67/MR 95). For both of us, there was something wonderfully refreshing about Heidegger's flat-out rejection of the objectifying ontology and the dualisms of mainstream philosophy. It was like coming up for air after being held under water. We felt, "Of course! That's the way things really are." The constructions of the tradition suddenly seemed wildly implausible. Philosophers had overlooked the "handiness" of things and had focused on the rather special cases of things appearing as objects, as "mere items on hand" (*vorhanden*) that show up in detached reflection. Heidegger helped us to see that our world is always already endowed with a significance and directedness from the outset—it is something we find ourselves in, not something we make.

Heidegger also recognized that the field of intelligibility is co-constituted by the practices and language of the wider culture where we grow up and first get a handle on things. Our typical relations to others are not something that can be understood in terms of some sort of abstract "I–Thou" relation. Instead, the all-pervasive context of intelligibility gains its meaning and order from what Heidegger calls "the One" or "the Anyone" (*das Man*, used in German in such remarks as "one doesn't do that sort of thing around here"). Humans discover themselves by finding their place within practical settings and dialogical communities as they become competent in the language of that world. So I can be a teacher only among other teachers, students, and administrators. My *being* the teacher I am is made possible by my ongoing intercourse with the "we" of a particular sort of world. We are tuned in to the shared world of the "one" in such a way that there is no way to disentangle ourselves from the local practices and ways of talking without shattering the "selves" we are. In this sense, we are placeholders in a public life-world: our identities as humans are defined by the cluster of roles we enact in playing out our parts on the big stage of life. The very notion of "the real me" or my being as an "individual" are, initially at least, components of what *we* are in our society, even if it is our contemporary individualistic, narcissistic society.

CARE

Another aspect of Heidegger's thought that resonated for both of us was his conception of "care" (*Sorge*). Heidegger's account of everyday being-in-the-world leads him to describe characteristic features of human being—the "*existentialia*"—that make us the worldly beings we are. Phenomenologists claim that these characteristics can be found by anyone who brackets or suspends the one-sided views of the tradition and describes what is transparently "there" in ordinary life. The conclusion of this part of Division One in *Being and Time* is that to be human is to *care* about things because we care about our own lives. Care takes the form of *concern* about particular things (e.g., my car, my career), or *solicitude* for others (e.g., my attachment to my wife), or larger scale cares such as "Who am I?" and "What is it all about?" (topics that will loom large in Division Two of *Being and Time*).

What is it that enables us to care about anything (even in the "privative mode" of trying not to care about things)? Heidegger identifies three broad aspects of human life that enable us to care. The first, called "understanding" (*Verstehen*), is our ability to make sense of things on the basis of an overview of what is going on around us. Second, there is "being-disposed" (*Befindlichkeit*, literally "how one finds oneself"), through which we have an orientation toward things based on what has historically come before. This sense of situatedness manifests itself in particular attitudes or moods that orient us toward things—in loving or hating, for example, or in fearing or being courageous. Third, there is "talk" or "discourse" (*Rede*), the opening of a "clearing" or "lighted space" (*Lichtung*) through which "what-is" (*das Seiende*) shows up.[2] To take a simple example, the spatula in the kitchen shows up for me as a tool for cooking in part because I feel like cooking, or am obligated to cook, or I want to make a dinner for my beloved.

What especially intrigued us was the notion of being "always already" enmeshed in a specific meaningful world, already having some sense of who or what we are and being already underway in projects that involve some degree of commitment to the future. Heidegger calls this "being already in" our "thrownness" (*Geworfenheit*); we always find ourselves thrown into a context of meaning we do not create or choose for ourselves (*pace* Sartre). Heidegger refers to this dimension of thrownness with the nineteenth-century technical term "facticity," a term referring to something that refuses to be mastered in conceptualizations because it contains tacit aspects discernable only in concrete involvements with things (as the appeal of something may only show up for particular people at special moments). Through being-disposed, we find not just where we currently are, but also that we have only particular "possibilities of being." What this dimension of thrownness reveals is that we humans are always bound up in a wider context of significance that defines in advance possible projects and situations of social involvement that demand decisions. The fundamental concept of thrownness, used to the end of Heidegger's career, opened Charles to work in psychology and Kevin to reflections on embodiment, where the human body is understood in the dynamic sense of the situated "lived-body" (*Leib*), not just the meat and bones of the "corporeal body" (*Körper*).[3]

Another innovative idea in Heidegger is that the meaning of the being of things is revealed not through cognition but through affective states or moods. Moods are the way our being-disposed takes a concrete form. For Heidegger, moods (*Stimmungen*, literally "attunements") are not fleeting interior states, like a gag reflex or a transient chill. They are rather "like an atmosphere" in which we are immersed and which attunes us "through and through" (GA 29/30: 100). Our moods tune us in to life and color the way things matter for us. Moods can be personal (like my dislike of romantic comedies) or, more likely, shared and "out there" in our community (e.g., fear of terrorists). The upshot of this view is that we find ourselves in a context of life where things matter for us and debates are already raging about the most worthy aspirations and projects. There is no objective vantage point for pure, unbiased observation of what is and what should be. At the same time, this facticity first gives us a window onto the world: only because we are attuned and "in on" things can we become functioning agents in the life-world we share.

ANXIETY

It follows that human beings are unique among other cases of what-is to the extent that we care about what it is "to be." We humans care not just in the sense that a dog might be said to care about its dinner, but in the specifically human sense of being articulate about what we want and being able to formulate and reformulate our concerns in the discursive interplay of a group's linguistic exchanges. In this sense, what we are is determined by what we care about in the ongoing life of a community. The conclusion is, again, that within the larger part of our lives, we tend to be placeholders in the "Anyone" of a specific social setting. We do what "one" does and thinks, and we suppose we are doing well so long as we "fit in" and "go with the flow." This mode of being of everydayness Heidegger calls "falling" (*Verfallen*, literally "addiction"). We drift along with the crowd in such a way that there is little need to see our lives as being in question for us.

This average, everyday way of being is so pervasive that Heidegger says it is an "essential trait" of human being, an *existentiale*. What especially fascinated the two of us in reading these texts was the suggestion that, underlying this typical way of life, there is a pervasive mood of "anxiety" (*Angst*), a mood that can crop up unexpectedly from time to time in what we usually call "anxiety attacks." Certainly Heidegger had experienced such attacks when he was expelled from training as a Jesuit because of "heart problems" (he lived to be 86) or in his total breakdown in 1946 when he was barred from teaching and spent months recovering in the Haus Baden mental asylum. But Heidegger does not propose the universality of anxiety solely on the basis of personal experiences. His line of thought, as we understand it, is that the fundamental nature of caring about things, together with a sense of the vulnerability and fragility of all worldly projects, sets us all up for the possibility of anxiety. In falling, we let our identity be defined by our ability to fit in with the prevailing forms of life of our community. Given the instability and impermanence of worldly things, however, this supposed grounding can fail us. I can, for example, find my dream of being a husband in a loving marriage shattered by divorce, and suddenly everything I held as definitive of my being collapses and slides away. In such an experience, the totality of what-is shows up as pointless, "completely lacking significance" (SZ 186/MR 231). In an outbreak of anxiety, "what-is as a whole . . . sinks into indifference," everything becomes "superfluous" (BW 102), and we are forced to confront our being as *solus ipse*, as a self alone, in an "existential 'solipsism'" (SZ 188/MR 233). In these situations, we are thrown into the midst of what-is with nothing to ground our being. The outcome is a "not-being-at home," a confrontation with the *uncanny* (*Unheimlichkeit*, literally, "loss of home-ness") (SZ 188/MR 233).

The description of anxiety in *Being and Time* has aroused a great deal of interest among scholars in fields such as psychology, psychiatry, literary studies, and film studies. For the authors of this piece, the section of *Being and Time* on anxiety (together with its 1929 companion piece, "What Is Metaphysics?") has a special meaning. Each of us has experienced a deep sense of anxiety for as long as we can remember. The feeling of anxiety, together with related feelings of disconnectedness and alienation, has provided an undercurrent for our lives. This affinity between us played a major role in bringing us together in the first place, and it keeps us inquiring into how Heidegger's description may be useful for the allied health professions and for understanding the ideal of authenticity. Where once we thought that such a feeling must be simply pathological, we now feel that it is an inevitable consequence of being-in-the-world and caring deeply about things.

The question about how to deal with this "problem" can be answered in different ways. One might see it as a reason to manifest one's care in social activism, or one might embrace a Buddhist or Daoist ideal of release from worldly concerns, or one might adopt some Christian form of "turning one's life over to God." The important thing is to see that anxiety is an unavoidable consequence of care, and for this reason is a condition intrinsic to being human.

HEIDEGGER'S LASTING CONTRIBUTIONS

So far we have tried to sketch out some of the key ideas in *Being and Time* in order to show how they might appeal to philosophy students of different ages and places of origin. A thorough account would also show how Heidegger's early ideas evolved into the very difficult but worthy later works after the so-called "turn" in his thinking. Instead of looking to these later works, however, we will point to a few of the key concepts in Heidegger's corpus we think will be of enduring interest to philosophy and to general readers in the future.

Part of Charles's first book, *Heidegger and the Problem of Knowledge* (1983), addressed the conundrum of realism versus anti-realism that has come down to us through the years. This is a good question to focus on in philosophy classes, because it ties into a number of dichotomies that any philosopher should question. The distinction between what is in the mind, on the one hand, and what is "out there" on the other, between the "subjective" and the "objective," seems to force the classical questions on us: Can we know about a world that exists independent of us? Or is what we call "reality" an invention of our own minds, a product of our mental categories and forms of perception? Or is it shaped by the language and conceptual schemes of a particular historical culture?

Heidegger's discussion of this issue is long and convoluted, and there is little agreement among Heidegger scholars about what he is saying. But his answer might be summed up in a couple of words that display his general strategy in dealing with old philosophical stumpers. Instead of defending one view over the other, he tries to show us that, although both sides have something right about them, overall the distinction is bogus. On the one hand, Heidegger insists that "what-is" in the broadest sense is already there, independent of our choices and creative activities. "Entities are never of our making," he says (GA 5: 39/BW 178), though we are self-making beings in the sense that we decide, within limits, our own fates. On the other hand, he shows us that what-is can show up as *counting* for anyone *as* such and such—as *being* something or other—only if Dasein *lets it be* what it is. Dasein "lets what-is be involved" in particular ways. A poker, for example, can show up *as* a fireplace tool or *as* a murder weapon. To say that, regardless of its uses, the poker is still an iron object is not to get at what it is independent of any way of being taken up in our letting-be. Instead, it is just one additional way of letting the poker be, in this case, the way of impartial, objective science. So what counts as "real" is always the result of an interplay between Dasein's way of letting-be and what we encounter as thrown into the midst of what-is.[4] This letting-be should not be thought of as a passive withdrawal in any sense. On the contrary, it involves receptivity, openness, and insight into the ways things are taken in our own community. Neither does this notion imply an "anything-goes" relativism. There are constraints on how we can let things be (though poets, artists, philosophers, and scientists can bring about shifts in our sense of how to let things be). It is because there are background constraints of this sort that we are largely in agreement concerning so much of our "sense of reality."

This example shows how even the most obvious puzzles of philosophy and the verbal distinctions that keep them going can be put in question. What we try to convey to our students in teaching Heidegger and what we see as the core contribution for future teaching and research "after Heidegger" is his insight into the *questionability of all traditional assumptions* and the *question-worthiness of the philosophical tradition as a whole*. Heidegger never thought of philosophy as one subject to be taught alongside other subjects in a humanities curriculum. For him, as we have come to see, it is part of the stance of critical reflection to always question—and to always try to be true to the way things actually show up in real life. This is the rejuvenating breath that Heidegger has brought to philosophy.

To say that Heidegger is a great philosopher and a powerful guide through the tangles of intellectual confusion is not to say that his thought should be bought whole hog. Criticizing everything also means criticizing Heidegger. But at the same time, it may be the case that even the most egregious errors in Heidegger's life and thought might be better understood in light of his times. As Heidegger saw it, there were two huge factions opposing one another in Germany in the twentieth century. There were the cosmopolitans, those who felt assured that the universally valid standpoint of science, logic, and reason would discover the truth. And there were what we might call localists who believed that, because we are always already "thrown" into the midst of a world we cannot totally control, we have to start from where we are, and we need to have some loyalty to the practices and forms of life of the communities that are "near" to us. Heidegger's lifelong play with the homonymous words *hören* ("listening," "hearing") and *Gehören* ("belonging to") made it plausible to think that belongingness to a particular community is not something we should necessarily try to cast off in order to achieve an enlightened "view from nowhere." To this end, we understand that we can't get out of our skins to see things from an impartial, detached standpoint. At the same time, we recognize the importance of striving for a truth that is not just the comfortable "truthiness" for a particular group or community. Moreover, we wholeheartedly reject any association, as apparently made by Heidegger, between the placeless "wandering Jew" and cosmopolitan ideas. But we also see that it is part of *our own* Western thrownness and sense of "home-ness" to be cosmopolitan and unprovincial about politics. The goal, put bluntly, is what people used to mean when they talked about not being so open minded that one's brains fall out.[5]

NOTES

1. The hyphens indicate that this is a "*unitary* phenomenon," not a result of piecing together a "mind" and a "body" (SZ 53/MR 78).

2. *Das Seiende* is often translated as "entities" or "beings," but that suggests that this singular term is to be thought of as items (e.g., objects) of some sort. In fact, for Heidegger, "everything we talk about, everything we have in view, everything towards which we comport ourselves in any way, is being [*seiend*]; what we are is being, and so is how we are" (SZ 6–7/MR 26).

3. See Frank C. Richardson, Blaine Fowers, and Charles Guignon, *Re-envisioning Psychology: Moral Dimensions of Theory and Practice* (San Francisco, CA: Jossey-

Bass, 1999) and James Aho and Kevin Aho, *Body Matters: A Phenomenology of Sickness, Disease and Illness* (Lanham, MD: Lexington Books, 2008).

4. The best discussion of this topic is found in John Haugeland's "Letting Be," in *Transcendental Heidegger*, ed. S. Crowell and J. Malpas (Stanford, CA: Stanford University Press, 2007).

5. David von Drehle writes, concerning the recent election in the United States, that American nationalism and exceptionalism have perplexed scholars from the beginning. "Old World nations hold fast to ethnic, racial or cultural identity—a particular people tied to a particular place. America, by contrast, has long perceived itself as a voluntary association of many races and ethnicities and cultures": "The Fight for the Meaning of America," *Time*, October 24, 2016, 82. The feeling of rootedness in the soil can collide with the cold and bloodless associationist view of political life, as was evident with Brexit and in the 2016 American election.

Chapter 17

Being at Issue

Richard Polt

The thought-provoking power of Heidegger's writings is evident to those who allow themselves to be moved by them. The depth of his thought is also undeniable: can there be deeper questions than the meaning of being and the essence of truth? So I am confident that Heidegger will continue to be appreciated, discussed, and rediscovered as long as his writings exist and there are readers to read them.

But to be thought-provoking and deep is not necessarily to be right. The sheer force and range of Heidegger's thought, together with his well-honed rhetoric, can persuade us that he must be on the track to answers—despite his repeated insistence that his thought is a series of *Holzwege*, "woodpaths" that do not issue in any solutions but only get us farther into the woods. At some point, a truly philosophical reader must establish some critical distance and try to decide which of the paths blazed by Heidegger are still promising and which are misguided.

Of course, our responsibility is made more acute by Heidegger's appalling enthusiasm for Hitler, his indefensible notes on "world Jewry," and his refusal to see any worth in liberal ethics and politics. This antiliberalism is part of an essential current of his thought: his relentless critique of the Enlightenment's faith that reason can rise above its circumstances, comprehend them, and improve them. For Heidegger, fact-gathering and logical explanations are ineluctably rooted in nonrational "thrownness"—our belonging to a given order whose givenness is ultimately inexplicable. We depend on our tacit familiarity with the norms and practices of our culture; we depend on unpredictable moments of illumination; we depend on our involuntary exposure to meaning itself. These shadowy preconditions of unconcealment sustain all our rational certainties and plans. When the Enlightenment forgets its roots, it distorts the human condition and destroys the richness and mystery of things.

The result, for Heidegger, is a growing wasteland—a world where all beings, including humans, are reduced to mere objects present for measurement and resources present for exploitation. For Heidegger, liberalism is simply the triumph of the calculating and rapacious subject.

It is not accurate to describe Heidegger as a convinced Nazi, since from the start he hoped for a questioning more radical than any party slogan. He comes to view Nazi ideology as an instance of the domineering and reductive metaphysics of modernity—thus, racial theory is nothing but "biological liberalism" (GA 65: 53). However, this metaphysical critique is not accompanied by a moral or political one, and he even explicitly dismisses such points of view (e.g., GA 95: 13). In texts such as the *Black Notebooks*, he portrays all modern movements and forces, including the phantasmagoric power of global Judaism, as instances of one and the same machinational metaphysics—thus indulging in a reductionism of his own. The Enlightenment's forgetting of its roots is associated all too easily in his discourse with the traditional prejudice against Jews as supposedly nomadic cosmopolitans. Despite his critique of Nazism on the theoretical level, he does not resist it, but submits to it (GA 95: 408). He seems to view Nazism as the ultimate modern destiny, an extremity of willfulness that must be played out to its catastrophic conclusion before a new inception can become possible (cf. GA 95: 50, 417).

Heidegger's reflections on modernity remain highly pertinent, even urgent. But again, we must be on our guard against following his critique all too readily, or abandoning the moral, political, and scientific ideals of the Enlightenment without articulating a responsible alternative.

We must be responsible. But what is the source of this responsibility? What makes it possible for us to be held responsible in the first place? *Being and Time* proposes an answer that, in my view, is one of Heidegger's most genuine insights. If so, then even the most valid criticisms of his own irresponsibility presuppose some phenomena that Heidegger himself can help us understand.

According to *Being and Time*, we are responsible—for ourselves, for others, for things, for the very meaning of it all—only because we are at the same time indebted. We are *schuldig*, "guilty"—that is, thrown into the predicament of having to be ourselves in our world, even though we did not bring ourselves into existence. Responsibility is not a matter of grounding one's own being; to the contrary, Dasein is responsible because it is beholden. We have been handed a burden that may feel heavy or light, that we may recognize or disregard, but that, as long as we exist, we cannot simply put down—for this burden is our existence itself.

Heidegger's insight into the burden of our being is genuine and revealing. The fact that our being is at issue is a crucial feature of our existence, a feature that often enough is either ignored or taken for granted in everyday discourse and in scientific and technological practice. Here is one truth, though surely not the only one, that Heidegger can offer us. If we explore a few of its ramifications, we can see not only how it connects to other themes in Heidegger, but also how he failed to reflect on some of its political implications. The insight into the burden of being may also help us see the limitations of the Enlightenment without leaping to the conclusion that it must be completely rejected.

WHO ARE WE?

Heidegger articulates a fundamental line of thought in §4 of the Introduction to *Being and Time*: Dasein's own being is at issue for it; Dasein is being-in-the-world; therefore, the being of all beings in the world is at issue for Dasein. Since our own existence is a problem, what it means for everything to be is also a problem—and we have an intrinsic mission to discover, question, and enrich our own understanding of being.

Let us look more closely at the elements of this idea. First, to say that Dasein's own being is at issue for it (*es geht um seinen Sein*) means that each of us is ineluctably concerned with *who* we are. Of course, most of the time we do not agonize over our identities; we simply accept who we are, and get on with the business at hand. Some of us never experience an existential crisis at all. But this is all consistent with Heidegger's idea; his view is that this normal way of existing is inauthentic everydayness, a "fallen" condition in which the question of selfhood appears to have been settled once and for all, or does not even appear but remains occluded. From a more insightful and authentic point of view, this fallenness of Dasein testifies to its higher calling. What might seem to be cases of indifference to one's own being—recklessness, ennui, automatism, the unexamined life in all its variations—really prove the ubiquity of care. Only an entity whose being is at stake for it can fail to take up the challenge, seek to unburden itself from itself, or forget its own responsibility.

In extraordinary moments of lucidity, we wake up to ourselves and realize how far we have fallen. But waking up to oneself does not mean retreating to a disembodied, noncommittal mind, for Dasein is always already being-in-the-world. "In" means engaged in, as when we say that someone is "into" politics or music. "World" means a network of meaningful and purposive relations. Each of us is into the network. I may care about my family, my neighborhood, and my career; I operate in these environments, interpret myself in terms of them, and encounter things and people as relevant because they play a part in these significant webs. Again, even a person who seems alienated or indifferent is being-in-the-world, albeit in a "deficient mode."

Even the experience of anxiety, where all the nodes of my network seem to recede into insignificance, does not destroy the network or my caring involvement in it. It is like standing atop Mount Everest, with an unparalleled view of the landscape, knowing that you will freeze or asphyxiate unless you descend. Anxiety shows me that my involvements cannot ground an essence that defines me as if I were a present-at-hand thing; my being remains at issue. But any viable response to the question of my being, any answer to the question of "who," no matter how provisional, must take the form of reengaging with the world.

My world is a shared world: the network constantly implies others, even if they are not currently on the scene. My habits are cultural, my language is dialogical, the traditions to which I am indebted were developed by others. To grapple with my own existence is, at the same time, to address what it means to be a member of my community.

Because I am-in-the-world, then, what is at issue for me is not just my own being in isolation, but the being of all those who matter to me—and in fact, the being of all the entities I can encounter within my significant network. The question of who I am cannot be answered by navel-gazing. For instance, if I am into music, then I am engaged with what it means to be an instrument, to be a musician, and to be a good or bad piece of music or performance. How I interpret music is part of how I interpret myself—how I manage to be somebody. If we extrapolate from this example and include lesser degrees of engagement, we see that every Dasein is necessarily concerned with beings as a whole and as such. No matter how circumscribed one's world may be, it forms some entirety, a field in which one plays a part and where things have their places. No matter how distant we may be from theoretical questions of ontology, it makes a difference to us that beings *are* at all, that they are something instead of nothing. And just as one's own selfhood is never settled, the meaning of all other beings remains in question: our interpretation of every region of entities is susceptible to a paradigm shift, and the meaning of the whole keeps calling for new responses. In this way, the question of being springs from the human condition itself. It is not the invention of philosophers, but is implied in the fact that our own selfhood is in question and that we can be someone only by engaging in a world where we care about all that there is.

Since being is at issue, we are constantly exposed to questions that cannot be definitively answered: What is the meaning of being? Who am I? Who are we? The issue of being cannot be displaced by an identity; any such identity turns its back on the persistent question.

This thought insists on a certain tension and incompleteness within our own being: rather than having a fixed character that we can simply discover, our selves are permanently at stake. Heidegger's position combats all "subjectivity," in his sense—that is, every view that takes the human being as a *subjectum*, an underlying thing that has ascertainable, unambiguous attributes. He thus insists that Dasein is a "who" rather than a "what"; this characteristic plays a part in all of our essential traits.[1]

If we adopt the fundamental insight that being is at issue for us, we should avoid three false steps that can spoil this insight. First, it does not follow that our being is a sheer abyss, void of meaning—a void that can then be filled by the arbitrary decision to pursue any project whatsoever. We find ourselves indebted to a tradition and community, and thrown into a world that is the only place where we can be anyone. This means that not every answer to the "who" is equally promising, viable, or coherent. If I set out to create a private language and a completely new culture, I will end in madness—or in a dated, clichéd fantasy that I fail to recognize as such.

Secondly, authentic existence does not have to avoid all stable personality. It may be quite appropriate to commit oneself to pursuing a single way of being in depth—as long as one remains aware that this pursuit is an ongoing response to a question that continues to be asked. In other words, even though identity cannot displace the issue of being, I can build an open and evolving personality for myself. I might authentically participate in a religious community, for example, as long as this participation is not a matter of dogma and inertia but a constantly renewed commitment, a lifetime of risking responses to ongoing questions. If I avoid all responsibilities or try to reinvent myself ex nihilo every day, I will just develop a shallow character, and my supposed freedom will be nothing but a cul-de-sac.

Finally, against some of Heidegger's own tendencies, there is no need to insist that only Dasein has the privilege of a problematic relation to its own being. Maybe other animals, or even all living things, are in the process of becoming themselves without ever settling into an essence or "species." Maybe all matter emerges from fields of potential that assume concrete forms under specific circumstances, but cannot be limited to those forms. Perhaps the ontology of presence at hand, where entities are objects in definite states, was never anything but a construct, not just when it comes to ourselves but as regards everything that is.

Heidegger's position, then, may exaggerate human uniqueness—but it is a virtue of his approach that it militates against all objectification of humanity. This is still a battle that needs to be fought. The biologism that he denounced in the 1930s has its counterparts in the "neurophilosophy" and evolutionary reductionism of today. Biology legitimately uncovers a wealth of interesting facts, but some interpretations of these facts assume that in order to understand the human condition, we simply have to explain the origin and structure of our bodies. As long as the body (including the brain) is grasped as a present-at-hand entity—an object, no matter how complex, that is not at issue for itself—then the deeper and distinctively human dimensions of our existence remain obscure.

Biological reductionism is often accompanied by an informational reductionism that represents "the mind" as hardware, software, algorithmic operations, or data. Partially valid analogies between humans and computers distract us from our own existence. If a computing machine ever becomes a problem for itself—if it experiences anxiety, has an identity crisis, and cares about being—then it will begin to make sense to speak of artificial intelligence.

As noted earlier, the point is not to insist on a quantum leap between humanity and all other beings; there seems to be an evolutionary continuum, and we cannot know a priori that it is impossible to build a silicon-based Dasein. The point is that our sciences and technologies often assume that all the entities they handle are simply present-at-hand objects, disregarding the possibility that such entities could become an issue for themselves. But this is to exclude Dasein's way of being in advance. As Heidegger always insists, in ontology we should begin with the richer phenomenon—our own, full-fledged existence—and then understand more restricted ways of being as kindred to it. Instead, we are constantly tempted to use our technoscientific knowledge to try to explain the rich in terms of the poor.

THE POLITICS OF THE "WHO"

Let us take a few steps now beyond Heidegger's own paths, extending his insight into the burden of being into areas he barely explored. First, how does the question of "who" lead to a wealth of issues in the political realm?

Against the prevailing ideology of the Nazi period, Heidegger insists that the mission of the people is a question, not an answer, and that the Germans should keep in view something greater than the *Volk* itself—the problem of being. A community is always becoming itself, without ever completing that journey; its members ought to remain alive to the questionable significance of all things, including themselves. "Who are we?" he constantly asks in the 1930s.[2]

Heidegger's best moment during his year of greatest complicity with the Hitler regime comes on January 30, 1934, when he denounces novelist and ideologue Erwin Kolbenheyer, a popular mouthpiece for theories of racial purity, who has just spoken in Freiburg. "Kolbenheyer does not see and cannot see that man as people is a *historical* entity, that to historical Being there belongs the decision for a particular *will to be* and *fate*—engagement of action, responsibility in endurance and persistence, courage, confidence, faith, the strength for sacrifice. All these fundamental modes of conduct of historical man are possible only on the basis of *freedom*" (GA 36/37: 210/160). Freedom exists because "man is a *self*, a being that is not indifferent to its own mode and possibility of Being; instead, its *Being is that which is an issue* for this being *in its own Being*" (GA 36/37: 214/163).

But if Heidegger understood national destiny as an open question, why did he go so wrong in politics? How could he ever have lent his support to a dictatorship that ultimately tried to settle the question of "who" in the worst possible way: by murdering those who "we" are not?

Despite Heidegger's promising philosophical beginning, he ignored or disdained several questions that are essentially political. Regardless of any ethical judgment we may pass on his behavior, he simply failed to consider these basic theoretical problems, and instead became increasingly bitter and alienated from the entire political realm. The absence of any serious reflection on these problems means that Heidegger does not engage in political philosophy as such.

First, to what communities does an individual belong, and how are they related? How do conflicts among them arise, and how should such conflicts be resolved? For example, a speaker of a certain language may find himself at odds with legislation passed by his state, and may have things in common with citizens of another state because they share his language.

Who gets to count as a member of a community? Can membership be established simply by legal status? Does it require participation in certain practices or allegiance to certain norms? Is it a matter of ancestry? Can individuals voluntarily join or leave the community?

A perfectly homogeneous community is impossible. Every group necessarily has differences and minorities. How far should a community go, then, in accommodating these subgroups—linguistic, racial, ethnic, or political? Should they have specific rights?

Likewise, a perfectly unified community is impossible. As Aristotle observes (*Politics* 2.5), an excess of unity destroys a *polis* as such, reducing it to a household or an organism. The question, then, is how much division, diversity, and dissent a community should tolerate, or even encourage.

Heidegger holds that some individuals can articulate a community's destiny—Hölderlin, for instance, is the preeminent poet of the German mission. But we are always faced with competing articulations of destiny. How can we tell which is preferable? Do we choose arbitrarily? Is it a matter of rhetorical force? Are these questions subject to debate and discussion?

Is there such a thing as the will of the people? Is it to be decided by one or a few prophetic leaders? Or by a majority vote?

Is a certain respect for fellow Dasein crucial to acknowledging them as "whos"? Does that respect entail certain norms and laws? Does it mean that a community should establish individual rights that recognize that each member is an issue for him or herself? (This need not mean subscribing to an unrealistic theory of individual autonomy.)

If there is some gathering into a community, is there always a complementary diaspora, in which members of the community explore other groups, mingle with them, and live abroad as expatriates or exiles?[3]

Can different communities find their way to mutual understanding? How can members of one group learn from those of another? Heidegger does reflect on such issues as regards the relations between Germany and France (GA 13: 15–21), the Germans and the ancient Greeks, and the East and the West.[4] Unfortunately, his thoughts never reach the level of concrete political problems.

All of these issues need to be explored well beyond what Heidegger's writings can offer us. His insight that Dasein's own being is at issue for it can provide an ontological starting point for basic questions of political philosophy, but his own political errors are examples of inadequate and unacceptable responses. By encouraging public debate about these questions, we erect the strongest obstacles to an authoritarianism that attempts to settle the questions by establishing a collective identity through force. The questions can never genuinely be settled—they can at most be silenced. Contests over them are a permanent part of authentic political life.

BECOMING AN ISSUE

Another problem implied by Heidegger's basic insight is how our being *comes* into question. If being is at issue, how does it become an issue? How do we enter selfhood?

It seems that there must be events of disruption, events in which a formerly unproblematic identity erupts into discord and becomes a problem for itself. In such happenings the sense of our own being, and thus of all being, is challenged. We could call these events emergencies—crises in which being emerges as a burden. We might even call them traumas, which wound a smoothly untroubled would-be whole and force it to acknowledge its incompleteness.

In *Being and Time*, Heidegger describes the experience of anxiety as such an event in which meaning itself is shaken. What was formerly taken for granted as an all-encompassing sphere of significance is revealed as contingent and alterable.

In the *Contributions to Philosophy*, the appropriating event (*Ereignis*), with its "expropriation" (*Enteignis*) and "de-rangement" (*Ver-rückung*), can also be read as such an emergency—but a more fundamental one, which not only sets the world trembling but establishes a world in the first place. In "the appropriating event of the grounding of the there" (GA 65: 183, 247), a "site of the moment" would be founded—a meaningful spatiotemporal center.[5]

However, in the *Contributions* and in all of Heidegger's later writings, this founding event remains vague and ambiguous. Does the thinker's thought happen as one with the event, or can we intimate the event only in a mood of longing and desolation? Does the event refuse to take place, remaining a remote possibility that would happen, if at all, only in an apocalyptic "other inception" of history?

Against this eschatological speculation, we need to recognize that appropriating events take place at many junctures in each of our lives. As we bring Heidegger's insights to bear on concrete experience, his sweeping account of the history of being must be replaced with a more modest position similar to the view in *Being and Time:* we tend to misconstrue and objectify ourselves, to fail to recognize our own, ineluctably problematic being. We fall and forget. This tendency can be exacerbated by certain elements of the philosophical tradition as well as by some tendencies in modern culture. But the response should not be to hope for an apocalypse, but to keep opening our eyes to how we actually exist, how we keep being faced with smaller and larger traumas that found and refound our "theres."

After Heidegger, then, we need a traumatic ontology that practices a traumatic empiricism. Such an empiricism attends to experience, but without misinterpreting it as the simple givenness of present-at-hand phenomena—be they sense data, objects, or essences. Experience is *Erfahrung*, a wayfaring in which the traveler is transformed by the passage. The most crucial experiences alter the identities of those who have undergone them, and break through the current bounds of sense.[6]

We must think not merely *about* these emergencies, but *in* them. We ordinarily try to get over emergencies as soon as possible and read them retrospectively, from a position of reestablished identity. To think *in* emergency would be to dwell in it and dwell on it. It would mean letting the transformation of identity come into language. Under conditions of emergency, concepts liquefy under pressure, as it were; words find their way into new possibilities. This event is poetry.

Another essential form of language, perhaps underestimated by Heidegger, is narrative—which will always appeal to us when it tells of emergencies, whether tragic or trivial, and confronts us with the question of who we are. Literature illuminates the human condition without objectifying experience and reducing it to a case of some universal law.

Traumatic ontology, then, goes hand in hand with narrative and poetic explorations of the experience of existing as a "who." It will push the edges of phenomenology, dwelling in the becoming of the sphere in which phenomena can be accessed and interpreted at all. It will explore questions in political philosophy by attending to the origin of communal configurations and the problem of the collective "who." It will promote individual self-knowledge by staying with the emergency of the self.

Finally, traumatic ontology must address the question of the limits of reason and the destiny of the Enlightenment. Can we preserve an awareness of the preconditions of rational thought while continuing to analyze and explain the beings around us? Can we keep in view the preconditions for rational action while continuing to try to act in ways that are rationally justifiable, and to show respect for other rational actors? Does reason have to shrink back from the turmoil of an emergency, or is there a traumatic logic—a logic of coming to be an issue for oneself? Can reason be flexible enough to build bridges of discourse across paradigms, to understand transitions, to avoid speaking only from within a constituted identity?

Those of us who are unwilling to discard the Enlightenment must articulate its most promising insights while considering Heidegger's incisive critique of the principles and concepts in terms of which those insights have often been articulated in the past. If we are to develop a more thoughtful Enlightenment, if we are to cultivate reason without rigid rationalism, we should take to heart Heidegger's insight that only entities whose being is at issue are able to engage in reasoning, and we will focus on events of becoming-an-issue as we pursue ethical and political reflections that steer clear of Heidegger's failures of responsibility.

There is no part of Heidegger's thinking that remains, and no part that does not endure. None of it remains as a settled, proven body of assertions. It all endures as a provocation that can inspire individuals to think more attentively—to deepen unconcealment—to become more enlightened.

NOTES

1. For more on this "existential" element in Heidegger's thought, see the contributions to this volume by Theodore Kisiel and by Charles Guignon and Kevin Aho.

2. See Julia A. Ireland's contribution to this volume for a reflection on the relationship between Heidegger's efforts to explore the problem of being German and cruder Nazi assertions of German identity.

3. Heidegger's 1933–1934 seminar briefly asserts a fruitful tension between rootedness in the homeland and interaction with the exterior: *Nature, History, State*, tr. and ed. Gregory Fried and Richard Polt (London: Bloomsbury, 2015), 55–56.

4. On the question of East–West dialogue, see Bret W. Davis's contribution to this volume.

5. For a detailed interpretation in these terms, see Richard Polt, *The Emergency of Being: On Heidegger's "Contributions to Philosophy"* (Ithaca, NY: Cornell University Press, 2006). William McNeill also elucidates *Ereignis* as event in his

contribution to this volume, and David Kleinberg-Levin's contribution explores what it means to say that we are "appropriated" in *Ereignis*.

6. See Richard Polt, "Traumatic Ontology," in *Being Shaken: Ontology and the Event*, ed. Michael Marder and Santiago Zabala (Basingstoke and New York: Palgrave Macmillan, 2014).

Chapter 18

Heidegger's Schematizations

Lee Braver

Part of Kant's project was to schematize the categories, taking something abstract and formal and putting flesh onto it, making it live and breathe in real existence. He used time to connect these transcendental categories to the mundane world of experience. But what if Kant's time remains too removed from experience, too conceptual to act as a bridge between concepts and phenomena? What if time itself needs schematization?

Kant took the formal relations of temporal succession and logical implication, for example, and fused the two into causality. *Pace* Hume, a match's ignition doesn't just succeed its being struck; striking it *makes* it burst into flame. The first event implies the second, with a temporal inflection. The implication follows, in both senses of the word.

This is a good step, but it remains rather abstract. It was Heidegger who brought the schematization of time home, and he did this by turning it existential. His question was not Kant's—how must time be in order for science to work?—but the much closer, more pressing question: how does time structure and suffuse our existence, the way we live everyday (itself a temporal term)? Lived-time—*that* is the fully schematized time and, it turns out, it behaves wholly differently than mere succession. For one thing, *lived*-time is, paradoxically, tied to death. Being-there is being-mortal; there is in the shadow of not-being-there. Death doesn't follow my life the way ignition comes after striking the match; no, death rushes toward me as I hurtle to meet it through every mundane moment of killing time. Apps on my phone are time-siphons, and my life seeps out like air from a leaky balloon. I don't show up to work today as the effect of yesterday's cause, as if the days of the week lined up as dominoes. Nor, on the other hand, is each day an entirely new, spontaneous decision as Sartre claimed, sounding for all the world like a very smart person who had never met an actual human (has anyone ever needed a dose of Aristotle as much as Sartre?). Today follows yesterday in a groove that is deepened with and by each day, activities following the path that they themselves make and further entrench with each step. My projects pull me forward while inertia and routine pass me along like the current of a river; I drift through my life more than I lead it. My present takes place in the place given by my past, in its wake that is not gone (the past is not an elapsed now—how absurd) but that remains in the shape of the landscape which, in turn, orients and guides my present and, at the same time (literally), opens up my future.

It is in this schematized sense of "after" that we, today and tomorrow, are after Heidegger. It is the way the American South lives after the Civil War. As one of its greatest writers, William Faulkner, put it, the past isn't dead; it's not even past. We, many of us, work and think in the aftermath of Heidegger's thinking. Part of his legacy is that he even taught us how to understand how legacies of thought work, how to work out an endowment of thought placed in us, and to work off the debt of gratitude such thoughts place us in.

I think this union of working and thinking and living, this fulfillment of schematization, is one of his lasting legacies. So much of the history of philosophy is made up of attempts to escape: to escape our bodies, our culture, our time, time in general, mortality, morality, the senses, our fallen nature, nature in general, and so on. As with so many things, Plato encapsulated the idea perfectly with an image (but representations and poets are to be condemned!): life, our very existence, is a cave, a mistake, a trap we have fallen into, and philosophy is what leads the way out.

I have argued elsewhere that this impulse to escape the mundanities of life has ruled philosophy for most of its existence;[1] it is part of what Nietzsche railed against in his diatribes against the weak and ascetic spirits who resent the grubby, undignified aspects of daily living, the stomachaches and minor humiliations, the thinning hair and fading memory, the ever-growing list of regrets and elapsed possibilities behind us and the ever-shrinking horizon ahead. In his early work Heidegger realized that, appearances to the contrary, phenomenology perfectly complements existentialism. For if we are to describe the things themselves, and us ourselves, faithfully to our experience of them, then we must not bracket or reduce anything; we must embrace the grime and detritus of daily living. We must settle into the cave rather than looking for a way out. We do not think in a vacuum; we think-in-a-world. In order to understand thinking we must understand the thinker, which means that we must understand the world, and the body and society and the life that are all part of that place, that enable it to take place, that give it space. Where Nietzsche preaches *amor fati*, love of all that happens to one, embracing both disappointments and triumphs, Heidegger encourages an *amor mundi*, or *amor essendi*, an awe-filled affirmation of all the ways beings manifest themselves to us (interestingly, both see art as one of the most successful forms of this attitude).

Heidegger's early work makes many basic categories philosophers have used more concrete, worldly, existence-infused: time, space, our selves, other people. Instead of the bloodless subjectivities Dilthey objected to, Heidegger discusses people: worried and working, occupied and preoccupied, death-bound mortals. We rarely encounter formal "objects," but we do use tools of various sorts all the time, so that's what he focuses on. Things aren't usually experienced as 2.3 meters northwest of our present position or located at (2,3) on the x–y axes, but rather just-out-of-easy-reach-without-getting-up. We worry less about doing the right thing morally than fitting in or passing the time. Instead of soaring into the heavens, Heidegger roots us in the earth, which is also the dust we will return to in time, in time.

One of his most important "schematizations" is his treatment of knowledge. Rather than disengaged acknowledgment of facts, sometimes called knowing-that, Heidegger focuses on skillful competence or know-how. Traditionally, philosophers have thought about thinking in terms of overt beliefs that one holds, facts one can state and justify. Indeed, one of the fundamental points of Plato's dialogues is that if you cannot articulate what you claim to know, then you do not actually know it. At best, it amounts to *doxa*, beliefs you have examined so little that it's questionable whether you can be described as actually believing them at all, at least in any robust sense of belief. This fetishization of explicit consciousness echoes throughout the centuries—from Augustine's worry about his tacit understanding of time that vanishes when examined, through Descartes's need to eject and reestablish the bolus of beliefs he had swallowed unthinkingly as a youth, to Hegel's transformation of the phases *Geist* has gone through in-itself or non-self-consciously into ones intensely examined and deliberately incorporated for-itself (*Geist's* development resembling Descartes's youthful acceptance and adult reexamination writ across history), to Nietzsche's insistence that we should only will what we ourselves have created, to Husserl's late discussion of geometry where he unfavorably compares a student's rote recitation of a proof with a geometer's deep comprehension of it.

Heidegger overturns this preference, following Aristotle instead, who said that the soldier who acts bravely but cannot provide a knock-down, internally consistent definition of courage that can withstand Socratic objections not only is more courageous, but understands courage better than the silver-tongued philosopher safely reading at home.[2] This requires a different conception of knowledge, epitomized in Aristotle's notion of *phronēsis*: judging a situation adroitly, taking into consideration all the nuances and shades of meaning that cannot be fitted into formulaic algorithms.

Heidegger thinks that while we lack explicit, articulate knowledge of many things, we must possess a tremendous amount of implicit understanding in order to live and navigate the world successfully. We must know the various kinds of things there are—we must understand the multiple forms of being—in order to interact appropriately with different entities, such that we treat, say, our students differently from our shoes (on good days, at least). It is this level of knowledge or understanding or skillful competence—what he calls pre-ontological understanding of being—that Heidegger is trying to access (and, ironically, articulate), and one part of his legacy has been the notion that artificial intelligence as originally understood cannot work since it leaves this level out, focusing exclusively on explicit knowledge of facts.

I believe that this task of schematization, of re-grounding abstract concepts and theories in the concrete details of our lives, remains one of the most important tasks for philosophy after Heidegger. Initiated perhaps by Kierkegaard and Dilthey, it was Heidegger who brought it to fruition. It appears to be a perennial task. Heidegger and Wittgenstein, the twentieth century's greatest philosophers, both see humans as prone to abstraction, such that we perpetually need intellectual ballast to keep our ideas from floating away.

Heidegger's later work continues this project of schematizing time, but in a different direction: time schematized is now history, thought schematized is historical. Not only do we think in a world, but also in and out of a tradition. These elements appear in *Being and Time*, but briefly, underdeveloped, whereas they come to take over the later work root and branch. Now time is thoroughly embodied in concrete events, albeit primarily cultural ones. It's not just that ignition follows friction, but that Kant follows Descartes and precedes Nietzsche. Such events become the landmarks of time because we think in their landscape, oriented by their compass points, as we live in particular societies at specific times. We always start from where the tides of time and tradition have deposited us, and philosophy is the moon for Heidegger. Instead of an individual wresting her place resolutely from the anonymous murmuring of the crowd, we must embrace our inescapable sociality, the multiple always alreadies that start us going. Heidegger has turned from Kierkegaard's heroic individuality to Hegel's historical *Geist*.

And what are the most prominent features of the intellectual landscape we find ourselves in today? I've been arguing for much of my career that the analytic-continental divide is one of them. Many people say that it is a thing of the past, that we have gone beyond it. Well, as we have just been saying, something can be of the past while still shaping the present. Sociologically, our profession is still largely laid out along the contours of this divide, with job openings, departments, figures, books, and so on, categorized as analytic or continental. And despite many assurances, I still see little scholarship that cross-pollinates or genuinely bypasses the divide.

I have argued elsewhere that drawing these two traditions into conversation is one of the great tasks lying before us, and I would say that Heidegger is one of the figures we should draw upon for this undertaking. For one thing, the treasure trove of insights in his texts could perhaps tempt some analytics to wander into continental territory. His work represents one of the towering achievements in the history of philosophy, in my opinion, and has something to teach many, as I have been trying to show in a number of works that have brought him into conversation with figures like Ludwig Wittgenstein, Nelson Goodman, Hilary Putnam, Donald Davidson, and others.[3] Hubert Dreyfus has been very successful in showing the significance of his early work for issues concerning artificial intelligence,[4] while the later work, which I consider even better, remains largely untapped.

Secondly, Heidegger has given us some of the tools and meta-level ways to think about this very conversation itself. While he only speaks overtly about hermeneutics in the early work, much of the later work is concerned with the classic hermeneutic issue of understanding alien texts. So much of his later work is taken up with wrestling with canonical texts that he once said, hyperbolically, that, "my whole work in lectures and exercises in the past 30 years has been in the main only an interpretation of Western philosophy."[5] He once spent eighty pages reading a single sentence of Parmenides—though, to be fair, it is one hell of a sentence (he says elsewhere that "the primal mystery for all thinking is concealed in this phrase"[6]).

The historical reconstruction of past ways of thinking was his central occupation for some forty years and dozens of books, and the significance of this project is rather complex. Part of it is the standard idea that we understand where we are by grasping where we have come from. This notion takes on a slightly different sense for someone who subscribes to a phenomenological ontology, which I think Heidegger still does in his later work. According to this view, being is only what it manifests itself as; there is no noumenal remainder behind, beneath, or above what appears. In his later work, he comes to appreciate the profound historicity of appearing, realizing not just that being is *said* in many ways, but that it has *appeared* in very different ways across the ages. Each kind of manifestation is fully real and legitimate (compared with what supra-phenomenal criterion could it be found wanting or less real?) and deserves study (in fact, it deserves a kind of resurrection by being allowed to manifest itself again through this attending-cultivating art-cum-phenomenology, but I'll leave that aside for now). We come to grasp these previous periods' forms of being by analyzing their metaphysics, and we can then piece together their progression.

Except that there is no progression. Heidegger diverges from Hegel on this point, seeing the changes between the epochs as radical leaps rather than rational transitions, such that they cannot be put into a logical evolution.[7] The point of studying these previous permutations of being comes closer to Foucault's archaeology, who overturns the rocks of history to uncover the perverse peculiarities scurrying around in the dark, to experience "the stark impossibility of thinking *that*."[8] It is the distance, not the similarity, the utter strangeness instead of familiarity that is the point. It is the shock that anyone could possibly see the world in such a foreign way rather than the recognition that deep down we're really all the same. It's Kuhn's notion that scientists from different periods work in different worlds and see different phenomena and reason about them in different ways rather than the Whig notion that earlier scientists or thinkers were stupid and superstitious, willfully ignoring what was right before their eyes, whereas we courageous souls have the clear eyes and full hearts to see things for what they are.

Now, if that is his goal, then we must ask why it is interesting, beyond merely gaping at the spectacle of the shock of the old? What gives this any more significance than a tourist's frisson at the darker, more bizarre corners of the past, the kind of history porn that Foucault's work occasionally suggests? Again, Heidegger has a number of things going on, but one of them is hermeneutic. Ever since Socrates compared himself to a gadfly, philosophy has been about waking people up. What normal people take for granted, what we all just take in and pass along in unthinking acceptance, philosophizing makes us think about and wonder on. Not only are the questions asked weird, but the topics discussed are those that we generally don't even notice, even as they pervade our lives—because they pervade our lives. We take things so much for granted that we even take for granted their being taken for granted or, as Heidegger puts it, we forget that we have forgotten them. Lacking a Socrates, how do we wake up? For that matter, how did Socrates awaken? Who dragged *him* out of the cave in the first place?

This is one service that these shockingly different understandings of the world can provide. Since understandings of being determine virtually everything else in our lives, and since they are shared communally for a period, the vast majority of people we encounter will have the same one as ours. Conversing with them, even disagreeing, reinforces our own, keeping it submerged, invisible, unthought. We only perceive these assumptions *as* assumptions, views that can be otherwise rather than simply the way things are, when they are challenged, which generally happens when we find people who lack them. Since these understandings of being are pegged historically, one of the best places to encounter people with different ones is in the past. Hence, Heidegger's extended readings of past metaphysical texts is a way to talk with people who understand being differently, who live in another world from us among not just different beings, but different *kinds* of beings. This provides a kind of reverse mirror: it lets us see ourselves, the deepest part of ourselves, but precisely by holding up an image that does not resemble us. Clashing with a profoundly different other can unearth this deeply buried level of ourselves.

This is, in some ways, an extension of Heidegger's early treatment of the hammer. As long as our assumptions or fore-understandings are operating smoothly, they withdraw invisibly into the background, leaving us unaware that they are even operating. Reading earlier metaphysical texts, however, provides encounters with contradictory views, producing clashes that throw off sparks which light up our own, sometimes for the first time. This can allow us to question and challenge our assumptions, philosophy's traditional task. His pupil Gadamer explores these ideas in depth, though I don't think this is quite Heidegger's goal.

Primarily, he wants us to celebrate our understanding, to rejoice in the fact that we have one at all. We do this by bringing understanding to a heightened state, nurturing it, allowing it to excel and become more fully what it is—bringing it to *eudaimonia* in an Aristotelian sense. Since this understanding is what enables us to have any kind of awareness at all, turning it back on itself by becoming aware of awareness would be a perfecting of it. That's why, in an essay whose title is quite relevant for the topic of this book—"The End of Philosophy and the Task of Thinking"—Heidegger writes about how "the clearing is the open region for everything that becomes present and absent. It is necessary for thinking to become explicitly aware of the matter here called clearing."[9] It is in the clearing that anything at all becomes present, but we are to become explicitly aware not just of the contents of the clearing or the cleared, but of the clearing itself. "The clearing grants first of all the possibility of the path to presence, and grants the possible presencing of that presence itself."[10] Reflection, reflexive awareness, self-consciousness (although Heidegger did not like that term), as many thinkers have said, is philosophy's true goal.

For this illumination to take place, we need differences to throw our views into relief; it doesn't particularly matter where we find those differences. Something like this process could also take place with those in our own time who do not share our philosophical views. Synchronic dialogue with those of a different tradition could serve just as well as diachronic reading of texts from another epoch, which means that talking with, say, Wittgenstein could take the place of Heidegger's obsessive rereadings of Parmenides, as sacrilegious as he would have found such a notion.[11] This means that the analytic-continental divide, as harmful as it has been to professional philosophy, also presents a remarkable opportunity, if Heidegger's model of understanding is correct, and if we talk to each other. This, to my mind, presents one of the most pressing, and promising, tasks for philosophy after Heidegger.

NOTES

1. Lee Braver, "On Not Settling the Question of Realism," *Speculations* IV (2013).

2. For a discussion of Aristotle as a predecessor of this view, see my *Groundless Grounds: A Study of Wittgenstein and Heidegger* (Cambridge: MIT Press, 2012), 168–70. Hubert Dreyfus is a pioneer of these notions (see note 4 below).

3. See especially my *A Thing of This World: A History of Continental Anti-Realism* (Evanston, IL: Northwestern University Press, 2007) and *Groundless Grounds*.

4. See especially Dreyfus, *Being-in-the-World: A Commentary on Heidegger's "Being and Time," Division I* (Cambridge: MIT Press, 1991) and *What Computers Still Can't Do: A Critique of Artificial Reason* (Cambridge: MIT Press, 1992).

5. " 'Only a God Can Save Us': *Der Spiegel*'s Interview with Martin Heidegger," in *The Heidegger Controversy: A Critical Reader*, ed. Richard Wolin (Cambridge: MIT Press, 1993), 109.

6. Heidegger, "Letter on Humanism," in *Basic Writings,* rev. ed., ed. David Farrell Krell (San Francisco, CA: HarperSanFrancisco, 1993), 238.

7. Of course, at other times he gives a quasi-Hegelian history of philosophy, where philosophy continuously devolves across the epochs with Nietzsche forming the inevitable ending point by reversing Plato. I find this view both incompatible with and inferior to the many comments he makes about leaps between epochs (and not just outside metaphysics). See my *A Thing of This World*, 261–73, 289–90.

8. Michel Foucault, *The Order of Things: An Archaeology of the Human Sciences* (New York: Vintage Books, 1970), xv.

9. Heidegger, *Basic Writings*, 442.

10. Ibid., 445.

11. See my *Groundless Grounds* and "Davidson's Reading of Gadamer: Triangulation, Conversation, and the Analytic-Continental Divide," in *Dialogues with Davidson*, ed. Jeff Malpas (Cambridge: MIT Press, 2011).

Chapter 19

Dasein

From Existential Situation to Appropriation in the Event

Theodore Kisiel

This chapter was originally conceived as a phenomenological account of Dasein as radically thrown into its existential and hermeneutical situation. But another chapter in this collection by Daniel Dahlstrom entitled "In Heidegger's Wake" served to point out how limited my treatment of Dasein, which I consider to be Heidegger's most genial coinage, is. While it plays a dominant role in Heidegger's magnum opus, *Being and Time*, "Da-*sein*" continues to play a central role ten years later in Heidegger's purported second magnum opus, *Contributions to Philosophy (Of the Event)*. Central in this later work is Da-*sein*'s relationship to the event (*Ereignis*), as an "appropriation in the event" (GA 65: 293/231) and by the event, where the appropriating event is "original history itself" (GA 65: 32/27), which proves to be the history of being. After a first beginning in the earliest Greek thinking upon the manifold mystery of being peaked in Plato and Aristotle, Heidegger's own philosophical history sees a millennial decline setting in that develops into an ever growing oblivion of being and its displacement by a metaphysics of constant presence. How to arrest this millennial decline? "The abandonment by being is the first dawn of beyng [*Seyn*] as self-concealing out of the night of metaphysics" (GA 65: 293/231). Bringing "beyng as self-concealing" to dawn in an other beginning is the first resolution to the crisis brought on by a centuries-long institution of the metaphysics of permanent presence. This is the task for what Heidegger called *seynsgeschichtliches Denken*, which is best translated as "thinking in accord with the history of beyng." But the task proves to be enormously intricate, and the transformation of oneself into truly being-here and receptive to what is coming to us on an epochal level is reserved for a courageous few. As Dahlstrom puts it, the later Heidegger leaves Da-sein's appropriation in the event that is to resolve this crisis "woefully under-determined" and it is left to us who come after Heidegger to find our way through this under-determined nexus.

1.1 Dasein as our existential situation. It is worth noting that Heidegger first mocked words like "existence" (*Existenz*) and "decision" as the then current fashionable words of his day (GA 20: 375/272)[1] shortly before he wholeheartedly introduced this existentialist terminology into the composition of his magnum opus, *Sein und Zeit*. "*Existenz*, as a designation of Being, will be allotted solely to Dasein" (SZ 42), understood as the way in which the human being stands out among other beings. "The Being itself toward which Dasein can comport itself in one way or another, and always does comport itself somehow, we call *Existenz*" (SZ 12). "*The 'essence' of Dasein lies in its existence*" (SZ 42), an "essence" that "resides in the fact that Dasein in each case has its Being to be as its very own" (SZ 12). We are approaching the need to place the companion mode word accompanying existence, decision or choice, in the text. "Dasein always understands itself in terms of its *existence*—in terms of a possibility of itself: to be itself or not to be itself" (SZ 12). It is the decision to be authentic (*eigentlich*) or not, to become one's own (*eigen*) and proper self or to cling to the anonymity of the anyone-self. Heidegger sets the poles of the decision between everydayness and lifetime considerations, following Kierkegaard's distinction between the crowd and the singular individual, or the public versus the self. The decision is by and large an ontical affair of the individual existence, whose underlying ontological structure is to be elaborated by way of an existential analytic of Dasein (SZ 13).

Economy dictates only the sparsest of presentations of the existentials of Dasein. Dasein first appeared in the guise of the situational I and the historical I or, taken together, the historically situated I (GA 56/57: 206/174, 208/175). This historically situated I would soon be designated more ontologically as Dasein. The German word *Dasein*, conveniently for our thematic, ordinarily means "existence," as in *der Kampf ums Dasein* (the struggle for existence). But in its etymological breakdown as Da-sein, it means "being-(t)here," being-in-its-existential situation. For Heidegger, the existentials for being-here are variously called situationality/facticity/thrownness, understanding/projection, and discourse, which invests all of Being with the possibility of meaning.

The crisis experience of angst evokes the comprehensive existential of care for Being itself. The question of the meaning of Being generated by such an extreme experience would focus its care for Being on its concern for the Being of its own Dasein, its *existence*. Human existence is bounded by the two limit situations of birth and death, in the vernacular sometimes called the two ends of life. Ends, bounds, limits: all underscore the commonplace and yet terrifying facticity of the *finitude* (*Endlichkeit*) of our respective

Beings. That I am and have to be and yet need not be at all and of necessity will not be and still am is precisely what calls for questioning. The questionable presence of finite Being is precisely what is most worthy of questioning. It is this question of finite Being asked by the being who identifies itself with its finite time that has been forgotten by millennia of philosophers. As Heidegger points out, "In the treatise *Being and Time*, the question of the meaning of Being is posed and developed explicitly *as a question* for the first time in the history of philosophy" (GA 40: 89/91–92).

The finitude of our Being is on full display in the overlapping existentials of situationality (*Befindlichkeit*), facticity, and thrownness. The facticity of human life, for example, refers to its irreducible and irrevocable givenness "behind which thinking can go no further." It is *unhintergehbar*, but it is not thereby a brute facticity, because of the human being's capacity for speech and so for intelligibility and meaningfulness. *Befindlichkeit* highlights the experience of finding oneself situated in existence, but in two very distinctive ways. One is in a sheer existentialistic way, finding oneself situated in existence willy nilly, "thrown" into a world I didn't make and a life I didn't ask for. The other is in the "naturally" historical way of being born into a historical-linguistic community of a particular people and into a particular historical generation of that people. Responsively taking over this finite historical situation as our very own, retrieving, re-viewing, re-vising, and so reinterpreting the possibilities transmitted to us by our heritage that are still relevant for our own time, being responsive to the solicitations and demands exacted by that temporally particular situation: all of these hermeneutic acts of enowning are consolidated in the protoaction (*Urhandlung*) of proper historicality, which resolutely recapitulates the movement of the thrown projection that is our originary temporality in its ownness and finite wholeness, from future to having-been to the present holistic moment of decision (SZ 384–86). This resolute retrieval of one's very own temporal-historical situation is the ultimately positive expression of our finitude, in statements of existential self-identification like "I myself *am* my time, We ourselves *are* our history."

1.2 Our hermeneutic situation. This enowned historical situation is at once a hermeneutic situation, charged with the meaningfulness transmitted to us by our tradition and brought up to date for our time by our reinterpretation. Indeed, interpretation is all-pervasive at all levels of our factic life-experience, which spontaneously articulates and contextures itself in a manifold of vitally concrete and meaningful basic relations that constitute our lifeworld. Gadamer, freely paraphrasing Dilthey, succinctly expresses the pan-hermeneutic character of human life as follows: "Das Leben selbst legt sich aus. Es hat selbst hermeneutische Struktur."[2] "Life itself lays itself out, explicates itself, interprets itself, articulates itself. Life itself has a hermeneutic structure." In such a pan-hermeneutic context, the basic form of knowing is interpretive exposition out of a tacit background of pre-reflective understanding (GA 20: 359/260).[3] This stands in the sharpest contrast to the tradition from Parmenides to Husserl, for whom the basic form of knowing has been the total transparency of illuminative seeing, intuition.

This pan-hermeneutic dimension is especially relevant to the life of a philosopher, who in his conceptual labor naturally draws his concepts from the meaningful context of life-experience already articulated in the native language into which he happens to have been born. In short, each and every philosopher necessarily lives and works, in Heidegger's terms, out of his very own hermeneutic situation in its already prepossessed, previewed, and pre-conceptualized form. In fact, at one point in his development of an ontology of being-here, Heidegger identifies one's own temporally particular hermeneutic situation as the sole object of philosophical research for a time and generation (BH 153). "The very idea of facticity implies that only authentic and proper [*eigentliche*] facticity—understood in the literal sense of the word: one's own [*eigene*] facticity—that is, the facticity of one's own time and generation, is the genuine object of research" (GA 62: 366/BH 167).[4] "Resolved to speak radically to the world—to question and to research" (GA 18: 40/29), each generation of philosophers is called upon to radically retake its unique hermeneutic situation for its own time, to appropriate its own past in order to recover its precedent possibilities that are especially appropriate for its time and generation. It is incumbent upon each generation of philosophers, by way of radical questioning, to explicate and interpret that situation for its own time. And by its very nature, it is something that a time "can never borrow from another time" (GA 62: 348/BH 156). So identified are we with our particular historical time that Heidegger makes existential assertions such as "I myself am my time" (BH 213) and "We ourselves are history"[5]—to be sure, not an objectified history but rather a history-in-actualization (*Vollzugsgeschichte*).

1.3 Our ontic-existentiell situation. With all this stress on the hermeneutical and *ipso facto* phenomenological dimension of Heidegger's philosophy, one may wonder where exactly the existential dimension plays a role, if any, in his multifaceted thinking. The answer lies in his seemingly abstract and much misunderstood idea of formal indication. For the formally indicative concepts of philosophy are designed to call individuals to transform themselves into the Dasein within themselves, that is, to perform the existential, or more accurately, existentiell action of authentication and self-transformation.

The course of WS 1929–1930 gives us Heidegger's very last and most definitive treatment of formal indication: In contrast to scientific concepts, all philosophical concepts are formally indicative. "The meaning-content of these concepts does not directly intend or express what they refer to, but only gives an indication, a pointer to the fact that anyone seeking to understand is called upon by this conceptual context to actualize a transformation of themselves into the Dasein within themselves" (GA 29/30: 430/297; cf. 428/296). Because such concepts—Heidegger's terse examples are "death, resolute openness, history, existence," in short, life's limit situations!—can only convey the call for such a transformation to us without being able to bring about this transformation themselves, they are but indicative concepts. They in each instance point to Dasein itself, which in each instantiation is my (your, our) Da-sein, as the locus and potential agent of this transformation. "Because in this indication they in each instance point to *a concretion of the individual Dasein* in humans, yet never bring the content of this concretion with them, such concepts are *formally* indicative" (GA 29/30: 429/296, em). But when concepts are generic and abstract rather than proper to the concrete occasion in terms of which they are to be interpreted, "the interpretation is deprived of all of its autochthonous power, since whoever seeks to understand would not then be heeding the directive that resides in every philosophical concept" (GA 29/30: 431/298). Yet the kind of interpreting that seeks out its very own facticity in each instance is not "some additional, so-called ethical application of what is conceptualized, but . . . a prior opening up of the dimension of what is to be comprehended" (GA 29/30: 428–29/296), namely, the "concretion of [each] individual Dasein," its proper selfhood. The concepts and questions of philosophizing are in a class of their own, in contrast to science. These conceptual questions serve the task of philosophy: not to describe or explain man and his world, "but to evoke the Dasein in humans" (GA 29/30: 258/174). Accordingly, philosophy is not a science but a directive exhortative protreptic, whose concepts are not generic and common, applicable to *all* indiscriminately and uniformly, but rather hermeneutically distributive and proper, applicable to *each* individually in accord with the unique temporal context in which each individual is situated. The same point is made in *Being and Time* in the distinction between categories and existentials, between the What-question and the Who-question, between the common anyone-self and the proper self of a unique one-time-only lifetime. "*All* men are mortal" is generic and common, stating a neutral scientific fact, while "*Each* of us must die our own death" is hermeneutically distributive and individuating, singling out each to come to terms with their very own facticity of being-here. These formally indicative, properly philosophical concepts thus only evoke the Da-sein in human being, but do not actually bring it about. There is something ultimate about philosophizing. Its questioning brings us to the very brink of the possibility of Dasein, just short of "restoring to Dasein its *actuality*, that is, its *existence*" (GA 29/30: 257/173). There is a very fine line between philosophizing and actualizing over which the human being cannot merely slip across, but rather must overleap in order to dislodge its Dasein. "Only individual action itself can dislodge us from this brink of possibility into actuality, and this is the moment of decision and of holistic insight" into the concrete situation of action and Being (GA 29/30: 257/173). It is the existentiell protoaction of resolute openness to our own concretely unique situation of Being, of letting it be, in each instantiation concretely reenacted in accord with our own unique situation and particular while (*Je-weiligkeit*) of history which authenticates our existence and properizes our philosophizing. It is in such originary existentiell action, repeatedly reenacted from one generation to the next, that ontology finds its ontic founding. Just as Aristotle (and so the metaphysical tradition) founded his *protē philosophia* in *theologia*, so Heidegger now founds his fundamental ontology in "something ontic—the Dasein" (GA 24: 26/19).

And it is in this ontic founding that is actualized by "individual [existentiell] action" that allows for the entry of selected biographical elements at least at the threshold of the transcendental level of philosophy. In the same vein, this individual existentiell action draws upon the content of the "*concretion of the individual Dasein*" in the human being that had been left unfilled because of the *formal* character of the indication. It is the individual Dasein itself, which, as the being that in its Being is concerned with this very Being, in its very nature straddles the ontological difference between Being and beings, the ontological and the ontic, that in its transcending/transforming move from the human being to its Dasein, from the ontic to the ontological, brings with itself certain elements of its ontic background that it regards as indispensable and irrevocable to its very identity as a self.

1.4 Heidegger's own ontic-existentiell founding of his philosophizing. This can be readily exemplified by the testimony of Heidegger himself in a letter to Karl Löwith in August 1921 in which he spells out the vital identity out of which he himself does his own philosophizing:

> I work concretely and factically out of my "I am"—out of my spiritual and thoroughly factic provenance [*Herkunft*], my milieu, my life contexts, and whatever is available to me from these, as the vital experience in which I live. This facticity, as existentiell, is no mere "blind existence"—this Dasein is one with existence, which means that I live it, this "I must" of which no one speaks. The act of existing seethes with this *facticity of being-thus*, it surges with the historical just as it is—which means that I live the inner obligations of my facticity and do so as radically as I understand them. This facticity of mine includes—briefly put—the fact that I am a "Christian theo*logian*." This implies a certain radical self-concern, a certain radical scientificity, a rigorous objectivity [*Gegenständlichkeit*] *in* this *facticity*; it includes the historical consciousness, the consciousness of the "history of spirit." And I am all this in the life context of the *university*. (BH 99–100)

"Ich bin 'christlicher Theo*loge*.'" Such deeply personal declarations of who "I am" are clear-cut statements of self-identity in which Heidegger is owning up to the deep Christian roots that ineradicably belong to his factic provenance, and so an admission of where he is in fact coming from (*Her-kunft*) in his thinking. Eventually this provenance will assume a note of necessity, of the inalterability and inescapability of a person's situation that cannot be denied without "denying who I am," and so being untrue to oneself. "I cannot do otherwise without rejecting myself and denying who I am" (BH 102). The note of possibility comes into play in how one takes up this inevitability and develops it. "I cannot make my 'I am' into something different, but can only take hold of it and be it in this or that way" (BH 101). In confessing where he is in fact coming from, Heidegger is at once translating "the inner obligations of my facticity" into "must do" tasks and projects, for example, by assuming the self-confessed role of "Christian theo*logian*" in his courses on the phenomenology of religion and on Augustine and Neoplatonism in 1920–1921.

The letter continues with Heidegger contrasting himself with his two best students at the time, Löwith and Oskar Becker, first of all in regard to where each is coming from and how starkly divergent these concrete backgrounds are. "It has always been clear to me that neither you nor Becker would accept the Christian side of me" (BH 100). But in spite of the disagreements and misunderstandings that such radically divergent backgrounds are bound to promote and the radically different paths that may therefore be taken, Heidegger nevertheless looks forward to a "meeting of minds" provided that each comes to terms with his temporally particular existentiell situation in its ownness and wholeness in full propriety and authenticity.

> Only one thing is decisive: that we understand each other well enough so that each of us is radically devoted to the last to what and how each understands the *unum necessarium* ["one thing necessary" (namely, our respective facticities)]. We may be far apart in "system," "doctrine," and "position,"—but we are *together* in the one way in which humans are able to be genuinely together: in *Existenz*. (BH 102)

What particularly distinguishes Heidegger from Becker, the scientifically oriented philosopher, and Löwith, the existentielly inclined thinker, in their respective facticities (concrete backgrounds) is that "the fact that I am a 'Christian theo*logian*' " is a side of Heidegger that neither one of them could be expected to empathize with. Behind this admission of identity lies an ontic-existentiell background experience that finds itself deeply embedded in a facticity of Christian religiosity that developed into the (here left unsaid and clearly ontic-existentiell) autobiography of a former Catholic seminarian who had broken with the religion of his youth to become a non-denominational "free Christian" and was now on the verge of proclaiming the atheism of philosophy in close conjunction with the rigorous fideism of Protestant theology. Thus the admission implies a "particular radical personal concern"

(Löwith's forté) and pathos that stems from this past life, but it also involves a "particular radical scientificity" (Becker's inclination) being cultivated by a university philosopher who had just completed two courses on the phenomenology of religion which had developed formal schemata that prefigure the concrete historical actualization of Christian life (its Da-sein) as it is depicted respectively in Paul's letters and Augustine's *Confessions*.[6]

2.1 Da-*sein* as appropriation in the event. The transformation of ourselves into the ownmost Dasein within ourselves allows us, among other things, to become our uniquely proper selves, a kind of self-authentication. How is this thematic carried over into the later Heidegger and its expanded sense of Da-*sein*? A pair of citations is in order:

> Da-sein is the turning point in the turn of the event, the self-opening center of the counter-play between call and belonging. Da-sein is the "domain of the proper" [*Eigen-tum*], understood in analogy with "domain of a prince" [*Fürsten-tum*], the sovereign center of the appropriating eventuation as the assignment of the ones who belong to the event and at the same time to themselves: becoming a self. (GA 65: 311/246–47)

As Heidegger explains later, "Inasmuch as Da-sein is assigned to *itself* as belonging to the event, it comes to its *self*" (GA 65: 320/253). Becoming its self thus happens concurrently with belonging to the event.

The ontic-existentiell roots of Dasein in the human being are highlighted in the following citation:

> The human being has an intimation of beyng [*Seyn*], is the surmiser of beyng, because beyng ap-propriates the human being, and indeed such that the ap-propriation [*Er-eignung*] first needs something of its own, proper to itself, a *self* whose selfhood the human being has to endure and withstand in that instantiation that lets the human being, standing in Da-sein, become *that* being [*Seiendes*] that is first encountered only in the who-question. (GA 65: 245/193)

These citations also show that "belonging to the event" is a more common formula for Da-*sein* than our somewhat richer formula of "appropriation in the event." Another common formula applied to Da-sein throughout this later text is the counterplay of "call and belonging" (*Zuruf und Zugehörigkeit*), which raises the question of whether the appropriately paired response to the call is buried deep within the German word for belonging, *Zugehören*, as in *hör' zu*, "Listen!" or the more archaic "Hark!" At any rate, such a response appears to be a more receptive "letting-be" than the resolute openness to our existential situation of being-here and active retrieval of our historical legacy. On the level of the history of beyng, it's more a matter of letting the future come to us *(uns zukommende Zukunft*) than of projecting toward it. And we have already seen earlier how acts of self-identification hearken back to our provenance (*Herkunft*). But most important of all and common to both phases of Dasein was the recovery from oblivion of a being that is finite through and through, the question of finite being, asked for the very first time in the history of philosophy, then the history of beyng (*Seyn*) as historical through and through, and accordingly finite.

NOTES

1. The full modish phrase was the "questionability of existence." Most of the other references to *Existenz* and the "existential" in the published version of this 1925 lecture course were Heidegger's handwritten insertions superimposed upon the stenographic typescript of the course (over a dozen times, from 218/162 to 402/291 and 408/295).

2. Hans-Georg Gadamer, *Wahrheit und Methode: Grundzüge einer philosophischen Hermeneutik* (Tübingen: J.C.B. Mohr, 1965), 213; *Truth and Method*, 2nd ed., tr. Joel Weinsheimer and Donald G. Marshall (New York: Continuum, 1994), 226. I am indebted to Eric Nelson for identifying the original source of this oft-cited line, sometimes mistakenly attributed directly to Dilthey himself.

3. "*Auslegung ist die Grundform alles Erkennens*" (GA 20: 359/260).

4. GA 62: 343–415 reprints the article entitled "Phänomenonologische Interpretationen zu Aristoteles: Anzeige der hermeneutischen Situation" written by Heidegger in the fall of 1922.

5. This is a remark that Count Yorck von Wartenburg is reported to have repeatedly made to his philosophical soulmate Wilhelm Dilthey.

6. The two formal schemata on "becoming a Christian" are to be found in Theodore Kisiel, *The Genesis of Heidegger's "Being and Time"* (Berkeley: University of California Press, 1993) on pages 184 (Paul) and 202 (Augustine).

Part V

PHENOMENOLOGY AND ONTOLOGY

Chapter 20

Of Paths and Method

Heidegger as a Phenomenologist

Steven Crowell

What are the most pressing and interesting tasks for philosophy after Heidegger? If one follows Heidegger's own narrative of the history of being, the question is ambiguous. In that narrative, philosophy is "metaphysics," the tradition of Plato and Aristotle, where being is reduced to representation (*eidos*) and thinking to logic (*logos apophantikos*). Philosophy culminates in nihilism; things are experienced as meaningless "resources" (*Bestand*). In contrast stands "thinking," a "mindfulness" (*Besinnung*) that recollects and ponders what early Greek figures such as Heraclitus and Parmenides experienced but did not bring into thematic view: *Seyn*, *Lichtung*, *Ereignis*. On this reading, the most pressing, if not the most interesting, task for philosophy is to "get over" itself and "learn to think." If, however, we allow the term "philosophy" to cover both metaphysics and "thinking," then the question concerns something we must formulate for ourselves, taking Heidegger's narrative as a contribution to a conversation that includes Heidegger but whose terms are not dictated by him. That's the way I will understand it here.

I am increasingly convinced that the most pressing task for philosophy is to become more phenomenological. Only as phenomenology—in the broad sense of carefully attending to the way things show themselves in first-person experience and inquiring into the inconspicuous conditions that make such self-showing possible—can philosophy cultivate the sort of experience-near sensibility that keeps it open for the unexpected, while retaining a kind of critical epistemic commitment that does not fetishize argument and arcane logical technique. Today such a phenomenological sensibility can be found in both analytic and continental philosophy, though it is rarely so named in either, and it is this sensibility that allows us to go along a path *together*, attentive to a ground of thinking accessible only through a first-person experience that is also responsive to what others have to say.

From this point of view, Heidegger's *Denkweg* presents a challenge. In all of Heidegger's writings, how many times does he admit to changing his mind thanks to an objection another thinker has brought against his views? Once? Twice? Karl Jaspers may have been exaggerating when he called Heidegger's thinking "dictatorial,"[1] but it is true that at some point after 1933 Heidegger began positioning himself beyond the reach of ordinary argument. The first published volume of the *Black Notebooks* (GA 94) documents Heidegger's transition to an "esoteric philosophy" that, like Nietzsche's, will be properly assessable only by some for us as-yet unimaginable future humanity.[2] One way of putting my conviction, then, is to say that the most pressing task of philosophy after Heidegger is to decline his invitation to esotericism.[3] To think philosophically is precisely to *refuse* to be "taught" by such esoteric revelations—as both Kierkegaard and Levinas understood, seeing in this refusal, however, philosophy's original sin.

Does this mean that in order to take up the pressing tasks of philosophy after Heidegger we must forget Heidegger? Not at all. But it does mean that we must find a way to *assess* his work, and not merely *understand* it. Hermeneutically, this would be a form of cherry-picking, and that's where phenomenology comes in. In my view, what is of enduring value in Heidegger's thinking can be *demonstrably* grounded in a kind of phenomenological reflection, if we ourselves practice that reflection. This means that while understanding Heidegger's thought as a whole requires seeing how all its pieces cohere—that is, do not appear as altogether unmotivated—understanding it as a contribution to *philosophy* requires a willingness to judge for yourself what is compelling and well supported and what is not. This judgment is what is of enduring value.

In my judgment, the "phenomenological" is what is of enduring value, but there is much in Heidegger's writings that cannot be supported phenomenologically. These writings are criss-crossed with various agendas, and perhaps it is more productive to assess some of what Heidegger says against the imperatives of those other agendas. Much of the "politics" of the 1930s and 1940s, for instance, derives from a non-phenomenological set of commitments and ought to be judged in political terms. Lawrence Hatab (in this volume) argues—correctly, in my view—that the phenomenological ontology of *Being and Time* is compatible with any number of political positions. So instead of asking whether Heidegger's politics is entailed by his philosophy, it might be more illuminating to explore whether elements of his philosophy are motivated by his politics, perhaps to cover for it, rationalize it. The question currently on the table, however, concerns the pressing issues for *philosophy*—including political philosophy—after Heidegger, and in this regard, I believe, phenomenology is the measure.[4]

To say that phenomenology serves as the measure, however, is not to say that everyone must adhere to some strict method or adopt a specific technical vocabulary.[5] As Heidegger held, method belongs to science, but philosophy is not a science; rather, all philosophy is path-following. In going along a path, you don't necessarily have a goal but you do have a direction (*Sinnrichtung*), and so you can stray from the path. To stray from a path of thinking is what Heidegger calls "errancy" (*die Irre*). Such straying belongs to all path-following, since the path's direction is not plotted out in advance. It is thus easy to lose sight of what measures a path of thinking, what keeps thinking, even at its most adventurous, responsive to the possibility of failure. Science is "method" because its measures are (relatively) fixed; philosophy follows paths because what it means to fail at it is always part of what is at issue in it. To say that phenomenology serves as philosophy's measure, then, is to say that thinking ought to be responsive to the things themselves, attuned more closely to the world as it is lived than to the stories we tell about it and the theories we use to explain it. This is the lesson of the phenomenological *epoché* which, for both Husserl and Heidegger, focuses thinking on its ownmost matter: "the meaning [*Sinn*] that prevails [*waltet*] in everything that is."[6] But this is also, in my view, to say that thinking finally cannot go it alone. Philosophy's attention to its own possibility of failure means that it must address itself to others.

It might seem that phenomenology, with its emphasis on first-person *singular* experience and evidence, on intuition before argument, is an unlikely candidate for the measure of a philosophy that *needs* to hear what others think. Heidegger's esotericism seems to exemplify this problem. It is not hard to imagine how an emphasis on experience prior to argumentation might lead one to believe that, at least when the matter of thinking is most pressing and most interesting, the thinker is a kind of oracle whose deliverances render dialogue and criticism beside the point. But this is not, in fact, a phenomenological attitude; on the contrary, it is to stray from the path. And it is precisely the phenomenological element in Heidegger's work that shows how phenomenology neither permits an oracular subjectivism, averse to dialogue, nor precludes even radical breaks with traditional ways of pursuing philosophy, serious reconsiderations of where the path is leading. Cherry-picking Heidegger's writings according to the measure of what is phenomenologically attestable provides many compelling examples of what philosophy could use more of today.

Being and Time is phenomenological in the sense I have in mind. It still has much to teach us about the issues it takes up. The same can be said for the lecture courses that precede it, all of which fly under the banner of phenomenology. None of these texts is "esoteric" in the relevant sense; they both invite and demand that Heidegger's students and readers attend to their own experience of the phenomena Heidegger is pointing out and, on that basis, judge the validity or assent-worthiness of the claims Heidegger makes about them.[7] Since *Being and Time* deals with issues of interest to every philosopher—intentionality, mind, language, self-identity, knowledge, action, reason, and being—perhaps the most pressing philosophical concern for Heideggerians after Heidegger is to show that the insights attained along the phenomenological path are *indispensable* for attaining a proper understanding of these issues. Addressing this challenge requires that we engage with work done in analytic philosophy and other philosophical approaches, since only so can it be shown why, and to what extent, these other approaches remain unsatisfactory in the absence of what Heidegger has to offer.

Elsewhere I have tried to make a start on one such issue: What is reason or ground?[8] Heidegger's ontology is radical because it substitutes the notion of care (*Sorge*) for the traditional definition of the human being as *animal rationale*, and in *Being and Time* this underwrites detailed demonstrations of the "derivative" character of rationalistic accounts of (among other things) meaning, action, and knowledge or truth. But this critical ground-clearing also makes possible a *positive* rethinking of what reason or reasoning is. Though Heidegger does not pursue this positive project explicitly, a phenomenological reading of the analysis of *Angst*, death, and conscience illuminates a path that we can follow. What shows itself along that path—elements of a dialogical concept of reason—would appear, further, to support the claim that philosophy ought to take phenomenology as its measure. Reason is not a mental "faculty," the kind of inference machine or "brain-power" that can be coded. Rather, it is grounded in Dasein's intrinsic norm-responsiveness as care: The factic "givens" of our being-in-the-world are not inert variables but are experienced as at issue for us, that is, they appear in light of a decision or choice about what is appropriate or inappropriate, better or worse. Their being at issue for us means that we are responsible—not for what things are but for the motivating force of the normative claim of what, in each case, is taken as "better," what speaks for or against something. And because we are not solipsists, this responsibility is also *answerability* to others for what we say and do. To be answerable to someone is to be accountable to them, to owe them an account, a reason. Reason is originally reason-*giving*.[9]

If something like this is correct, then esoteric thinking falls short of the measure of philosophical responsibility. Fortunately, understanding reason in terms of care suggests a different path along which we might recover at least some of later Heidegger's insights into how technology (logistics, monological reason, calculative thinking) distorts philosophy and our contemporary world—without necessarily adopting his history of being (*Seinsgeschichte*), in which philosophy itself is the culprit.

Here, however, we face another pressing issue: How should we evaluate Heidegger's apparent dismissal of his own early approach? If we follow the phenomenological path we will not be inclined to believe that Heidegger's global rejection of "transcendental" philosophy as nihilistic "metaphysics" undermines the truth of, for instance, his earlier account of why mental content or act-intentionality is possible only for a being who can act for the sake of being something. Instead, we might be inclined to look in the other direction: If a certain analysis proves to be phenomenologically compelling, we are likely to discover that it haunts Heidegger's later writings at those places where he finds himself in need of something like it.[10]

Phenomenological cherry-picking, then, need not stop with the early work. It seems to me that most of Heidegger's later lectures and writings on historical figures remain "phenomenological interpretations" as this term was understood before 1930, and contemporary philosophy can learn much from this practice. Traditional philology retains its rights, but a *philosophical* history of philosophy must respect traditional historical scholarship while finding its own distinctive measure elsewhere. Where? Today it is common to ask how some past philosopher would address matters that occupy contemporary philosophers, though the terms be anachronistic: Is Descartes an "externalist" or "internalist" about justification? Is Kant a "conceptualist" or "non-conceptualist" about mental content? Phenomenology proceeds in a somewhat different way: it starts not with a contemporary conceptual conundrum but by calling upon one's own experience of the phenomena that are at issue for some philosopher in the past; attending to the way the language in which those things are described both enables a certain view of them and necessarily leaves aspects "unthought." This path is not a one-way street: those who follow it may discover, by thinking about things in the idioms of the past, dimensions within their own experience that challenge the conceptual complacency of "today."

One striking example is found in Heidegger's 1928 treatment of Leibniz's *Monadology* (GA 26: 70–100). In exploring how the monad can contain *in esse* all the predicates that will ever be true of it, Heidegger draws upon phenomenological concepts ("intentional implication" and "horizon") to explain what Leibniz had in view in calling *perceptio* and *appetitus* modes of *representatio*. Thus he makes sense of Leibniz's doctrine not *only* by appeal to textual sources but *also* in terms the things themselves—that is, here, the kind of "having in advance" characteristic of mentality as such. This, in turn, highlights what remains unthought in Leibniz's own presentation: What Leibniz saw as two irreducible capacities of the monad are actually abstract moments of a more fundamental unity: *representatio* is "already a perceptive striving or striving perception" (GA 26: 114). Such unity does not derive from the *ego cogito*—hence Leibniz's inability to get to the bottom of it—but has its phenomenological source in Dasein (care) as the "equiprimordial" belonging-together of *Verstehen* and *Befindlichkeit*.

Details aside, Heidegger's practice shows that, when conducted phenomenologically, a "violent" reading can also be a close reading, because it measures the author's concepts and arguments against what Gadamer called the shared "matter [*Sache*]" at issue in the dialogue between author and interpreter. Thus when Heidegger suggests that for Husserl "there was something that did not exist, namely the deep meaning of history as tradition,"[11] this cannot mean that in order to do justice to such meaning we must depart from the phenomenological path; instead, Heidegger's practice shows that a philosophical dialogue with tradition *presupposes* phenomenology. My hunch is that Heidegger's late reflections on language are a rich source of phenomenological insight into the practice of historical thinking—far removed from any "linguistic idealism" or historicist skepticism about "experience"—though I cannot pursue that hunch here.

On the other hand, Heidegger's own dialogue with traditional thinkers somehow led him to believe that philosophy should be "thinking in terms of the history of being" (*seinsgeschichtliches Denken*), that philosophy today should be measured by its awareness of its place in a specific historical narrative. The history (*res gestae*) of being is the happening of successive sendings (destinings; *Geschicke*) by being; these "modes of revealing" (truth) constitute how things as a whole can be experienced. The history (*historia rerum gestarum*) of philosophy is the story of the "names" philosophers have found for the experiences that define such "epochs," fundamental concepts such as *eidos*, *energeia*, *subiectum*, *Macht*, *Bestand*, and so on. Heidegger's narrative does draw partly on phenomenological insight—its obvious foil is Hegel's philosophy of history, and Heidegger's critique of Hegel's "dialectic" is a phenomenological one—but it is also committed to the (perhaps mistaken) view that the designs of being (*Seyn*) itself can be discerned in the workings of ordinary history. It is one thing to recognize that the phenomena of an historical period often align with the period's philosophical ideas; it is quite another to hold that these ideas *explain* the phenomena because they are "sent" by being itself. I say that this view is "perhaps" mistaken. How can we tell if it is or not? The question of how historical narratives are to be evaluated is, at least in part, a philosophical one, and those who go along the phenomenological path will not be inclined to abandon specifically philosophical measures of thinking for the supposed authority of storytelling.

For those who want to think with Heidegger while retaining their own judgment, then, a pressing question is how to gain independent, critical access to this narrative. This might *also* be a pressing issue for philosophy in general, *if* Heidegger's main point in constructing such a narrative turns out to be compelling. That point is to establish the "closure" of philosophy as "metaphysics" (nihilism as the result of philosophy's "forgetting" of "being itself" [*Seyn*]), thereby motivating a "step back" that will overcome such forgetfulness and open us to an "other" beginning. Derridean deconstruction offers one example of how difficult it is to take this narrative seriously while simultaneously trying to maintain an independent stance with respect to it. For my part, I don't find the story at all compelling as a putative *measure* for thinking. Here I side with Gadamer: there is no such thing as "the" language of metaphysics.[12] Even if it does not provide an inescapable norm for thinking, however, Heidegger's narrative is not vacuous, since it incorporates phenomenological analyses that do not depend on the etiological story in which they are found, and these reflections can be independently compelling. For instance, his description of the contradictory way in which we experience ourselves today—as "lords of the earth" and as "human resources"[13]—is deeply illuminating, even if we reject the idea that this is a *necessary* outcome of what began with Plato and Aristotle.

These reservations about Heidegger's history of being force us to confront the ontological elephant in the room: Heidegger always claimed that his exclusive concern was with the question of being. What becomes of this question after Heidegger? Is it a pressing and interesting concern of phenomenological philosophy? Perhaps predictably, my answer is "yes and no." First the yes, and then the no.

It is noteworthy that today a certain aspect of Heidegger's approach to the being-question in *Being and Time* has found resonance in discussions of "ontological pluralism."[14] This is a salutary development and illustrates a kind of *Verkehr* between phenomenology and analytic philosophy it would be nice to see more of. This development also points toward a second, and from a phenomenological perspective even more important, aspect of Heidegger's way of raising the question of being: his recognition of the "ontological difference." If being is not itself *a* being, then it is not a property of beings, a relation between beings, a category "in the mind," a Platonic form, a process, an event, or anything of that sort. If, from a phenomenological point of view, the ontological difference is the distinction between an entity and what it is/means to be that entity, then even after Heidegger the question of being—concerned with conditions of possibility of meaning, with "being in the sense of truth" (*on hos alēthes*) and the clearing (*Lichtung*) that enables things to show up *as* what they in truth are—remains perhaps *the* pressing question of philosophy.[15]

What, then, is to be done with Heidegger's later claims about being—for instance, his claim that the ontological difference, with its focus on the being of *beings*, obscures the real issue; that what needs to be thought is not the "is-ness [*Seiendheit*] of beings" but *Seyn selbst*, the "it" which "gives," *Ereignis*, and so on? Here I can only reiterate my commitment to a phenomenological measure. To the extent that these notions are attested in reflection on first-person experience and can be shared with others through the kind of discussion and reasoning that puts all of us in a position to evaluate the truth or bindingness of that reflection, then they must have a place at the table. They will be encountered on the path. So then, *do* such "names"—*Seyn, Ereignis, Lichtung*—call forth something that does not float entirely free of first-person experience? This is not a matter that can be dispatched all at once, but pursuing it a bit will show where the "no" side of my equivocal answer about the question of being arises.

On the one hand, we have some reason to think that Heidegger takes these late terms to be phenomenologically attestable, since even when he embraces the idea of a "phenomenology of the unapparent," he insists that we must *experience* the matters at issue.[16] The "unapparent" (*das Unscheinbare*) cannot be what does not show itself at all but rather what is *inconspicuous* and in need of being pointed out. On the other hand, Heidegger's texts also provide many instances of language that seems to abandon phenomenology altogether. A good example of the ambiguity is found in a phrase from the *Beiträge*, versions of which often appear in Heidegger's late work: "*Das Seyn braucht den Menschen*" (GA 65: 261).

Here everything depends on what thoughtful translation makes of the (intentional) ambiguity in the German. If we translate *braucht* as "uses," then it will be tempting to think of *Seyn* as some sort of agent or cosmic event or process. Being would somehow do whatever it does, occasionally "using" the human being—perhaps to establish the destiny of the German *Volk*. However one may describe it, this independent "power"—the Heideggerian version of the physicalist's Big Bang—would clearly run afoul of the ontological difference between being and beings.[17] But since Heidegger himself criticized the ontological difference as a relic of transcendental philosophy, maybe he was indeed working toward this sort of speculative concept of being. If so, I just say "no."

On the other hand, if we translate *braucht* as "needs," we can find our way back to the phenomenological path from which the other translation might tempt us to stray, since it preserves the correlation that is essential to phenomenology. To say that being "needs" the human being is to say that being cannot be what it is, cannot "hold sway," without the participation of its "shepherd." Less metaphorically, there is no addressor without an addressee; we cannot think being without also thinking the way our own thinking of being "lets" being "be." This is essentially the position of *Being and Time*, where "there is" being (meaning, truth) only so long as Dasein is—because Dasein's being is defined as being at issue, and only so long as there is such a being who measures itself against a norm of success or failure can beings be, that is, mean, something.

It might be possible to understand Heidegger's late discourse about *Seyn*, independently of his historical narrative, in something like these terms—namely, as an attempt to follow the path of a phenomenology of meaning opened up by *Being and Time* while being attuned to phenomena unsuspected in that work. When Heidegger identifies thinking with *Besinnung* and describes it as "admitting oneself into meaning [*sich auf dem Sinn einlassen*],"[18] we may see in this a pathmark. If, as I believe, Heidegger's writings are not always consistent on this matter and pull in different directions, this just means that they contain cherries ripe for picking.

One final word, off the beaten path. In these paragraphs, I have proceeded as though the most pressing issues concerning philosophy after Heidegger are internal to philosophical questioning. A completely different sort of pressure, however, is exerted on philosophy today in the form of a radical transformation of the institution in which, in the West, it has found its home since the late eighteenth century: the university. This institution has lost its way—a fact not unconnected to Heidegger's thoughts about "reason" as the most "stiff-necked adversary of thought"[19]—and with it are disappearing the conditions for the kind of *scholē* or *contemplatio* that even dialogical-phenomenological philosophy requires. *This* sort of "pressing issue" is not really in philosophy's power to control (though, obviously, we—philosophers and nonphilosophers alike—can take steps to mitigate it). Here, it seems to me, Heidegger's late thinking about thinking, and his reflections on language and poetry, when taken up along a phenomenological path open to dialogue, are among the most valuable things we have in the way of fragments shored against our ruins. For a certain sort of person, myself included, pondering the *Glasperlenspiel* of Heidegger's winding and surprising thought is deeply pleasurable, and such pleasure is nothing to sneeze at these days. But as Rorty put it, this is first of all a "private" matter, not a world-historical "esoteric doctrine" for the *Eingeweihten.*[20] It is *possible* that the words of the poet—be it Hölderlin or some other—may put us on the path to the pressing issues of philosophy today, but phenomenology is what allows us to go along a path *together*, and philosophy is something we share.

NOTES

1. Karl Jaspers, "Letter to the Freiburg University Denazification Committee (December 22, 1945)," in *The Heidegger Controversy: A Critical Reader*, ed. Richard Wolin (New York: Columbia University Press, 1991), 149.

2. The phrase "esoteric philosophy" comes from Peter Trawny, *Adyton: Heideggers esoterische Philosophie* (Berlin: Matthes & Seitz, 2010). See also Steven Crowell, "Reading Heidegger's Black Notebooks," in *Reading Heidegger's Black Notebooks 1931–1941,* ed. Ingo Farin and Jeff Malpas (Cambridge: The MIT Press, 2016), 29–44.

3. Several other contributors to this volume note Heidegger's frustrating resistance to dialogue and call for an end to esotericism. See, for instance, Braver, Dahlstrom, Fried, Gordon, Polt, and Sheehan.

4. In addition to helping us avoid the thoughtless claim that Heidegger's politics is a necessary consequence of the ontology of *Being and Time*, applying this phenomenological measure allows us to see exactly where the pressure of non-phenomenological commitments in *Being and Time* itself distorts the argument. See Steven Crowell, "The Middle Heidegger's Phenomenological Metaphysics," in *The Oxford Handbook of the History of Phenomenology*, ed. Dan Zahavi (Oxford: Oxford University Press, forthcoming).

5. Several contributors to this volume also suggest, in various ways, that phenomenology remains part of what is enduring in Heidegger's legacy (see, for instance, Critchley, Figal, Dahlstrom, Kisiel, Mitchell, Raffoul, Scharff, and Sheehan). Since there are many senses of "phenomenology" in play here, one of the most pressing tasks of philosophy after Heidegger is to think about whether there are core principles at work in this diversity.

6. Martin Heidegger, *Gelassenheit* (Tübingen: Neske, 1977), 13.

7. Heidegger's technical term for such pointing out is "formal indication" (*formale Anzeige*), illuminating accounts of which are given by Hatab and Kisiel (this volume). See also Steven Crowell, *Husserl, Heidegger, and the Space of Meaning: Paths Toward Transcendental Phenomenology* (Evanston, IL: Northwestern University Press, 2001), chapter 7: "Question, Reflection, and Philosophical Method in Heidegger's Early Freiburg Lectures" (pp. 129–51).

8. Steven Crowell, *Normativity and Phenomenology in Husserl and Heidegger* (Cambridge: Cambridge University Press, 2013).

9. Richard Polt's contribution to this volume highlights the connection between the basic feature of Dasein—that in its being that being is at issue for it—and the question of our own responsibility for establishing a "critical distance" from Heidegger's writings. Gregory Fried's reflections on "daring" also point in this direction, and Dennis Schmidt takes up the idea of what it is to be "answerable" for oneself and to others. Drew Hyland's contribution adds a key element here: Though Hyland is criticizing the "ethical and political vacuity" of Heidegger's ontological thinking when he claims, following Plato, that all philosophy is "concerned with the Good," this concern is already implicit in Heidegger's phenomenological analysis of authenticity, becoming explicit in *Vom Wesen des Grundes*. See Crowell, *Normativity and Phenomenology*, Part III.

10. For an example, see Steven Crowell, "Measure-Taking: Meaning and Normativity in Heidegger's Philosophy," *Continental Philosophy Review* 41/3 (2008), 261–76. More generally, *Being and Time's* phenomenological analysis of conscience as taking over being a ground (*Grundsein-übernehmen*) pops up whenever Heidegger comes to discuss how norms or measures function—for instance, in the analysis of the "rift-design" as the instauration of the "struggle between earth and world" in *The Origin of the Work of Art* and in the explanation of why the "destining of revealing" is "danger as such" in *The Question Concerning Technology*.

11. Martin Heidegger, *Four Seminars*, tr. Andrew Mitchell and François Raffoul (Bloomington: Indiana University Press, 2003), 16.

12. Hans-Georg Gadamer, "*Destruktion* and Deconstruction," in *Dialogue and Deconstruction: The Gadamer-Derrida Encounter*, ed. Diane P. Michelfelder and Richard E. Palmer (Albany: SUNY Press, 1989), 107.

13. Martin Heidegger, "The Question Concerning Technology," in *The Question Concerning Technology and Other Essays*, tr. William Lovett (New York: Harper & Row, 1977), 27.

14. See, for instance, Kris McDaniel, "Ways of Being," in *Metametaphysics: New Essays on the Foundations of Ontology*, ed. David J. Chalmers, David Manley, and Ryan Wasserman (Oxford: Oxford University Press, 2009), 290–319. Versions of this idea, starting from Heidegger's "history of being," can be found in Braver and Thomson (this volume).

15. See Crowell, *Husserl, Heidegger, and the Space of Meaning* (2001); Dahlstrom and Sheehan (this volume).

16. François Raffoul addresses this topic in his contribution to this volume, but I am skeptical of what appears to be his view that the "unapparent" is what neither does nor can show itself, the "invisible." In contrast, I think we must recall here Heidegger's claim, in *Being and Time*, that the "phenomenon in the phenomenological sense" (being) is what "proximally and for the most part does not show itself." That is, while being *proximally* and for the *most* part does not show itself, it can and does show itself to a thinking attuned to it. What such self-showing is, and in what kind of first-person experience it becomes salient, are, of course, issues that require careful thought, above all if we wish to extend the *Being and Time* model into Heidegger's later work.

17. In Dahlstrom's terms (this volume), it would not pass the "duck test." For an alternative interpretation, see Richard Capobianco (this volume).

18. Martin Heidegger, "Wissenschaft und Besinnung," in *Vorträge und Aufsätze I* (Tübingen: Neske, 1967), 60.

19. Martin Heidegger, "The Word of Nietzsche: 'God Is Dead," in *The Question Concerning Technology and Other Essays*, tr. William Lovitt (New York: Harper & Row, 1977), 112.

20. Richard Rorty, "Proust, Nietzsche, Heidegger," in *Contingency, Irony, and Solidarity* (Cambridge: Cambridge University Press, 1989), 118–19.

Chapter 21

Still, the Unrest of the Question of Being

Katherine Withy

Being and Time begins by asking, "Do we in our time have an answer to the question of what we really mean by the word 'being' [*seiend*]?" (SZ 1/MR 19). Heidegger's project is thus often understood as an attempt to answer this question of being. But Heidegger immediately goes on to say that the problem is not that we lack an answer to this question so much as that we do not even have a sense of the question: "But are we nowadays even perplexed at our inability to understand the expression 'Being' [*Sein*]? Not at all" (SZ 1/MR 19). Instead of, or at least before, giving us an answer to the question of being, Heidegger wishes to gift us the openness of that question. So, to understand Heidegger's project and to assess what of it, if anything, remains of interest and importance, we must bring ourselves into the experience of the questionability of being and ask whether we still are, or can be, beset by the unrest of that question.

BEING IS PRESENCING

As any true novice knows, one must have a fairly good sense of what is going on before one can feel, much less formulate, a question. To be moved by the question of being, then, we must first have *some* sense for what "being" names. Intuitively, *to be* is to exist or to be real. Since the Greeks, such being real has been thought quasi-temporally as *being present*. Thus Thomas Sheehan reconstructs the genesis of the question of being in this way: the metaphysician looks at entities, which are real or present, and asks what accounts for them as real or present.[1] She answers: realness, presence. Being, as that by virtue of which entities are (real or present) is thus realness or presence. The question of being starts from here, according to Sheehan, and it asks: What is the source of such realness or presence?

But while Sheehan's metaphysician may be portrayed with historical accuracy, she has put her Heideggerian foot wrong. Being is not the realness or presence of things—whether in the most capacious sense of "presence" or in the narrowest sense as some static property of *thereness*, such as substantiality or materiality. Instead, as Heidegger thought the pre-Socratics knew, being is the "emerging and abiding" of entities into and in such presence (e.g., GA 40: 16/16). In plainer language: what accounts for entities as real or present is not their realness or presence but their *being* real or *being* present. Consider that a painter is such by virtue of painting, and a singer by virtue of singing. So too, an entity is an entity—something that *is*—by virtue of is-ing. The painter paints, the singer sings, and the entity *ises*, *bes*, or *presences*. The peculiarity of these locutions reflects the peculiarity of the phenomenon for which we are searching. For while be-ing or is-ing is grammatically just like the painter's painting and the singer's singing, it is ontologically different. It is not something that some entity *does* but the very *doing* that makes for an entity in the first place.

Where can we look for guidance in thinking this odd phenomenon? According to Heidegger, the pre-Socratic insight into being as emerging and abiding has been lost. It persisted into, but deteriorated in, Plato's philosophy. In Plato, the entity emerges and abides in its "look" or form (*eidos*, *idea*) and this emerging and abiding is its "participating" or "sharing" (*metechein*) in the form. But such participating remains deeply mysterious for Plato. He comes to locate true being elsewhere: in the forms themselves. He thus makes the same mistake that Sheehan's metaphysician did. He takes being as an abstract property—such as blueness, or justice, or presence—in which the (blue, just, present) entity participates, instead of the *emerging into* and *abiding in* blueness, justice, or presence.

Heidegger gives no real explanation of why Plato, and following him Aristotle, neglected the dynamic presencing, or emerging and abiding, of entities. But we can see why one might come to do so: language. First, the mere fact that we must use a noun (being, *Sein*) to make the verbal phenomenon of be-ing (*seiend*) the grammatical subject of our sentences, and so the object of our investigation, can mislead us into thinking that we are pursuing an abstract property that entities have (i.e., presence) rather than a happening in which they are implicated (i.e., presencing). Second, Heidegger himself is sometimes led to make this mistake in part because he investigates being in the German language. He thus pursues a verbal phenomenon in a language that is utterly in love with nouns—the more abstract the better. While this penchant for abstraction makes the German language appropriate for certain kinds of philosophizing, it does again encourage one to treat being as an abstract property of entities rather than as their being or is-ing.

Of course, Heidegger struggles mightily against his language in order to preserve the verbal character of being. Many of his more distinctive neologisms are a product of this effort. Still, much of his corpus would need to be rewritten in order to guarantee that any gloss on "being" or "presencing" belonged to the same part of speech and so tracked the same sort of phenomenon. *Being and Time*, for example, is on the right track when it names the entities that we are (with a view toward our distinctive is-ing) "Dasein": being or to be (*sein*) there (*da*). But it errs when it nominates our distinctive is-ing "existence" (*Existenz*) rather than "existing" (*Existieren*). Such existing should in turn be constituted by disclosing (*Erschliessen*) rather than disclosedness (*Erschlossenheit*)—and while such disclosing certainly takes as a component moment understanding (*Verstehen*), it should also include not findliness (*Befindlichkeit*) but finding (*Befinden*). Similarly, the being of the world cannot be worldhood (*Weltlichkeit*) but must be worlding (*Welten*), and the being of equipment must be readying-to-hand or being-ready-to-hand (*Zuhandensein*) rather than readiness-to-hand (*Zuhandenheit*). Such lexical violence is warranted in order to preserve the verbal character of be-ing. Should such violence be charged with hubris, I would only echo Schleiermacher and insist that, after Heidegger, we are in a position to name Heidegger's topic better than he named it himself.

PRESENCING IS MEANINGFUL PRESENCING

To be is to be present, and being is presencing. But what is it to be present? Is it to be meaningfully present to us, or to be present independently of such being meaningful? Richard Capobianco, for example, maintains the latter.[2] According to him, the being of entities is a precondition for, but is not the same as, their showing up meaningfully to us.

Note first that the emerging and abiding of an entity in its form or look—its "look-ing"—is always a looking *for* or *to* someone. Entities *look* or *appear* always for a seeing that receives that look (GA 34: 70/52). This is not just a Platonic point but a phenomenological one. Entities are *ta phainomena*: that which show themselves in themselves (SZ 28/MR 51). Their presencing or is-ing is thus self-showing, and self-showing is inherently dative. Entities show themselves *to* someone. This is why the being, presencing, or self-showing of entities always "needs" Dasein; the two are necessarily correlated. The presencing of entities is not simply their being *there*, available for subsequent encounter, but their being *presented* to someone. Even dinosaurs and distant galaxies are present only by presenting themselves to us—in imagination, through the fossil record, or through infrared light specks. Positing this necessary dative is the distinctive move of phenomenology.

Do entities present themselves to us without being meaningful? Some take the experience of angst to be an experience of precisely this. But angst is properly the experience of one particular entity, Dasein, in its meaningful being what it is—that is, as being-in-the-world (SZ §40). It is because angst is a direct insight into Dasein's being that it must be analyzed in the existential analytic and experienced in order to become authentic.[3] Of course, the flipside or condition of being exposed to its own being is that for Dasein "the totality of the involvements of the ready-to-hand and the present-at-hand discovered within-the-world, is, as such, of no consequence," such that "it collapses into itself" and "the world has the character of completely lacking significance" (SZ 186/MR 231). But Heidegger's point is that angst has an ontological rather than an ontic object. In it, we are concerned with our being and not with the entities we ordinarily engage with. Such entities do not press upon us with their non-meaningfulness (as they might in Sartre's nausea). At most, their meaning (i.e., the totality of involvements) becomes temporarily uncoupled from our projects (i.e., significance). Angst is an experience of ontological insight that disconnects us existentielly from meaningful things. It is not an experience of entities beyond meaning.

Yet the mood of angst does raise the question: Why are there entities at all rather than nothing (GA 40: 3/1; GA 9: 122/96)? One might take *this* to ask about an extra-meaningful presencing of entities: the sheer fact that entities *are*. Richard Polt calls this fact the "excess" of entities.[4] The naked and excessive fact *that* entities are is a sort of substratum for their meaning, and this meaning is in turn identified with *what* entities are.[5] But Heidegger never treats the fact *that* entities are (their that-being, or existing) as a basis for what they are (their what-being, or essencing), and he never limits meaningfulness to entities' what-being alone. There is, in fact, a plurality of modes of that-being, including factuality, facticity, and availability. Each of these is correlated with a particular kind of what-being: presencing-at-hand, existing, and readying-to-hand, respectively. Thus the that-being of entities is always reciprocally implicated in their what-being, making these two dimensions of meaningfulness. As a result, there are as many modes of that-being as there are of what-being: multiple ways in which entities can make sense with regard to the fact that they are. It may be the case that some factuality of bare presence lies behind this multiplicity (SZ 71/MR 101), but even such factuality remains a way in which entities are meaningful to us. Even presencing-at-hand needs and depends on Dasein's understanding of being—as all modes of being, including all modes of that-being, do (SZ 212/MR 255). Indeed, it is *this* remarkable fact that is interrogated in the question of why there are (meaningful) entities (for Dasein) rather than not: the fact that Dasein, as essentially open, is there and so able to co-constitute, by actively receiving, the meaningful presencing of entities. And this fact—Dasein's facticity—consists precisely in Dasein's showing up to itself meaningfully as that and what it is (SZ 56/MR 82).

MEANINGFUL PRESENCING IS BEING HELD UP TO NORMS

All presencing is meaningful presencing, and all entities are meaningfully present in terms of both the fact that they are and what they are. We have thus won some sense of what we are talking about when we ask after being. But we have yet to reach the unrest of that question. We must ask: In what does the meaningful presencing of entities consist? What is it for entities to emerge and abide?

When entities show up to us, they always show up *as* something or other—even if just as the liminal "some sort of thing" or the "I know not what" of the unidentifiable contraption. Heidegger's great insight in *Being and Time* is that entities (other than me) show up *as* something or other in terms of my projects (i.e., Dasein's *for-the-sakes-of-which*). By taking up some possible identity or way of being me—whether being a singer, painter, grandparent, chemist, lover, activist, introvert—I open up a field of possible ways in which things can be meaningful (i.e., the world). Entities can be usable for, serviceable in, or detrimental to (SZ 144/MR 184) my *being* a painter, lover, introvert. They might be *in order to* apply paint to a surface, that *with which* I express my affection, or that *toward which* I aim in conversation (SZ §15). It is because cases of Dasein are in the business of living out concrete identities that entities *can* show up as that and what they are.[6]

Entities *do* show up as that and what they are when I project them onto possibilities. To be a paint brush, for example, is to be *in order to apply paint to a surface*, and an entity shows up as a paint brush when it shows up in terms of—is projected onto—such usability as a possibility. *In order to apply paint to a surface* is a possibility not in that it is potential rather than actual but in that it implicitly lays out what is possible and impossible for an entity that counts as a paint brush: it must be able to make contact with both paint and the painting surface, it must be capable of transferring that paint to that painting surface, it must not introduce foreign elements to or damage the painting surface, it must be wieldable by the painter, and so on. It is because I grasp the entity in terms of this range of possibilities and impossibilities that it shows up to me as that and what it is: a paint brush.

In laying out what is possible and impossible for entities, the possibilities in terms of which entities make sense are normative: they function as ontological standards for counting as that and what entities are. To project entities onto their possibilities is to hold them up to these norms. Entities' showing up as that and what they are is thus a matter of *being held up to norms* or *being grasped in light of norms*. This insight is present already in Plato: the metaphysical participating of entities in the forms is epistemologically rendered as the recollecting of the forms in encountering particular entities. According to the recollection argument in the *Phaedo*, something comes to count as, say, a paint brush, when I grasp that entity, grasp the form of the paint brush, compare the one with the other, and find the entity to "measure up" to the ontological standard (74a). It is in such measuring up to a paradigmatic form that the entity shows up meaningfully as that and what it is.

The question of being thus becomes: What is it for entities to be held up to norms or grasped in light of them?

BEING HELD UP TO NORMS IS . . . QUESTIONABLE

Here, perplexity looms. The meaningful presencing of entities is their being held up to or grasped in light of norms. What does this mean? We are working with a series of metaphors—and mixed ones at that. We do not literally throw (project, *pro* [out, to] + *iacere* [to throw]; *entwerfen*, *ent-* [away from] + *werfen* [to throw]) entities onto possibilities. We do not literally grasp (i.e., touch) things in the (visible) light of something else. We do not even really hold entities up to the light—and in any case, norms do not actually give off light. What, then, is this be-ing of entities? Our ways of speaking of this phenomenon are too saturated in metaphor to give us any real purchase.

The source of these metaphors is plausibly Plato's allegory of the cave, in which the forms are pictured as objects illuminated by the light of the sun (*Republic*, 516a), which represents the form of the good (508b). In Heidegger's framework, the form of the good is the governing identity that Dasein takes up as its for-the-sake-of-which. This is so, first, because (as Aristotle knew) the good is that at which all things aim, just as the for-the-sake-of-which is Dasein's *telos* and that which organizes the world; and second, because Heidegger explicitly identifies the for-the-sake-of-which with the sun in Plato's allegory of the cave (GA 26: 237/184; GA 9: 161/124). To say that the sun illuminates the forms is thus to say that Dasein's chosen identity—whether painter, lover, or introvert—organizes the world, which is exactly what Heidegger does say. The world as a network of possible meanings thus corresponds to the realm of the forms, in light of which we grasp entities. But this in turn means that the forms must themselves be illuminating—which is presumably why Heidegger identifies them with Plato's sun, or the form of the good (GA 34: 57/42–43). But how can the allegory's illuminated objects (i.e., the forms) be identified with the sun that illuminates them (i.e., the form of the good)? How can the possibilities in terms of which entities make sense, such as *in order to apply paint to a surface*, be the same as the identity that Dasein takes up, such as *being a painter*?

How can the forms even be thought as illuminating? Here is one suggestion. As flicking on a light switch makes clear, light traverses and opens up distance. Perhaps the metaphor of illuminating refers to this: to see x in light of y is to traverse the distance between x and y—that is, to *compare* x to y. It would then most properly be *we* who illuminate, not the forms. The light would allegorically represent our comparing the entity with the form.

But in what does this comparing consist? Plato's term *ennoiein* (*Phaedo* 74a) suggests an explicit, cognitive activity, of the sort that we might undertake when we meticulously compare a likeness such as a painting with the original. Yet such explicit comparing does not plausibly take place in ordinary acts of perceiving entities as that and what they are. Further, according to Heidegger, we paradigmatically make sense of entities as that and what they are in our skillfully engaging with them. As he would put it, I grasp the paint brush most fully as a paint brush not when I consider its resemblance to the form of the paint brush, or when I simply perceive it as a paint brush, but when I pick it up and paint with it (cf. SZ 69/MR 98). But where in my *picking up and painting* do I compare the entity with the ontological standard for being a paint brush?

There is a still deeper problem. Whatever our comparing, holding up to, or illuminating consists in, it cannot be some action that I undertake or event that happens. The reason is that the ontological difference between being and entities holds that the meaningful presencing of entities, or my holding them up to the light of ontological standards, is not itself an entity. If it is not an entity, then it cannot be an event that happens or an action that I carry out, since—although they are not the usual examples that we discuss—all actions and events are, after all, entities. They are things that *are*. But what, then, are we looking for? How can we even begin to think what it is to grasp things in light of norms, if this is neither something that we do nor something that happens? What possible path forward is there for thought about being?

Here, we reach *aporia* in the literal sense: there is no (*a*-) way (*poros*) to proceed in thinking through the question of being. Perhaps this is why Plato did not succeed (at least in his exoteric writings) in understanding either participating or recollecting but only in identifying his confusions about them. Thus stilled yet still restless, we reach the perplexity of the question of being.

AND THE QUESTION REMAINS

The question of being asks what we could possibly mean by "being": the meaningful presencing of entities, which is entities' being grasped (or our grasping them) in light of ontological standards. Heidegger attempted to analyze this phenomenon in *Being and Time* and *The Fundamental Concepts of Metaphysics* in terms of projecting entities onto possibilities. Later, he tried to think it as *Ereignis*, the event of the happening of being. But the former attempt stalled and was abandoned, while the latter was more of a designation of the problem than a solution to it. Indeed, Heidegger came to think that being cannot be grasped because it is inherently self-concealing.

Heidegger means many different things when he speaks of concealment and concealing, but the self-concealing of being is (at the very least) the fact that, because it is not an entity, being cannot show up meaningfully.[7] If being cannot show up meaningfully, then our efforts to make sense of it will always be stymied. Yet, as entities for whom all entities show up meaningfully, we are essentially meaning-constituting. Thus we are driven to make sense of being—while always failing to do so. We find ourselves in the curious position that Kant described as being "burdened by questions which [we are] not able to ignore, but which [we are] not able to answer."[8] Being will always be inherently question-worthy for us.

If we are *after* Heidegger in the sense that we are still pursuing the direction of his thought—*out to get* whatever he was after—then our task is to continue to sharpen the questionability of being. But even if we are *after* Heidegger in the sense that we are *over* his thought—whether no longer inspired by his avenues for thinking, or dismayed by his politics, or both—we still cannot stay the question. The question of what it is to grasp things in light of norms is an ontological-epistemological question that extends well beyond the boundaries of Heidegger's philosophizing and has been with us since at least Plato. In whatever sense we are after Heidegger, then, there remains—still—the unrest of the question of being.[9]

NOTES

1. Thomas Sheehan, *Making Sense of Heidegger: A Paradigm Shift* (London: Rowman & Littlefield International, 2015), 14.
2. See, for example, Richard Capobianco, *Heidegger's Way of Being* (Toronto: University of Toronto Press, 2014), as well as his contribution to this volume.
3. See my "The Methodological Role of Angst in *Being and Time*," *Journal of the British Society for Phenomenology* 43:2 (May 2012): 195–211.
4. See, for example, Richard Polt, "Meaning, Excess, and Event," *Gatherings: The Heidegger Circle Annual* 1 (2011): 27.
5. This point is sometimes made in terms of Heidegger's concept of "earth," which I do not have space to address here.

6. The path from what Heidegger says in *Being and Time* to the reading I sketch here is more convoluted than my brief summary suggests. For details, see my "Haugeland's Heidegger and the Metaphysics of Normativity," *European Journal of Philosophy* 25:2 (June 2017): 463–84.

7. For a sketch of a taxonomy of concealments and concealings in Heidegger's thought, see my "Concealing and Concealment in Heidegger," *European Journal of Philosophy*, published online 13 March 2017, DOI: 10.1111/ejop.12236.

8. Immanuel Kant, *Critique of Pure Reason*, tr. Norman Kemp Smith (Boston: The Macmillan Company, 1929), 7 (A vii).

9. Many thanks to the editors of this volume, Gregory Fried and Richard Polt, as well as to Quentin Fisher, for their helpful comments on a draft of this chapter.

Chapter 22

What Is the Meaning of the Meaning of Being?

Simon Critchley

Martin Heidegger's 1927 book *Being and Time* is considered by some (including me) to be the most important and influential work of philosophy written in the twentieth century. Yet, as readers of this monumental and monumentally difficult book know to their cost, there is precious little discussion of the ostensive subject matter of the book—the meaning of being. Heidegger keeps nudging the question of being's meaning into the future, postponing it until it falls over the edge of the published tome. Heidegger focuses rather on trying to define the meaning of the being of that being for whom being is an issue, as he puts it, namely the human being or *Dasein*. Yet, about five chapters into the First Division of the book, Heidegger momentarily pulls back and expands the focus of his concern. He writes:

> If we are inquiring about the meaning of being, our investigation does not then become a 'deep' one [*tiefsinnig*], nor does it puzzle out what stands behind being. It asks about being insofar as being enters into the intelligibility of Dasein. The meaning of being can never be contrasted with entities, or with being as the 'ground' [*'Grund'*] which gives entities support; for a 'ground' becomes accessible only as meaning, even if it is itself the abyss of meaninglessness [*Abgrund der Sinnlosigkeit*]. (SZ 152/MR 193–94, tm)

That is, meaning is not deep. It is not a question of looking behind what appears for some hidden meaning which structures appearance. Inquiry into the meaning of being is not deep either. It just sounds deep. It sounds like we are after a ground, something determinate but hidden, something behind the scenes that pulls the strings of the world's stage. This is what we might call a metaphysical misconstrual of both the meaning of meaning and the possible meaning of the meaning of being. The problem with being-talk is that it sounds as if being has some fantastic agency of its own, or that it is "miraculously transcendent," as Glaucon ironically replies to Socrates as he is about to introduce the three similes for the relation of the soul to the Good at the enigmatic center of the *Republic*.

One can easily be persuaded of the mistaken idea that being is pulling the strings behind the scenes, like some sort of puppet master, and doing amazing things like shaping human action in the world and producing various historical epochs. This is an error. Worse still, it succumbs to the sort of obscurantist temptation that continually seduces readings and readers of Heidegger. Too many readers of Heidegger see being as some kind of rabbit in a hat. There is no rabbit. The point is to learn to see the hat without wanting the rabbit.

Heidegger only asks (*can* only ask) about the meaning of being insofar as being enters into the intelligibility of Dasein, namely into *our* understanding. From the first pages of *Being and Time*, Heidegger characterizes Dasein in terms of its possession of understanding of being (*Seinsverständnis*), although this is admittedly vague and average. So, meaning can only mean insofar as there is Dasein. That is, meaning is Dasein-dependent, or as Heidegger puts it, "Meaning is an existential of Dasein, not a property attaching to entities, lying 'behind' them, or floating somewhere as an 'intermediate domain'" (SZ 151/MR 193, tm). As Heidegger says, meaning is the "upon which" (*das Woraufhin*) in terms of which something becomes intelligible *as* something. But this "upon which" is nothing other than Dasein itself insofar as Dasein lays itself out (*sich auslegt*) as that being that understands meaningfulness.

This is the meaning of interpretation or *Auslegung* in Heidegger, where interpretation is understood as the laying out (*auslegen*) of the understanding, or the act by which understanding becomes aware of itself. In interpretation, Heidegger writes in one of his characteristic tautologies, "understanding appropriates understandingly that which is understood by it [*eignet sich das Verstehen sein Verstandenes verstehend zu*]. In interpretation, understanding does not become something different. It becomes itself" (SZ 148/MR 188). Of course, this is to say that the act of interpretation is retroactive: it is the retroactivity or reactivation of a prior understanding. Here we enter what Heidegger sees as the hermeneutic circle. Interpretation already understands, and what interpretation lays out is already understood and must have been already understood. Heidegger suggests that interpretation differs from what we might call "normal" scientific proof, or the logic of discovery, where it is illegitimate to presuppose what it is our task to provide grounds for. With everyday human life in the world, or what we may call "social being" (Heidegger would be rightly suspicious of the seeming self-evidence of the concept "social"), it is precisely the other way around and we have to presuppose that which we provide grounds for, namely understanding. We are always stuck in a circle, and it is therefore a question of entering the circle in the right way and not trying to get out of it.

I think this is also profoundly true of poetry (not *all* poetry, obviously, but some), which can be said to move within a hermeneutic circle. The poet issues reminders for what we already know and interprets what we already understand but have not made explicit. Poetry takes things as they are and as they are understood by us, but in a way that we have covered over through force of habit, a contempt born of familiarity, or what Fernando Pessoa's heteronym Alberto Caeiro calls "a sickness of the eyes." Poetry returns us to our familiarity with things through the defamiliarization of poetic saying; it provides what Caeiro calls "lessons in unlearning," where we finally see what is under our noses. What the poet discovers is what we knew already, but had covered up: the world in its plain simplicity and palpable presence. In this way, we can perhaps reach lucidity. But this lucidity is not a propositional explicitness, it is not the cognitive awareness that water is everywhere and at all times two parts hydrogen to one part oxygen, or that Benjamin Franklin was the inventor of the lightning rod. It is rather a lucidity at the level of feeling, of what Heidegger calls mood (*Stimmung*), that the poetic word articulates without making cognitively explicit, as when Pessoa writes in a text on sensationism, "Lucidity should only reach the threshold of the soul. In the very antechambers of feeling it is forbidden to be explicit." Poetry produces felt variations in the appearances of things that return us to the understanding of things that we endlessly pass over in our desire for knowledge.

Now, Heidegger's inquiry into the human being is phenomenological, it is concerned with trying to elicit Dasein's being-in-the-world phenomenologically. Crucially, this is also not a deep inquiry. Heidegger defines the Greek word *phainomenon* as "that which shows itself" and *logos* as "that which lets see." Therefore, phenomenology is that which lets us see what shows itself, which is a tautology, as Heidegger was perfectly well aware. Phenomenology also moves within the hermeneutic circle, and this is not a matter of occult, hidden, or deep meanings; it is a question of surfaces. The phenomena, as those surfaces that show themselves, have to be brought to appearance through the activity of *logos* or what Heidegger calls discourse, talk, or *Rede*, which is perhaps the most important and elusive concept in *Being and Time*. (The word was common in Shakespearean English, as when Ophelia suspects that her brother Laertes is being one of those moral hypocrites who "recks not his own rede.") It is discourse that lets us see what shows itself; it is the activity of talking that reactivates our prior and a priori understanding of things.

Yet, if I say that phenomenology is not deep inquiry, then that does not mean that it is superficial. Phenomenology is the refusal of metaphysical or mystical depth and the cultivation of surfaces. It is a matter of opening one's eyes and seeing the palpably obvious fact of the world that faces one and that one faces. Human life in the world is two surfaces that touch and resonate each with the other. Or perhaps life in the world is two faces of the same surface, the unity of the phenomenon of being-in-the-world that Heidegger fervently wants to preserve and which philosophy continually splits apart into mind and world, subject and object, *res cogitans* and *res extensa*, or soul and things.

Phenomenology gives lessons in unlearning that allow us to relearn how to see the world. Now, in my fancy at least, I want to imagine poetry as phenomenology, as an art of surfaces or the cultivation of what we might call *surfaciality*. The problem is that these surfaces only show themselves with great difficulty, they are enigmatic surfaces that come to appearance through the felt variations that flow from the poet's words. I think this is what Heidegger has in mind in an important sentence from the discussion of *Rede* or discourse in *Being and Time*:

> In 'poetical' [*'dichtenden'*] discourse, the communication of the existential possibilities of one's state-of-mind can become an aim in itself, and this amounts to a disclosing of existence. (SZ 162/MR 205)

Poetry, in the broad sense of *Dichtung* or creation, is the disclosure of existence, the difficult bringing to appearance of the fact that things exist. By listening to the poet's words, we are drawn outside and beyond ourselves to a condition of being there with things where they do not stand over against us as objects, but where we stand with those things in an experience of what I like to call, with a nod to Rilke, *openedness*, a being open to things, an interpretation which is always already an understanding (hence the past tense) in the *surfacial* space of disclosure.

If this sounds a little mystical, then I'd like to say with Caeiro, *está bem, tenho-o*—"that's fine, I have it." If there is a mystery to things, then it is not at all other-worldly, or some mysticism of the hidden. On the contrary, the mystery of things is utterly of this world, and the labor of the poet consists in the difficult elaboration of the space of existence, the openedness within which we stand.

Of course, one might respond that Caeiro (and maybe Heidegger too) is simply replacing one kind of mysticism with another: that is, rejecting an other-worldly mysticism of the transcendent beyond with the here-and-now mysticism of immanent presence. To which Caeiro might also say, *está bem*; his would be a mysticism of the bodily presence of things to the senses. The contrast is between what we might call a mysticism of gnosis that claims to see beyond appearances to their invisible source of meaning and an agnostic mysticism that just sees appearance. Caeiro does not claim to *know* anything about nature; he simply sings what he sees:

Se quiserem que eu tenha um misticismo, está bem, tenho-o.
Sou místico, mas só com o corpo.
A minha alma é simples e não pensa.

O meu misticismo é não querer saber.
É viver e não pensar nisso.

Não sei o que é a Natureza: canto-a.
Vivo no cimo dum outeiro
Numa casa caiada e sozinha,
E essa é a minha definição.

If you'd like me to have a mysticism, that's fine, I have it.
I'm a mystic, but only with the body.
My soul is simple and doesn't think.

My mysticism is not wanting to know.
It is to live and not to think about this.

I don't know what nature is: I sing it.
I live on the top of a small hill
In a whitewashed and solitary house,
And this is my definition.

For Caeiro, we need an apprenticeship in unlearning in order to learn to see and not to think. We need to learn to see appearances and nothing more, and to see those appearances not as the appearances of some deeper, but veiled reality, but as *real* appearances. Of course, it is often hugely difficult to even see those appearances as our vision becomes obscured by habit, by what Pascal called the machine. Such machinic habit is what Caeiro calls the "sickness of the eyes" that happens when we think and do not see: *Pensar é estar doente dos olhos*. In our sickness, we pass over what is most *obvious*, most familiar and closest to us, namely the phenomenon of the world, the fact that things simply are, in their plain, palpable, and everyday presence. What Caeiro counsels, and one finds similar advice in Wallace Stevens, is that we give up both the skeptical and metaphysical impulses that are distrustful of the world of appearances. If we follow the path of Caeiro's lessons in unlearning, then what we might learn to cultivate is the art of appearances, the prose of things that surround us, those things that escape our attention because of their sheer obviousness, because they are under our noses.

That is, we understand things already, always already as Heidegger might add, and the purpose of the poem or of thinking is to point this out. This means that poetry, as nothing more but nothing less than the enactment of the poem itself, is the pointing out of that which we understand already, but have forgotten or passed over. That is, the poem gives us reminders; it functions as what I like to call, following my teacher Frank Cioffi, "everyday anamnesis," the recollection that brings us back to the fact that things are what they really seem to be. Such a notion of anamnesis does not, as it might do on a certain caricatural metaphysical reading of Plato, invoke the existence of some world behind the scenes, some invisible and hidden meaning that supports visible and manifest meaningfulness. On the contrary, as Caeiro insists, "Things have no meaning," *As cousas não têm significação*, in the sense of a hidden signification. What we can say of them, what the poet says of them, is that they exist, or better that they *have* existence, *têm existência*. Things merely are—or better, they are in and through their mere existence in the world. Everyday anamnesis returns us to the recalcitrant and enigmatic surfaces of things.

Chapter 23

The Future of Thought

Of a Phenomenology of the Inapparent

François Raffoul

To reflect on what comes "after Heidegger," to address the question, "What do you consider to be the most pressing and the most interesting tasks for philosophy after Heidegger?" is to reflect on the future and the possibilities of thought that he has opened for us. Precisely, I would like in the following pages to reflect on the future of thought itself—on "futural thought" (which Heidegger calls at times "preparatory thinking," GA 14: 75/60) or "the thinking that is to come" (*das künftige Denken*, GA 9: 364/276)—by focusing on the motif of phenomenology. Indeed, in "My Way to Phenomenology" (1963), Heidegger makes the claim that phenomenology is not a given school or movement in philosophy, not a past discipline or method, but a possibility for the future of thought.

> And today? The age of phenomenological philosophy seems to be over. It is already taken as something past which is only recorded historically along with other schools of philosophy. But in what is most its own phenomenology is not a school. It is the possibility of thinking, at times changing and only thus persisting, of corresponding to the claim of what is to be thought. (GA 14: 101/82)

This of course echoes the famous pronouncement from *Being and Time*, in which Heidegger stated that the "essential character of phenomenology does not consist in its actuality as a philosophical 'movement,' " and that "We can understand phenomenology solely by seizing upon it as a possibility" (SZ 38). In an addition from 1969 to the essay "My Way to Phenomenology," Heidegger himself referred to that passage, reiterating the claim that phenomenology is to be approached in its *possibility* and not as actuality (GA 14: 101/82). What would it mean for phenomenology, indeed for the future of thought, if it were indeed seized as possibility? What of these possibilities for phenomenology? Heidegger always remained faithful to this promise of phenomenology, which explains why he returned to it even in the last seminars to characterize his own path of thinking. Remaining faithful to the promise of phenomenology, he thereby profoundly transformed the senses in which phenomenology ought to be taken. I would like in the following pages to delineate this possible future of phenomenology as Heidegger approaches it, namely as what he called in a late seminar a "phenomenology of the inapparent" (*Phänomenologie des Unscheinbaren*) (GA 15: 399/80). What will be most striking is to discover how this very withdrawal, this "refusal," is constitutive of the future of thought.

Phenomenology is traditionally considered to be a thought of presence, assigned to a phenomenon that is identified with the present being, or with an object for consciousness. The very term "phenomenon" has its roots in the Greek verb *phainesthai*, "to appear," "to show itself." As a middle-voice construction of *phainō*, *phainesthai* means to bring to light, to place in brightness, where something can become visible and manifest. The phenomena are thus the "totality of what lies in the light of day or can be brought to light."[1] One may conclude from these passages that by definition the phenomenon is what appears and shows itself, and shows itself to a perceiver or to a consciousness. The phenomenon would be synonymous with presence itself, with what manifests itself in a presence that can be attested in a conscious experience. Indeed, is consciousness itself nothing but a form of presence, that is, a presence to self? As Jacques Derrida remarks: "But what is consciousness? What does 'consciousness' mean? Most often, in the very form of meaning, in all its modifications, consciousness offers itself to thought only as self-presence, as the perception of self in presence," which also explains why the "privilege granted to consciousness therefore signifies the privilege granted to the present."[2] Phenomenology would be a thought of presence, and of presence to consciousness (itself, then, a form of presence). However, I will suggest in the following pages that phenomenology is haunted by the presence of a certain unappearing dimension, a claim that was made by Heidegger in his last seminar in 1973, when he characterized the most proper sense of phenomenology as a "phenomenology of the inapparent." Such "inapparent" names a certain alterity that escapes presentation, and which yet belongs to the phenomenon, and to phenomenology as such. I will attempt to show in what sense the "inapparent" plays a role in phenomenality and in phenomenology, and then suggest that such a withdrawal harbors the possibilities of a future.

As just mentioned, a certain presence of the *inapparent* can be traced in Heidegger's very definition of the phenomenon, and indeed of phenomenology. This claim might seem at first paradoxical and even go against the very definition that Heidegger gives of the phenomenon in §7 of *Being and Time*: "Thus we must *keep in mind* that the expression '*phenomenon*' signifies that which shows itself in itself, the manifest" (SZ 28). Now, we should clarify from the outset that a phenomenon for Heidegger, that is, the phenomenon with which phenomenology is concerned, cannot be reduced to an empirical intuition or an ontical given, to a present being. In fact, Heidegger rejects explicitly the Kantian notion of an "empirical intuition" to designate the phenomenon with which phenomenology is concerned (SZ 31). Why? Because the phenomenon is approached by Heidegger *in its verbal sense*, that is, as that which shows or manifests itself of itself and from itself. The phenomenon is defined as "the-showing-itself-in-itself" (*das Sich-an-ihm-selbst-zeigen*) (SZ 31), and not simply as the ontical given or as the entity. The term "phenomenon" thus immediately refers to the event of a self-showing, and the "given" is consequently assigned to the event of its *giving*. A phenomenological approach to the phenomenon is not turned toward the ontic phenomenon, but rather toward the event of its manifestation. This is why phenomenology is not about beings but about the *being* of beings. For Heidegger, phenomenology is the very method of ontology, and the phenomena are to be referred not to a constituting consciousness, but to the *event* of being as such. Unlike his former mentor, Husserl, Heidegger defines phenomenology in relation to ontology, as giving us access to the being of beings. "With regard to its subject-matter, phenomenology is the science of the being of entities—ontology" (SZ 37). In turn, and most importantly, "*Ontology is possible only as phenomenology*" (SZ 35). Indeed, Heidegger stresses that phenomenology is concerned about the *being* of phenomena, their modes of givenness, or of happening. Phenomenology is thus rigorously approached as *ontology*, that is, concerned with being in its event.

In this ontological understanding of phenomenology (phenomenology as concerned with the being of beings), the emphasis shifts from phenomena (things) to the *being* of these phenomena (their happening or eventfulness), from phenomena to phenomenality. As Jean-Luc Marion clarifies, phenomenology consists in showing not the appearance itself, but the *appearing* in the appearance: "If in the realm of metaphysics it is a question of proving, in the phenomenological realm it is not a question of simply showing (since in this case apparition could still be the object of a gaze, therefore a mere appearance), but rather of letting apparition show *itself* in its appearance according to its appearing."[3] Such a phenomenology would bring to light the appearing of appearances, and bring to light what Françoise Dastur calls "the conditions of all appearing."[4] Here one glimpses for the first time the presence of the inapparent in phenomenology: the phenomenon is not the appearance but the appearing of the appearance, an appearing that, precisely because it itself is not an appearance, *does not appear*. Because such appearing is not itself an appearance, because, in other words, *it does not appear*, it could be said to be invisible, although, as Dastur remarks (following Merleau-Ponty), we are here speaking of an invisibility *of* the world, and not a metaphysical, transcendent invisibility. Merleau-Ponty wrote famously in *The Visible and the Invisible* that the invisible is "not a *de facto* invisible, like an object hidden behind another, and not an absolute invisible, which would have nothing to do with the visible. Rather it is the invisible *of* this world, that which inhabits this world, sustains it, and renders it visible, its own and interior possibility, the Being of this being."[5] The invisible is "an idea that is not the contrary of the sensible," but rather "its lining and its depth."[6] There is thus an invisibility *of* the visible, an invisibility of phenomenality itself, concealed and nonetheless sheltered in the visible.

By understanding being in distinction from beings, Heidegger allows us to approach being itself as an event, the event of presence. Although in the tradition being was indeed understood as presence, *Anwesenheit*, its eventfulness was nonetheless "repressed" through the reference to *constant* presence (*beständige Anwesenheit*), or substantiality; Heidegger thus speaks of how the temporal meaning of *Anwesenheit* was "repressed" (*abgedrängt*) in the tradition of substantiality (GA 34: 144/104).[7] Now, the very movement of presence seems to harbor a certain *withdrawal*. In fact, the very term *Anwesenheit* reveals a withdrawal at the heart of manifestation. The *an-* in *An-wesen* or *An-wesenheit* suggests a coming into presence, a movement, a motion, from concealment to unconcealment, from withdrawal to visibility. Thus, to characterize a being as *an-wesend* (which "is to implicitly understand presence as an *event*"[8]), also shows that the preposition *an*, as Dastur notes, "indicates a movement of approach that enters in a conflict with a movement of withdrawal,"[9] a play between unconcealment and concealment already captured by the Greeks in the contrast between the prepositions *para* and *apo* in *parousia* and *apousia*. This implies, in turn, a break with the model of constant presence, that is, with a kind of "stability" that represses the temporal happening in the phenomenon of presence, including the phenomenon of withdrawal that seems to affect, each time, the event of presence. This is why Heidegger could write that the phenomenon, precisely as that which is to be made phenomenologically visible, does not *show itself*. "And just because the phenomena are proximally and for the most part *not* given, there is need for phenomenology" (SZ 36). The very concept of phenomenology, insofar as it is defined as a "letting something be seen," necessarily implies the withdrawal of the phenomenon.

Indeed, if phenomenology is a "letting be seen" (*sehen lassen*), then the phenomenon of phenomenology cannot be simply that which is apparent or manifest; the phenomenon, precisely as that which is to be made phenomenologically visible, *does not show itself*, while nonetheless belonging to what shows itself, for Heidegger also stresses that " 'behind' the phenomena of phenomenology there is essentially nothing else" (SZ 36). What does not appear in the phenomenon is not some noumenal reality hidden behind the phenomenon, but a dimension that belongs to it.

> What is it that must be called a "phenomenon" in a distinctive sense? What is it that by its very essence is *necessarily* the theme whenever we exhibit something *explicitly*? Manifestly, it is something that proximally and for the most part does *not* show itself at all: it is something that lies *hidden*, in contrast to that which proximally and for the most part does show itself; but at the same time it is something that belongs to what thus shows itself, and it belongs to it so essentially as to constitute its meaning and its ground. (SZ 35)

Now, for Heidegger, what does not appear in what appears is its *being*: "Yet that which remains *hidden* in an egregious sense, or which relapses and gets *covered up* again, or which shows itself only '*in disguise*,' is just not this entity or that, but rather the being of entities" (SZ 38). Let us note here that Heidegger explained in *On the Way to Language* that *Ereignis* was the least apparent of such inapparent: "The *Ereignis ist das Unscheinbarste des Unscheinbaren*—the least apparent of the inapparent" (the English translation has: *Ereignis* "is itself the most inconspicuous of inconspicuous phenomena") (GA 12: 247/128). This accounts for Heidegger's late pronouncement: phenomenology, in its very essence, is a *phenomenology of what does not appear, a phenomenology of the inapparent.*

Being, in its advent, is concealed. Indeed, the structures of the being of beings are not accessible in some kind of immediate clarity, are not presented to some pure, contemplative gaze, which accounts for the task of an existential analytic as a hermeneutics: an opacity affects Dasein's being, requiring a hermeneutic (and "destructive" or de-constructive) approach.[10] Indeed, Dasein's "privilege," that is, the fact that it comes to the fore in the ontological inquiry, does not mean that it would be immediately and fully accessible in its *being*. On the contrary, Heidegger emphasizes a paradoxical structure by which the ontical proximity to one's own self is always accompanied by an ontological distance and obscurity. This structure can be read in all its enigmatic simplicity in this passage from §5 of *Being and Time*: "Dasein is ontically 'closest' to itself and ontologically farthest; but pre-ontologically, it is surely not a stranger" (SZ 16). Dasein is "closest" to itself because it is, itself, that entity. This ontical proximity to one's self nevertheless cannot provide an appropriate *access* to Dasein's *being*. On the contrary, it takes place in a vague and ordinary understanding that obscures the most proper constitution of our being. This is why Heidegger adds: "In spite of this, *or rather, for just this reason*, it is ontologically that which is farthest" (SZ 15, em). Dasein's ontological opaqueness or distance from itself must be referred to its tendency to understand itself on the basis of the simply given being, and it is *against* this tendency that its being could be elucidated.

This is indeed why there is a need for a genuine *phenomenological forcing*, the goal of which is to elucidate, to bring to light and to uncover that which remains hidden, covered over, or dissimulated. There is thus an unavoidable *violence* of thought or interpretation. This necessity of a philosophical violence turned *against* the self-concealment of being is described in the early courses Heidegger gave when he was engaged in the so-called "hermeneutics of factical life." It was then a matter for him of deriving "the phenomenological interpretation out of the facticity of life itself" (GA 61: 87/66). Now life is characterized by a constant moving-away from itself (*Abfallen*), a constant fleeing from itself. Life is "inclined" toward the world, and this inclination takes the form of a "propensity" to becoming absorbed in the world, and be taken along by it—a movement that is a falling away. Heidegger speaks indeed of this falling away, which he characterizes as "ruinance," as "the ownmost character of movement belonging to life." In this movement of falling away into ruins, life is opened to its own possibility and becomes an issue for itself in an originary self-estrangement. We recall in this respect how in the 1929–1930 lecture course, drawing from Novalis, Heidegger defined philosophy as homesickness (*Heimweh*), exiled as it is in the "not-at-home" of expropriated existence (GA 29/30: 7–8/5–7). *Homelessness* is the origin of philosophy. Thinking begins in life's self-estrangement or *expropriation* from itself, and is itself a part of this movement of life, a sort of *countermovement*, a response to the event of life, a counter-event to such event. That is the origin of what Heidegger calls the "counter-motion" of thought, going against life's "own" tendency to fall into expropriation. Thinking originates from the need to go counter to life's tendency to move away from itself. Heidegger writes of "the constant *struggle* of factical, philosophical interpretation *against its own factical ruinance*, a struggle that accompanies the process of the actualization of philosophizing" (GA 61: 114). Thought: a movement going against life's ruinance. Thought is counter-ruinance. "Phenomenological interpretation . . . manifests by its very essence a 'counter-movedness'" (GA 61: 99). Thought is a counterviolence to the originary violence of the ruinance and self-estrangement of life. The violence of interpretation responds to the violence of the self-estrangement of life and goes against it.

In *Being and Time*, the necessity of this violence was explained by reference to Dasein's hermeneutic situation: the ontological interpretation of this being must go "against" its own tendency to conceal, and can only be "won," Heidegger explains, by "following an opposite course" from the tendency that distances Dasein from its being by throwing it toward beings. "The laying-bare of Dasein's primordial being must rather be *wrested* from Dasein by following the opposite course from that taken by the falling ontico-ontological tendency of interpretation" (SZ 311). The existential analytic thus recognizes its phenomenological violence. "Dasein's *kind of*

Being thus *demands* that any ontological Interpretation which sets itself the goal of exhibiting the phenomena in their primordiality *should capture the being of this entity, in spite of this entity's own tendency to cover things up.* Existential analysis, therefore, constantly has the character of *doing violence*, whether to the claims of the everyday interpretation, or to its complacency and its tranquilized obviousness" (SZ 311). Thought is a struggle with this obscurity, this inapparence, this concealment. *Phenomenology is a wrestling with the inapparent.*

The entire phenomenological problematic is thus rooted in the concealment of being, its *non-appearing*. In a passage from the essay "*Moira*," Heidegger thus speaks of how the play of the calling, brightening, expanding light "is not actually visible." That play, he writes, "shines imperceptibly [*scheint so unscheinbar*], like morning light upon the quiet splendor of lilies in a field or roses in a garden" (GA 7: 256/EGT 96). Being withdraws to only let the being appear. As Heidegger puts it in a crucial passage from "Anaximander's Saying" (repeating that statement twice in the essay), stating a veritable law of the givenness of being: "By revealing itself in the being, being withdraws [*Das Sein entzieht sich, indem es sich in das Seiende entbirgt*]" (GA 5: 337/253–54). Heidegger posits that being is the mystery because "Being itself withdraws [*entzieht sich*] into its truth. It saves [*birgt*] itself in its truth and conceals [*verbirgt*] itself in such shelter [*Bergen*]" (GA 5: 265/197 tm). This is why in the essay "Nietzsche's Word: 'God is Dead,' " Heidegger also clarifies: "Being does not come to the light of its own essence. In the appearance of beings as such, being itself stays away. The truth of being escapes us. It remains forgotten" (GA 5: 264/197).

With respect to this forgetting, Heidegger distinguishes between the concealment proper to metaphysics (which "is the oblivion of Being," GA 14: 50/41) and the concealment proper to *Ereignis*: "the concealment which belongs to metaphysics as its limit must belong to Appropriation [*Ereignis*] itself. That means that the withdrawal which characterized metaphysics in the form of the oblivion of Being now shows itself as the dimension of concealment itself" (GA 14: 50/41). The difference between the two concealments lies in whether the concealment itself is concealed or not! Whereas in metaphysics there is a forgetting of the forgetting, since the withdrawal of being itself withdraws ("Metaphysics is the oblivion of Being, and that means the history of the concealment and withdrawal of that which gives Being," GA 14: 50/41), in the thinking of the truth of being such concealment is meditated upon and *remembered*: "now this concealment does not conceal itself. Rather, the attention of thinking is concerned with it" (GA 14: 50/41). Indeed, Heidegger determines the thinking of being, as early as *Being and Time*, as a *remembering*, which is itself to be understood paradoxically as a standing in oblivion. Remembering is not the overcoming of oblivion, but its *guarding*:

one remembers that there is forgetting, *and nothing else*. Heidegger's thinking is grappling with an irreducible concealment and expropriation at the heart of the event of being. This is why, as we noted, Heidegger characterized phenomenology as a phenomenology of the inapparent: "We are here in the domain of the inapparent: presencing itself presences . . . phenomenology is a path that leads away before . . ., and it lets that before which it is led show itself. This phenomenology is a phenomenology of the inapparent" (GA 15: 399/80).

Phenomenology is now assigned to a secret or mystery, as Heidegger recognizes in "My Way to Phenomenology" (1963):

> And today? The age of phenomenological philosophy seems to be over. It is already taken as something past which is only recorded historically along with other schools of philosophy. But in what is most its own phenomenology is not a school. It is the possibility of thinking, at times changing and only thus persisting, of corresponding to the claim of what is to be thought. If phenomenology is thus experienced and retained, it can disappear as a designation in favor of the matter of thinking [*Sache des Denkens*] whose manifestness remains *a mystery* [*Geheimnis*]. (GA 14: 101/82, em).

We see here how the future and possibility of thinking is associated with the presence of the inapparent, of the mystery that emerges in the event of being. This conjunction of the mystery and the opening of a future is best captured in a famous passage from *What is Called Thinking?* where Heidegger states that "Most thought-provoking in our thought-provoking time is that we are still not thinking" (GA 8: 7/6). We are still not thinking because what must be thought about turns away from the human being and "withdraws from him." In fact, being happens by and in withdrawing. Being is the withdrawal, being withdraws (GA 8: 10/8), and from such a withdrawal it calls us . . . to think: *the future of thought arises out of the withdrawal of being*. "Whatever withdraws, refuses arrival. But withdrawing is not nothing. Withdrawal is an event. In fact, what withdraws may even concern and claim man more essentially than anything present that strikes and touches him" (GA 8: 10/9). The event of withdrawal is what opens the future of thought, it is what makes us think: "What withdraws from us, draws us along by its very withdrawal, whether or not we become aware of it immediately, or at all" (GA 8: 11/9). As if the future of thought was harbored in the withdrawal that refuses thinking: "Thinking must first learn what remains reserved and in store for thinking to get involved in. It prepares its own transformation in this learning" (GA 14: 75/60). As if the future itself lodged in what is held in reserve, as if it is only by dwelling in the mystery that a future becomes possible.

Let us in closing gesture toward such a future by evoking the ethics that is involved in this presence of the inapparent in phenomenology. Derrida evokes an ethics of the secret (the French *secret* translates Heidegger's *Geheimnis*). There is no knowledge of the secret, but there is, Derrida suggests, an *ethics* of the secret, a respect and a responsibility for the secret. Indeed, the demand for the revealing of a secret, the demand that the other confess, for instance, that he or she explain him - or herself and reveal his or her secret, may be the greatest violence. "Is there any worse violence than that which consists in calling for the response, demanding that one *give an account of* everything, and preferably *thematically?*"[11] In fact, the secret is non-thematizable, "not phenomenalizable." The secret is not a phenomenon, in the sense of what can become present, although its inappearance does not mean that it belongs to some noumenal realm. Not locatable, not presentable, not knowable, it is the object of *respect*: one must respect the secret, not do violence to its withdrawal, its non-appearing. "Nowadays, there is perhaps an ethical and political duty to respect the secret, a certain kind of right to a certain kind of secret," writes Derrida. The lack of respect for the secret is a quest for total transparency (and thus for control), the sign of any totalitarianism, which can also *use* and instrumentalize the secret: "The totalitarian vocation is manifested as soon as this respect is lost. All the same—and this is where the difficulty comes in—there are also forms of abuse in relation to the secret, political exploitations of the 'state secret,' like the exploitations of 'reasons of state,' and police or other archives."[12] This responsibility to a secret is developed in Heidegger's thought, which, it is perhaps not stressed enough, entails a major thought of responsibility, as I have tried to argue elsewhere.[13] The response to a call, whether the call of conscience in *Being and Time* or the address of being in later writings, is always a response to what remains *inappropriable* in such calls.

In its very eventfulness, being withdraws is the mystery: such a withdrawal, Heidegger stresses, *calls us*. Responsibility to being would then be a responsibility to a secret and an inappropriability. Responsibility is the "carrying" of the inappropriability or unpresentability—the secret—of being. This secret of being represents an unappearance that constantly haunts phenomenology, to which it belongs, and which constitutes, whether it knows it or not, its very future.

NOTES

1. SZ 28. I will draw from both extant English translations (MR and SS).
2. Jacques Derrida, "*Différance*," in *Margins of Philosophy*, tr. Alan Bass (Chicago: University of Chicago Press, 1984), 16.
3. Jean-Luc Marion, *Being Given: Toward a Phenomenology of Givenness*, tr. Jeffrey L. Kosky (Stanford: Stanford University Press, 2002), 8.

4. Françoise Dastur, "Phenomenology of the Event: Waiting and Surprise," *Hypatia* 15:4 (Fall 2000), 181.

5. Maurice Merleau-Ponty, *The Visible and the Invisible*, tr. Alphonso Lingis (Evanston, IL: Nortwestern University Press, 1968), 151.

6. Ibid., 149.

7. The English translation reads: "The concept of being loses its primordial innermost meaning, i.e., presence; the *temporal* moment is completely shaken off."

8. Françoise Dastur, "Présent, présence et événement chez Heidegger," in *Heidegger, le danger et la promesse*, ed. G. Bensussan and J. Cohen (Paris: Kimé, 2006), 121.

9. Ibid., 121.

10. "Philosophy is universal phenomenological ontology, taking its departure from the hermeneutic of Dasein" that is an "analysis of *existence* [Existenz]" (SZ 38).

11. Jacques Derrida, "Passions," in *On the Name* (Stanford, CA: Stanford University Press, 1995), 25.

12. Jacques Derrida, *Paper Machine* (Stanford, CA: Stanford University Press, 2005), 162.

13. See my *The Origins of Responsibility* (Bloomington: Indiana University Press, 2010).

Part VI

THINKING WITH LATE HEIDEGGER

Chapter 24

On the Essence and Concept of *Ereignis*

From Technē *to Technicity*

William McNeill

In what follows, we shall think after Heidegger in attempting to follow what is indicated by the keyword of his mature thinking, namely, *Ereignis*.

Heidegger famously remarks that the term *Ereignis* has been the guiding word of his thinking from 1936 on, a date that coincides with his beginning to write the *Contributions to Philosophy (Of Ereignis)*. In the present chapter, I shall attempt to argue the following: (1) That Heidegger's appropriation of the concept of *Ereignis* has its roots in his 1934–1935 reading of Hölderlin; (2) that the meaning of *Ereignis* is essentially related to the problem of the origin of the work of art; (3) that *Ereignis* does mean, and may appropriately be translated as "event," contrary to what is sometimes claimed; (4) that this "event" is never anything actual, nor can it be understood in terms of actuality; and (5) that *Ereignis* must be understood in relation to the temporality of the enigmatic *poiēsis*, or "bringing-forth," at the root of *technē*, the Greek word for the kind of know-how enabling both works of art and products of utility. *Ereignis* is thus also implicated in that outgrowth of *technē* that is modern technicity. In examining these points, I will move from the first Hölderlin course, via the "Origin of the Work of Art," to the *Contributions* and the later writings on technicity as the essence of technology. I conclude with some remarks on the significance of this thematic for thinking "after Heidegger."[1]

In a marginal note to his 1946 essay "Letter on 'Humanism,'" Heidegger remarks that "since 1936, '*Ereignis*' has been the guiding word of my thinking" (GA 9: 316/241). The note implies that Heidegger's use of the term *Ereignis* to designate the key to his thinking coincides with the writing of the text known as *Contributions to Philosophy (Of Ereignis)*, a series of reflections composed during the years 1936–1938. While this may be true, it should not, however, obscure the fact that Heidegger's use of the word *Ereignis* has its roots in his earlier reading of the poet Hölderlin in 1934–1935, and that the term is also used in the 1936 essays "The Origin of the Work of Art" and "Hölderlin and the Essence of Poetizing."[2] This genesis of the term *Ereignis* in Heidegger's thinking suggests that this concept is intrinsically bound to the question of art—in Greek, *technē*—and more specifically to the *poiēsis* that lies at the "origin" of the work of art and the happening of truth that occurs therein. It should come as no surprise, then, not only that *Ereignis* in the *Contributions* is repeatedly characterized in terms of the strife of world and earth that was regarded as central to art and poetizing in those earlier texts, but also that Heidegger later returns to Hölderlin when meditating on *Ereignis* in relation to technicity, as another historically configured form of *technē*. In what follows, I attempt to trace something of the genesis of Heidegger's appropriation of the term *Ereignis* in the texts predating the *Contributions*, and to show how this genesis remains critical to understanding what this concept means in the later Heidegger (as well as what it does not mean). It should go without saying that a short chapter such as this cannot claim to give an exhaustive account of the problematic. It limits itself to outlining the essential features of what I take to characterize Heidegger's thinking of *Ereignis*.

In his first lecture course on Hölderlin, on Hölderlin's hymns "Germania" and "The Rhine," Heidegger reflects on Hölderlin's understanding of the time that characterizes authentic creators—poets, thinkers, and the founders of a state, each of whom ground in their own way the historical Dasein of a people. The times of these creators are "the peaks of time," times of supreme solitude, of a dwelling on the mountain peaks exposed to the lightning flashes of the gods—the gods themselves, however, being nothing other than time. Meditating on these lightning flashes of time, Heidegger cites the lines from Hölderlin's hymn "Mnemosyne" that read, "Lang ist/Die Zeit, es ereignet sich aber/Das Wahre": "Long is/The time, yet what is true/Comes to pass."

If the time of the everyday is long in the sense of the "long while" of boredom (*Langeweile*), the time on the peaks is long in a different sense, remarks Heidegger, as a preparation and awaiting of the event (*Ereignis*) whereby what is true comes to pass. Heidegger even underlines the word *Ereignis* in this context:

> The time of the peaks is long, because on the peaks reigns a persistent waiting for and awaiting *the event* [Ereignis], not boredom or diversion. . . . The time on the peaks is *essentially* long; for a making ready for the true that shall once come to pass [*sich ereignen*] does not happen overnight or to order, but consumes many human lives and even "generations." (GA 39: 56/53)

This authentic time of the creators, however, Hölderlin also calls *die reissende Zeit*, "the time that tears," and Heidegger explicitly understands this in terms of the originary temporality that he thematized in *Being and Time*:

> The poet on a number of occasions names this time the "time that tears," because it is within itself the oscillation that tears us away into the future and casts us back into having-been. Within the rhythm of this being torn back and forth into an ever-new preservation of what has been and an ever-new awaiting of that which is to come, there is temporalized the time of a people. By virtue of this time, a people enters into the standing open of valley and flowing rivers for that which is told from the mountains concerning what is to come, from those peaks of time upon which the creators dwell. (GA 39: 109/99–100)

The event of that which is truc is thus a moment that is temporalized within ecstatic temporality, within the oscillation of having-been and future. Significantly, however, and by contrast with the account given in *Being and Time*, this moment or *Augenblick* is not that of the present. It is never simply present. Heidegger indicates this in citing Hölderlin's thinking of the moment, as poetized in the fragment "O Mother Earth":

> And ever knowing the measure, with protective hand, a God
> Touches the dwellings of humans,
> Just for a moment,
> And they know it not, yet long
> They ponder it, and ask who it was.
> But when a time has passed, they know it. (GA 39: 111/101)

The event, as the temporalizing of the moment, is never present, but can be known only in retrospect, only after the event—which is to say, only as a trace. This time, "our" time, as the time of a people among the peoples, the historical time of authentic community, is concealed from us. Even the creators who dwell on the peaks of time do not know it. Not only is the event never present, but it cannot be understood in terms of something present—it cannot be "dated," as Heidegger emphasizes, invoking the phenomenon of datability that in *Being and Time* was said to be a "reflection"—but really more a spectral image, as it turns out—of the ecstatic structure of originary temporality (GA 39: 56/53; SZ 408). The event is the event of "the true," of truth, an event that is temporalized in and as "the authentic time of poetizing" (GA 39: 112/102). It is founded in and through the poetic work. Poetizing, as a telling, is a founding of truth, the founding of a locale of historical Dasein, of a locale where humans may "dwell poetically upon this earth" (GA 39: 113/103, 36/34).

I cannot pursue here how Heidegger reads and unfolds this temporal founding of the event and time of poetizing in and through the fundamental attunement of mourning in his account of "Germania," and in relation to the origin and origination in his account of "The Rhine." Instead, I want to turn briefly to "The Origin of the Work of Art" to examine how *Ereignis* is deployed there and to show its consistency with the earlier account in the first Hölderlin course.

In "The Origin of the Work of Art"—an essay that exists in three versions—the term *Ereignis* appears only in the third and final version, dating from 1936. It arises once again in the context of a discussion of artistic creation, and in particular of the createdness of the work of art. In the case of a "great" work of art (for Heidegger, a work that first institutes or founds the truth of a historical people), the fact of its having been created is not a self-evident or circumstantial fact: rather, it announces itself in and through the work itself as the announcement of its temporal and historical singularity. Heidegger first describes this event in terms of the more common verb *geschehen*, "to happen":

> the simple "factum est" is to be held into the open in the work: this, that unconcealment of that which is has happened here [*daß Unverborgenheit des Seienden hier geschehen ist*], and first happens as this event that has happened [*als dieses Geschehene erst geschieht*]; this, that such a work *is* rather than is not. (UK 66/190)[3]

What is significant here is that this event can manifest itself only after the event, only "after the fact," so to speak: it first happens as already having happened. In itself, therefore, this event is nothing present. It has always already withdrawn in such a way as to first let presence happen, to first let happen the presencing of the work as something that has happened. That the event of the work's origination, of its coming to presence, can manifest itself only after the fact, however, does not mean that it is a mere aftereffect of the actual work. Rather, as the event of its origination, it always precedes the work, goes ahead of it in its very presencing. Heidegger now describes this phenomenon as an *Ereignis*:

> The event [*Ereignis*] of its having been created is not simply a subsequent resonance in the work; rather, the work casts this event-like fact [*das Ereignishafte*]—that the work is as this work—forth before itself and has constantly cast it about itself. (UK 66/190)

This discussion responds to the questions that were posed concerning the happening of truth toward the end of the first part of the essay:

> Can truth in general happen [*geschehen*] and thus be historical [*geschichtlich*]? Truth, so people say, is surely something timeless and supra-temporal. (UK 32/163; cf. 56/182)

What is truth itself, such that it can at times happen [*sich ereignet*] as art? (UK 34/165)

Truth, Heidegger's inquiry has shown, is originarily not the correctness of representation, but the happening of unconcealment, and art is one way in which the event of unconcealment happens. Artistic creating, as this event, is at once the opening up of a world and the setting it back into the earth. It is a bringing forth out of concealment into unconcealment. As such a bringing, Heidegger notes, "it is more a receiving and taking within the relation to unconcealment" (UK 62–63/187). The event or *Ereignis* that first gives rise to presence is "not simply" a subsequent resonance, but presumably it is also that: *Ereignis* can manifest itself only in and through the work, but that means: only as trace of the non-simple "origin" of presence, of the "origin" (*Ursprung*) that lets something come into Being by way of a leap (*Sprung*), a leap that in advance must already have leapt over that which is to come into presence (UK 78–80/201–2). Heidegger in fact writes here of a "trembling" or "reverberation" that follows in the wake of such an event.

Yet what is true of the work of art, of the temporality and event of its emergence, now shows itself to be true for all bringing-forth, for the temporality of Being in general. This temporal understanding of *Ereignis*, its relation to presence and to the moment, is at once continued and extended in the more esoteric texts written between 1936 and 1942. In the *Contributions to Philosophy (Of Ereignis)*, a structured series of reflections that begin in 1936, the same year as "The Origin of the Work of Art," Heidegger on the one hand relates the understanding of *Ereignis* back to the temporal analysis of Dasein—and more importantly, to the horizonal Temporality (*Temporalität*) of Being itself, in which *Ereignis* is already implicit and prefigured. He remarks that "The unexpressed intimation of *Ereignis* presents itself on the surface and at the same time in historical recollection (*ousia* = *parousia*) as 'Temporality'" (GA 65: 73–74/59).[4] *Ereignis* is itself the origination of the *Augenblicks-Stätte*, the "site" of and for the moment, and continues to be understood in terms of the strife of world and earth. As the "site" of the moment, however, *Ereignis* is now understood as not simply temporal, but in terms of the unfolding of time-space in the originary (that is, originating) configuring of truth as unconcealment: "Time-space is, as the configuring of truth, originarily the site of the moment of *Ereignis*. The site of the moment essentially unfolds from out of the latter [i.e., *Ereignis*] as the strife of earth and world" (GA 65: 30/26).

Here already Heidegger implicitly retracts the attempt in *Being and Time* to ground the spatiality of Dasein in originary temporality. Space and time, in the event of their origination, are co-implicated in the happening of

Dasein—and yet the fact that time is named first still seems to suggest a certain "priority" of time over space. The happening of Dasein itself, for its part, springs forth and originates from *Ereignis*:

> Dasein is the fundamental happening [*Grundgeschehnis*] of the history to come. This happening springs from *Ereignis* and becomes a possible site of the moment for the decision concerning the human being—his history or the corruption thereof as its transition into downgoing. (GA 65: 32/27)

At the same time, as this passage intimates, *Ereignis* is now to be understood historically, in relation to the first beginning of Western thought as metaphysics and to the possibility of another beginning. The reflections on *Ereignis*, which attempt to think and speak from out of *Ereignis* itself, indeed understand themselves to be an attempt (but "only an *attempt*") at "the transition from metaphysics into Beyng-historical thinking," that is, into thinking from out of the happening of Beyng as *Ereignis*, a happening that is "abyssal" (GA 65: 3/5).[5] The "historical" understanding of Beyng and its "essence" (*Wesen*) does not mean a historiographical account or story of how Being has been thought or failed to be thought in Western thinking hitherto, in being reduced to presence, or *parousia*. It is not a presentation at all, for "the essence [*Wesen*] of Beyng no longer means only presence [*Anwesenheit*], but the full essencing [*Wesung*] of the abyss of time-space, and thereby of truth" (GA 65: 32/27–28). The boldness of the *Contributions* as a work is that they venture to speak from and to point toward that dimension from which presence and the moment of presence first emerge. *Ereignis* names the trace of such emergence.

Despite the multiple twists and turns that Heidegger's thinking of *Ereignis* undergoes—where the thinking "of" *Ereignis* means not a thinking "about" *Ereignis*, but a thinking from out of *Ereignis*—this implication of *Ereignis* in the bringing-forth and founding of Beyng in the unconcealment of beings, its implication in the bringing-forth that in Greek is called *poiēsis*, remains central to Heidegger's thinking of *Ereignis* from early to late. *Ereignis* demands to be thought within the orbit of *poiēsis* in general, and in particular in relation to that bringing-forth of the work that goes by the name of *technē*. That this is so becomes evident from a brief consideration of the seminal 1953 essay "The Question Concerning Technicity."

The verb *sich ereignen* and the noun *Ereignis* are used throughout "The Question Concerning Technicity," almost inconspicuously, and yet, as I shall indicate, in a way that remains in continuity with their earlier usage, not just in the *Contributions*, but extending all the way back to "The Origin of the Work of Art" and even the first Hölderlin course. Following his introductory discussion of Aristotle's four causes, Heidegger states that what is ultimately at stake in the interplay of the four causes is that they let something come into presence, something that, prior to that, was not present and thus might not have been. "They let that which is not yet present arrive into presencing," as he puts it (TK: 10/10). This letting is also a bringing, a bringing something forth into appearance that in Greek was called *poiēsis*. Such bringing something forth into appearance and presencing, Heidegger notes, is not restricted to the process that occurs in art and artisanship, but occurs also in and as *phusis*, "nature." What happens in this event of bringing something into appearance is *Ereignis*. Heidegger writes:

> Yet how does bringing-forth happen, whether in nature, or in craftsmanship and in art? . . . Bringing-forth brings forth from out of concealment into unconcealment. Bringing-forth happens [*ereignet sich*] only insofar as that which is concealed comes into the unconcealed. This coming resides and oscillates within what we call revealing [*Entbergen*]. For this, the Greeks have the word *alētheia*. (TK: 11/11–12)

Once again, Heidegger first uses the verb *geschehen* here, and then *sich ereignen* to name this happening or event of revealing that occurs in both *phusis* and *technē*, nature and art. He hyphenates *Her-vor-bringen* to draw attention to the movement implicit in this event: forth (*her*) from out of concealment, and to the fore (*vor*) into unconcealment, into appearance (*Vorschein*).

Modern technicity too is a mode of revealing, and as such a happening or event of unconcealment, yet it is not a bringing-forth, but rather a challenging-forth that Heidegger names *Ge-stell*, "enframing," and identifies as the essence of technicity: "In *Ge-stell*, unconcealment happens [*ereignet sich*]" (TK: 20/21). Nevertheless, the central point in Heidegger's entire essay is that the event of unconcealment—whether in nature, art, or modern technicity—is nothing human: "the human being does not dispose over unconcealment" (TK: 17/18). "Unconcealment itself . . . is never something made by humans" (TK: 18/18). To appreciate this, Heidegger indicates, we need only consider in an unprejudiced manner that which has already claimed us, indeed in such a way as to constitute our "essence," that is, the mode of our presencing:

> Wherever the human being opens his eyes and ears, unlocks his heart, and freely gives himself to meditating and striving, shaping and working, entreating and thanking, he finds himself everywhere already brought into the unconcealed. The unconcealment of the latter has already happened [*hat sich schon ereignet*] whenever it calls the human being forth into the modes of revealing allotted to him. When the human being, in his way, from within unconcealment reveals that which presences, then he only responds to the call of unconcealment, even when he contradicts it. (TK: 18/18–19)

Let us be clear about what Heidegger is indicating here. Human beings can indeed, whether through art or artisanship, or through the mode of revealing that is modern technicity, bring or challenge beings forth into unconcealment. *That* unconcealment (presencing) happens, however, is not something that humans bring about. And is precisely this "fact," as we heard earlier, that the great work of art brings to the fore: "this, that the unconcealment of that which is has happened here," as Heidegger put it in "The Origin of the Work of Art." Moreover, the temporality of the event of unconcealment is here delineated in the same way as it was in "The Origin of the Work of Art": The event of unconcealment has *already* happened, and humans find themselves *already* brought into the unconcealed. That the event of unconcealment has already happened means not only that the event itself is nothing present as such, but also that it both precedes and exceeds the human. If we humans do not dispose over unconcealment and its event, it is because we always come too late. We arrive too late on the scene, after the event, and in this sense the essence of the human is itself nothing human (just as, in Heidegger's opening remarks, the essence of technicity is said to be nothing technical). All human doing and making occurs only after the event, as a response to the call or address of unconcealment.

If *Ereignis*, as the event of unconcealment, is itself nothing present, it itself can be indicated or revealed only as a trace. This is just what the great work of art was said to accomplish in the earlier essay. Heidegger might, therefore, just as well have appealed to art in "The Question Concerning Technicity" in order to make his point about the ever excessive happening of unconcealment and the always too late arrival of the human. And in fact he does. Once again, and unsurprisingly, it is Hölderlin's poetizing that he appeals to here. Hölderlin's presence is in fact palpable at several points in the essay, not just in the concluding pages that, as is well known, meditate on the lines "Yet where danger is, grows/The saving power too" and "poetically the human dwells upon this earth."

Early in the essay, while acknowledging that the instrumental and anthropological definition of technology as a means to an end and as a human activity is correct, yet not for that reason true, Heidegger insists that only where something is unveiled in its essence does that which is true come to pass. He does so using Hölderlin's words that we heard earlier from "Mnemosyne": "Only where such unveiling happens, does that which is true come to pass [*ereignet sich*]" (TK: 7/6). This is in fact the first occurrence of *Ereignis* in the essay. Once again, the language of *Ereignis* is prefigured as a happening. The word used for unveiling, moreover, we might note, is also a word used by Hölderlin in the hymn "The Rhine": "Even the song/ May scarcely unveil it"—it, that is, the enigma of the origin of that which has "purely sprung forth," the Rhine as poetic work. The river Rhine too appears twice in the essay, first where there is mention of the hydroelectric power plant on the Rhine (TK: 6/5), and then later in the essay when we are invited to compare the Rhine as dammed up and integrated into the power plant with " 'The Rhine' as told by the work of *art* in Hölderlin's hymn by that name" (TK: 15/16). It should come as no surprise, then, that Heidegger returns to the question of art and to Hölderlin's poetry toward the end of the essay.

Within the realm of *technē*, *Ereignis* occurs essentially as language—language not as a foreground phenomenon, nor as an instrument at human disposal, but language as "that *Ereignis* that disposes over the highest possibility of human being," as Heidegger puts it in the 1936 essay "Hölderlin and the Essence of Poetizing" (GA 4: 38/56). The essential *Ereignis* of language is dialogue (*Gespräch*), not only dialogue between humans, but in the first instance dialogue between humans and the gods, between humans and time itself. This entails, as Heidegger explains in the same essay, that "the time that tears" must itself be torn open into the ecstases of past, present, and future. This tearing open of time as time is the founding or instituting (*Stiftung*) of Being itself as that which remains.[6] And this, as "The Origin of the Work of Art" also explains, is what is accomplished by poetizing as the essence of all art. "Poetizing," as Heidegger puts it in the Hölderlin essay, "is the founding of Being in and through the word" (GA 4: 41/59). In the later work, such as "The Question Concerning Technicity," such "tearing" is understood as the *Ereignis* of a "destining" (*Geschick*) of Being, as a gathering that "first brings the human being onto a path of revealing" (TK: 24/24). Such gathering first opens and founds a historical epoch. This opening occurs as an ever-excessive freeing and granting that remains "inexplicable to all thinking" (TK: 30/29).

It should be noted, finally, that while Heidegger certainly appeals, especially (though by no means exclusively) throughout the more esoteric reflections, to the sense of *eigen*, of "own" or "proper" that lies within the German *Er-eignis*, thus lending it the sense of beings coming into their own, being appropriated into their own Being or presencing by *Ereignis*, he also knows this etymology to be suspect and unrelated to the original derivation of *ereignen* from *eräugen*: to strike the eye, to come into view, to appear.[7] It is this more original sense to which he appeals in the essay "The Turning," composed at the same time as the first version of "The Question Concerning Technicity" and belonging to the series of four Bremen lectures delivered in 1949. *Ereignis* can announce itself only in and as the "lightning flash" of Being itself that strikes our eye, the lightning flash of the divine, as in Hölderlin, whose lines from "Patmos" appear again in this essay. *Ereignis*, Heidegger writes here, is *eignende Eräugnis*: the lightning flash of Being that flashes before us, first bringing things into the clearing light of their proper Being.

Let me try to summarize what I hope to have indicated, though not exhaustively demonstrated, with regard to *Ereignis* and what we might call its minimal meaning in Heidegger's work. *Ereignis* most certainly names an event and a happening in Heidegger, but it is not an event that happens within time as an already given or constituted realm. *Ereignis*, rather, names a singular event that first opens time itself, thereby first enabling presence. Since it first enables presence, this event can never be something present. It thus never refers to an "actual" event, if by "actual" we mean present within the field of actuality. *Ereignis* thinks what was earlier called the finitude of ecstatic temporality and its productive temporalizing, but now with respect to the finitude of Being itself, thought in terms of *poiēsis* and granting. Heidegger's mature appropriation of the concept of *Ereignis*, moreover, has its roots in his reading of Hölderlin, and can be adequately understood only in terms of *technē* and the work of art. In relation to *technē* and the work of art, it becomes evident that *Ereignis*, as the event of unconcealment, can itself become manifest only as a trace, only as always already having withdrawn in favor of the opening and granting of presence. *Ereignis* names the trace or trace-structure of Being.[8] In the work of art, if it succeeds, the "that it has happened" of the event of unconcealment becomes manifest as the reverberation of Being (Beyng) in a being, in a work.

It is in and through *Ereignis*, as the keyword of his mature thinking, that Heidegger thinks the poietic moment within the happening of Being as time. His thinking thereby thinks the unthought of the Greek understanding of Being as producedness and presence-at-hand, an understanding of Being that tacitly governs the entire subsequent history of philosophy, and indeed of science too, as a series of efforts to comprehend theoretically the Being of that which is. As emerging from a reductive interpretation of *technē*, science is in its essence already "technical" through and through, and enters the phase of the consummation of its essence only with its complete subjection to technicity, which we are witnessing today. One need only think of the virtual disappearance of "pure" research and the emphasis on "applied" (including the increasing funding of universities and research centers by private and corporate concerns), and the emphasis in even our finest educational establishments on the "production" of knowledge for the so-called "real world." Scientific advances are everywhere instantly deployed (if not already designed) for the ordering, not simply of nature, but of human beings everywhere—of "human resources," as we are now known.

And after Heidegger? The question of what becomes of philosophy, or of what remains for philosophical thinking "after Heidegger," seems an obvious question to ask—above all in an age of technicity, when we are constantly oriented toward what comes next, toward the next newest thing, product, or thinking, all in the naive belief that what comes next will constitute some form of progress over and beyond what has gone before. Yet perhaps, for that very reason, we should be suspicious of the question. Is not the thought of "after Heidegger"—at least if understood in this way—itself complicit with the essence of technicity and entirely under its sway? Above all, we of today, even those of us who may think of ourselves as Heidegger scholars, do not come after Heidegger, but remain well before him. His thought still awaits us, as something yet to be understood in its trans-epochal significance. Perhaps, therefore, rather than thinking "after" Heidegger in that sense, our task might be to follow his thought into a meditation on the essence of technicity—that is, into one configuration of *Ereignis* as a particular epochal destining of Being—and on its enigmatic proximity to the work of art. If, that is, our era is indeed one in which not only our actions, but our thinking too, are pervasively determined by technicity, about whose essence, as Heidegger once remarks, "much has been written, but little has been thought" (GA 9: 340/259).

NOTES

1. An initial version of this chapter was presented at the 51st meeting of the Heidegger Circle, held at Whitman College in Walla Walla, Washington from March 30 to April 2, 2017. I am grateful to Julia Ireland for the invitation to present there, to my respondent Jeffrey Powell for his thought-provoking questions, and to the participants at that conference for their questions and feedback.

2. The word *Ereignis* is, of course, used earlier (indeed, significantly earlier) in Heidegger's work, but these earlier usages should not be conflated with the meaning of *Ereignis* that emerges in the mid-1930s. See, for example, GA 56/57: 75, GA 26: 274/212. Of these earlier terminological usages, the latter, in describing the "world entry of beings" that results from the "peculiar inner productivity of temporality" (GA 26: 272/210), comes closest to the later sense attributed to *Ereignis* in the mid-1930s in emphasizing the *poiēsis* within the temporalizing of temporality. However, it still understands such productivity within the transcendental-horizonal perspective of the temporality of Dasein, and not yet in terms of the Temporality of Being itself beyond its transcendental inscription.

3. Translations from UK are modified from the existing translation by Albert Hofstadter.

4. "*Da-sein* essentially in terms of *Ereignis*; *thus* already (only transcendental Temporality) in *Being and Time*" (GA 71: 213/182).

5. The archaic spelling *Beyng* here translates the archaic German spelling of *Sein* (Being) as *Seyn*—a spelling also found in Hölderlin, and which Heidegger adopts in order to indicate a non-metaphysical understanding of Being.

6. On this, see my essay "Remains: Heidegger and Hölderlin Amid the Ruins of Time," in *Philosophers and Their Poets: Reflections on the Poetic Turn in German Philosophy since Kant*, ed. Charles Bambach and Theodore George (Albany: State University of New York Press, forthcoming).

7. See GA 71, §194; also *Identität und Differenz* (1957), 24–25.

8. On Beyng as trace, see GA 66: 202/178 and GA 70: 41.

Chapter 25

Learning to See Otherwise

The Transformative Appropriation of Vision

David Kleinberg-Levin

In a letter to his friend, Rilke wrote:

> It is certain that the divinest consolation is contained within humanity itself—we would not be able to do much with the consolation of a god; only that our eyes have to be a trace more seeing, our ears more receptive, the taste of a fruit would have to penetrate us more completely, we would have to endure more odor, and in touching and being touched be more aware and less forgetful—in order promptly to absorb out of our immediate experiences consolations more convincing, more preponderant, more true than all the suffering that can ever shake us to our very depths.[1]

Five years earlier, the eponymous character in his work of prose fiction, *The Notebooks of Malte Laurids Brigge*, penned this reflection: "I am learning to see. I don't know why it is, but everything penetrates more deeply into me [. . .]. I have an inner self of which I was ignorant."[2]

In "The Turn" (1947), Heidegger expressed a lament: Philosophical thought, accustomed to working with a conception of history as mere occurrence, can never bring us to discover the historical destiny that awaits in the fulfillment of our intrinsic potential (GA 79: 76–77/72–73).[3] Thought has not only failed to guide us toward the proper relation to our essence, our ownmost potential, so that we might realize more fully what we are capable of; it has also failed to guide us toward creating the *world* in which our humanity might be redeemed. Reflecting critically on our time, Heidegger tells us: "we do not yet hear, we whose hearing and seeing are deteriorating because of radio and film under the dominance of technology" (GA 79: 77/72 tm). What he is lamenting is an ever-spreading, ever-deepening nihilism, leaving us empty of spirit, lost in a meaningless world, a world in which the things we have made, the things we have brought forth in the world, are turning against us, threatening our way of life, in part because of the violent way we see and envision things—a way Heidegger repeatedly described as an assault, an expression of what Nietzsche called our will to power. There is a challenge for us in Heidegger's critique: to transform our way of looking and seeing. After Heidegger, that work on ourselves still remains to be undertaken.

Vision is a wonderful gift. From the earliest years of Greek philosophy into Husserl's phenomenology, vision has served as the paradigm for interpreting knowledge, truth, and reality. But this same vision, which in Plato favored an otherworldly idealism that could oppose the corruption of truth in everyday perception, has increasingly been mobilized to serve the nihilism that threatens in the will to power. And yet, at the same time that Heidegger challenged this paradigm for encouraging a metaphysics he sought to overcome because of its inherent and increasingly manifest objectivism and nihilism, he continued to draw on Plato's metaphors of vision and light in order to indicate a radically different experience in relation to knowledge, truth, and reality: as critical as Plato of the common understanding, but without reference to illumination by non-sensible Ideas.

We, gifted with vision, may notice or look at something, and yet not really see it. Sometimes, we see things we do not want to see; and we look away. And there are times and ways of seeing such that we are as if blind, the consequence of passions, prejudice, habits, limitations in experience and knowledge. There are times and ways of seeing such that, while our *eyes* are open, *we* are steadfastly closed.

Our eyes are organs of sight. But our eyes can also weep, pained by what they see, as when, confronting horror and tragedy, a cold lucidity unclouded by emotion is no longer possible. Or they can weep in joy, as when the emotion is too intense for words. What is the significance of this uncanny affinity between seeing and weeping? We might consider this: weeping, as the expression of an affective connection not structured by the positions of subject and object, is the *root* of seeing. But our vision, our way of seeing, can get uprooted, detached from its connectedness to life in the world, detached from its source in sense and sensibility. According to Heidegger, it is in our world, a world belonging to the epoch of the will to power and its nihilism, that the uprooting of our vision has taken place. There is violence in the uprooted character of our seeing. And that violence has been transferred to the things we see, turning their thing-being into object-being and standing reserve. We ourselves have undergone corresponding changes in character: we have become subjects, encapsulated subjectivities, emptied-out interiorities without truth. Without truth, because modern subjectivity recognizes truth only in objectivity. For Heidegger, this misses and conceals the *essential ground* of truth.

Vision is a capacity. That means: our seeing is *capable* of learning and development. That we can look and see things is not merely a *fact* about us;

it is also an opportunity for learning and achievement. What would it be (like) for our eyes to become *ontologically attuned* organs? That is the question Heidegger's lectures are asking us. It calls for learning to see differently. But how so? I suggest that, if there is a connection between (1) the *Ge-stell* defining our time as the epoch of the totalizing imposition of an order of constant availability and (2) the prevailing character of the perceptual *Gestalt*, then Heidegger's critique of the *Ge-stell* implies ways in which, after him, we might work on how vision functions in our lives and in philosophical thought.

In a 1951 lecture, "Logos (Heraclitus, Fragment B50)," Heidegger took up for thought a saying attributed to Heraclitus: "When you have listened not to me (*my* words, my *logoi*) but to the *Logos* itself, you realize it would be wise to be in accord with the One unifying All."[4]

Heidegger takes Heraclitus to be saying that "mortals, whose [propriate] essence remains appropriated in *homologein*, are fulfilling their given potential when they measure up to the *Logos* as the *Hen Panta* [One unifying All] and submit themselves to its measure" (H 226/75 tm). In other words, it would be wise (and most appropriate to our a priori nature) for us to correspond to, become like, or become near in character to, the *Logos* (i.e., being), which, in its *Legein*, gathers and unifies all in the layout of a clearing that makes possible the disclosing of things in their meaningful presence.

In bringing further into the light a potential in our vision that each of us can develop, I would like to demonstrate the significance of the phenomenology of vision that we might adduce from Heidegger's reading of this fragment. The key to the learning at issue revolves around the notions, as Heidegger interprets them, of *legein* (a verb signifying what speech, and all other forms of articulation, including perception, are, namely a gathering-laying-down, a disclosive bringing-forth) and *homologein* (a term designating a becoming-like, a drawing-near, hence a *correspondence*, say, between actual human forms of articulation and the ontological dimension of articulation constitutive of the *Logos*, i.e., being).

I will show that, in this short 1951 text on Heraclitus, Heidegger's way of thinking about our capacity for vision is strikingly similar to his way of thinking about vision in a 1949 text, "The Turn," even though their thematic contexts and orientations are different. Despite the differences, however, the two lectures draw on the same metaphorical imagery, creating for our thought a startling prosopopoeia, charging us with the task of learning a vision appropriate to the "truth of being," vision no longer belonging to the total imposition of the reifying *Ge-stell*.

In "The Turn," Heidegger invokes "the lightning-flash of being," "the glance of being," and "the looking of being" (GA 79: 73ff/69ff). The lecture is saturated with thoughts in which ontological matters concerning being are expressed in the language of vision—and, most surprisingly, in phrases that seem to attribute vision to being itself. Similarly, in the lecture on Heraclitus, where Heidegger connects fragment B50 to fragment B64, he draws our attention to the "flash of lightning" that "steers the totality" of what is present (H 222/72) and suggests that the "flash" in this image represents the glance of being. This connection between vision (looking and seeing) and being that Heidegger made in "The Turn" is reinforced when, a few years later, in the 1951 lecture on Heraclitus, he would speak of the "lightning flash of being" (H 227/76) and "the [lightning] storm of being" (H 229/78). So we find that, in this lecture on Heraclitus, Heidegger *envisions* being by using the very same imagery he had used in the earlier 1949 lecture, concerned as it is with a turning regarding the meaningful presencing of beings that is both a turning in the human relation to being and a turning in the history of being that is manifest in metaphysics.

What does Heidegger's prosopopoeia in these two texts mean? Why does he resort to this strange rhetorical conceit, speaking as if *being* could look, cast a glance like lightning, and see in a flash of light? After all, he repeatedly tells us in numerous texts and in unequivocal terms that what "being" signifies is not an entity, not a being. Why then is he using this rhetorical construction? A quick answer, correct but far from telling the whole story, would be that, like the Greek philosophers before him, Heidegger wanted to say something important about the predominant *character* of human vision in our time and about the historical possibility of a certain transformation. Being, we suppose, cannot see; but it is, in one of its significations, the clearing of a meaningful world, that which makes the visibly meaningful presencing of beings possible. So if, counterfactually, we were to *imagine* being as capable of seeing, how might we attempt, in *our own* seeing, to emulate, hence correspond to, *its* way of seeing?

In "The Turn," Heidegger reflects on an ever-increasing nihilism in the world—a nihilism interpreted in terms of the *Ge-stell*, namely the imposition of an order that submits absolutely everything to constant presence—total availability—for the sake of the human will to power. He also reflects there on the possibility of turning our future, our destiny, away from its violence, its devastating destructiveness, even finding strength precisely in its danger and drawing, as he so often does, on the vocabulary of vision in order to convey his thinking. As in the lecture on Heraclitus, his argument takes shape in a prosopopoeia. His thought is that, if we can be brought to an understanding of the danger challenging our time as the epoch in which being comes to presence in and as configurations of the *Ge-stell*, then the oblivion of being into which we have fallen might be overcome and our unfathomably deep relation to being, a relation deeper than we could ever succeed in representing, could perhaps be retrieved from such forgetfulness. However, the form of expression that Heidegger employs to lay out the phenomenology of such a turn is perplexing, because it seems that he is attributing vision, a human capacity, to being itself. Is "the lightning-like flash" describing a subjective insight that engages and turns our vision—or is it describing the objective turning of *being itself*? Might this question take us in the wrong direction, perpetuating the very metaphysics we must get free of?

According to Heidegger, "the turning of the danger [inherent in the nihilism operating in the epoch ruled by the regime of the *Ge-stell*] suddenly comes to pass" in the "self-lighting" of being, a "lightning-flash" that lights up the essence of being, showing it as the clearing (GA 79: 74/69).

Continuing the imagery, in which, as in Plato, a certain visualism figures in philosophically consequential ways, Heidegger tells us that "'To flash,' thought in terms both of its derivation and of what it designates, is 'to look in a glance.' [. . .] Moving through the element of its own illumination, the flashing glance retrieves that which it catches sight of and brings it back into the brightness of its own looking" (GA 79: 74ff/70ff). However, the reduction of the world in the *Ge-stell* turns the openness for meaningful presencing in unconcealment ("the truth of being") into a reifying closure ("truthless being"). Nevertheless, what shows itself in this world is always an event that makes an ineluctable claim on us: it is always a coming-into-sight that *appropriates* our vision, claiming us for insight into its ownmost nature, its role in the realm of the visible and invisible.

Thus, near the end of this text, Heidegger argues that, despite the rule of the *Ge-stell*, there are still grounds for hope, because the bright open space of the world still lights up and the truth of being can always suddenly show itself, as when the essence of *Ge-stell* clearly reveals itself as the danger, but also shows thereby the way to a saving power. The *Ge-stell* is "no blind destiny," no "completely ordained doom" (GA 79: 75–76/71).

When we understand the Parmenidean bond between seeing and being, then we will understand with insight that in all our visual experience, we human beings are "the ones who are caught sight of" (GA 79: 75–76/71).  For the beings we see are like mirrors: they reflect back to us the way we are seeing them. We are not only beings who behold as meaningful what shows itself; we are also ones—perhaps the only ones—caught and held in the sensible realm of sight, called into question, and held to account in our way of beholding, by the beholding of what presences: what Heidegger here calls "the lightning-glance of being." So how are we to respond to the questions this text leaves us with, not only regarding the *character* of our seeing and but also regarding *what it is* we are willing and resolved to see. We need to see with understanding what is happening to our world: the nihilism and its ever-increasing devastation.

The textual passages I have quoted might seem perplexing in at least two respects. First of all, they *seem* to present "being" in unmistakably anthropomorphic terms, rendering it as if it were an entity—a something—somehow capable of agency. We are familiar with the experience in which we, we human beings, have a sudden insight—an insight so unexpected, so surprising, and so very sudden, that, as we are wont to say, it happened in a flash, striking like a bolt of lightning. But here Heidegger does not want the flash to describe only the sudden insight turning our vision, bringing to light, so we can see it, the truth about our plight. He also seems to be describing *being itself* as a look or glance that, like lightning, clearing and lighting things up, suddenly flashes. Why?

Heidegger's metaphorical language persists in moving ambiguously, swinging between *our* being and being *itself*. This two-sided reference, however, is *not* the anthropomorphism it seems to be, turning being into something that is capable of casting a flashing glance. So what does the ambiguity mean?

If we are determined to avoid taking his words as treating being as a singular being, or a higher kind of being, then we are compelled to construe the formulation as constructing an elaborate metaphorical thought. It serves as a provocation, a challenge for thought—indeed, as I shall argue, an *appropriating claim* on our vision. But this is an argument which requires that we understand how metaphor functions in Heidegger's thinking. For Heidegger, what needs to be said always comes "from out of the experience of thinking." Metaphor is accordingly never merely a figure of speech, a fiction; it is always a medium for expressing a thought that, drawing attention to our experience, might move us, taking our experiencing and thinking to a different or new place. Heidegger rejects metaphysical interpretations of metaphor, which miss the essence by forcing it into its dualisms: literal or figurative, fact or fiction, truth or falsehood, subjective or objective, real or imaginary? The crucial point is that Heidegger's metaphorical constructions always perform an important philosophical function: in this context, his metaphors are attempts to lay claim to the *ontological responsibilities* of our vision for the sake of a future *after* the regime of the *Ge-stell*.

Using metaphor, Heidegger is arguing that being—all that in any way meaningfully presences—shines or flashes a critical spotlight on our way of seeing: the way things are reflects back to us, like a mirror, the character of our way of seeing them. Shining directly on us, the metaphorical "light of being" claims us for questioning: Is our way of looking and seeing realizing and actualizing the character (*ēthos*) of our vision that most befits the dignity of our humanity? Is our way of looking and seeing realizing and actualizing the disposition of character to which, in their essential nature, they have already—a priori—been claimed, appropriated? Does the *actuality* of our looking and seeing "correspond" to their endowed potential?

As the ones "caught sight of" from the hypothetical and metaphorical standpoint of "the glance of being," we are appropriated to—and for—the history-making task of overcoming, by virtue of the *character* of our perceptivity, the *Ge-stell* that rules our time, securing for a different future "the truth of being," securing an *openness* for the meaningful presencing of things—*whatever* in any way, any sense, *is*.

To understand Heidegger's prosopopoeia, we also need to work with his concept of the *Ereignis*—and, related to it, the notion of correspondence, inspired by what Heraclitus says in fragment B50 about the *homologein*. Although in ordinary German usage, *Ereignis* means the happening of an "event," Heidegger brings out a meaning operating within it, namely, a claim on us to achieve a "correspondence," a nearness of belonging and attunement. Thus, the meaning of *Ereignis*, signifying at first the phenomenological *event* that is the encounter between a human being (*Dasein*) and being (the meaningful presencing of something that in some way *is*), undergoes a profound semantic shift, so as to signify that such encounters always activate a claim—an *appropriation*—calling us to take up and develop our ownmost potential. In other words, the *Ereignis*, understood first as (1) a phenomenological *event*, or *situation*, of meaningful presencing in a *Dasein*'s life, is unfolded into (2) an *Er-eignis* in the sense of an *appropriation*, a claim that summons us to (3) an *Er-eignis* in the sense of a *propriation*. And because of the association of *Er-eignen* and *Er-äugen*, Heidegger argues that our *perception* is subject to this appropriation.[5] The point is that the event or situation, the so-called "event of being" that is the meaningful presencing of beings, summons us to become the fulfillment of our ownmost essence as mortal human beings, *taking some responsibility* for the way things are. This is because the happening of "being," understood as signifying the phenomenology of the clearing—that which makes possible meaningful presencing, and the presencing itself—*is* in essence *Da-sein itself*; and that means that, living up to our essence *as Da-sein*, we bear some responsibility for the historical conditions enabling and limiting both that clearing and whether and how what-is can presence. This point demands critical reflection on the *character* of our perceptual engagements and on our developing of the potential inherent in our perceptual capabilities. The most fundamental dimension of this potential is the openness of the clearing itself within which vision receives whatever might, given prevailing historical conditions, come into its presence.

Having interpreted Heidegger's use of prosopopoeia in "The Turn," I will now consider his use of that rhetorical strategy in the text on Heraclitus, in order to suggest how, in the *legein* ("the laying-out that gathers") and the *homologein* (a becoming-like or corresponding that draws near in its character), our vision is opened to possibilities that bear on our future. In the *homologein*, we take over the potential given in our nature as embodied mortal beings gifted with a certain capacity for vision. Through a process of propriation, our vision is charged with corresponding (*daseinsmäßig*) to what is called for by our appropriation. The *correspondence* Heraclitus urges in the *homologein* constitutes an *ontological appropriation* of our capacity for visual perception, summoning us to a mindfulness that would enable our vision to become more fittingly what, in its essence, its inherent disposition, it already is: *a clearing*, a *disclosive laying-out-that-gathers*.

I hope in this way to bring out for further thought the importance of perception—especially seeing and hearing—in Heidegger's Greek-inspired conception of "the worthy life." To follow this conception, we need to reflect, after Heidegger, on the *possibilities* in perception as an endowment of capacities capable of learning and development, not only in regard to various skills, but also in regard to ethical and aesthetic character.

In what sense could our looking and seeing, our glance, our gaze become (like) the glance or look or gaze *of* being? If we parse the "of," reading it in terms of the subjective and objective genitive, these phrases are claiming *us* for *an appropriated correspondence*: there is always, inherent in the taking place of perception, the call for such a correspondence. The presencing of beings always claims our vision for a *homologein*, the developing of a character *corresponding* to its inherent potential as a mode of unconcealment or disclosiveness, bringing something forth into the gathering layout (*legein*) of a delimited field formed by the interplay of visibility and invisibility.

This interpretation hinges on understanding that *it is not only language* which is a gathering-and-laying-out; our vision is also a *legein*, a laying-out-that-gathers—a clearing for presencing, an unconcealing or disclosing in the interplay of concealment and unconcealment. Since the *Logos* (the language of being) is a *Legein*, a disclosive laying-out-that-gathers (the laying-out of an open clearing in the gathering of which the unconcealment and presencing of what-is can take place), the Heraclitus fragment is telling us, through his word *homologein*, that it would be *correspondingly* wise, and most appropriate, most fitting for our vision to become, through its self-recognition, a laying-out that disclosively brings-forth and gathers into unconcealment, while at the same time preserving and protecting the encompassing darkness that conceals.

Heidegger's use of prosopopoeia gives rhetorical force to an ontologically motivated challenge to the current historical, culturally shaped character of our vision. It makes no sense to speak of being as looking, seeing, glancing, beholding, clearing, or lighting up. But he is using these figures of speech to address us with regard to *our capacity* as beings gifted with sight. What Heidegger invites us to contemplate in his reading of Heraclitus is our achievement of the *homologein* in our vision, an achievement *corresponding to* the clearing, the openness, attributed to the *Logos*—Being itself. Thus, the meaning of Heidegger's rhetorical conceit lies in the challenge of a question: How might our perceptual abilities, feeble and finite though they are, attain a fitting and worthy measure of disclosive openness, a clearing in our world, *corresponding* to the immeasurable openness in vision that we *imagine* in contemplating the idea of being—*as if* being itself could look and see?

We are still learning to see, still learning to think with philosophical insight about both the actuality and the potential operative in our perception. Since the way we see the world is determined by, and reflects, the way the world is, but also, and reversibly, since the world we see is shaped by, and reflects, the way we see it, to understand our world and think critically about it requires understanding and thinking critically about how our vision is implicated in maintaining the *Ge-stell* that prevails in our time. Heidegger leaves us with critical thoughts about vision, and about the vision-generated metaphysics—the paradigm of knowledge, truth, and reality—that belongs to the epoch of the *Ge-stell*; but we, coming after him, can take Heidegger's project further by reflecting critically on the *character* of our seeing in the two-way relation between it and the regime of the *Ge-stell*. This means, for instance, that, inasmuch as the *Ge-stell* depends on the reification of the subject–object structure, one of our tasks must be to learn how to keep our seeing *connected and belonging* to the open dimension underlying the differentiation of subject and object, maintaining awareness of the emergence of that structure from the formative dimension—the "truth of being" underlying, and grounding, the possibility of truth as correctness.

Using the German word for perception (*Wahrnehmung*), Heidegger reminds us that, in its essence, perception involves protecting, preserving, and safeguarding the "truth [*Wahrheit*] of being": the openness of the clearing, as that which is needed to make meaningful presencing in our world possible. Perhaps the taking up of this appropriation of our perception could prepare us for overcoming the epoch of the *Ge-stell*.

Heidegger summons us to a future beyond the continuum of history—beyond more of the same. How might we receive and engage, in the way of our vision, the promise in the possibilities of this future—*after* Heidegger?

NOTES

1. Rainer Maria Rilke, *Letters of Rainer Maria Rilke 1910–1926*, tr. Jane Greene and M. D. Herter Norton (New York: Norton, 1947, 1972), 139–40.

2. Rilke, *The Notebooks of Malte Laurids Brigge*, tr. M. D. Herter Norton (New York: Norton, 1949), 14–15.

3. Mitchell's translation is excellent, but I have occasionally altered it. I have also consulted William Lovitt's earlier translation: "The Turning," in QCT.

4. Heidegger, "Logos (Heraklit, Fragment 50)," in *Vorträge und Aufsätze* (Pfullingen: Günther Neske, 1954), 207–29; "Logos (Heraclitus, Fragment B 50)," in EGT, 59–78 tm. Hereafter designated by H, followed by the page numbers, German first.

5. See Heidegger, "Der Satz der Identität," GA 79: 124–128/117–119. And see the translation of a different version of this text in a bilingual edition: "The Principle of Identity," in *Identity and Difference*, tr. Joan Stambaugh (Chicago, IL: University of Chicago Press, 1969), esp. 30–37. Also see "Zeit und Sein" and "Protokoll zu einem Seminar über den Vortrag 'Zeit und Sein,' " in GA 14/*On Time and Being*.

Chapter 26

On the Meaning and Possibility of Thought

Miguel de Beistegui

"After Heidegger." Should we read this as an invitation—in spite of everything—to think in the manner of Heidegger, to imitate him, to the point, perhaps, of becoming more Heideggerian than him, of extending his thought in new directions? Or should we read it as an invitation to leave it behind, to move on, albeit by way of something resembling an *Aufhebung*, as if one could use his thought as a ladder, a useful but ultimately dispensable piece of equipment? Is this an invitation to be done with Heidegger? Or is it perhaps a matter of something altogether different, of asking after the nature of thought itself, not as an afterthought, but as the question underlying all questions, as the question which, more or less explicitly, is always at work in every body of thought, every philosophical system? To think after Heidegger, then, would be to think about the meaning or, more precisely and decisively, about the *event* of thought: How does thought come about? Is it bound to happen, necessary? Or is it entirely contingent, a matter of chance? Is thought something that is given in advance, if only as a possibility? Is it something that we are all capable of, and which, either by sheer will or training, either through a decision or an adequate method, or possibly a combination of both, we can set in motion? Or is the vocabulary of possibility, necessity, and even chance entirely inadequate to understand the nature of thought? Of course, thought is a possibility for human beings. This is (trivially) true. But does this possibility every guarantee that we are "capable" of thinking? Furthermore, should we think of this capacity for thought as an innate, possibly transcendental faculty, which we apply to a range of objects? Or should we think of it as a power that comes from without and originates in a place that draws us in, despite ourselves, as it were? In short, is thought something that we *can* do, or something that we are *forced* to do?

It is perhaps not entirely surprising that Heidegger's very last lecture course at the University of Freiburg, which spanned two semesters (1951–1952), was devoted to the question which animated him throughout his life: not the so-called question of being, but the question of thought: *Was heißt Denken?* What, he seems to ask in that lecture course, is this activity I have been engaged in all my life? What is this state, height, or depth I have been trying to reach, this *ethos* I have been trying to develop? Does its event, its coming into being, depend on me, or on something else, and should its conditions of emergence be sought elsewhere?

In this paper, I will try to extract and justify the following axioms of thought, before offering a critical assessment of the last (and key) one:

1. Thought is not a *given*, at least in the sense of something that is innate, a potentiality that could be activated at any time. Thought is a *gift*. What is the difference between a given and a gift? A gift comes from without, and exposes us to an Outside, which is the origin of thought.
2. Is this gift something that I receive passively, and for which there is no preparation? In no way: thought is an apprenticeship (*Lernen*). We never think, we only ever learn to think—not as a result of some flaw or deficiency, but as a result of the nature of what calls for thinking. We do not learn rules, techniques, or a method, which we then apply to situations and objects. This (Kantian) model of thought is in fact a model of cognition, recognition, and representation. But thought differs *essentially* from cognition.
3. To acknowledge that thought is a matter of apprenticeship is to acknowledge that we are never done with thought, that thought is always to come as well as underway, that we are not quite yet able (*vermögen*) to think. Far from being a matter of mere method, that is, of discovering the correct and most direct path (*hodos*) to a truth to which we are naturally inclined, as Descartes and many others tried to convince us, thought is itself the way, path, or voyage born of the call or invitation to think. To call (*heissen*) or invite (*einladen*), Heidegger reminds us by drawing on a passage from Matthew's Gospel, means *keleuein*, to get something on the road, to set it underway (*auf den Fahrweg, auf den Weg bringen*).[1] If *keleuthos* "means" path, it is in the sense of a path that one follows as a result of a call that comes from without, and not as a result of a will to think. The parallel with the call of conscience as described in *Being and Time*, the roots of which are themselves Christian, is obvious, and raises the crucial question of whether the model of thought at issue here, beyond Heidegger's own intention, does not itself remain deeply Christian.

4. It follows that far from facilitating thought, or allowing it to happen, the will to think (*Denkenwollen*) is itself an obstacle to thought. This means that thought does not require any goodwill, or any will at all. It means that thought is involuntary or, better said perhaps, a-voluntary. The capacity for thought is thus not activated by another faculty, the will. In fact, the will is not a mere faculty or power of the human soul, but a dimension and even a constitutive feature of modern times, an onto-historical constraint and disclosure: the world is Will (as well as Representation). Is thought activated by another faculty, then, another dimension of the human Dasein?
5. It would seem so. Memory (*Gedächtnis*), Heidegger claims, is the modality of thought that retains what can be thought (*das Bedenkliche*). But this retaining (*be-halten*) is to be distinguished from remembrance, that is, from our capacity to retain the past in a representation. It is even to be distinguished from retention in the phenomenological, Husserlian sense. It is not a psychological (whether empirical or transcendental) feature of human subjectivity, a faculty that works alongside other faculties, such as the understanding, the imagination, reason, or intuition. Rather, this retaining is to be understood as the minding and tending (*Hüten*), preserving (*Bewahren*), safekeeping (*Verwahren*), rescuing (*Bergen*), and sheltering (*Verbergen*) of what can be thought. It is through memory that we are able to think. As such, memory is the gathering (*Versammlung*) of thought itself, or the very unfolding of thought. It is *how* thought happens. Memory originally designates the *Gedanc* or "the soul as a whole" (*das ganze Gemüt*), "in the sense of the constant and intimate abiding by [*Versammlung bei*] that which essentially speaks to the sentiment as a whole [*was sich allem Sinnen wesenhaft zuspricht*]" (GA 8: 143–44, cf. WCT 140). From this point of view, *Gedächtnis* originally designates roughly the same as *An-dacht* (one of the senses of which is the state of being completely absorbed, devoted), which Heidegger understands as a way of remaining in constant proximity, or as a form of gatheredness and togetherness—not just of the past, but also of the present and what may come. Far from resembling something like an idea or a representation, thought indicates our ability to gather what we are essentially exposed to, to re-collect.
6. Thought (*Denken*) is thus Memory, or recollective thinking (*Andenken*). But what exactly is being remembered in thought? The Origin. The Origin is not the beginning: it does not designate a specific point in time, an intra-temporal or chronological event. It does not take place *in* time, but takes place *as* time. It is the event of time, or what we could call *pure* time. That is the phenomenon which, ever since *Being and Time*, Heidegger sought to reveal as the origin or horizon of experience,

or as the transcendental pure and simple, and as the task and future of thought.

7. *Andenken* re-collects thoughtfully, or gathers in thought, that which withdraws (*entzieht*) and effaces itself in what comes to presence; that which has been (*das Gewesene*), and continues to have been, in everything that is present, without itself ever having been present, and thus without ever becoming something that is no longer, something past (*das Unvergängliche*); that which conceals itself in every unconcealment or configuration of truth; that which, from the start, has withdrawn from presence (in making present) and thus has fallen into oblivion, an oblivion that needs to be attended to, minded (*in-die-Acht-genommen*), and safeguarded *as such*—not, therefore, through a willful act or an effort of remembrance, not, that is, by making it (finally) present, or re-presenting it, and thus erasing it as *das Gewesene* in all that endures (*Währen*) (for that is what metaphysics does).
8. The very possibility of thought is thus caught up with the distinct temporality of what calls for thinking, what sets it in motion or provokes it. For thought happens only when confronted with a past that does not pass, that is, with a pure past, irreducible to any present, to re-presentation and re-cognition—in short, to metaphysics. Thought is the recollection that greets and gathers this past that exceeds all presence—all actuality and object-ness, all constant and continual presence (*Beständigkeit*). Metaphysics is the system of representation that is in the way of thought, and not the way of thought. Yet the Origin continues to speak in and through metaphysics, as its unthought.
9. If we are "not yet thinking," and if this "not yet" is itself "what most calls for thinking" (*das Bedenklichste*), it is not simply because of metaphysics, and this in such a way that, were metaphysics to be overcome, we would finally be thinking. Rather, it is because thinking is oriented toward, or drawn into, this past that never was, and never will be, present, this founding event that does not take place *in* time. What most calls for thought, and in which we learn to think, is thus not this or that "interesting" problem, this timely, untimely or timeless question, but this *other* time, this doubling of (chronological, worldly) time: that we are not yet thinking comes the fact that what calls for thinking turns away (*sich abwendet*) from the human, and has done so "for a long time" (GA 8: 8). For how long? Forever: this "for a long time" is in fact an "always already" that indicates not a promised land, a future present or a time when we will be able to say: "at long last, we have reached the shores of thought," but a past without present, or the pure form of time in which everything present comes to pass. This other time is in fact the founding event, but one that is not inscribed within the chain of events

known as history: "The event of withdrawal [*das Ereignis des Entzugs*] could be what is most present [*das Gegenwärtigste*] in everything that is currently present, and so infinitely exceed the actuality of everything actual" (GA 8: 11/9, tm). It is this original turning away or withdrawal that makes history—and the specific history, *our* history, which is not that of thought, but of *ratio*, knowledge, science, representation, calculation, technics, in short, metaphysics. Between metaphysics and thought, there is no space for something like a transition, mediation, or bridge. There can only be a leap (*Sprung*).

10. This raises the question of access. How does this leap come about? One way is through metaphysics itself—through the metaphysical text and its unthought or forgotten origin, which deconstruction is to bring out; but, also and more importantly, through the manner in which the world itself unfolds metaphysically, as a series of historical horizons, technology being the latest and most extreme, insofar as it signals the utter concealment and forgetting of the self-concealment of the process by which "there is" (something rather than nothing). Technology, Heidegger argues, is the paradoxical epoch par excellence, in that it designates the time in which thought has never been more necessary and urgent, and yet never more remote and threatened: the other time is entirely buried in real, actual time, and the event of presence is entirely covered up by pure, constant, and readily available presence. But if the event of time is concealed to that extent in what it opens up, how can thought ever be awakened to it? How can the paradoxical nature of our time actually generate thought? This, I think, is where Heidegger's answers fall short of the question he opens up. This is the issue we need to revisit.

Let me address this problem of access in greater detail, and attempt to take it in a slightly different direction, aimed at overcoming the problematic place in which Heidegger's own thought on the matter leaves us.

In the period of fundamental ontology (and the brief period of metontology that followed it), the question of access was addressed via two different routes: one, deconstructive, attempted to reveal time as the unthought or blind spot of the metaphysical text; the other, which Heidegger ran in parallel, was ontological, and sought to reveal existential—that is, ecstatic, finite, and horizontal—temporality as the hidden condition of experience, phenomena, and the world as a whole. He identified the possibility of the awakening of thought, as that which brings us into contact with the transcendental, or the event of time, in specific, rare and seemingly unattractive moments of existence, such as anxiety, profound boredom, guilt, and the call of conscience.

From the mid-1930s, however, Heidegger understood metaphysics to cover not only the history of philosophy, but the history of the sciences that emerged from philosophy, the mathematization of nature as a whole, the quantifying, measuring and modeling of all phenomena, the will to predict, control, exploit, and dominate, all of which culminate in what he refers to as *die Technik*, which is not so much a phenomenon as an epoch, the essence or origin of which, he argues, is itself nothing technological. Metaphysics thus came to designate a historical phenomenon, or, better said still, the very unfolding of Western history. Our history, Heidegger claims, is metaphysical through and through: the beginning of Western thought corresponds with the forgetting of origin, and not with the thinking of what calls most for thinking. This, in turn, means that the origin speaks in and through this forgetting, as its unthought. To think the unthought of metaphysics is to think the origin that is hidden behind and in the beginning. Metaphysics is both access to, and a concealing of, the origin. And at this particular point in time, a time of deep crisis, our history is out of joint, precisely because it is absolutely cut off from its origin, unable to access the ground from which it sprang, the roots from which it grew. Cut off from its origin, it errs—and this erring takes the form of planetary domination and exploitation.

Where, in this gloomy picture, is the point of inflection, the pivot around which thought might arise? Heidegger no longer speaks of anxiety, or boredom, or guilt, as what jolts us out of our torpor and forgetting, and exposes us to what is worthy of thought. He does, as we saw, speak of thought as *Andenken* (memory, recollective thought), as well as *Besinnung* (meditative thinking), or *Gelassenheit* (a letting-go and letting-be, a relinquishing and releasement, in and through which we gain a certain serenity, or composure). *Gelassenheit* signals a dwelling that is not a dominating, a proximity to the world and to things that is not an appropriation. Similarly, we should be lucid regarding the origin of calculative thought, and the manner in which it has become the only recognized form of thought, or knowing (*technē*). We should take into consideration its peculiarity. This peculiarity, Heidegger claims, has to do with the fact that whenever we plan, research, and delimit a domain, we always reckon with circumstances that are given. And the way in which we reckon with them or take them into account is by calculating the specific purposes they will serve. Thus we can predict or count on definite results. This is the calculation that is the mark of technological thought. It remains calculation even when it neither works with numbers nor uses computers. Calculative thought always computes. It computes ever new, ever more promising and at the same time ever more economical possibilities. Calculative thinking races from one prospect to the next. It never stops, never collects itself. As such, while it realizes an essential possibility of the metaphysical destiny of the human, calculative thinking runs the risk of alienating the human from its own essence. Meditative thought, by contrast, abstracts itself from calculation and directs thought back toward that which calculation covers over, back toward the origin of the forgottenness that reigns in calculation. It is the thought that stops, collects itself as well as the world in which we live, and "ponders." It is the thought through which, once again, a free relation to technology, born of a reflection upon its provenance, becomes possible.

But Heidegger does not tell us how thought understood in that way arises immanently, from within the world and history. He does not tell us what, in machination or technology, provokes or forces us to think. In the 1930s, Heidegger still seems concerned to identify ways in which something like a philosophical disposition could be awakened from within the German (and European) Dasein. Following his analysis of facticity, attunement, and moods as a structural feature of human existence in *Being and Time*, he seems to want to anchor the possibility of thought in a shared, collective disposition. But amid the social misery and political confusion that defined Germany at the time, he sees no room for the disposition conducive to thought which the Greeks called enthusiasm (*enthousiasmos*) and wonder (*thaumazein*), and in which they felt something like a distress and an urgency (*Not*), an oppression (*Bedrängnis*) and a blissful liberation at the same time.[2] All he sees, in this most confused time, is a sense of emptiness and nihilism: "we" are bored with ourselves, he says, and no longer have answers to the questions "what for?" and "where to?" The cultural activity, if not frenzy, in which the German Dasein finds itself is itself a distraction from that boredom, and thus its confirmation. And yet, Heidegger claims, reiterating the structure of conscience and resolute disclosedness (*Entschlossenheit*) revealed in *Being and Time*, it is from the very depths of our boredom that a voice (*Stimme*) can be heard—the very voice that appeals to our essence and demands that we own up to our own being (GA 29/30: 254/171). The basic structure remains, but the problem is now amplified: the possibility of thought is now a historical problem, and the question of its emergence an increasingly elusive matter. There is, it seems, not a single experience (in the philosophically rich sense of *Erfahrung*, and not in the impoverished, empty sense of *Erlebnis*) that is strong enough to wrest us from the state of extreme oblivion (*Vergessenheit*) and abandonment (*Verlassenheit*) in which we find ourselves, or from the position of radical separation from our own essence. If anything, the technological world as we know and experience it today is that of an absolute and, it seems, irreversible dispersion, of an increasingly fragmented time-space that reflects the imperatives of consumption and of the construction of oneself as lived experience. To be sure, only the *essence* of technology, rather than anything technological, can be thought, that is, recollected and meditated. But does thought not need to be already at work in order for the question of essence to be raised, and the essence of technology to be held in view?

Heidegger's messianic tendencies stem from his inability to pose that question with sufficient clarity. By messianic, I mean the tendency to attribute the leap of thought, and the transformation of our collective and historical Dasein, to a "saving power," whether it be that of a hypothetical "custodian" (*Verwalter*) capable of reawakening us to our own essence in 1929–1930 (GA 29/30: 244/163), of the actual *Führer* himself in 1933, of art in "The Question Concerning Technology," or of a "god" in the interview with *Der Spiegel* in 1966.

I am not claiming that those figures all operate on the same level. In fact, and for reasons that will become apparent, I should want to isolate art as a very specific, and indeed pivotal, experience in which thought is indeed called upon and opened up, set in motion as it were, and in such a way that it moves away from the messianic climate of the promise, salvation, and patient expectation. To save, Heidegger suggests in "The Question Concerning Technology," is not to draw something or someone away from the danger they face. Rather, it is to fetch something home into its essence, in order to bring the essence for the first time into its genuine appearing. To rescue, or to save, means to undo, to frank, to free, to look after and protect, to shelter, to take under one's wing, and safeguard (TK 41). As such, it is synonymous with recollective thought. As the saving power understood in this sense, art does not save us *from* technology, as if technology signified this ultimate danger to be avoided. Rather, art forces us deeper into technology by bringing us face to face with its essence. The work of art, whether visual or poetic, and so long as it hasn't been subjected to the demands and norms of the *Kulturindustrie* (a condition that is increasingly rare), is thus a site of resistance, that is, a self-reflective mode of production that discloses its own disclosedness, or the process by which it came into being. In the work, it is not just the product and its sheer presence that speak. Nor is it the artist, that is, his or her "experience" or "worldview." Rather, it is that which, of itself, does not show itself, or that which withdraws in what it discloses. Art, along with a certain relation to language, which poetry incarnates, indicates the opening up of a sphere of experience—of experience as such—which technology has always already sealed off. It is at once closest to technology, in that it is a form of *poiesis*, and farthest from it, inasmuch as it stems from a response to, and a gathering of, that which remains hidden and suppressed in the technological mode of production and manifestation. Art is the unnamed, unknown, and unsurpassed "other" of technology. The history it opens up is not so much outside that of technology, as folded into it. And the unfolding of this fold, in which something else takes place, is the realization of the hidden and preserved essence of technology:

> Because the essence of technology is nothing technological, essential reflection upon technology and decisive confrontation with it must happen in a realm that is, on the one hand, akin to the essence of technology and, on the other, fundamentally different from it. Such a realm is art. (QCT 35)

Heidegger, as we know, rejects the term "aesthetics" as metaphysical: it operates within a distinction, that between the sensible and the intelligible, which "thought" tries to move away from; and as a theory of art rooted in the problematic of feeling and taste, it fails to address the question of the origin of the work of art, and of the beautiful.

My claim is that what is missing in Heidegger's account of the emergence of thought is precisely a strong account of the aesthetic, understood as a double theory of the sensible and art, and in which the sensible includes the affective, or what Heidegger thinks under the category of attunement (*Stimmung, Befindlichkeit*). For once we have acknowledged that thought is not an innate faculty that can be activated through an act of the will, or through a free accord between faculties, once we have recognized Memory as the thought of the transcendental, do we not need to locate in the sensible itself, and our sensible experience of the world, the (perhaps minimal) spark that lights up pure time, or the trigger of Memory? How could thought not originate in the sensible? This does not commit one to a metaphysical aesthetics: for the sensible does not open onto the intelligible, as if the realm of Ideas were the truth of that of the sensible. Instead, the sensible, conceived under very specific conditions, appears as the site from which we are *forced* to think. It is the shock that sets thought in motion, that is, the sign that takes us to the limit of the sensible, or to the point at which it becomes Memory. Exemplary, if not programmatic, in that respect, is Proust's great novel, and the role that the involuntary plays in it. For what does the taste of the madeleine, the sound of the knife against the plate, the feeling of the uneven pavement beneath the narrator's feet make possible, if not a window into the past not as it was once lived, and was once present, but as it exists (or rather insists) in a state of purity that exceeds chronological, linear time, and the ordinary organization and distribution of space? This aesthetic provocation is what gives food for thought, and forces the different faculties—sensibility, memory, and thought—into a different arrangement, a different regime, beyond representation and recognition. Out of this shock, thought is wrested from its torpor, and exposed to the *being* of the sensible.[3] The sensible can, in that respect, be connected to a work of art, or to an affect, whether individual or collective, from boredom to indignation or disgust. But it is conducive to thought only to the extent that it takes aesthetic experience, or a given mood, to a new threshold and a new power, which disrupts the order of things, and of the world, and demands another kind of response. Failing such an account, we will inevitably fall back into a sort of *deus ex machina*: a God, a "call," a gift (*Gabe*), or an "address." Thought, as distinct from cognition, representation and calculation, will not have been accounted for immanently, but only axiomatically posited as the response to an address or sending that emanates from the depths of our time.

NOTES

1. GA 8: 121/117. The passage in question reads: "Seeing a large crowd around him, Jesus called to them to go to the other side of the lake" (Matt. 8:18).

2. For a detailed discussion of *thaumazein*, see GA 45: §§36–37.

3. I have tried to develop those thoughts in *Proust as Philosopher: The Art of Metaphor* (London: Routledge, 2012) and *Aesthetics After Metaphysics: From Mimesis to Metaphor* (London: Routledge, 2012).

Chapter 27

Clearing and Space

Thinking with Heidegger and Beyond

Günter Figal

Philosophy, from Plato on, has always been a particular kind of clarification devoted to matters of a particular kind. These matters are, in a certain way, well known, often familiar, but nevertheless not to be determined offhandedly. They are different from normal objects of linguistic determination, and accordingly it is difficult to find adequate words for them. Matters of philosophy in general are as time is according to Augustine's characterization: One intuitively knows what time is, but only as long as one does not make attempts to articulate this knowledge.[1] Challenged to do this, one will normally have no precise idea what to say.

Philosophizing begins with this lack of adequate words, and it does not only begin so. Philosophical attempts to determine something never are definite, but always preliminary, and accordingly matters of philosophy remain indefinite, at least to a certain degree. There is nothing mystical about this indeterminacy, as if philosophical matters would withdraw from experience and perception. Philosophical matters, this may be repeated, are well known, and their indeterminacy only applies to attempts at determination. This can be so because the knowledge of philosophical matters is of a particular kind. According to Wittgenstein, the knowledge of time as Augustine describes it is like that of the sound of musical instruments, for instance of a clarinet. One may almost hear this sound as soon as the question how a clarinet sounds is asked, or as soon as just the word "clarinet" is uttered. To describe and to determine this sound, however, is difficult if not impossible.[2]

The indeterminacy of philosophical matters as indicated has its parallel in the indeterminacy of philosophical discourse. Philosophizing never comes to an end because the language of philosophy cannot avoid being indeterminate at least to some degree. Philosophizing always is searching and finding; it is never the firm possession of definitely articulated knowledge, since there is no standard language of philosophy that would guarantee a standard description of philosophical matters. Philosophy never is "normal science." Its questions arise again and again, and accordingly philosophical clarifications can always be complemented or replaced by other ones. Philosophical matters cannot be clarified except in the web of many incomplete clarifications.

Since there is no standard for philosophical thinking and for the language of philosophy, one might seek orientation in philosophies already developed and manifest in philosophical writings. In such writings philosophical matters in question have already found a certain determinacy, and thus these writings may appear as a basis for attempts to find adequate words or even just words for them. On the one hand, such reference to philosophical writings, indeed, can be helpful. Clarifications already elaborated may function as pre-clarifications for one's own philosophical attempts, and, going along with this, one may learn that philosophical clarifications are not isolated, but rather have as context the discourse of philosophy that always has to be taken into account. One may learn that philosophy has many different ways to investigate a particular subject matter and to seek for clarifications. On the other hand, philosophies already elaborated may be regarded as authoritative or even as canonical doctrines, which cannot be disputed. As a consequence of this view, one may subordinate one's own attempts at philosophical thinking to such an authoritative philosophy. This, however, is philosophically problematic. With the presupposition of philosophical certainty one will lose the true sense of philosophizing and thus fail to do philosophy at all.

The supportive and also the problematic functions of philosophies already elaborated may, possibly at best, be illustrated by the effective history of Heidegger's philosophical work. Many philosophers who have been motivated and inspired by Heidegger's work have found their own way in philosophy. They have shared Heidegger's questions, his ways of reading traditional philosophical texts, and many of his insights without being subordinate to him. Others, however, have followed Heidegger as if his work were a doctrine, and thus they have become Heideggerians.

Heidegger himself has enabled and supported both attitudes. His keen sense for philosophical questions, his scrutinizing readings, and his discoveries of new philosophical ground have encouraged many philosophers to ask questions anew and to read the main sources of philosophy with new eyes. But Heidegger's thinking also has given remarkable support to various types of dogmatism. Though he claims to avoid the conceptual predeterminations of the philosophical or, as he puts it, "metaphysical" tradition, his own language has turned out to be canonic for those who unhesitatingly follow him. Even more, Heidegger's vision of history, namely his conviction that modernity, dominated by science and technology as it is, has to be overcome by a "New Beginning," has been adopted by many of his readers. This, however, has proved to be deeply problematic. As the publication of Heidegger's so-called *Black Notebooks* has revealed, his worldview includes ideological presuppositions and resentments that cannot be neatly separated from his "pure" philosophical considerations.[3] This does not mean that Heidegger's thinking in general should be regarded as ideological. Despite Heidegger's problematic and even disgraceful convictions, his thinking should be taken seriously as philosophy. This includes, however, finding out which aspects of his philosophy allow or even favor ideology. For this purpose one should try to determine, so to speak, the essence of Heidegger's philosophy, or, as he himself would have called it, the matter of his thinking. If this matter can be brought into sight, one can ask whether and to which degree the problematic aspects of Heidegger's thinking are grounded in this matter. And one can make attempts to clarify whether conceptual elaborations of this matter different from Heidegger's own are possible, perhaps more convincing, and in any case less problematic.

So what is the matter of Heidegger's philosophy? Is there only *one* such matter or is there a manifold of them? Heidegger's philosophy, this almost goes without saying, can be discussed in many respects. But without one single matter that, more or less explicitly, would be present throughout in Heidegger's philosophical considerations, his philosophy could not be a unitary and consistent philosophy at all. In any case, Heidegger himself saw his philosophical work as led by one single philosophical matter. He determines this matter most clearly in a text from 1964, "The End of Philosophy and the Task of Thinking."[4] This very title is instructive. It indicates that the task of thinking, which is tantamount to the matter of thinking, cannot be that of philosophy. As it were, the task and matter of thinking does not come into play before philosophy has come to an end. So this task and matter is *transphilosophical*, just as "thinking" in its devotion to this matter is beyond philosophy. Accordingly, thinking in Heidegger's sense has to be understood in relation to philosophy, more precisely in relation to philosophy's inability to experience and to articulate the matter of thinking.

First, however, one should say what the matter of thinking for Heidegger is. It is not, as one might expect, "Being" or "Beying," but rather "Clearing" (*Lichtung*). Heidegger had used this word earlier, already in *Being and Time*, but without taking it then as a word for his matter of thinking. Heidegger explains this matter by referring to the word's ordinary meaning. "Clearing" (and also the German word *Lichtung*) means an open site in a forest, a site that has been cleared from trees and, accordingly, is a clear site. Since it is free from trees, one could also call it a free site. "Clear" or "free" in this sense both mean "uncovered," "void" and thereby also "accessible" and, more basically, "open." A clearing is a site that may be lightened and then allow an unimpeded view that would be impossible in a dense forest or in a thicket. In the openness of a clearing, something or someone can appear so that it or she or he can be seen in its or her or his appearance.

Heidegger's explication of the word "clearing" directly applies to the matter of thinking. The matter of thinking *is* clearing in the way just explained. It is nothing that only could be compared to clearings in forests. As Heidegger says, he is not "extracting mere notions from mere words, e.g. *Lichtung*, at it might appear on the surface," but "rather, we must observe the unique matter that is named with the name 'clearing' in accordance with the matter" (442). According to this explication, clearings in forests are particular cases, concretions of Clearing as the matter of thinking. As this matter, Clearing is clear or free openness in which something can appear and can be experienced in its appearing. As Heidegger says, appearing is in need of lightness that as such belongs to an openness, which, at times, can be lightened. Also the play of brightness and darkness, of sounding and trailing away belongs to the clear or free site of Clearing (442).

The explications just given implicitly determine the conceptual status of Heidegger's matter of thinking. Clearing, as Heidegger explains it, is a *phenomenological* matter and task—more precisely, the essential matter and task of a version of phenomenology that seeks to clarify the *possibility* of appearing and of its experience. This possibility was already the task and matter of Heidegger's phenomenology as developed in *Being and Time*. In his early magnum opus, however, Heidegger had identified the possibility of appearing and of its experience with the "disclosure" (*Erschlossenheit*) of the Being of human beings, which he calls *Dasein*. Compared with Heidegger's later version of Clearing, this is a remarkably different conception. But despite their difference, Heidegger's earlier and later versions of phenomenology are revisionary in the same respect. Both versions are meant as critical revisions of Husserl's phenomenology. They claim to clarify what Husserl, according to Heidegger's conviction, had just taken for granted. Heidegger's argument against Husserl in his late text, namely that original intuition and evidence in Husserl's sense are not possible without Clearing (443), is basically the same as his argument in *Being and Time*. But now, in his later text, Heidegger no longer makes attempts to revise Husserl's phenomenology on the basis of the ontology of Dasein. The openness that enables appearing as well as its experience is no longer conceived as the "disclosure" of Dasein, but rather as an openness that encompasses the experience of appearing and appearing itself. As one would say in reference to the language of *Being and Time*, the openness called "Clearing" *transcends* not only the intentional correlates of Dasein, but Dasein itself. This transcending openness is the later Heidegger's matter of thinking.

But why is this matter supposed to be exclusively the matter of thinking as strictly distinguished from philosophy? Heidegger's answer to this question is a simple assertion: Philosophy in Heidegger's sense is not able to understand what Clearing is. From its very beginning on, philosophy has only considered appearances, everything that is present, but not appearing and presence as enabled by Clearing. Heidegger admits that Parmenides, in the very beginning of philosophy, had caught a glimpse of Clearing when he spoke of *Alētheia*, but "afterward it is not explicitly thought as such by philosophy" (446). Heidegger does not say directly why this should have been the case. He suggests, however, that philosophy might have missed Clearing because of the very "nature" of Clearing itself. As he says, "self-concealing, concealment, *lēthē*, belongs to *a-lētheia*, not as a mere addition, not as shadow to light, but rather as the heart of *alētheia*" (448). Appearing might only be enabled along with the withdrawal of the enabling as such. The very possibility of appearing, then, must be concealed in order to allow appearing.

But why should this be so? At least, Clearing cannot be completely concealed if it can be the matter and task of thinking. But why, then, did no philosopher before Heidegger, for example Parmenides, discover Clearing as the matter of his thought? As Heidegger indicates, this might have been the case because of the ambivalent "nature" of *Alētheia*. Whereas *Alētheia* can be understood as Clearing, it can also be correctness (*Richtigkeit*) and reliability (*Verlässlichkeit*), and that is what truth is for "natural" experiencing and speaking. According to Heidegger, philosophy has exclusively adopted this second option, so that philosophy essentially has been bound to "natural" experiencing and speaking. Phenomenologically speaking, philosophy has been bound to the "natural attitude" (*natürliche Einstellung*) in Husserl's sense. As a consequence, philosophy as such cannot be phenomenological. The decisive phenomenological operation, namely the suspension of the natural attitude, leads beyond philosophy.

Why, however, should thinking in Heidegger's sense be able to think what essentially remains concealed for philosophy? Why should thinking, in contrast to philosophy, be phenomenological? Again Heidegger's answer is a simple assertion: because philosophy has come to an end and thus has lost its binding power. Philosophy is no longer an option for those who seek to think.

The end of philosophy, as Heidegger understands it, is neither perfection nor decline. According to Heidegger, philosophy, rather, came to an end already in "the age of Greek philosophy." Already then, "a decisive characteristic of philosophy appears," namely "the development of the sciences within the field that philosophy opened up" (433). This development has meanwhile become dominant and it has led to the "separation" of the sciences from philosophy and to "the establishment of their independence" (433). Independent as they have become, the sciences replace philosophy and bring it so to an end. This does not mean that there is no longer something that could and would be called "philosophy." Just as Hegel's conviction that art has come to an end does not imply the ending of all artistic production, Heidegger's statement about the end of philosophy allows for activities called "philosophical" of whatsoever kind. As Heidegger assumes, however, these activities have no credibility. Heidegger regards them as imitations of what philosophy formerly was, without having original power. They are just "an epigonal renaissance and variations of that renaissance" (433).

As a consequence, the impulse that originally was philosophical has to reach beyond philosophy and thus become "thinking." Thinking in Heidegger's sense reflects its philosophical prehistory and realizes what has remained in concealment during the philosophical age of thinking as the hidden enabling of philosophy—Clearing, the possibility of appearing, and of its experience. Heidegger also assumes that a new general orientation in the age of science could go along with thinking. In this sense he speaks of the "possibility that the world civilization that is just now beginning might one day overcome its technological-scientific-industrial character as the sole criterion of man's world sojourn" (437). Heidegger does not say how a "transformation" (436) of philosophy into "thinking" should be possible. He does not discuss why and how it can be possible for "thinking" to consider what has been concealed during the centuries of philosophy. He is just convinced of a historical caesura that allows him a retrospect on philosophy in general and also a new beginning with a matter of thinking that, in a different version, was already his matter in *Being and Time*.

So far, the matter of thinking as Heidegger understands it should have become sufficiently clear, as well as the contour of the thinking that is devoted to this matter. This thinking, thinking in Heidegger's particular sense, may have become intelligible as a very special version of phenomenology combined with an interpretation of history hitherto, including the modern age, that is mainly a history of philosophy and science. One may assume that Heidegger's interpretation of the modern age is meant to legitimate the transformation of philosophy into thinking. Thinking, Heidegger is at least convinced of that, is the only chance not to be entrapped in modernity's "technological-scientific-industrial character."

Is this conviction plausible? This question may initiate a critical examination of Heidegger's considerations concerning the end of philosophy and the task of thinking, not the least because it includes another, more specific question, namely whether philosophy really is unable to understand Heidegger's matter of thinking. Is thinking in Heidegger's sense really the only chance to reach beyond the "technological-scientific-industrial character" of the present age? If this proves not to be the case, Heidegger's understanding of the present age will become dubious. There would be no need, then, to assume that this age is shaped by nothing but the independence of the sciences from philosophy and that there is no longer a chance for philosophy in the traditional sense.

Surely the independence of the sciences from philosophy cannot seriously be disputed. It was as recently as the nineteenth century that, via scientific emancipation, psychology and sociology were established as self-contained, independent sciences. This scientific emancipation and independence, however, do not imply the end of philosophy. Perhaps philosophy has only lost some burden, so that it may have become easier to concentrate on tasks that are really and exclusively philosophical—tasks that better should not be treated in the sciences, because there is no scientific solution for them. Heidegger very likely would argue against this option; he would or could say that philosophy, in the century of its bloom, has proved to be scientific and therefore is essentially unable to reach beyond the sciences. But this is not true. Plato already reflected critically on the presuppositions of the sciences. Unlike the sciences, however, such a reflection cannot be based on these presuppositions, and accordingly philosophy cannot be scientific or scientifically bound at all.

Philosophy as a competence for critical reflection can go along with the sciences without any competition. Sciences never will be able to rule philosophy out, if science and philosophy are essentially different from each other. And if philosophy can be a critical reflection of science, the "technological-scientific-industrial character" of the present age cannot be as firm and all-encompassing as Heidegger assumes. The contrast between a homogeneously technological, scientific and industrial age on the one hand, and "untimely" thinking that goes beyond the "character" of this age on the other hand, is all too simple. Simplifications like this led Heidegger to his refusal of modernity in general, and so also to his most problematic exaggerations and resentments.

If philosophy, despite Heidegger's assertion, has not come to an end, a general retrospect on the age of philosophy is impossible. Philosophy is not as homogeneous as Heidegger assumes it to be, and accordingly his general statements about the limits of philosophy are no longer convincing. If philosophy has not come to an end, there is no viewpoint outside philosophy from which the supposed presuppositions of philosophy could be critically reflected. If critical reflection of philosophy is nevertheless necessary and possible, it must be a philosophical affair—and this it has always been, as long as philosophy has existed. Philosophy, then, cannot be a conceptual version of the "natural attitude." Rather, the suspension of the natural attitude is a philosophical option. Phenomenology belongs to philosophy. It is not transphilosophical at all.

Accordingly, there is sufficient evidence to doubt that the single matter of phenomenology is a phenomenon that has essentially been concealed from philosophy. Why should phenomenology be devoted to such an exclusive matter, and why should this be its only distinction from other versions of philosophy? According to Husserl's phenomenological program, the so-called "Principle of Principles," no particular matter constitutes phenomenology, but rather its specific way of considering subject matters, whatever they may be. As Husserl says, phenomenology accepts everything "originarily," "in its bodily actuality, so to speak," "as it gives itself, but also only in the limits in which it gives itself there."[5]

Heidegger explicitly rejected Husserl's program. But his reasons for doing so are difficult to maintain. Quite surprisingly, Heidegger states that Husserl's program "contains the thesis of the precedence of method" and that it "requires absolute subjectivity as the matter of philosophy" (440). With the "Principle of Principles," nothing like this is said. Instead of being committed to method in a Cartesian manner, Husserl's principle adheres to the primacy of perception that originally presents its subject matter. This is a general statement. It is not restricted to "absolute subjectivity" and it cannot even apply to "absolute subjectivity," since nothing absolute can be given within "limits." For Husserl—this may be repeated—the matter of phenomenology is not "absolute subjectivity," but everything originarily given in perception. Because of this, and contrary to Heidegger's argument, the Principle of Principles and Husserl's statement according to which "matters and problems" should be the motivation for phenomenological research basically have the same intention.

Heidegger's critical remarks on Husserl's Principle of Principles thus prove not to be plausible. This, however, does not per se refute Heidegger's own contribution to phenomenology. Husserl, in contrast to Heidegger, did not investigate the possibility of phenomena, perhaps because he took it as assured by the immanent givenness of phenomena in consciousness. As Husserl is convinced, phenomena are to be experienced as soon as the assumption of reality made in the natural attitude is suspended and, as a consequence, the contents of consciousness can be contemplated in pure, immanent reflection. A letter that Heidegger wrote to Husserl on October 22, 1927 (GA 14: 129–32) gives clear evidence that Heidegger, already in the twenties of his century, doubts the plausibility of this assumption. He agrees with Husserl that the transcendental constitution of the "world" of beings cannot be elucidated in reference to some being of the same kind. But, as Heidegger adds, this does not necessarily mean that the "place of the transcendental" could not be a being at all (GA 14: 131). Heidegger, indeed, takes the "place of the transcendental" as a being, albeit a being of another kind, and he claims to have elucidated the kind of being (*Seinsart*) of the being that constitutes the world of beings in the analytic of *Dasein* in *Being and Time*. Husserl resolutely rejects Heidegger's proposal. For him, the "philosophy of human existence" (*die Philosophie des menschlichen Daseins*) is a regression to a kind of naivety, the overcoming of which has been the sense of modernity (*der ganze Sinn der Neuzeit*). Heidegger, on the other hand, rejects Husserl's phenomenology as a transcendental philosophy of pure consciousness, and he sticks to this rejection till his late years. As he states in a seminar on his lecture "Time and Being," with the "invasion of philosophy into phenomenology (in the shape of Neo-Kantianism)," "the principle of phenomenology was relinquished" (GA 14: 53). But Heidegger does not stick to the anthropological foundation of phenomenology as elaborated in *Being and Time*. This gives support to the assumption that he has taken Husserl's critique seriously. Heidegger's late answer to the question of the possibility of phenomena, the thinking of Clearing, is not anthropological at all, but rather regards human experience as also being enabled by Clearing.

At least one problem of Heidegger's earlier philosophy is conserved in his later thinking. One could call it the problem of regressive foundation. Whereas the earlier Heidegger was sure that a particular being could constitute the world of beings, the late Heidegger regards the possibility of phenomena as a phenomenon, more precisely as a "primal phenomenon" (*Urphänomen*) (442). Heidegger does not explain this word invented by Goethe, and thus it remains unclear how to understand it in the context of his argument. Of course one could agree with Goethe's advice—Heidegger quotes it—not to seek something "behind phenomena," since "they themselves are what is to be learned" (442). This advice can help to avoid the presupposition of something "real" or "ideal" from which phenomena could be deduced, thus deviating from the phenomenological way of philosophy. But Goethe's advice would not help to understand how Clearing could be a "primal phenomenon" and just as little to answer the question of how the possibility of phenomena can be a phenomenon, even the only phenomenon of phenomenology. This assumption appears as problematic as an assumption made in the sixth and seventh book of Plato's *Republic*, namely that the possibility of the ideas is an idea. It should be more plausible to neatly distinguish the possibility of something from what is made possible and, accordingly, to say that the possibility of phenomena as such cannot appear. It must be non-appearing in contrast to the appearing of phenomena—a particular kind of non-appearing, however, that is different from concealment, because otherwise it could not be experienced at all. The possibility of phenomena understood in this way could be called "inconspicuous." It would be experienced together with phenomena, like the background together with something that can draw attention because of a background. A background, understood in this way, is not just background but the main feature of appearing. The inconspicuous, understood in this way, is neither appearing nor concealed.

Though the inconspicuous is no "primal phenomenon," Heidegger's considerations on Clearing can help to see more concretely how it can be conceived. As free and open site, Clearing must be *space*—not just one particular site among others, but rather the openness of every particular site. It is not metaphorical to speak of Clearing in this sense since every particular site and every particular clearing *is*, as such, spatial openness.[6] Every particular site, if it is clear, is ready to *receive and hold* something. It is *transparent* so that it allows free appearing and a free view on everything that appears. And it is *open wideness*, in which there can be distances so that everything that has found its place in this wideness can be beside something else and in relation to it, in such a way that one may take distance from it, more or less distance, and experience it from closer by or from farther away. *Places* that may receive and hold something, *free spaces* that allow free appearing and experience in freedom, *wideness* that lets something be in distance from something else and thus in relation to each other—these are possibilities of space.

Though it seems plausible to conceive Clearing as space, Heidegger did not take this way. He only suggests this option in a certain way, but he does not realize it. Instead he considers whether Clearing must be beyond space and time, in such a way that Clearing as free openness may be "that within which alone pure space and ecstatic time and everything present and absent in them have the place that gathers and protects everything" (442–43). This consideration, however, is strange. A place for space and time—what should that be? How should space be at a place? Whereas this does not make sense, it appears intelligible to understand Clearing as space—as place, free space, and wideness.

If Clearing proves to be space, then space is the possibility or the enabling of phenomenality. The sketchy remarks on place, free space, and wideness just made may at least indicate how this can be understood. This understanding could be made explicit, and that, again, would show in detail that phenomena cannot sufficiently be described without referring to their spatial character. Then the experience of phenomena, too, must be spatial. Something seen or heard is at a place, it needs free space in order to appear and to be experienced, and it appears as closer by or as farther. Thus, the enabling of phenomena is "there" with every phenomenon. It can be philosophically considered and described.

In the history of philosophy space has been discussed in different ways—seldom extensively, however, seldom sufficiently, and only once, namely in Plato's *Timaeus*, in its complexity. Nevertheless, there is no "metaphysical" forgetfulness of space, as if "metaphysics" as a whole would not have been able to consider this singular matter, Clearing, so that there would be need to overcome "metaphysics" in a kind of thinking that, as nonphilosophical original phenomenology, would be totally different from it. The exclusivity of this conviction generates the revolutionary gestures and authoritative claims of Heidegger's thinking. In contrast to such an attitude, the exploration and description of space as the enabling of phenomena and of their experience is something normal. Spatial phenomenology is not supposed to revolutionize philosophy, but rather to cultivate it. It is only possible in letting philosophy be as it is. Spatial phenomenological thinking does not mark a new beginning, much less one that begins differently. It just goes on, and it does so in the context of philosophical tradition.

The normality of such a philosophical exploration of space does not imply that its matter, space, would be easily accessible. This, however, also is philosophically normal, assuming that all matters of philosophy are like time as characterized by Augustine—well known, even familiar, but difficult to conceive and to describe. What should be known better and be more familiar than space? Space is there in every look, in every listening, in every movement, and in everything experienced. Space is also there in language, in every sentence referring to something that is "there" and is also "this," something objective over there that can be pointed to; likewise with every sentence that refers to things as being in juxtaposition, or "under" or "above" something else, or "in" something or "outside" of it; finally, in every sentence that localizes its speaker as "here," in such a way that one may experience that this "here" belongs to oneself, since one is always "here," no matter at which place one is. Maybe just because space is "everywhere" and "nowhere," it is so difficult to grasp and to describe. Space, in its inconspicuousness, indeterminacy, and nonobjectivity, withdraws from straightforward conception. Presumably no small reason for this is that conception as such is spatial—the word "to conceive" has a spatial meaning. Is everything spatial, at least everything inconspicuous? Is language spatial and also time? These are questions concerning matters of philosophy. They cannot be elucidated without original perception and without discussing philosophical conceptions already elaborated, again and again.

NOTES

1. Augustinus, *Confessionum Libri XIII*, Corpus Christianorum Series Latina XXVII, ed. Lukas Verheijen (Turnholt: Brepols, 1981), XI, 14: "Quid est ergo tempus? si nemo ex me quaerat, scio; si quaerenti explicare velim, nescio."

2. Ludwig Wittgenstein, *Philosophical Investigations,* tr. G.E.M. Anscombe, P.M.S. Hacker, and Joachim Schulte, revised 4th ed. (Oxford: Wiley-Blackwell, 2009), §§78, 89.

3. For a more extensive discussion, cf. Günter Figal, "Die andere Seite der Philosophie: Zu Heideggers *Schwarzen Heften*," *Journal Phänomenologie* 45 (2016): 101–18.

4. In *Basic Writings*, revised ed., ed. David F. Krell (San Francisco, CA: HarperSanFrancisco, 1993), 427–49. All quotations from the text are from this edition. The original German text, "Das Ende der Philosophie und die Aufgabe des Denkens," is published in GA 14: 67–90.

5. Edmund Husserl, *Ideen zu einer reinen Phänomenologie und phänomenologischen Philosophie: Erstes Buch: Allgemeine Einführung in die reine Phänomenologie*, Husserliana III.1, ed. Karl Schuhmann (The Hague: Martinus Nijhoff, 1976), §24, 51. Translation by David Farrell Krell in Heidegger, *Basic Writings*, 439.

6. For an extensive discussion of the conception of space as sketched, cf. Günter Figal, *Unscheinbarkeit: Der Raum der Phänomenologie* (Tübingen: Mohr Siebeck, 2015).

Chapter 28

Thinking Bodily Time-Spaces with and Beyond Heidegger

Daniela Vallega-Neu

When one looks at academic philosophy programs in the United States and in many European countries, a strong emphasis on analytic philosophy as well as on social, political, and moral philosophy is hard to miss. Everywhere there appears the demand that philosophy adhere to a language rationally accessible that operates with clearly defined concepts, and that it show "practical" outcomes and thus contribute to what are considered to be "concrete" problems. In Continental philosophy, this demand applies especially to issues of diversity in terms of gender and race or ethnicity, but also to environmental matters (climate change, animal rights). In such a scenario, it would seem, Heidegger has little to contribute, since he criticizes the very demand for practical outcomes as testifying to the oblivion of the question of being and, as he would say in the 1930s, the abandonment of beings by being under the dominion of "machination" and "technology." Furthermore, one cannot but denounce his poor political judgments and his newly confirmed anti-Semitism as they appear, for instance, in the *Black Notebooks*. And yet, for Heidegger, his question of being was nothing lofty or abstract but was rooted in what he experienced as a historical plight. He found a necessity to revive philosophy and to ground it in true historical being. Heidegger thinks that historical being claims each of us and determines how things appear to us and how we relate to things and to each other. I (like so many Heidegger scholars) am critical with respect to the way Heidegger frames the question of being in the 1930s: he frames it in terms of a history of being that commences with the Greeks and for which he seeks to prepare another beginning in which the Germans (above all Hölderlin and Heidegger himself) are supposed to play a prominent role. Still, there are many aspects of Heidegger's approach to the question of being in the 1930s and 1940s that are important and pressing for philosophy today because they open up possibilities for fostering sensibilities and transformations of our fundamental approach to living and nonliving beings and events.

In what follows, I will address a number of aspects of Heidegger's thinking that open important venues and possibilities of thinking beyond Heidegger's own work. Among these aspects are how the question of being is opened up and directed by attunements and dispositions and the profound work with listening and language this requires; Heidegger's rethinking of Da-sein (literally "t/here-being" or "being-t/here") in terms of a concrete spatiotemporal site of being; his move away from the primacy of subjectivity and thinking in terms of subject–object relations; and the middle-voice thinking he fosters. I will furthermore propose that we "unhinge" Heidegger's notion of Da-sein in the 1930s from its reductive being-historical framing, and attempt to rethink it in terms of plural, embodied, historical sites of being, not only of humans but of any thing or event. I thus find resources in Heidegger to give accounts of things and events as complex interconnected spatiotemporal occurrences, and this in the effort to do justice to the complex senses of being in our "globalizing" world.

For Heidegger, being (whether in terms of the sense of being as such or of a historical sense of being in the West) manifests itself in fundamental attunements (*Grundstimmungen*) that unsettle us from our everyday involvement with things and show how our being is fundamentally exposed and finite. In order to think being as such, one needs to stay with these attunements and attempt to think and speak from them. Fundamental attunements are distinguished from non-fundamental attunements in that they do not relate to this or that thing or event. In *Being and Time* Heidegger notably found in *Angst* (which is to be distinguished from fear of something specific) a venue to think how Dasein occurs as a finite and groundless temporalizing in which possibilities of being open up, possibilities into which we find ourselves at the same time thrown. He writes of how in *Angst* there emerges a call ("the call of conscience") that summons Dasein to take over its most extreme possibility of being, namely death. It is in sustaining the possibility of not being that Dasein discloses being as such in its temporalizing. It is then that Dasein exists authentically or properly (*eigentlich*) (singularized with respect to its own possibilities of being) instead of being lost in the *Man* of everydayness, that is, in how "one" does things.

In the lecture course from the winter semester of 1929–1930, *The Fundamental Concepts of Metaphysics*, Heidegger thinks through another fundamental attunement, deep boredom, and now he begins to think this fundamental attunement in a historical context as revealing a historical sense of being for a people. Deep boredom (which reminds one very much of a sense of alienation and which is to be distinguished from a boredom arising in relation to something or someone) is constituted by "being left empty"

(*Leergelassenheit*) and "being held in limbo" (*Hingehaltenheit*). In deep boredom we are not bored because we have to wait at the bus station or a date does not show up. We cannot give any specific reason for our being bored; rather beings as a whole are indifferent and don't offer any possibility of engagement. Beings "refuse themselves," writes Heidegger, and in this refusal, in this not-being, there occurs a "spellbinding" or "entrancement" (*Gebanntsein*) of time (with its unitary horizon of past, present, and future) that harbors possibilities that are yet to be decided and that as such "press forward." The way Heidegger thinks here is similar to the relation between being-toward-death and the possibility of authentic being as Heidegger described it in *Being and Time*. Authentic or originary possibilities arise (disclose or press forward) in relation to a nonbeing, a lack—only that in *The Fundamental Concepts of Metaphysics*, Heidegger thinks of the lack and the possibilities as historical. Thus he ends his analysis of deep boredom by calling it the "fundamental attunement of *our* Dasein" (GA 29/30: 238, em), which points to how he understands what is revealed in deep boredom as a sense of being determining not only an individual but a people.

The relation between fundamental attunements and history becomes even more manifest in Heidegger's *Contributions to Philosophy (Of The Event)*, written 1936–1938. In this work, Heidegger will think of fundamental attunements in the context of the history of beyng (written with a "y" to mark this now more originally understood, historical sense of being). He understands this history of beyng in terms of its first beginning in Ancient Greece (where there prevailed the attunement of wonder that revealed a sense of being as surging and coming to presence) and the possibility of the other beginning into which he understands his thinking to begin to transition. His transitional thinking occurs in an attunement that reveals in shock, restraint, and diffidence (see section 5 of *Contributions*) a sense of being as withdrawal and abandonment (which reminds one of the "being left empty" he speaks of in 1929–1930) and at the same time (much as also in *Being and Time*) springing from the sense of lack, a call to which thinking finds itself responding, a call to ground a concrete site that may allow being to occur no longer only as withdrawal but as an event (*Ereignis*) in which humans (not only as individuals but also as a people) and all beings are appropriated into their own (*eigen*) and *are* in a more original way. This site of being (of which I will write more further down) Heidegger calls Da-sein (now written with a dash) and he addresses it as well as time-space.

One may (I certainly do) find it difficult to follow Heidegger in his presentiment of the possibility of another beginning for a people, especially when he frames it in terms of the Greeks and the Germans; one may also maintain a healthy suspicion with respect to the epochal implications in Heidegger's thinking of fundamental attunements. (How can he be so sure of the epochal dimension of the attunements that determine his thinking, i.e., that the historicality of beyng in the West is at stake? What if the complexity of attunements that he acknowledges has to do as well with an implication—a co-attuning, so to speak—of attunements that are of a more culturally specific or "personal" or local nature?) Still, the very notion that thinking and all human comportment are always attuned, and that attunements can carry historical dimensions well beyond so-called individual human lives, harbors important and fruitful insights and opens possibilities of thinking with and beyond Heidegger. In our prevalently scientifically oriented Western societies, attunements are usually understood as subjective feelings that are opposed to a rationally accessible objective world. But Heidegger draws our attention to how attunements (or moods) are experienced as overcoming us and not as arising in a supposed human subject. In *Being and Time*, where Heidegger addresses the notion of attunement as well as *Befindlichkeit* (one may translate *Befindlichkeit* perhaps better with "disposition" in order to distinguish it from *Stimmung*), he points out how attunement testifies to our thrownness into our possibilities of being and with this, into relations with things. Attunements testify to the fact that we are not first encapsulated subjects with inner feeling who then relate to things in the world. Rather, how we find ourselves to be is already a historically rooted, exposed being-with things, events, others, or—in rare moments—an exposure to the fact of being and nonbeing as such (in the case of fundamental attunements). Pervasive, historically determining attunements for many people in Western society are, for instance, fears connected with incumbent ecological disasters or the collapse of the economy. The insight that attunements like fear, hope, desires, and aversions predetermine our relation to things also has consequences with respect to the belief in rational judgments or how we understand thinking to occur. It invites a critical work and self-reflection not simply on the level of rational judgment but on the level of attunements and bodily dispositions. That we favor a political party or a political decision over another, for example, or that we argue for legalizing or deporting immigrants, is never only a matter of rational judgment but is predisposed by attunements rooted in historical lineages, habits, and relations to situations and people that "affect" and dispose us at the precognitive level of attunements. That we are able to listen and hear what someone means is also made possible or inhibited by attunements; even the elements we take into account when making decisions have already undergone a process of selection indebted to attunements that allow us to hear matters, to see possibilities, or remain deaf to them.

Heidegger's description of how in fundamental attunements lies a silent call, a summons, points to the close relationship between language and attunement. He does not think of language on the basis of words (written or spoken) that would signify something but rather as the very arising of meaning or sense. From the 1930s on, he questions the surging of language as he experiences it in his own thinking, namely as a response to a groundless silent call that has much to do with how his own thinking finds itself to be attuned or disposed in what he calls (in *Contributions to Philosophy*) the plight of the abandonment of beings by being. Beings, that is things and events, are encountered as not truly being since they are from the outset reduced to mere means of production, calculation, or enjoyment. The world is emptied of meaning, which relates to the domination of a scientific worldview that focuses only on those aspects of the world that are scientifically accessible and calculable. It is in this experience of lack that possibilities "press forth," to use a phrase from the 1929–1930 lecture course, or that Heidegger's thinking finds itself responding to a summons or call, intimating the possibility of a fuller, original sense of being.

Prior to being uttered or written, in Heidegger's understanding, language occurs as a saying (*Sagen* or *Sage*) that is to be distinguished from speaking "about" something. Saying (Heidegger thinks this notion in relation to the ancient Greek *logos*) is a disclosing and letting be seen. Rather than a speaking about something already there, saying is that through which something appears to us as *being there* in the first place, and only because something is thus disclosed to us can we talk about it. Starting in the 1930s, Heidegger's thinking becomes a practice of what I call (in reference to the Greek word *poiēsis*, "bringing forth") "poietic" saying and thinking, that is the practice of letting a sense of being arise in the very saying and thinking. This requires that thinking beforehand lets itself be attuned or determined by "what" calls to be said. I am writing "what" with quotation marks because "what" calls to be said is nothing before the saying. We may be familiar with this experience in creative writing or when we try to give words or meaning to "what" comes to be, perhaps at first, as an uneasy feeling: Prior to finding the words there is nothing already there. Whatever surges in the words we find, surges only in the finding of the words, which requires a certain attunement and—I would add—a particular bodily disposition. We do not experience such saying as something we "do," but neither are we simply passive in this event. This experience of "something" coming to word is a "middle voice" event; it is neither active nor passive nor simply a combination of the two. "Language speaks," writes Heidegger in his essay of 1950 titled "Language." The phrase evokes the ancient Greek middle voice—a voice that designates neither activity nor passivity and that does not exist in modern Indo-European languages. It can be approximated in passive verb form constructions such as when we speak of an event unfolding itself or in phrases such as "x occurs," "there is." Poetry often speaks in the middle voice, as may be exemplified by the famous short poem of Angelus Silesius: "The rose is without 'why'; it blooms simply because it blooms. It does not care about itself and does not ask whether it is seen."

Heidegger's emphasis on thinking in the middle voice carries significant possibilities for thinking beyond the subject–object distinction that has contributed to thinking in terms of a separation of the human subject and the world. It allows for a sense of the happening of things and events "in themselves." It works powerfully in Heidegger's attempt to think non-subjectively in the attuned exposure to what eventuates without having to reinstall a human subject either as the actor or as the passive recipient of an action. Heidegger's discipline of thinking with or out of attunements in attentiveness to the arising of sense thus also is a discipline of thinking in the middle voice. It opens up venues for what one may crudely call a more "embodied" thinking, or perhaps better said, "bodily thinking." Such a thinking does not take an observing or objective stance toward what it questions (which would imply thinking in terms of active or passive relations) but questions out of its attuned exposure to what is in question, such that attunements are like connective tissues through which we are bodily exposed and bound to what we question.

Heidegger himself famously wrote very little about the human body, a fact that has much to do with his effort to think human being not in terms of an entity but in terms of how it happens or how we find ourselves to be (ecstatically projected into possibilities of being into which we find ourselves always already thrown, always already being with others, things, and events in the openness of a world). In the *Zollikon Seminars* (1959–1969) Heidegger extends to the human body his effort to think human being not as an entity, by approaching the human body as lived body (*Leib*) (which is to be distinguished from *Körper*, the body understood as an object) in terms of its *Leiben*, its "bodying-forth." This bodying-forth is fundamentally ecstatic, in Heidegger's account. The limit of bodying-forth is not the skin, not even what lies within the scope of our senses, but rather the horizon of being in which I dwell (ZS 87). Heidegger develops bodying-forth in terms of the spatiality of our being and not by questioning further the relation between attunement and bodying-forth. He does, however, indicate that the way we "take place" or are spatial, the way we body-forth, is determined by language and that language is "also" a bodily phenomenon, for instance in hearing: "The listening to something is in itself the relation of bodying forth to what is heard" (ZS 96–97). If we consider the relation between language and attunement as indicated earlier, we can intuit how Heidegger opens a window to think (with and beyond what he writes) the relation between the lived body and language through the notion of attunement. We might explore how we find ourselves attuned not only in relation to how we find ourselves addressed or claimed by something or a sense of being, but also how this being claimed and being attuned configures our lived bodies, orients, and directs them, opens them up and lets them stay concealed; or—vice versa—how the dispositions of our bodies may allow us to listen and be open to what calls to be thought. What we see or hear when walking through the streets of a city is determined by (disclosive) attunements that dispose us toward looking up, or looking in a certain direction, or not looking at all as we are absorbed in our thoughts. In turn, what calls our attention and makes us move in determinate ways or say determinate things is at the same time dependent on the openness and orientation of our lived body. Places, cities, institutions, gardens, mountains, living beings, and groups of people carry attunements that dispose our bodies, not only how we feel but also how we find ourselves to be oriented and what we are able to hear and to say. Lineages and histories—mixed with "the news"—predispose our bodies also in determinate ways such that an event does or does not spark our attention, our attraction or aversion, or such that we can hear or not what a friend or a stranger has to say. Violence suffered through racial or gender discrimination attunes and disposes bodies in ways that determine how one moves, what calls one's attention, and, again, what one hears and has to say. Heidegger's own anti-Semitism is rooted, I would say, in attunements and dispositions associated with lineages he incorporated that disposed what he thought and wrote in his *Black Notebooks* about world Jewry.

Another possibility of thinking with and beyond Heidegger that has impacted my thinking is one that brings into play his notion of Dasein. In *Being and Time*, Dasein designates human existence, but in his non public writings of the 1930s, Heidegger attempts to think Da-sein (now written with a hyphen) in terms of a not-only-human site of being in which a world discloses itself in a fuller way. He thinks of Da-sein as a concrete time-space in which truth occurs. Such a time-space (Da-sein) happens only with beings, with words, works of art, or deeds that "shelter" truth and configure a concrete site of being, something that Heidegger elaborates, for instance, in his essay from 1936 "The Origin of the Work of Art." Thus, we may be struck by words or works of art that open up for us a fuller sense of being or a fuller sense of world. In essays from the 1950s (for instance, "Building, Dwelling, Thinking" and "The Thing"), Heidegger writes how things "gather" the world understood as the fourfold of earth and sky, mortals (humans), and divinities. His meditations on how in partaking in the configuration of a concrete site of being, things may occur in a way that they shelter truth or gather a world—these meditations occur against the backdrop of his experience of how currently in the West, things don't really happen in this way, how they don't shelter truth and don't gather a world but are encountered in advance as disposable commodities swallowed up in the demand for calculability, productivity, and enjoyment. In other words, Heidegger's thinking of the relation between being and beings, between truth and things, is determined by his account of the history of beyng as a further and further withdrawal of being, concealment of truth, and abandonment of beings; a lack that now necessitates—as he sees it—his own thinking and announces new, again inceptual possibilities of being. Thus Heidegger's interpretation of Da-sein as well as his account of things remain caught in the framework of the history of being, of a quest for an originary event of being on the one hand, and his interpretation of pretty much everything happening around him as being deprived of true being (the *Black Notebooks* testify to this). His history of being works like a gravitational power that does not allow him to see Da-sein in a perhaps more "humble" way (not only as an originary or authentic opening for "the" truth of beyng) and to consider things and events perhaps more on their own terms that seem to me mostly indifferent to human affairs. There are moments we experience when things or events appear to happen freely (in a middle-voice manner) in a way that lets a fuller sense of being emerge; this may occur in a conversation, a silent sharing of a moment of stillness, a musical performance. Do these not deserve to be called Da-sein? There is also much that happens indifferently to human affairs even when we find meaning in them, like the motion of celestial bodies, the flow of a river, the grazing of a deer, the aging of our skin, or digestion. It seems to me that a certain sense of indifference is necessary to begin to have a sense for things happening "on their own," and not primarily in relation to human being.

If we release the notion of Da-sein from the framework of the history of being, Heidegger opens up again possibilities of thinking beyond the tradition and beyond his own work. We may rethink Da-sein in the plural as configurations of sites of being that occur through or with things and events in manifold, either related or unrelated ways. Da-sein carries a middle-voice character that can allow us to approach things and events in attuned receptiveness to their interconnected or indifferent happening. This leads to a dynamic ontology that allows for an approach to things and events that does not operate with traditional conceptual frameworks such as subject and object, cause and effect, activity and passivity, substance and accidents; it leads to an ontology close to Merleau-Ponty's. (I am thinking here, for instance, of his second lecture course on Nature, where he writes of the unfurling of the life of a living being occurring like a melody that sings itself.) Such an ontology calls for attuned, bodily thinking in exposure to and directed by the interconnected or indifferent happening of living and nonliving beings and events. Such an ontology would not gravitate around human subjectivity, nor around a history of being, nor around any other single *archē* or principle, and thus would be an implicitly plural ontology according to the many ways in which things (in the largest sense) take place. Getting accustomed to think in an attuned way and in the plurality of "there-being" or of time-spaces fosters sensitivity to differences without the need to subsume them under common denominators, a way of thinking that responds to and can be responsible to the complexity of the worlds we inhabit.

Chapter 29

The Appeal of Things

Ethics and Relation

Andrew J. Mitchell

Where I see Heidegger most appealing for today is in his thinking of things. This is a concern of his later, postwar work; indeed, in my view, it is the crux of that later work. After the war, when Heidegger turns his attention to things he does so in a manner that is informed by all that has come before—the fundamental ontology of *Being and Time* and the being-historical thinking of *Contributions to Philosophy*, especially—while nevertheless achieving nothing short of a new way of thinking. I believe that this thinking of things still remains underthought in Heidegger and remains to be thought "after" Heidegger. In what follows, I will sketch Heidegger's development from the early *Being and Time*, through the middle period's *Contributions to Philosophy*, and on to his postwar thinking of things. I conclude with some reflections on an ethics of things.

Being and Time is a breakthrough in the thinking of subjectivity. It can easily be read as a work in the tradition of subjectivist philosophy, from Descartes through Kant and on to Husserl. This is not all that it is, nor all it seeks to be, but it is a core concern of the book. *Being and Time* proposes itself as the first part of a larger investigation into the "meaning of being." Heidegger does not propose investigating being as such, as though this were something on its own, apart from Dasein, but rather the "meaning" of being, that is the relation of being to a particular being non-indifferently disposed to it (the being for whom being's meaning is an issue). But since the meaning of being is an issue raised by a particular being, Dasein, the first portion of this larger project will be an investigation of the particular being that raises the question of being.

The relationship we see here, between the questioner and the question, is key to the hermeneutic nature of *Being and Time*. The questioner does not stand outside the matter under discussion. When it is a matter of being, the questioner itself is a particular being. It is always a particular being that asks after being. As such, the questioner cannot take an outside stance, in a position of indifference, to what is questioned. The questioner is "in" the question, and this fact propels the hermeneutic character of the book.

Being and Time is a book about being "in." Indeed, this "in" character of the book is so strong, Dasein is so fully "in" a world, that it can no longer be extracted from it to take the position of a "subject" over and against an "object." This separation and division endemic to subject–object metaphysics plays no role here. The emphasis in *Being and Time* on being "in" is its greatest and most transformative contribution to a philosophy of "subjectivity," as traditionally construed. That subject is now understood as being "in" a world. What "in" names in the phrase "being-in-the-world" is a non-indifferent relation with that world. Dasein is not in the world like a marble in a bag. It is not indifferent to the world as the marble is to the bag. Dasein is always disposed to the world in some way or another. Dasein is always affected by the world in one way or another and is always affecting that world in one way or another. "In" names the reciprocal nature of this mutually affecting relation. Dasein is marked by its world and is itself the marker of world. Dasein is marked by the world it marks in turn.

What such a reciprocal relation means is that there is no place where the world does not touch you. The reciprocity of the relation ensures that no subject will raise itself above the world in total detachment from it. There is neither a purely active subject here, nor a purely acted upon object. "In" names this conflation of subject and object in worldhood. More simply put, being "in" means no longer being "out," that is, outside of the world regarding it as object. What happens in the world, stays in the world, we might say.

With this understanding of Dasein as being-in-the-world, Heidegger has made a decisive and transformative contribution to the thinking of subjectivity as traditionally understood. No longer is the subject held to be an abstract I hovering above the world. Indeed, such an I knows no "world" at all, only object after object after object. The breakthrough of *Being and Time* is this insistence on the situatedness of the subject. Dasein occurs in a context. Dasein is worldly. Heidegger has "concretized" the subject. Where philosophy dealt with generic subjects in its history, Heidegger welcomes that subject to the world. And insofar as worlds are fields of difference (every place in a world is different from every other place), the subjects "in" those worlds, affected and affecting them, are different as well.

Being and Time can thus be seen as a progenitor of more contemporary attempts at thinking subjective identity in still greater "concretion," in terms of sex, gender, race, and so on. Insofar as each of these identity strata are concretizations of subjectivity, *Being and Time* offers an account of the conditions for their emergence. Adherents of these conceptions of subjectivity might object that *Being and Time* still only concretizes the subject at a formal level and that such a formal concretization (this emphasis on the conditions of concretization) still remains overly general and abstract. While this may be true, the objection nevertheless suffers from bad faith, in that no subject can ever be so concretized as to be fully specified in advance. In the name of defending the singularity of the subject, such views overlook that singularity and formality are not opposing terms.

If *Being and Time* rethinks subjectivity as being-in-the-world, with the *Contributions to Philosophy (Of the Event)* Heidegger offers us a new account of the beings of that world. Those beings are now understood in terms of abandonment and withdrawal. Beings are "abandoned" by being. Being has "withdrawn." If there is a "turn" in Heidegger's thinking, it happens as he works through these ideas in his notebooks. However we might characterize that turn, it brings a renewed interest in particular beings. The relation of these beings to being comes more to the fore.

What Heidegger proposes is that the beings we interact with today, the beings all around us, are so many markers of withdrawal. If "being" is what constitutes beings, then a withdrawal of being would appear to leave these beings as something less than whole. Heidegger's notion of ontological difference, first developed in his early work, has always insisted upon this distance between being and beings. Ontological difference is the name of that distance, but with the *Contributions* that distance has been pushed to the extreme. The withdrawal of being has led to the construal of beings as discrete, self-contained entities, that is as objects. The *Contributions* details an itinerary of objectification operative in the world today, from processes of "machination" (a progenitor of Heidegger's concern with technology) that place the world at our disposal to the emphasis on "lived experience" that converts existence into a game of collecting objectified experiences. Being's withdrawal would thus give the appearance of eliminating the difference between being and beings, leaving beings on their own, "abandoned," to fend for themselves.

But "abandonment" is still a relation. One is abandoned by someone, and in being so abandoned, one is (paradoxically) tied to the one who abandoned one in the first place. Beings are abandoned by being. Being and beings maintain a relation, but it is a peculiar one, for if abandonment, the attempt to be free of something, nonetheless remains tied to what is abandoned, then all such attempts at severing relations must fail. The abandonment of being names the impossibility of an abandonment of beings by being. Beings can never be so fully independent as to achieve metaphysical objectivity. Beings will always remain tied to being, especially when abandoned by being. Abandonment so understood takes what should be a non-relation (the withdrawal of being) and proves it to be the most extreme relation.

There is thus a kind of fragility of beings named in abandonment. Abandoned beings are endangered, they run the risk of objectification. But they simultaneously maintain a relation to what is no longer present, the being that has withdrawn. Beings are tied to a being that is no longer thinkable as present. This non-presence is essential to beings qua abandoned. Even abandoned beings are to be understood relationally, they feign being objective.

Heidegger's work after the war brings together the rethinking of both "subjectivity" and "objectivity," found in his early and middle work, respectively, in the new figure of the "thing." More precisely, Heidegger's later work details an interrelation of thing and world that I view as the culmination of his thinking and a challenge to all who would think "after" him, *nach ihm*, in accordance with him, which likewise entails diverging from him.

Heidegger's new understanding of things is a new understanding of the world. As noted earlier, understanding the subject as a being-in-a-world was a capital achievement of *Being and Time*. So much so that Heidegger doubles down on the notion in the 1929–1930 lecture course *Fundamental Concepts of Metaphysics*, where he proclaims Dasein to be "world building" in contradistinction to the "world poor" animal and "worldless" stone. Any such hierarchization of world-forming activity recedes in the later thinking of the world. The world is no longer the product of Dasein's privileged activity of construction. Rather, Heidegger relocates the world around things.

The world is the effulgence of things. Otherwise put, things "gesture" world, to use Heidegger's language. Things are the moments around which the world unfolds. Things localize the world, determine it. But this is not to identify the world with things. Heidegger's predilection for reciprocal relations is operative here as well. If things "gesture" world, then, in Heidegger's language once again, world also "grants" things. This play of gesture and granting is the world of things. A thing is more than simply what it is. It is no object. An object is a discrete and self-contained entity, a hallmark of modern metaphysics. Things, on the other hand, exceed themselves, are understood relationally. Things relate to what lies beyond them. Things are "ecstatic," in other words, to use another term previously reserved for Dasein. Things are determined by the relations they hold. This network of relations (not all of them relations of use) is what allows the thing to be the thing that it is. Relationality is essential to the thing and the world is the name for the "space" (physical or otherwise) through which these relations stream. The world is the medium of things.

But if these things are not objects, what are they? Heidegger's answer is that things are gatherings of relation. To emphasize that things are "gathered" is to insist on their non-substantive and nonhomogeneous nature. The unity of a gathering is a unity that bears separation at its core; the proof is that it had to be gathered together in the first place. Things are gatherings of relation, and Heidegger specifies four components, if you will, that gather at the thing:

earth, sky, divinities, and mortals. Heidegger names the gathering of these the "fourfold" and the active relating of these (their "fouring") constitutes the things that gesture forth world (and let us note that the mortal is only one component of this fourfold and one that holds no hierarchically privileged role in world formation).

Only a thing outside itself could gesture, that is implicate, something beyond itself. The fourfold gives us such a thing outside itself, or opened and fissured within itself (along those lines of relation). Simply put, Heidegger thinks things as phenomenally (if not materially) composed (as earthen, in his locution), but as always radiating beyond their limits (into the sky), in a way that is meaningful (marked by the absence of gods, the paradoxical role of the divinities in this fourfold) due to our mortality (with the mortals understood as those who are defined by finitude and limitation). Things are the material tethers of the unfurling world.

This is where I think a thinking "after" Heidegger can take place. Heidegger's work has guided our phenomenological gaze back to the things themselves. To come after him, we would continue the momentum of his thinking toward these things, further exploring their relational character. Heidegger sees things as relational, which is to say, opened onto the world beyond them. But that opening is not a unilateral one; it also means the world enters the things. And for Heidegger that world is given over to technological domination. The thing is in an essential relation to technology. Heidegger terms it a danger; things are endangered by technology.

But today's technology may be of a different kind than that of the 1960s and 1970s, not merely of a different degree. The challenges it poses to things may be different, too. Is the Internet of the twenty-first century continuous with the cybernetics that so concerned Heidegger some seventy years prior? Has the Internet not changed our relation to things? Online shopping and delivery would seem to embody what Heidegger had to say of positionality (*Ge-stell*) and its concentration of ordering and delivery, but is there not more to the Internet than this? Then again, perhaps the online presence of a thing is simply another relation in which it finds itself; perhaps the Internet does not destroy the relationality of things, but somehow is capable of fostering such relations. Heidegger could not know this, but we can, after him. Can we definitely say no new epoch of being awaits? Heidegger himself already perceived that the technological advances of his time (his contemporary technology) marked a break with the technologies of the modern epoch. Our current technological landscape may well mark a further break with that of Heidegger's lifetime. A thinking after Heidegger could explore this.

Heidegger also shows us that the things around us are tied to our own comportments toward them, that things appear as objects when we objectify them, that things appear as commodities (or standing reserve) when we commodify them. We take part in these procedures, but he is also insistent that we are not their source. It is not something we can simply stop "on our own." Commodification happens even against our will. The whole relation of commodification is historically bequeathed to us. Heidegger would say it is "sent" to us. But as every sending entails a concomitant holding back, the "epoch" of commodification that is sent to us can never be complete. On the one hand, there is always more that could be commodified, things can always get worse, and more of what we consider unique, singular, even sentimental will be converted into the replaceable. But on the other hand, this incompletion also means that things will never be so commodified that nothing remains of the unique and singular. It will be the task of those who think after Heidegger, a task he sometimes associates with the work of the poet, to find and detect these singularities and to guard them.

And for us today this is a difficult task; it never was easy. We live in a world with a tendency to maximization; we want the most of everything and appreciate most that which fully accomplishes its task in performing at the highest level. But the singular is never the maximal; it is more often the slight. Those who would detect singularities would do well to work against these drives to optimal performance. To do that means acknowledging loss, the non-maximal, it means foregoing the optimization of all functions for their own sake. Guarding this latitude in our approach to the world also grants things a space in which to show themselves not fully, but singularly. This is one way, but things may be guarded in many ways.

To be a thing is to exist relationally, not objectively. Such a state thus requires that there be no subject present who objectifies the thing in question. But this is not to say that the human is to do nothing in the face of things. Doing nothing is still doing something. Rather it is a matter of doing that which facilitates the relational unfurling of the thing. Heidegger terms this comportment guarding (*bewahren*). This non-objectifiying coming-into-relation with things allows them to reach us. And because we are not doing nothing in this relation, it allows us to reach them as well. This contact is the appeal of things—that we might touch them and that they might touch us. Heidegger does not term this relation ethical, but, in my view, it is the ethical end of any thinking after Heidegger. Across the history of philosophy, there seems to have been an increasing expansion of the beings toward which we are willing to behave ethically. We have accorded such respect to other rational beings, to other human beings, to other living beings, and now after Heidegger we should continue the thought and accord that respect to things (and objects and commodities as well!). Ethical action would be measured action and measured action need not be restricted to beings like us. It can apply to all, especially those least like us. Perhaps that is where both an ethics after Heidegger and a thinking after Heidegger should begin.

Chapter 30

Overcoming the Subjectivisms of Our Age (or Why Heidegger Is Not a Phenomenologist)

Richard Capobianco

> Yet Being is never dependent upon existing humanity.
>
> —Heidegger, "Recollection in Metaphysics," 1941

> The human being for itself has no power over truth, which remains independent of the human being.
>
> —Heidegger, "Three in Conversation on a Country Path," 1944–1945

Why, still, Heidegger after Heidegger? For many reasons, but an especially important one is to help free us from the many and varied "subjectivisms" of the contemporary age, including the persistent Cartesianism and Kantianism of classical phenomenology as inaugurated by Husserl. Husserl's basic position was strongly inflected toward the dependence of "being" on human subjectivity: "It is a being [*ein Sein*] that consciousness in its own experiences posits, . . . but *over and beyond this*, is nothing at all" (*Ideas I*, §49). The later Heidegger refused all such human-centric perspectives, and I have attempted to show the manifold dimensions of his critique in both *Engaging Heidegger* and *Heidegger's Way of Being*. His heralded turn to *Sein/Seyn* (henceforth, Being), as he worked this out over the course of his lifetime of thinking, represented a decisive turn away from all prevailing modern versions of the human being *as the measure of all things*.

Yet rather than restate the case already made, I would like to consider the matter afresh and highlight several of his signature themes along the way. In 1967, Heidegger delivered an address to the Academy of Arts and Sciences in Athens, Greece, under the title "The Provenance of Art and the Determination of Thinking." This lecture is not well known, and it has not yet been published in Heidegger's *Complete Works* (*Gesamtausgabe*).[1] The address is one of several that he delivered in the 1960s that speak to similar themes, yet what is especially notable in this particular talk is his appeal to the figure of the Greek goddess Athena in order to highlight the core matter of "*Alētheia*" and how *Alētheia* is not only the "provenance" of "art," but also "older," "more primordial," and "more enduring" than the human being and all that is brought forth as "art" by the human being. In other words, *Alētheia* (as Being), although cor-related with the human being in the expanse of the time of human beings, is nonetheless *independent* of the human being. Yet let us approach this conclusion slowly by way of a consideration of the lecture text.

ATHENA SPEAKS

Heidegger opens the address by stating in a characteristic manner that the matter of the inception of the "arts and sciences" among the Greeks is not fundamentally an "historical" matter that lies in the distant past, but rather a matter—and an experience—that remains "present" to us. The task before us, he states, is to "meditate on the provenance of art in Hellas" (136/119). Note that he uses the word "Hellas," and not "Greece" (*Griechenland*), as he begins his reflection. This is his reminder, familiar to us from many other places in his work, that, in his view, we must peel back the layers of Romanized and Latinized thinking that have accrued over the centuries in order for us to arrive again at the originary matter for thought; thus, our seeking must find its way back not to Roman *Graecia*, but to *Hellas*. In the following line, he sets out the aim of the meditation: "We shall try to get a glimpse into the region [*Bereich*] that already prevails prior to all art and that first bestows to art its ownmost character" (136/119). This "region" that "prevails" and is "prior" to all art—and therefore "prior" to the human being—is "*A-lētheia*," as he will tell us in due course, but at the outset he has already clearly signaled the destination of his thinking.

To proceed, he calls upon "the goddess Athena" for "counsel and guidance." This is not simply a polite rhetorical gesture to his Athenian hosts. The later Heidegger was deeply moved by the "invocation" to the gods or muses that opened the great poems of the ancient Greek poets such as Homer and Pindar. These ancient invocations honored the gods for their "wisdom" and expressed an abiding human humility to listen and learn—which Heidegger laments has been increasingly lost in the present "egoist" age.

The matter of the significance of "the gods" in the later Heidegger's thinking is complex, but we should at least keep in view that he always insisted that "the gods" are never mere projections of the human being; that is, "the gods," no less than we "mortals," emerge from out of Being, the temporal-spatial emerging/unfolding "way" (or ontological process) wherein and whereby all beings issue forth and come to be. Certainly, for Heidegger, the "gods" or "divinities" are not traditional ontotheological timeless entities, for they, too, are "temporal" as they emerge from out of the temporal way itself—Being—their "source." Some recent readings of Heidegger—which are no more than variations of Husserl's transcendental idealism—are entirely off the mark to suggest that for the later Heidegger the human being is the "source" of "Being," and, accordingly, these readings are also mistaken in trying to settle the matter of "the gods" in his thinking by claiming them for the human being, that is, by claiming that "the gods" are only insofar as the human being is. Heidegger—at every turn—upends this kind of position. In this talk, not only does he "invoke" the goddess Athena, but he adds that even as we look to her for counsel and illumination on the core matter for thinking, we must ever keep in mind that "we cannot penetrate into the plenitude of her divinity" (136/119). What is more, he states, "We are only attempting to explore what Athena says to us about the provenance of art." He recalls that our human task is to be attentive and *listen* to "what Athena says." In other words, it is not simply humans who "say" and "speak"; the goddess "says" and "speaks," too.

Admittedly, what and how "the gods" "are" as they emerge from out of the Being-way, and what and how "the gods" "say" and "speak," are considerations that remain for us to reflect upon further—and this only testifies to the continuing resonance of Heidegger's thinking. Even so, let us recognize that what he opens for our thinking in such passages is altogether closed off in every kind of reductive human-centric reading that insists on positing the human being as the singular "source" of all "saying." In other words, what is lost in these reductive human-centric readings is Heidegger's abiding call for us to be "open" to how all things "speak" to us. As he put this in a seminar in Le Thor a couple of years later in 1969: "The Greeks are those human beings who lived immediately [*unmittelbar*] in the manifestness of phenomena—through the specifically ek-static capacity of letting the phenomena *speak to them*, [yet] modern man, Cartesian man, *se solum alloquendo*, speaks only to himself" (GA 15: 331/38). For us to be "open" in this Greek way is for us to be "open" to hearing how the sea, the trees, the animals—all that is, even "the gods" and "muses"—how *everything* "speaks" to us.[2] Yet it seems that we are no longer listening—or we are listening only for what we need and demand to hear.

Heidegger recalls that Homer names Athena *polumetis*, "the manifold counselor" (136/119), the one who helps in many and varied ways. It is Athena who "prevails" over everything that human beings bring forth, and it is she who "dispenses her special counsel to humans who produce tools, vases, and jewels." All who are skilled and masters at crafting we may call *technitēs*, but he cautions that "we understand this word in too limited a sense when we translate it as 'artisan.'" The *technitēs* is one whose activity "is guided by a comprehension whose name is *technē*," yet this word does not simply mean "a doing and making"; rather, *technē* is fundamentally "a form of knowing." This "knowing" is a seeing in advance of what is to be brought forth, and what is to be brought forth is not simply a crafted chair or sculpture or building—but also "a work of science or of philosophy, of poetry or of public rhetoric." In this way, then, "art is *technē*, but not *technicity* [*Technik*]," and "the artist is *technitēs*, but not a technician or even an artisan" (137/120).

Thus "art," according to Heidegger, is a kind of *technē*, and *technē* is a "knowing" that is a looking ahead to the creation and completion of *any work*. This "knowing" as a "looking ahead" therefore requires "exceptional vision and brightness and clarity," and again he invokes the goddess Athena, who is not only the manifold counselor, *polumetis*, but also well known as the bright and shining one, *glaucopis*. He considers the Greek word *glaucos* and observes that the adjective *glaucos* usually refers to "the radiant gleaming [*das strahlende Glänzen*] of the sea, the stars, the moon, but also the shimmer of the olive tree" (137/120). The published translation opts for "lustre" to translate his word *Glänzen*, and this is acceptable, of course, but I think that the word "gleaming" gets us much closer to the "shining forth" that he always had in view. In chapter 2 of *Heidegger's Way of Being*, I highlight and discuss how this word *glänzen* is widely used by Heidegger and is one of his most favored words in speaking of the "shining forth" of beings and of the Being-way itself—and not surprisingly, he himself had pointed out that this very word was widely used and highly favored by Hölderlin in the first place.[3]

Athena's eyes are *glaucos*, that is, "gleaming and illuminating." It is for this reason, he adds, that the owl, whose eyes are "fiery-blazing," has the name *hē glaux* in Greek and is forever associated with her, "a sign of her essence." The owl's bright eyes are able to see at night as well, and, correspondingly, Athena's bright and gleaming glance is able to "make visible what is otherwise invisible" (120/137). Yet where is Athena's illuminating glance directed? What is the "invisible" she has in view? The clue, he says, is to be found on the sacred relief on the Acropolis museum where Athena appears as the *skeptomenē*, "the meditating one."

What follows is a familiar motif, but now unfolded in terms of Athena as the meditating one. Athena's glance is turned toward "the boundary stone, to the boundary." Athena's bright eyes watch over meditatively the "boundary" or "limit" of things, but this limit is not a mere limitation or marker for the end of something. Rather, "limit," understood in a genuinely Greek manner, is what determines something coming to be in its ownmost character and fullness. Indeed, something *cannot* come to be unless it enters into its limit or boundary; its boundary is its very *being*. In this sense, then, Athena does not cast a meditative look only upon that which is brought forth by humans, but more broadly—and "above all," Heidegger states—upon that which allows all things of the earth and sky that require *no* human action and production to come into their "limit" and therefore their being. This *that-by-which* all such beings come to be is what the ancient Greeks named *physis*. Again characteristically, he warns of the narrowing of the Greek understanding of *physis* in the Roman appropriation of *physis* as *natura*, but his central point is that the Greeks recognized (and therefore we may recognize once again) that *physis* is "that which emerges from itself forth into its respective limit and therein lingers" (138/121).[4]

Indeed, even today, he observes, "we are able to experience the fullness of the mystery of *physis* in Hellas, where in an astounding yet at the same time restrained manner there appears a mountain, an island, a coast, an olive tree." He admits that there is something to be said for the exceptional Greek visible "light" that allows us this experience, but this visible light is itself granted by another kind of light that is much more difficult to see (and for this reason is comparatively "invisible," although Athena, like the owl, is able to see it). Yet before naming this unique light, he emphasizes that it was the Greeks who first recognized that *physis*—"the whole of the world"—always already addresses human beings and lays claim upon them so that human "knowing and doing" is compelled to cor-respond to this claim. Athena has her gleaming eyes upon *physis*, and as we know from the wealth of Heidegger's other reflections on the earliest Greek thinkers and poets, *physis* is another name for Being. Recall, for instance, his decisive statement in *Introduction to Metaphysics* (1935): "*Physis* is Being itself" (GA 40: 17). Accordingly, although he does not name Being in this address, we may say that it is Being as *physis* that ever rises up to us, opens us, and draws us into cor-respondence (*Entsprechung*). As I have expressed this in *Heidegger's Way of Being*: "*physis* endlessly arising, and we endlessly astonished."[5]

Art, then, is a "cor-respondence" to and with *physis*, and this belonging together of *technē* and *physis* is but another way of characterizing the relation of the human being to Being. He returns to the primordial "light" by which and through which everything comes to be gathered into what it is. This is the "lightning-flash" (*der Blitz*) of which Heraclitus speaks in fragment 64: "But the lightning steers everything." The lightning brings everything into its "limit" and "steers" everything into place. From Heidegger's many other elucidations of this fragment we know that he reads this "lightning-flash" as another name for Being as "the primordial *Logos*" that lets be and gathers all that is, but here he does not restate this. He simply observes that the lightning is hurled by Zeus, "the highest god," and that Athena is Zeus's daughter. Athena alone knows where the lightning is kept, as she herself tells us in Aeschylus's *Eumenides*. Heidegger sums up by observing that it is precisely because Athena has this "knowing" that she is the manifold counselor, *polumētis*; the brightly seeing one, *glaucopis*; and the goddess who meditates on *physis*, *skeptomenē*. We must hearken to Athena if we are "to understand even a little of the mystery of the provenance of art in Hellas."

OPENING TO *A-LĒTHEIA*: "OLDER" AND "MORE ENDURING" THAN THE HUMAN BEING

What follows in the lecture is a disquisition on the perils of the contemporary age that is dominated by cybernetic and technological modeling and thinking. The age of unremitting calculative thinking has largely cut us off from that very "region" that is the provenance of art. The ground that he covers here is familiar; he had been making these same observations in much the same way throughout the 1960s.[6] This is not to say, of course, that the details of his critique in this particular lecture are not worth examining, yet I am more interested in distilling one crucial component of his critique in order to get to the heart of the matter.

To do this, let us restate in another way what we have already discussed. For Heidegger, *technē*, all human making, doing, and thinking—all human creation of whatever kind—emerges by virtue of our openness to that "region" in which all things emerge. We may call this "region," along with the ancient Greeks, *physis*. Our unfolding "belongs" with the unfolding of *physis*. We create along with *physis*. Our "artful" gathering cor-responds with the primary gathering of *physis*. We might say, then, that our creation of any kind of "work" is always a "working with" Athena (or the other gods); that is, it is a "working with" *physis*, which Athena ever has her gleaming eyes upon. Ultimately, then, our "working with" entails that, on one level, we yield, give way, release ourselves to *physis*, which is beyond our making and control. So what, then, is the fundamental problem in the present age? If we distill Heidegger's message, it is this: The thoroughgoing *subjectivism* in the contemporary age has cut us off from our "source," *physis*. Two statements from his lecture bring this into sharpest relief:

> Industrial society constitutes the ultimate elevation of egoity [*Ichheit*], that is, of subjectivity. In it, the human being rests exclusively on itself and on the domains of its lived world, reworked into institutions. (124/144)

> This is subjectivity resting only on itself. All objects are attributed to this subject. Industrial society arrogantly proclaims itself as the absolute norm of every objectivity. (125/145)

At root, then, it is this conviction that we are the "source" of all that "is" that has so deformed and disabled us in the contemporary age by blocking us from entering into the fullness of our "essence" *in relation* to Being as *physis*. Heidegger specifically points to the dominance of "industrial society," but what he is assailing more generally is the insistence, embedded in our contemporary culture in manifold ways, that the human being measures out all that "is" and that "world" refers to no more than the sum of all human meaning and naming, interests and concerns, action and producing. We have become forgetful that any particular being (*ein Seiendes*) is always more than how it is measured out by the human being, and that Being (*Sein*), the ontological temporal way or process wherein and whereby all beings issue forth, is always more than this human measure as well. The contemporary insistence on the human perspective (including the phenomenological insistence on the "first-person perspective") is the chief impediment to our opening to Being as *physis*—as *Alētheia*.

Alētheia. Finally, we arrive at the other Greek *Ur*-word. He calls upon us to take a "step-back" from the prevailing "egoity" of the present age in order to enter again into the fullness of our existence. This means recovering and restoring our relation to "the open and free domain" that bestows and grants all things, and this domain was named by the Greeks *A-lētheia*. *A-lētheia* or "un-concealment" is the primordial "openness" that "does not do away with concealment; rather unconcealment is invariably in need of concealment" (127/147). He adds the hyphen in the Greek word *A-lētheia* in order to emphasize that the dimension of concealment and reserve—the *lethe* dimension—is intrinsic to all unconcealment.

Yet we note, too, that he capitalizes the Greek word *Alētheia* as he had done on many occasions in his earlier work, and especially in the brilliant lecture courses on Parmenides, Heraclitus, and Anaximander in the early 1940s.[7] In those places, Heidegger repeatedly stated that *Alētheia* is another name for Being—and we recognize this as his truly original and distinctive position on "truth": "Truth" is in the first place the unending temporal unfolding, the radiant emergence, of all that is. To put this succinctly, "is-ing" is "true-ing."[8] The capitalization of *Alētheia* signals the continuity with the earlier work. *Alētheia* as Being (Being as *Alētheia*) is the "open and free" domain or region that grants all unconcealment and yet also holds back in reserve. *Alētheia* as Being is, in the first place, the locus of unconcealment and concealment—*not the human being*, whatever our own activity of unconcealing and concealing.

This tells us most clearly that all persisting philosophical positions that posit the human being as the "source" of Being—that is, as the "source" of all unconcealment and concealment—are simply symptomatic of the hubris and narcissism of the prevailing modern subjectivism that the later Heidegger identified again and again as blocking us from entering into the fullness of our *Da-sein*.[9]

The Greeks glimpsed the "region" that bestows all things, including human beings and their "art," and they gave the name *alētheia* (*A-lētheia*) to this region—but also *physis*, provided that we keep in view the originary indication of this word. That is, insofar as *physis* names only the pure "light" or pure transparency of unconcealment as it came to be understood among the Greek philosophers (Plato's *eidos* or Aristotle's *morphē*, for example), then this name is not yet fundamental. Nevertheless, the earliest Greek thinkers and poets, and especially Heraclitus, had in view *physis* in the richest and fullest sense as the unending temporal emergence from concealment that ever shelters concealment. Heidegger cites Heraclitus's fragment 123, as he had so many times before, *physis kryptesthai philei*, or as he translates this saying here: "To emerging-forth from itself, self-concealing properly belongs." What Heraclitus already knew we are called upon to know—and experience—once again for ourselves in the present age.

With a series of concluding questions, Heidegger makes the point that for us to restore and embrace our relation with (Being as *physis* as) *Alētheia* is for us to experience once again "awe" and "wonder" and "humility" (all translations of *Scheu*) before the unending temporal-spatial unfolding of all things and what "cannot be planned or controlled, or calculated and made" by us. In other words, our releasement to Being is a releasement from our subjectivist prisons, and this holds out the promise of our "dwelling" once more, of our finding our home again "upon the earth." A dwelling and abiding, he says, that is once again open to listening to "the voice" (*Stimme*) of *A-lētheia*.[10] An openness that is not necessarily opposed to ontic mastering, but rather an openness, a releasement, that tempers and keeps humble these ontic efforts. He adds that while we do not know what will become of the present age, we do know that "the *A-lētheia* that conceals itself in the Greek light, and which grants this light in the first place, *is older and more primordial and consequently more enduring* than every work and fabrication devised by human beings and brought forth by the human hand" (128/149; my italics).

This is the culminating statement. He maintains that *A-lētheia* grants the Greek light in the first place. What does this mean? He appears to be speaking of the "Greek light" of sheer unconcealment (*eidos*, *idea*, *morphē*), which was the focus of Plato and Aristotle and the later medieval metaphysicians (*essentia*, *quidditas*, *actualitas*). Yet recall that the primordial light of *A-lētheia* (as unconcealment-concealment) was indeed glimpsed by the earliest Greek thinkers Parmenides, Anaximander, and Heraclitus; it is the "lightning" of Zeus that grants and "steers" all things, the "lightning" that is intimately known by Athena.

But to the crucial part of the line: *A-lētheia* is "older, more primordial, and consequently more enduring" than the human being and the full spectrum of "art." Let us be clear on the significance of what he is saying: *A-lētheia*, this ancient Greek *Ur*-word for Being, is not dependent upon the human being. Being as *A-lētheia* is *independent* of the human being; in other words, the "is-ing" of all things unfolds both before and after the human being. The later Heidegger made this point in several places, not simply in this lecture, and it captures the fundamental thrust of his thinking after *Being and Time*.[11]

Thus, what is at issue here is not the cor-relation of Being and the human being in the expanse of the duration of human beings; indeed, Heidegger always highlighted this cor-relation. What is at issue, and what he is repudiating in this talk (and elsewhere in the later work), is any human-centric position—including a strict transcendental-phenomenological position—that holds that Being "is" only insofar as the human being is. To put this more pointedly: The later Heidegger is *not* a phenomenologist in this strict sense. Indeed, it is any understanding of the "cor-relation" *that makes Being dependent upon the human being* that is ruled out by his emphatic statement—and it must be ruled out if we are to take a step in thinking toward breaking free of the prevailing and unrelenting "egoity" or "subjectivism" that has taken hold of the modern and contemporary age and that has installed the human being as the measure of all things. We are called to recall, as he states in another place, that "[Being as] *kosmos* is the measure-giving; the measure that *kosmos* gives is it itself as *physis*."[12]

Being (as *physis* as *alētheia* as *kosmos*) is the "measure" that is not made by us, and Heidegger is perfectly clear about this: "It [Being itself (*Sein selbst*)] is nothing made and has therefore also no determinate beginning at a point in time and no corresponding ending of its existence."[13] Yet this is so hard for us to understand and accept in the contemporary age—except most notably in the *best* thinking of theoretical physics and science (which cannot be dismissed as mere "scientism"). It is possible, then, for us to consider (even if Heidegger did not) that his later thinking joins the deepest reflections of theoretical science in setting all things free from our measure.

So, why, still, Heidegger after Heidegger? No small matter: To free all things from ourselves; to free us from ourselves.

NOTES

1. "Die Herkunft der Kunst und die Bestimmung des Denkens," in *Denkerfahrungen: 1910–1976*, ed. Hermann Heidegger (Frankfurt am Main: Klostermann, 1983), 135–49. English translation by Dimitrios Latsis, amended by Ullrich Haase: "The Provenance of Art and the Destination of Thought (1967)," *Journal of the British*

Society for Phenomenology 44:2 (2013): 119–28. Parenthesized references will refer to this lecture unless otherwise indicated. References follow this form: (English/German), but I have modified the English translation, especially in the last key line on *Alētheia*. The German text will be included in GA 80.2.

2. In my *Heidegger's Way of Being* (Toronto: University of Toronto Press, 2014), I point out the affinities of Heidegger's later thinking with American authors such as Walt Whitman, E.E. Cummings, and John Muir. With respect to Heidegger's "gods," one may also consider these lines from John Muir on being in the presence of Yosemite Falls at midnight: "How interesting does man become considered in his relations to the spirit of this rock and water! How significant does every atom of our world become amid the influences of those beings unseen, spiritual, angelic mountaineers that so throng these pure mansions of crystal foam and purple granite" (from his letter to Mrs. Ezra S. Carr, April 3, 1871).

3. Capobianco, *Heidegger's Way of Being*, especially chapter 2, "On Hölderlin on 'Nature's Gleaming.'" See also Richard Capobianco, "Heidegger on Heraclitus: *Kosmos*/World as Being Itself," *Epoché: A Journal for the History of Philosophy*, 20:2 (Spring 2016): 465–76.

4. Yet, for Heidegger, Hölderlin's "Nature" (*die Natur*) does indeed name *physis* in the richest Greek way; see chapter 2 of *Heidegger's Way of Being*.

5. Capobianco, *Heidegger's Way of Being*, 64.

6. See especially his 1965 talk in honor of Ludwig Binswanger titled "On the Question Concerning the Determination of the Matter for Thinking," trans. Richard Capobianco and Marie Göbel, *Epoché: A Journal for the History of Philosophy*, 14:2 (Spring 2010): 213–23.

7. See especially GA 55, *Heraklit*. For many translations and discussion of these brilliant lecture courses, see Capobianco, *Heidegger's Way of Being*, chapters 5 and 6, as well as "Heidegger on Heraclitus."

8. For more on the matter of Being as "primordial truth," see Capobianco, *Heidegger's Way of Being*, especially chapter 4.

9. Heidegger studies need to be open to consider how the best thinking in contemporary theoretical astrophysics (which is by no means mere "scientism" or "technicity") may dovetail with Heidegger's later thinking of Being as "time-space" (*Zeit-Raum*), as *physis* and *alētheia*. We should consider, too, the remarkable nearness *in spirit* of the later Heidegger's theme of *Gelassenheit* ("releasement") with several of Albert Einstein's broader reflections: "A human being is part of the whole, called by us 'Universe,' a part limited in time and space. He experiences himself, his thoughts and feelings as something separated from the rest—a kind of optical delusion of his consciousness. This delusion is a kind of prison for us, restricting us to our personal desires and to affection for a few persons nearest to us. Our task must be to free ourselves from this prison by widening our circle of compassion to embrace all living creatures and the whole of nature in its beauty": from a letter Einstein wrote at age of seventy (dated March 4, 1950) to Norman Salit (Einstein Archives, 61–226). See also a similarly worded letter by Einstein dated February 12, 1950 to Robert Marcus (Einstein Archives, 60–424/425/426). In document 60–425 (in German), he also states: "Not to nourish the illusion but to try to overcome it is the way for us to

reach the attainable measure of inner peace." With thanks to Chaya Becker, Archivist, Albert Einstein Archives, The Hebrew University of Jerusalem.

10. For more on "the voice" of Being as the primordial *Logos*, see chapter 6 of Capobianco, *Heidegger's Way of Being*.

11. See especially Capobianco, *Heidegger's Way of Being*, chapter 1, and "Heidegger on Heraclitus." The later Heidegger "turned" away from his own transcendentally inclined statements about *Sein* in *Being and Time* and in other places in the early work—for example, in *Being and Time*, section 43(c). For more on this, see my article "In the *Black Notebooks*: Heidegger's 'Turn' Away from the Transcendental-Phenomenological Positioning of *Being and Time* to the Thinking of Being as *Alētheia* and *Physis*," in *Zur Hermeneutik der "Schwarzen Hefte,"* Heidegger-Jahrbuch 11, ed. Alfred Denker and Holger Zaborowski (Freiburg/München: Verlag Karl Alber, 2017).

12. Capobianco, "Heidegger on Heraclitus," 473; GA 55: 171.

13. Capobianco, "Heidegger on Heraclitus," 470; GA 55: 166.

Part VII

OPENINGS TO OTHERS

Chapter 31

Thinking Heidegger's Postmodern Unthought

From Ontotheology to Ontological Pluralism in Technology, Education, Politics, and Art

Iain Thomson

In *Heidegger, Art, and Postmodernity*, I sought to show that Heidegger is best understood not simply as another regressive or reactionary "antimodernist" (the way critics often portray him) but, instead, as a potentially progressive and so still promising "postmodernist"—if I may be forgiven for trying to rehabilitate a term that has become so thoroughly "unfashionable" (or *unzeitgemäß*, as Nietzsche aptly put it, literally "not cut to the measure of the time"). Sounding like some hipster conservative, Heidegger contends in *Being and Time* that a formerly hyper-trendy term like *postmodern* "can first become free in its positive possibilities only when the idle chatter covering it over has become ineffectual and the 'common' interest has died away" (BT 218/SZ 174). In other words, once everyone stops talking about "The Next Big Thing," it becomes possible to understand what was so inspiring about it in the first place, letting us uncover those enduringly inspirational sources that tend to get obscured by the noise that engulfs a major trend during its heyday.[1]

It remains true and important that Heidegger is highly critical of modernity's metaphysical foundations, including (1) its axiomatic positing of the Cartesian *cogito* as the epistemological foundation of intelligibility; (2) the ontological subject/object dualism generated by (1); (3) the fact/value dichotomy that follows from (1) and (2); and (4) the growing *nihilism* (or meaninglessness) that follows (in part) from (3), that is, from the belief that what matters most to us world-disclosing beings can be understood as "values" projected by human subjects onto an inherently meaningless realm of objects.[2] I continue to find myself provoked and inspired by Heidegger's phenomenological ways of undermining *modern* Cartesian "subjectivism," but my own work is even more concerned with Heidegger's subsequent deconstruction of *late-modern* "enframing" (*Ge-stell*), that is, with his ontological critique of global *technologization.* Heidegger's critique of the nihilism of late-modern enframing develops out of his earlier critique of modern subjectivism but goes well beyond it. Enframing is "subjectivism squared": As modernity's vaunted subject applies the technologies developed to control the objective realm back onto human subjects, this objectification of the subject is transforming us into just another intrinsically meaningless resource to be optimized, ordered, and enhanced with maximal efficiency—whether cosmetically, psychopharmacologically, eugenically, aesthetically, educationally, or otherwise "technologically."[3]

Taken together, Heidegger's ontological critiques of modern subjectivism and late-modern enframing helped establish his work as an uncircumventable critical touchstone of twentieth-century "continental" philosophy. And I say this while fully acknowledging that Heidegger deliberately and directly involved himself and his thinking with history's greatest horror (greatest thus far, at least), thereby rendering his work even more controversial than it would have been anyway. All of us would-be *post*-Heideggerians have to work through the significance of Heidegger's deeply troubling Nazism for ourselves, as I have long argued. Indeed, that critical task is new only to those who are new to Heidegger (or who have somehow managed to avoid it by bunkering down in untenable and so increasingly desperate forms of denial). The critical task of working through and beyond Heidegger's politics remains difficult nonetheless, because (as I showed in my first book) the most insightful and troubling aspects of Heidegger's thinking are often closely intertwined. Disentangling them thus requires both care and understanding, and so a capacity to tolerate ethical as well as philosophical ambiguity, traditional scholarly skills that seem to be growing rare in these days of one-sided outrage and indignation.[4]

Yet, despite Heidegger's sustained critiques of modernity and late modernity, he is not simply an *anti*-modernist (or even an *anti*-late-modernist). To try to think *against* something, he repeatedly teaches, is to remain trapped within its underlying logic. (The proud atheist often remains caught in the traditional logic of theism, for instance, insofar as both theist and atheist presume to know something outside the realm of possible knowledge. Like Hölderlin, Heidegger himself ended up a romantic polytheist, open to the relevant phenomena and so capable of different kinds of religious experience.)[5] Many people find it difficult to muster the hermeneutic charity and patience we need in order to be able to understand Heidegger. But one of the deepest and most universal axioms of the hermeneutic tradition (one still shared from Gadamer to Davidson) is that the only way to understand other thinkers is to presume that they make sense, that they are not just passing off meaningless nonsense as profundity. (There is a detectably post-Christian wisdom in the hermeneutic tradition here. "Thinking . . . loves" [GA 8: 22/20]: Love even thine enemy, as it were, because hatred can never *understand*.)[6] When Heidegger is read charitably (rather than dismissed polemically), it becomes clear that his overarching goal is not only to undermine but also to *transcend* modernity.

By working to think modernity from its deepest Cartesian presuppositions to its ultimate late-modern conclusions, I believe Heidegger helps open up some paths that lead beyond those problematically nihilistic modern axioms mentioned earlier, paths that also allow us to preserve and build upon the most crucial and irreplaceable advances achieved in the modern age.[7] As that suggests, we need to acknowledge—much less grudgingly than Heidegger himself ever did—that humanity has made undeniable and precious *progress* in the domains of technology, science, medicine, art, language, and even (I try to show, thus going well beyond Heidegger) in *politics*. According to the perhaps heterodox, *left-Heideggerian* postmodernism I espouse, Heidegger's central *postmodern* insight into the inexhaustible *plurality of being* serves best to justify and promote a robust liberal tolerance, a tolerance intolerant only of intolerance itself. That may initially sound relativistic, but this is a tolerance with teeth, because ontological pluralism undermines *all* fundamentalist claims to have finally arrived at the one correct truth about how to live, let alone to seek to impose those final answers on others.[8]

Questions concerning how best to understand the implications of Heidegger's central insights remain complex and controversial, of course. But I think it is clear—in light of Heidegger's distinctive attempts to combine philosophy and poetry into a thinking that "twists free" of and so leads *beyond modernity*—that Heidegger was the original *post*modern thinker. Here I say "original" even while acknowledging that Heidegger's postmodern vision drew crucial inspiration from many others (including the Romantic tradition, especially Hölderlin, Van Gogh, and Nietzsche, as well as from his creative readings of pre-Socratic philosophy). For Heideggerian "originality" (*Ursprünglichkeit*) is less concerned with being first than with remaining *inspiring*; that is, it is less about planting flags and more about continuing to provoke important insights in others.[9]

This view of Heidegger as the *Ur-postmodernist* gains a great deal of support, moreover, from the fact that almost every single significant contemporary continental philosopher was profoundly influenced by Heidegger. The list is long, because it includes not just more recognizably "modern" philosophers like Arendt, Bultmann, Gadamer, Habermas, Kojève, Marcuse, Merleau-Ponty, Sartre, Taylor, and Tillich, but also such "postmodern" thinkers as Agamben, Badiou, Baudrillard, Blanchot, Butler, Cavell, Derrida, Dreyfus, Foucault, Irigaray, Lacan, Levinas, Rancière, Rorty, Vattimo, and Žižek—*all* of whom take Heideggerian insights as fundamental philosophical points of departure. Each of these thinkers seeks to move beyond these

Heideggerian or post-Heideggerian starting points (more and less successfully, it must be said, but with lots of significant advances along the way).

Taken as a whole, one thing *all* of these major thinkers help confirm is that we think best with a hermeneutic phenomenologist like Heidegger only when we learn to read him "reticently"—that is, slowly, critically, carefully, thoughtfully, with reservations and alternatives left open rather than too quickly foreclosed. If we can adopt a critical yet charitable approach to Heidegger's views on the matters of deep concern that we continue to share with him, then we can find our *own* ways into *die Sache selbst*, the matters themselves at stake in the discussion. Focusing on the issues that matter in this way can also help us avoid getting too bogged down in the interminable terminological disputes that too often turn out to be merely "semantic" misunderstandings or confusions of translation, noisy distortions in which those trained in different traditions and languages continue to unknowingly talk past one another.[10] Our hermeneutic goal should instead be genuine understanding and so the possibility of *positive disagreement*, that is, disagreements that generate real alternatives and so do not remain *merely* criticisms (let alone pseudo-criticisms, confused epiphenomena of unrecognized misunderstandings, distortions passed down through generations or sent out across other networks). The modestly immodest goal of post-Heideggerian thinking, in sum, is to *think* the most important issues at issue in Heidegger's thinking further than he himself ever did. At the very least, such attempts can succeed in developing these enduringly important issues somewhat *differently*, in our own directions and inflections, in light of our own contemporary concerns and particular ways of understanding what matters most to our time and generations.

Heidegger's provocative later suggestion about how best to develop the deepest matters at stake in the thinking of another can be helpful here: We need to learn "to think the unthought."[11] Thinking the unthought of another thinker means creatively disclosing the deepest insights on the basis of which that thinker thought. When we think their unthought, we uncover some of the ontological "background" which rarely finds its way into the forefront of a thinker's thinking (as Dreyfus nicely put it, drawing on the Gestalt psychology Heidegger drew on himself). Thinking the unthought means seeing something otherwise unseen or hearing something otherwise unheard, but such hermeneutic "clairvoyance" (as Derrida provocatively dubbed it) should not presume that it has successfully isolated the one true core of another's thinking (a mistake Heidegger himself too often committed).[12] But nor should we concede that "death of the author" thesis which presumes that there is *no* deep background even in the work of our greatest thinkers. We post-Heideggerian postmodernists should just presume, instead, that any such deep background will be plural rather than singular, and so irreducible to any one overarching interpretive framework. In that humbler hermeneutic spirit of ontological pluralism, we can then set out to develop at least *some* of a thinker's best insights and deepest philosophical motivations beyond whatever points that thinker was able to take them.[13]

In such a spirit, my own work focuses primarily on some of the interconnected issues of enduring concern that I think we continue to share with Heidegger, including (1) his deconstructive critique of Western metaphysics as *ontotheology*; (2) the ways in which the ontotheology underlying our own late-modern age generates troublingly nihilistic effects in our ongoing *technologization* of our worlds and ourselves; (3) Heidegger's alternative vision of learning to transcend such technological nihilism through ontological *education*, that is, an education centered on the "perfectionist" task of "becoming what we are" in order to come into our own as human beings leading meaningful lives. My interest in those interconnected issues (of ontotheology, technology, and education) led me to try to explicate (4) the most compelling phenomenological and hermeneutic reasons behind the enduring appeal of Heideggerian and post-Heideggerian visions of *postmodernity*; and so also (5) the continuing relevance of *art and poetry* in helping us learn to understand being in some enduringly meaningful, *postmodern* ways. The point of this postmodernism, to put it simply, is to help us improve crucial aspects of our understanding of the being of our worlds, ourselves, and each other, as well as of the myriad other entities who populate and shape our interconnected worlds.

Beneath or behind it all, I have also dedicated much of the past decade to working through some of the philosophical issues that arise, directly and indirectly, from the dramatic collision between Heidegger's life and thinking (as I have been working on a philosophical biography of Heidegger). I have thus taken up, for example, Heidegger's views on the nature and meaning of *love* (which prove surprisingly insightful, once again, when approached with critical charity), while also continuing to participate in that ongoing reexamination of the significance of Heidegger's early commitment to and subsequent break with Nazism, as well as the more recently revealed extent of his ignorant anti-Semitism (fraught and difficult topics).[14]

In all these ways, then, I remain most interested in developing a Heideggerian and post-Heideggerian view of the role that *thinking* can play in helping us learn to live meaningful lives, forging existential trajectories that help transcend the nihilism of late-modern technologization. To develop Heidegger's thinking on technological nihilism beyond the point he himself left it, I think we need to learn both (1) to recognize the undertow of technologization's drift toward nihilistic optimization and also (2) to find ways to use particular technologies (including word processing software, synthesizers, Facebook, and all the other proliferating technological media of our worlds) so that they help move us beyond that nihilistic technologization rather than merely reinforcing it. Heidegger himself was more directly helpful with the first than the second of these tasks, but his work also helps us respond to the second task by teaching us to cultivate a receptivity to that which overflows and so partly escapes all the willful projects in which the modern subject understands itself as the source of what matters most in the world (as the foundation of all "values," all "normativity," and other such widespread but deeply problematic, modern philosophical ideas). We think Heidegger's unthought, then, when we disclose this postmodern understanding of being, learning to understand and so encounter being not as a *modern* domain of objects for subjects to master and control, nor as a late-modern "standing reserve" of resources to be efficiently optimized, but instead as that which continues to both inform and exceed our every way of making sense of ourselves and our worlds.[15] By learning to cultivate a phenomenological receptivity to this postmodern understanding of being, we can address the nihilism of our technological understanding of being by directly discerning and transcending its *ontotheological* foundations.

Heidegger, Art, and Postmodernity begins with the words, "What does Heidegger mean by *ontotheology*—and why should we care?" Here is a greatly simplified answer: If, like Parmenides, we think of all intelligible reality as a sphere, then ontotheology is the attempt to grasp this sphere from the inside-out and the outside-in at the same time. More precisely, ontotheology is Heidegger's name for the attempt to stabilize the entire intelligible order (or the whole space of meaning) by grasping *both* the innermost "ontological" core of what-is *and* its outermost "theological" expression, then linking these innermost and outermost "grounds" together into a single, doubly foundational, "ontotheological" understanding of the being of what-is. An ontotheology, when it works (by uncovering and disseminating those grounds beneath or beyond which no one else can reach, for a time), establishes the meaning of being that "doubly grounds" an historical age. Such ontotheologies shape and transform Western history's guiding sense of what being "is" (by telling us what "Isness" itself is), and since everything is, they end up shaping and reshaping our understanding of everything else. (Heidegger's notorious antipathy to metaphysics thus obscures the pride of place he in fact assigns to ontotheologies in the transformation and stabilization of history itself.)[16]

One of the crucial points to grasp here is that Heidegger's critique of technology follows directly from his understanding of ontotheology. Indeed, the two are so intimately connected that his critique of technology cannot really be understood apart from his view of ontotheology. One of Heidegger's deepest but most often overlooked insights is that our late-modern, Nietzschean ontotheology generates the nihilistic technologization in whose currents we remain caught. The deepest problem with this "technologization" of reality is the nihilistic understanding of being that underlies and drives it: Nietzsche's ontotheological understanding of the being of entities as "eternally recurring will-to-power" dissolves being into *nothing* but "sovereign becoming," an endless circulation of forces, and in so doing, it denies that things have any inherent nature, any genuine meaning capable of resisting this slide into nihilism (any qualitative *worth*, e.g., that cannot be quantified and represented in terms of mere "values," so that *nothing is invaluable*—in the full polysemy of that crucial phrase).[17]

Heidegger, Art, and Postmodernity explains Heidegger's radical philosophical challenge to the deepest presuppositions of modernity and his attempt to articulate a genuinely meaningful postmodern alternative by drawing on key insights from art and poetry—especially insights into the polysemic nature of being and the consequent importance of creative world *disclosure* (as contrasted with the willful, subjective *imposure* of "value"). Heidegger's view is that even great late-modern philosophers like Nietzsche, Marx, and Freud remain trapped within unrecognized modern presuppositions, including the nihilistic view that all meaning is projected onto or infused into an inherently meaningless world of objects through the subject's conceptual and material labors (both conscious and unconscious). These unnoticed metaphysical presuppositions undermine their otherwise important attempts to forge paths into a more meaningful future. Drawing on Kierkegaard, Hölderlin, Van Gogh, and others, Heidegger teaches that more genuinely enduring meaning cannot come from the subject's imposing its values on the world but, instead, only from a poetic openness to those meanings that precede and exceed our own subjectivity. Such meaningful encounters (or "events") require us to creatively and responsibly disclose their significance, unfolding their meaning throughout the lives they can thus come to transform, guide, and confer meaning on.

This difference between *imposing* and *disclosing*—or between technological imposition and poietic disclosure—can be understood as the crucial distinction between the meaninglessness of our technological understanding of being and those meaning-full encounters that a postmodern understanding of ourselves and our worlds helps give rise to, nurture, and encourage.[18] Genuinely enduring, meaningful events, the kinds around which we can build fulfilling lives, do not arise from imposing our wills on the world. This modern view, as Kierkegaard already taught, turns us into sovereign rulers over a land of nothing, where all meaning is fragile because it comes from us, from the groundless voluntarism of our own wills, and so can be rescinded as easily as it was projected. Genuinely enduring meanings emerge, instead, from learning to creatively disclose those often inchoate glimmers of meaning that exist at least partly independently of our preexisting projects and designs, so that disclosing their significance creatively and responsibly helps teach us to partake in and serve something larger than ourselves (with all the risk and reward that inevitably entails).

In short, a truly *postmodern* understanding requires us to recognize that, when approached with a poetic openness and respect, things push back against us, resisting our wills and so making subtle but undeniable claims on us. We need to acknowledge and respond creatively and responsibly to these claims if we do not want to deny the source of genuine meaning in the world. For only those meanings which are at least partly independent of us and so not entirely within our control—meanings not simply up to us human beings to bestow and rescind at will—can provide us with the kind of touchstones around which we can build enduringly meaningful lives (and loves). Heidegger sometimes describes our encounter with these more genuinely meaning-full meanings as an "event of enowning" (*Ereignis*), thus designating those profoundly significant events in which we come into our own as world-disclosers by creatively enabling things to come into their own, just as Michelangelo came into his own as a sculptor by creatively responding to the veins and fissures in a particularly rich piece of marble so as to bring forth his "David," just as a woodworker comes into her own as a woodworker by learning to respond to the subtle weight and grain of each individual piece of wood, and just as teachers come into their own as teachers by learning to recognize, cultivate, and so help develop the particular talents and capacities of individual students.[19]

This poetic openness to that which pushes back against our preexisting plans and designs is what *Heidegger, Art, and Postmodernity* calls a sensitivity to *the texture of the text*, that subtle but dynamic meaning-fullness which is "all around us" phenomenologically, as Heidegger writes (GA 77: 227/147).[20] The current of technologization tends to sweep right past the texture of the texts all around us, and can even threaten to render us oblivious to it (most plausibly, if our resurgent efforts at genetic enhancement inadvertently eliminate our defining capacity for creative world-disclosure). When we learn to recognize the onto-historical current feeding technology, however, we can also learn to resist its nihilistic erosion of all inherent meaning, and so begin to develop a "free relation to technology" in which it becomes possible to thoughtfully use technologies against nihilistic technologization, as we do, for example, when we use a camera, microscope, telescope, or even glasses creatively to help bring out something there in the world that we might not otherwise have seen, a synthesizer or computer to make a new kind of music that helps us develop our sense of what genuinely matters to us, or when we use a word processor or even the Internet to help bring out our sense of what is really there in the issues and texts that most concern us.

In my view, the role human beings play in the disclosure and transformation of our basic sense of reality thus occupies a middle ground between the poles of voluntaristic constructivism and quietistic fatalism. Heidegger is primarily concerned to combat the former, "subjectivistic" error—that is, the error of thinking that human subjects are the sole source of meaning and so can reshape our understanding of being at will—because that is the dangerous error toward which our modern and late-modern ways of understanding being incline us. But this tendency toward overcorrection has led to some widespread misunderstandings of his more considered view. Indeed, Heidegger's oft-quoted line from his famous *Der Spiegel* interview, "Only another God can save us," is probably the most widely misunderstood sentence in his entire work. By another "God," Heidegger does not mean some otherworldly creator or transcendent agent but, instead, another *understanding of being*. He means, quite specifically, a post-metaphysical, post-epochal understanding of "the being of entities" in terms of "being as such," to use his philosophical terms of art. Heidegger himself equates his "last God" with a postmodern understanding of being, for example, when he poses the question "as to whether being will once more be capable of a God, [that is,] as to whether the essence of the truth of being will make a more primordial claim upon the essence of humanity."[21] Here Heidegger asks whether our current understanding of being is capable of being led beyond itself, of giving rise to other world-disclosive events that would allow human beings to understand the being of entities neither as modern "objects" to be mastered and controlled, nor as late-modern, inherently meaningless "resources" standing by for optimization, but instead as *things* that always mean more than we are capable of expressing conceptually (and so fixing once and for all in an ontotheology). That the "God" needed to "save us" is a postmodern understanding of being is one of the central theses of my own work.[22]

Rather than despairing over the possibility of such an inherently pluralistic, postmodern understanding of being ever arriving, moreover, Heidegger thought it was *already* here, embodied in the "futural" artwork of artists like Hölderlin and Van Gogh, simply needing to be cultivated and disseminated in myriad forms in order to "save" the ontologically abundant "earth" (with its seemingly inexhaustible plurality of inchoately meaningful possibilities) from the devastation of technological obliviousness. When Heidegger stresses that thinking is at best "preparatory" (*vorbereitend*), what he means is that great thinkers and poets "go ahead and make ready" (*im voraus bereiten*), that is, that they are ambassadors, emissaries, or envoys of the future, first postmodern arrivals who, like Van Gogh, disseminate and so prepare for this postmodern future with "the unobtrusive sowing of sowers" (GA 5: 210–11/158), as Heidegger puts it (nicely intimating the deep and illuminating parallel between his teaching and Van Gogh's painting that I explain in *Heidegger, Art, and Postmodernity*). As this suggests, new historical ages are not simply dispensed by some superhuman agent to a passively awaiting humanity. Rather, actively vigilant artists and particularly receptive thinkers pick up on broader tendencies happening partly independently of their own wills (in the world around us or at the margins of our cultures, e.g.,), then make these insights central through their artworks and philosophies.

For good and for ill, then, Heidegger ends up as a profoundly *hopeful* philosopher, not some teacher of despair and resignation, as he is often polemically portrayed.[23] As I began by saying, he is not an anti-modern who exhausts himself critiquing modernity but rather the original *postmodern* philosopher, a thinker who dedicates himself to disseminating a postmodern understanding of being in which he places his hope for the future. I continue to find myself inspired by Heidegger's poetic thinking of a postmodern understanding of being (as well as by many of those Heidegger helped inspire in turn), especially by the deeper philosophical insights behind his provocative proclamations that we need to think through art and poetry's distinctive ways of disclosing the world in order to help find ways through and beyond the growing noontime darkness of technological nihilism. Perhaps such concerns partly reflect middle age and its attendant anxieties, but if so, then I have been partly middle-aged my whole life, and suspect that many of us feel similarly, as if we were all living in a time in the middle or *between* ages, an historical period of radical change and transition—or at least we, some of us, still *hope*.

NOTES

1. That "hipster conservativism" sounds rather paradoxical does not make it false—just falsely totalizing in this case: What is false is imagining that *only* latecomers can truly understand something. As anyone who has ever been there at the beginning of something important will probably recognize, first-comers often understand something too, and can do so at least as deeply (if not often as cogently) as those who come later. Rather than define "understand" more cognitively than Heidegger himself did, let us just admit that we need *both*: Early arrivals help create and draw our attention to potentially important and inspiring phenomena; latecomers remain crucial to preserving what remains inspiring beneath traditions whose day in the sun might otherwise have come and gone. That we need both "creators" and "preservers" is something Heidegger himself recognized by the time he wrote the *magnum opus* of his middle period, "The Origin of the Work of Art" (1934–1935), which goes so far as to posit creators and preservers as the two equally important sides of the *work* of art. On the creative role of such interpretive "preservers," see Iain Thomson, *Heidegger, Art, and Postmodernity* (Cambridge: Cambridge University Press, 2011), ch. 3.

2. For more on these points, see *Heidegger, Art, and Postmodernity*, pp. 53–57, and Thomson, "Ontology and Ethics at the Intersection of Phenomenology and Environmental Philosophy," *Inquiry* 47:4 (2004): 380–412.

3. See *Heidegger, Art, and Postmodernity*, 57–62.

4. See Thomson, *Heidegger on Ontotheology: Technology and the Politics of Education* (Cambridge: Cambridge University Press, 2005), esp. chs. 3–4.

5. I discuss Heidegger's provocative views on polytheism, atheism, and on the phenomenological relation between humanity and "the divine" in *Heidegger, Art, and Postmodernity* (esp. chs. 1 and 6); and in Thomson, "The Nothing (*das Nichts*)," in *The Heidegger Lexicon*, ed. Mark Wrathall (Cambridge: Cambridge University Press, forthcoming). See also Hubert Dreyfus and Sean Kelly, *All Things Shining* (New York: Free Press, 2011).

6. On this point, see Thomson, "Heidegger's Nazism in the Light of His Early *Black Notebooks:* A View from America," in *Zur Hermeneutik der "Schwarzen Hefte,"* Heidegger-Jahrbuch 11, ed. Alfred Denker and Holger Zaborowski (Freiburg: Karl Alber, 2017).

7. This hermeneutics of philosophical "fulfillment" (*Vollendung*)—or what *Heidegger, Art, and Postmodernity* also calls the strategy of "hypertrophic deconstruction" (p. 149)—is premised on the insight that, where the deepest historical trends are concerned, *the only way out is through.*

8. See Thomson, "Heideggerian Phenomenology and the Postmetaphysical Politics of Ontological Pluralism," in *Phenomenology and the Political*, ed. S. West Gurley and Geoffrey Pfeifer (Lanham, MD: Rowman & Littlefield, 2016).

9. See *Heidegger, Art, and Postmodernity*, 99–120, 213–20.

10. See Thomson, "In the Future Philosophy Will Be Neither Continental Nor Analytic but Synthetic: Toward a Promiscuous Miscegenation of (All) Philosophical Traditions and Styles," *Southern Journal of Philosophy* 50:2 (2012): 191–205.

11. See *Heidegger, Art, and Postmodernity*, 31–32.

12. On this still metaphysical mistake, see *Heidegger, Art, and Postmodernity*, ch. 3.

13. Heidegger's personal limitations have become increasingly glaring in the four decades since his death. However much distance we might like to put between Heidegger's perspective and our own, the fact that all of our perspectives remains limited (in ways more and less visible to us) may help to motivate the open-minded, hermeneutic humility that we still need in order to approach Heidegger's work in ways that remain charitable as well as critical, so that we can both learn something and go further ourselves.

14. See, for example, Thomson, "Thinking Love: Heidegger and Arendt," *Continental Philosophy Review* (2017); and Thomson, "Heidegger's Nazism in the Light of his early *Black Notebooks*."

15. See *Heidegger, Art, and Postmodernity*, 216.

16. For more on the way the great metaphysical ontotheologies temporarily dam the flow of historicity by grasping the innermost core of reality and its outermost expression and linking these dual perspectives together into a single "ontotheological" account, see *Heidegger on Ontotheology*, ch. 1. On why even atheistic sciences like astrophysics count as "theological" for Heidegger, see *Heidegger, Art, and Postmodernity*, 12.

17. *Heidegger on Ontotheology* thus seeks to develop and defend the core of Heidegger's "reductive yet revealing" (and so rightly controversial) reading of Nietzsche

as the unrecognized ontotheologist of our late-modern age of technologization (see ch. 1). I argue that Heidegger's view is not itself metaphysical, because it is not doubly foundational the way ontotheologies are; see ch. 1 of *Heidegger, Art, and Postmodernity* (ch. 3 shows that Heidegger does believe in essences, but understands them as both historically unfolding and conceptually inexhaustible). On the crucial polysemy of the nothing, see *Heidegger, Art, and Postmodernity*, ch. 3.

18. On this crucially important difference between imposing and disclosing, see *Heidegger, Art, and Postmodernity*, esp. ch. 3, and Thomson, "Rethinking Education after Heidegger: Teaching Learning as Ontological Response-Ability," *Educational Philosophy and Theory* 48:8 (2016): 846–61.

19. For more on such events of ontological truth, see Thomson, "Heideggerian Perfectionism and the Phenomenology of the Pedagogical Truth Event," in *Phenomenology and Virtue Ethics*, ed. Kevin Hermberg and Paul Gyllenhammer (London and New York: Bloomsbury, 2013), 180–90.

20. "The texture of the text" is also the seditious way in which *Heidegger, Art, and Postmodernity* tries to re-Heideggerize Derrida's famous, anti-Heideggerian *aperçu*: "There is nothing outside the text."

21. See GA 5: 112/85. Here the "truth of being" is shorthand for the way an understanding of "the being of entities" (i.e., a metaphysical understanding of "the truth concerning entities as such and as a whole" or, in a word, an *ontotheology*) works to anchor and shape the unfolding of an historical constellation of intelligibility. Its "essence" is that apparently inexhaustible source of historical intelligibility the later Heidegger calls "being as such," an actively *a-lētheiac* (i.e., ontologically "dis-closive") Ur-phenomenon metaphysics eclipses with its ontotheological fixation on finally determining "the being of entities." (That "being as such" lends itself to a series of different historical understandings of "the being of entities" rightly suggests that it *exceeds* every ontotheological understanding of the being of entities.) The "essence of humanity" refers to Dasein's definitive world-disclosive ability to give being as such a place to "be" (i.e., to happen or take place); it refers, that is, to the *poietic* and maieutic activities by which human beings creatively disclose the inconspicuous and inchoate hints offered us by "the earth" and so help bring genuine meanings into the light of the world.

22. See esp. *Heidegger on Ontotheology*, ch. 4 and *Heidegger, Art, and Postmodernity*, chs. 3, 6, and 8.

23. As the Black Notebooks show, Heidegger becomes extremely dark and pessimistic in the midst of the war, with recurring bouts of despair that grow into a severe postwar depression. But it is central to my understanding of Heidegger's philosophical biography that he passes through—and is crucially transformed by—such deaths and rebirths. For more on this point, see Thomson, "The Failure of Philosophy: Why Didn't *Being and Time* Answer the Question of Being?" in *Division III of Heidegger's "Being and Time": The Unanswered Question of Being*, ed. Lee Braver (Cambridge: MIT Press, 2015), 285–310. I would like to thank Gregory Fried and Richard Polt for asking me to contribute to this volume and for their many helpful comments and suggestions.

Chapter 32

East–West Dialogue After Heidegger

Bret W. Davis

People interested in Heidegger's thought should also be interested in East–West dialogue. And people interested in East–West dialogue should also be interested in Heidegger's thought. The aim of this chapter is to make a concise case for these correlative claims.

WHY THOSE INTERESTED IN HEIDEGGER'S THOUGHT SHOULD BE INTERESTED IN EAST–WEST DIALOGUE

Baldly stated, the reason for making my first claim is as follows: Heidegger's entire path of thinking can be understood—as he himself suggests on more than one occasion—as preparing the way for what he calls "the inevitable dialogue with the East Asian World" (GA 7: 41/QCT 158). And so, while many readers of Heidegger may be satisfied to focus on this or that text or period, this or that issue or step on his path, those who pursue the entire trajectory of his thinking will eventually find themselves faced with the inevitability of this dialogue. Following the "step back" of Heidegger's path of thought returns one not only to a dialogical encounter with the "first inception" of the ancient Greeks but also, in the end, over to an even more radical and more difficult, yet for that very reason potentially even more fruitful, dialogical encounter with East Asian traditions of thought. Given that still relatively few students and scholars of Heidegger's thought are pursuing his path to this end, such a claim will likely strike some readers as controversial; yet, if they carefully follow Heidegger's own inclinations and indications, it should appear rather as incontrovertible. After Heidegger, in the wake of his thought, more philosophers should therefore be engaging in—or at least oriented toward—East–West dialogue.

Heidegger is of course not the first modern Western philosopher to have taken a serious interest in Eastern traditions of thought; Asian philosophies have exerted a significant impact on numerous modern Western philosophers ranging from Leibniz to Schopenhauer and Emerson. Yet it is no exaggeration for Rolf Elberfeld to write that "Heidegger is the first great European thinker . . . whose entire path of thought has been accompanied by dialogues with Asian philosophers,"[1] especially if what is meant by this is direct encounters and exchanges. Some of Japan's leading philosophers studied with Heidegger starting in the early 1920s, including Tanabe Hajime,[2] who published the first article on Heidegger's thought in 1924;[3] Kuki Shūzō, who, after introducing Heidegger's thought to Sartre in 1926, published what is perhaps the first substantial introduction to Heidegger's thought in 1935;[4] Nishitani Keiji, who studied with Heidegger in 1937–1939 and was reportedly given a standing invitation to come to his house on Saturdays to teach him about Zen;[5] and Tsujimura Kōichi, who studied with Heidegger in 1956–1958 and was asked to give the commemorative address (*Festrede*) at Heidegger's eightieth birthday celebration in 1969.[6] A visit from Tezuka Tomio, a Japanese scholar of German literature, occasioned Heidegger's composition of one of his most important and far-reaching later texts: "From a Conversation on Language (1953–1954): Between a Japanese and an Inquirer" (GA 12: 79–146; OWL 1–54 tm).

In addition to his interest in Zen Buddhism, Heidegger also demonstrated a keen interest in the original texts of Daoism. In 1930, he reportedly referred in conversation to chapter 17 of the *Zhuangzi* in order to elucidate his conception of being-with-others (*Mitsein*).[7] At the end of his *Country Path Conversations* (1944–1945), Heidegger quotes a passage from another chapter of the *Zhuangzi* on the "necessity of the unnecessary" (GA 77: 239/156). This is no tangential matter: in a letter to his wife at this time, Heidegger wrote: "On the essence of the unnecessary (which is what I mean by 'Being') I recently found the short conversation between two Chinese thinkers that I am copying out for you."[8] It is also in *Country Path Conversations* that Heidegger first comments on the emptiness of the jug as being what is most essential to it (GA 77: 130–31/82–84). This idea, which he returns to later (PLT 167), clearly echoes chapter 11 of the *Daodejing*. In 1946, Heidegger reportedly even worked on a co-translation of the *Daodejing* with Shih-yi Hsiao.[9]

A number of scholars have endeavored to take up and carry forth the dialogue Heidegger began between his post- or non-metaphysical thinking and Asian traditions of thought. In 1969, a groundbreaking conference was held at the University of Hawaii on the theme of "Heidegger and Eastern Thought."[10] In 1987, Graham Parkes published a landmark collection entitled *Heidegger and Asian Thought*.

While some scholars have related Heidegger's thought to Indian as well as East Asian thought, Heidegger's own attention was clearly oriented toward the latter. The fact that Sanskrit and other Indian languages belong to the same language family as do European languages may have led Heidegger to surmise that Indian thought would be implicated in the same kind of metaphysics as are Western philosophies. Moreover, especially in the 1930s, Heidegger's most ethnocentric period, he reiterated in his own manner the all too familiar trope that Greek philosophy was born out of a confrontation with—rather than an innovative inheritance of—"Asiatic" thinking (e.g., GA 39: 134/118). As late as 1962, Heidegger still claimed that "the *Auseinandersetzung* with the Asiatic was for the Greek *Dasein* a fruitful necessity" (GA 75: 228). Heidegger never pursued the dialogical encounter with Near Eastern, Egyptian, and Indian traditions that contributed to the birth of Greek philosophy.[11] For the most part he remained stuck—as do many philosophers still today—in the late-eighteenth-century invention of the idea of philosophy's autochthonous and exclusive origins in ancient Greece.[12] Nevertheless, even though Heidegger did not care to look back behind the horizons of ancient Greek philosophy, he did concern himself, and urged us, to look beyond the current horizons of Western philosophy. In a text from 1959, he wrote that the modern Western world, which derives from the great Greek inception, "can no longer remain in its Occidental isolation" and he affirmed that "it is opening itself to the few other great inceptions" of thinking (GA 4: 177/201 tm).

Among non-Western traditions, Heidegger was most interested in the great inception of East Asian thought, especially the tradition rooted in the foundational texts of Daoism and blossoming later in Zen Buddhism (which he evidently, and problematically, viewed as a purely East Asian rather than a hybrid Indian/Chinese/Japanese tradition). In part, it seems, he was interested in entering into a conversation with ways of thinking that are rooted in languages—that is, "houses of being"—that are entirely different from those of Europe (GA 12: 85, 89/OWL 5, 8). After all, if even the most radically—that is to say, inceptually (*anfänglich*)—different linguistic houses of being could be understood to "well up from a single source" (GA 12: 85, 89, 109/OWL 5, 8, 24), then this would presumably be the source of the essence or essencing (*Wesung*) of being and language as such.

Yet Heidegger was not only interested in East Asian thought because of its inceptual difference from—and hence the depth of its possibly originary sameness with—Western thought. He was also strongly attracted to the specific content of Zen Buddhism and Daoism, in which he saw striking similarities to his own thought. He reportedly exclaimed upon reading a book on Zen by D. T. Suzuki: "If I understand this man correctly, this is what I have been trying to say in all my writings!"[13] At the end of a dialogue in 1958 on art with the Zen thinker Hisamatsu Shin'ichi, Heidegger stated: "It has become clear that, with our ideas . . . we can hardly get to where the Japanese already are."[14] Perhaps referring to Hisamatsu, Heidegger reportedly spoke to C. F. Weizäcker of "the deep impression left on him by a visit from a renowned Japanese Zen Buddhist, who spoke of what is decisive in an entirely unmetaphysical manner; it was as if here a door had been opened" for Heidegger.[15]

In fact, Heidegger may have found inspiration by looking—if not quite stepping—through that doorway starting much earlier. In 1989, Reinhard May published *Ex oriente lux: Heideggers Werk unter ostasiatischen Einfluß*,[16] which was translated by Graham Parkes as *Heidegger's Hidden Sources: East Asian Influences on His Work* in a volume that also includes Parkes's own supplementary essay, "Rising Sun over Black Forest: Heidegger's Japanese Connections." May and Parkes have assembled a compelling body of textual evidence that testifies not only to Heidegger's deep and abiding interest in Daoism and Zen, but also to the largely unacknowledged influence that these sources appear to have exerted on key concepts of Heidegger's thinking such as the nothing (*das Nichts*), the clearing (*die Lichtung*), the Way (*der Weg*), and saying (*die Sage*).[17]

While not admitting to influence, on several occasions Heidegger did point out these congruences himself. In particular, he acknowledged a profound affinity between what East Asian traditions refer to as "nothingness" or "emptiness" and his own conception of "being" which, in its ontological difference from determinate beings, including the highest being of theology, is "no-thing." Heidegger was fond of noting that his non-nihilistic notion of *das Nichts* was understood better by the Japanese than by his fellow Westerners, since what he was trying to think as "being" resonates with what the Japanese have traditionally understood in terms of "emptiness" (*kū*) or "nothingness" (*mu*), namely an essentially indeterminate wellspring of possibilities as opposed to either the fixed form of a being or the inert vacuity of a nihility.[18]

Aware that *dao* can mean "saying/showing" as well as "way," in a text on language from 1953 Heidegger goes so far as to proclaim: "The *Dao* could thus be the Way that moves everything [*der alles be-wëgende Weg*], that from which we might first be able to think what reason, mind, meaning, *logos* properly—i.e., from their own essence—mean to say" (GA 12: 187/OWL 92 tm).

We should add to this list of connections the resonances between, on the one hand, Heidegger's critique of the will and his notion of *Gelassenheit* and, on the other hand, Daoist and East Asian Buddhist critiques of artificiality and egoistic willfulness and notions of "non-doing" (Ch. *wuwei*, Jp. *mui*) and "naturalness" (Ch. *ziran*, Jp. *jinen*). Several Kyoto School philosophers have fruitfully pursued connections between Heidegger and Zen in this regard.[19]

Yet Heidegger's notion of *Gelassenheit*—which entails both a releasement *from* the will and a releasement *into* a non-willful correspondence with the open-region (*Gegnet*) of being (GA 77: 145/95)—arguably resonates even more deeply with an East Asian tradition that Heidegger unfortunately seems to have remained unfamiliar with, namely Shin Buddhism, a most radical form of Pure Land Buddhism established by Shinran Shōnin in the thirteenth century. Heidegger's non-willful comportment of *Gelassenheit* evinces striking similarities to Shinran's notion of *shinjin*, "the entrusting heart." This resemblance is especially significant, given that these terms name for the later Heidegger and for Shinran the most authentic manner of being human. Analogies can be drawn not only between Heidegger's critique of "the will" and Shinran's critique of "self-power" (*jiriki*), but also between the manners in which they both deal with the paradox of "willing not to will." In both cases, the resolution of the paradox is found in a realization that the very source of releasement/entrusting is that unto which one is released/entrusted.[20]

The "inevitable dialogue" envisioned by Heidegger concerning such themes as sketched here is just beginning; yet it cannot proceed unless more students and scholars follow his path of thought all the way to the point of engaging in it.

WHY THOSE INTERESTED IN EAST–WEST DIALOGUE SHOULD BE INTERESTED IN HEIDEGGER'S THOUGHT

It is not just readers of Heidegger who need to be convinced of the relevance of his thought to East–West dialogue. Among my fellow cross-cultural philosophers, my second claim—that people interested in East–West dialogue should be interested in Heidegger's thought—may appear to some even more controversial than my first. Lately the name Heidegger is not very popular or "academically correct" among the voices seeking to pluralize the field of philosophy. These days, one is more apt to hear offhand references to Heidegger as an unrepentant Nazi or anti-Semite than as a radical critic of Western metaphysics and modern technological reductionism and homogenization who lamented the "Europeanization of human being and of the earth" (GA 12: 99/OWL 16), much less as a precursor and catalyst for a genuine East–West philosophical dialogue. Some recent scholarship on this topic has stressed the limitations, misunderstandings, and Eurocentric prejudices embedded in Heidegger's gestures toward East–West dialogue rather than his actual and potential contributions. Whereas twenty-five years ago Florian Vetsch[21] had sympathetically interpreted Heidegger as having provided a viable path to, and model for, intercultural encounter and dialogue, more recently Lin Ma for the most part critically portrays Heidegger as an inveterate Eurocentrist caught in "the irresolvable dilemma" of "how to include and how not to include East Asia in the history of Being."[22] Given this polemical trend of the times, cross-cultural philosophers are understandably hesitant to turn to Heidegger for assistance with their endeavors.

To be sure, Heidegger's gestures toward East–West dialogue are frequently marred by errors and arrogance. Yet removing Heidegger from the forum of East–West dialogue would be as shortsighted and simpleminded as would be removing Aristotle and Kant from ethics syllabi on account of their condemnable misogyny and racism. Heidegger's thought and texts, like those of all great philosophers, should be critically engaged with, not apologetically defended or polemically attacked. Philosophies are as complex and often conflicted as are the men and women who produce them, and our job is to critically sift what is not valuable and viable from what is, so that we can excise the former and develop the latter. In that spirit, in a recent article I argued that toward the end of the 1930s, his most ethnocentric decade, Heidegger's interest in East Asian thought was rekindled and he began to see his prolonged engagement with the Greeks and the history of Western philosophy as preparation for dialogue with East Asian thought.[23]

It is true, however, that Heidegger remained ambivalent to the end regarding the role that the "inevitable dialogue with the East Asian world" can play in a recovery from the willful technological nihilism with which the Western history of metaphysics has culminated. In the 1966 *Spiegel* interview Heidegger wavered on this point: moments after having said, "And who of us can decide whether one day in Russia and in China ancient traditions of a 'thinking' will awaken which will help enable human being to have a free relationship to the technical world" (GA 16: 677), Heidegger reversed course and claimed that "any reversal of the modern technological world can only occur from out of the same location in which it arose, and . . . cannot happen by means of an adoption of Zen Buddhism or other Eastern experiences of the world" (GA 16: 679). Then again, just two years later, in a foreword written for the Japanese translation of one of his essays, Heidegger explicitly affirmed that a dialogue between a "transformed European thinking" and Eastern thinking "can assist in the endeavor to save the essence of the human from the threat of an extreme technical calculation and manipulation of human Dasein."[24] Heidegger is surely right to say that we cannot resolve problems that arose in the Western tradition by means of any uncritical and wholesale adoption of an Eastern replacement. But the idea that only the West can fix what it broke in the first place strikes me as more of a stubborn remnant of Eurocentric arrogance than a genuinely hermeneutical or onto-historical insight. Heidegger's own alternative suggestion—that a genuine dialogue with other ways of thinking can assist in the endeavor to think through certain problems and move beyond certain impasses—is far more compelling.

Heidegger's Eurocentric definition of "philosophy" is another irritant to many cross-cultural philosophers. Heidegger did indeed claim, on more than one occasion, that "Occidental philosophy" is a tautology, given that philosophy was born in ancient Greece and, since then, has essentially defined the Western, and only the Western, tradition (GA 55: 3; WP 31; WCT 224). But these statements of his are often taken out of context and mistakenly criticized by lumping them together with similar sounding claims made by others, such as notably his teacher Husserl. There are, in fact, crucial differences between their assertions: Whereas Eurocentric rationalists such as Husserl mean to unequivocally praise the West and denigrate other traditions, charging that the latter remain mired in the particularity of their mythical discourses while the West, and the West alone, has managed to transcend its particularity by means of the universally valid logos of philosophy, Heidegger's point is very different. Whereas Husserl claims that only the Western tradition has developed philosophy as a "rigorous science" (*strenge Wissenschaft*),[25] Heidegger claims that "science does not think" (*die Wissenschaft denkt nicht*) (WCT 8). After around 1940, that is to say, in the later period of Heidegger's thought during which he makes the claims in question about philosophy being essentially Western, the term "philosophy" is for him equivalent to "metaphysics," and his own project entails announcing the "end of philosophy and the task of thinking" (BW 431–49). Heidegger aims to overcome or recover from philosophy as metaphysics and to take up the task of developing a "non-metaphysical thinking" (GA 77: 187/122), that is to say, a nonphilosophical thinking. "The thinking that is to come is no longer philosophy because it thinks more originally than metaphysics—a name identical to philosophy" (GA 9: 364/276).

One may of course want to take issue with Heidegger's restrictive definition of "philosophy" as equivalent to "Western metaphysics." Indeed, unless and until we were to change the name of our academic field, departments, societies, and journals to "thinking," I agree with those who argue for the inclusion of certain non-Western texts and traditions in the semantic scope of the term "philosophy"—and, moreover, I think we should welcome rather than fear the ways in which such inclusion challenges us to stretch the range and perhaps even redefine the methods and aims of the discipline. We should celebrate the end of Eurocentric philosophy and the task of engaging in a worldwide dialogue among philosophical traditions.

While Heidegger's equation of "philosophy" with "Western metaphysics" may be questioned, there is little doubt that Heidegger frequently displayed an immense respect for and a profound interest in East Asian traditions of "thinking." Nevertheless, it cannot be said that Heidegger contributed to East–West dialogue by studying in depth any Asian texts or traditions, or that he ever made an effort to learn any Asian language. Gadamer, who has said that "Heidegger studies would do well to pursue seriously comparisons of his work with Asian philosophies," suggests that a German philosopher of Heidegger's stature and generation would be hesitant to refer in print to any text he could not read in the original language.[26] There may well be elements of scholarly pride and academic politics involved in his reticence, as there apparently still are today for many Western professors of philosophy who refuse to allow into the den of their department a faculty member who works on a tradition of philosophical thinking they are unfamiliar with, especially if this new area may attract the interest of students, thus diminishing his or her (usually his) own authority and popularity.

There is, however, a more legitimate concern indirectly expressed in Heidegger's reticence to refer explicitly in his writings to the East Asian texts and ideas in which he otherwise expressed great interest. In his letter to the director of the conference held at the University of Hawaii in 1969 on the theme of "Heidegger and Eastern Thought," Heidegger reaffirmed that "Again and again it has seemed urgent to me that a dialogue take place with the thinkers of what is to us the Eastern world." Yet he went on to write that "the greatest difficulty in this enterprise always lies, as far as I can see, in the fact that with few exceptions there is no command of the Eastern languages either in Europe or in the United States."[27] There are, in fact, an increasing number of Western scholars who have attained competence, and even fluency, in Eastern languages. But arguably too few of these scholars also have sufficient competence in Western philosophy. One may become an expert in a field of "area studies" without knowing enough about the "area" *from which* one is studying other cultures and traditions. For a genuine dialogue to take place, one cannot just learn about others but must also come to "know thyself." For Heidegger, this meant that "the dialogue with the Greek thinkers and their language . . . remains for us the precondition of the inevitable dialogue with the East Asian world" (GA 7: 41/QCT 158). Too often, he would say, Western students and scholars who work primarily on non-Western traditions do so with an insufficient understanding of their own presuppositions, that is to say, of the ways in which their conceptual approach to non-Western traditions is shaped by their own insufficiently foregrounded background.

But this hermeneutical point (which coalesces with significant ethical and political critiques of Orientalism), while valid and important, can be taken too far—as Heidegger perhaps did when, in a conversation with Hellmuth Hacker in 1952, he reportedly suggested that "we must first develop the questions from out of our own Occidental thinking. Our heretofore philosophy must first become question-worthy. For the process of the encounter between Occident and Orient I suppose 300 years [is needed]."[28] Did he mean that the encounter itself would take three centuries, or that it would take this long for Westerners to prepare for the encounter? The former would not be an unreasonable estimate. Yet if he meant the latter, imagine what it would sound like to Japanese philosophers—who for their part have been intensely engaged in the encounter between Eastern and Western traditions for more than a century, and with Heidegger's thought itself for nearly a century—to be told that they need to wait two more centuries for Western philosophers to prepare themselves to reciprocate!

The problem with the step-by-step approach Heidegger sometimes suggests—according to which Westerners and Easterners must first "step back" into a dialogical encounter with the "venerable inceptions" (GA 12: 124; OWL 37 tm) of their own traditions before being ready to step outward into a dialogical encounter with one another—is not just that the globalizing world will not wait on such hermeneutically plodding preparations, but also that it fails to understand that learning about others and learning about oneself are in fact mutually supportive and enriching endeavors. I come to know myself better by way of knowing others, just as I come to know others better by way of knowing myself. In an important sense, as David Foster Wallace has pointed out, a fish has no idea what water is, since it has never left this medium in which it dwells and so has nothing to compare it to. As Max Müller once said, "He who knows [only] one, knows none." Or as the Japanese philosopher Nishida Kitarō remarked, someone who does not know other languages does not even know his or her own language.[29] In this sense, a Westerner cannot really understand the Western tradition unless he or she has acquired a vantage point from which to view it from the outside. Perhaps someday "cross-cultural philosophy" will be recognized as a tautology. In the meantime, let us at least acknowledge the important sense in which cross-cultural and multilingual "turtles" make for better philosophers than monocultural and monolingual "fish."

In short, and in terms of the second of my correlative claims in this chapter, I think that critically engaging both with Heidegger's at times excessive cautiousness as well as with his occasionally bold willingness to take a "leap" into East–West encounters can help reveal to us how very difficult, though not impossible, a genuine intercultural or intertraditional dialogue is. In such a dialogue the participants become aware of the particularities of the language, culture, and tradition in which they have heretofore been immersed and from out of which they tend to think and speak, and they become aware of this by way of being exposed to the words and thoughts of someone speaking from out of a different language, culture, and tradition. Such a dialogue thus involves a deepening of self-awareness and self-understanding at the same time as other-awareness and other-understanding. And on the basis of such mutual understanding, we can begin again, after Heidegger, and now together, to think.

NOTES

1. Rolf Elberfeld, "Heidegger und das ostasiatische Denken: Annäherungen zwischen fremden Welten," in *Heidegger Handbuch: Leben-Werk-Wirkung*, ed.

Dieter Thomä (Stuttgart: Metzler, 2003), 469. Unless otherwise noted, translations in this chapter are my own.

2. Japanese names are written in the order of family name first.

3. *Tanabe Hajime zenshū* [Collected Works of Tanabe Hajime] (Tokyo: Chikuma Shobō, 1972), 4: 17–34; available in German translation as "Die neue Wende in der Phänomenologie—Heideggers Phänomenologie des Lebens," in *Japan und Heidegger*, ed. Harmut Buchner (Sigmaringen: Thorbecke, 1989), 89–108.

4. Kuki Shūzō, "Haideggā no tetsugaku" [Heidegger's Philosophy], in *Tetsugaku: Gendai no tetsugaku* [Philosophy: Contemporary Philosophy] (Tokyo: Iwanami, 1933).

5. Reported by Graham Parkes in "Rising Sun over Black Forest: Heidegger's Japanese Connections," in *Heidegger's Hidden Sources: East Asian Influences on His Work*, ed. Reinhard May, tr. with a complementary essay by Graham Parkes (New York: Routledge, 1996), 100.

6. Kōichi Tsujimura, "Martin Heideggers Denken und die japanische Philosophie," in *Japan und Heidegger,* 159–65; Kōichi Tsujimura, "Martin Heidegger's Thinking and Japanese Philosophy," tr. Richard Capobianco and Marie Göbel, *Epoché* 12:2 (2008): 349–57.

7. Heinrich Wiegand Petzet, *Encounters and Dialogues with Martin Heidegger 1929–1976*, tr. Parvis Emad and Kenneth Maly (Chicago, IL: University of Chicago Press, 1993), 18.

8. Martin Heidegger, *Letters to His Wife: 1915–1970*, ed. Gertrud Heidegger, tr. R. D. V. Glasgow (Cambridge, UK: Polity Press, 2008), 187.

9. See Shih-yi Hsiao, "Heidegger and Our Translation of the Tao Te Ching," in *Heidegger and Asian Thought*, ed. Graham Parkes (Honolulu: University of Hawaii Press, 1987), 93–103.

10. The papers were subsequently published in a special issue of *Philosophy East and West* 20:3 (1970).

11. See the mere passing reference to a Sanskrit term in GA 40: 76/79. On the seminal exchanges of thought and culture in the ancient world stretching between Greece and India, see Thomas McEvilley, *The Shape of Ancient Thought: Comparative Studies in Greek and Indian Philosophies* (New York: Allworth Press, 2002).

12. See Peter K. Park, *Africa, Asia, and the History of Philosophy: Racism in the Formation of the Philosophical Canon, 1780–1930* (Albany: SUNY Press, 2013); and Robert Bernasconi, "Heidegger and the Invention of the Western Philosophical Tradition," *Journal of the British Society for Phenomenology* 26:3 (1995): 240–55.

13. William Barrett, Introduction to *Selected Writings of D. T. Suzuki* (New York: Doubleday, 1996), xi.

14. Martin Heidegger and Shinichi Hisamatsu, "Die Kunst und das Denken: Protokoll eines Colloquiums am 18. Mail 1958," in Bucher, *Japan und Heidegger*, 215.

15. Willfred Hartig, *Die Lehre des Buddha und Heidegger: Beiträge zum Ost-West-Dialog des Denkens im 20. Jahrhundert* (Konstanz: Universität Konstanz, 1997), 29.

16. Reinhard May, *Ex oriente lux: Heideggers Werk unter ostasiatischen Einfluß* (Stuttgart: Steiner Verlag Wiesbaden, 1989).

17. On the relation of East Asian thought to Heidegger's notions of *Weg, Lichtung,* and especially *Nichts*, see my "Heidegger and Asian Philosophy," in *The Bloomsbury*

Companion to Heidegger, ed. François Raffoul and Eric S. Nelson (New York: Bloomsbury Academic, 2013).

18. See GA 12: 103; OWL 19; and Heidegger's 1963 letter to Kojima Takehiko, in Buchner, *Japan und Heidegger*, 225. For more references and for analysis, see the latter half of my "Heidegger and Asian Thought."

19. See my *Heidegger and the Will: On the Way to Gelassenheit* (Evanston, IL: Northwestern University Press, 2007), 56–59, 319–21.

20. See GA 77: 122/79, 145/95; and *The Collected Works of Shinran*, ed. and tr. Dennis Hirota et al. (Kyoto: Jōdo Shinshū Hongwanji-ha, 1997), vol. 1, 496–97. I have pursued these analogies in "*Gelassenheit* and the Entrusting Heart: Toward a Dialogue between Heidegger and Shinran," to be included as a chapter in a book edited by Dennis Hirota.

21. Florian Vetsch, *Martin Heideggers Angang der interkulturellen Auseinandersetzung* (Würzburg: Königshausen & Neumann, 1992).

22. Lin Ma, *Heidegger on East-West Dialogue: Anticipating the Event* (New York: Routledge, 2008), 213; see also 208–9. I have reviewed this book in *Journal of the British Society for Phenomenology* 41:3 (2010): 327–29.

23. Bret W. Davis, "Heidegger on the Way from Onto-Historical Ethnocentrism to East-West Dialogue," *Gatherings: The Heidegger Circle Annual* 6 (2016): 130–56.

24. Martin Heideger, "Zur Frage nach der Bestimmung der Sache des Denkens (1968)," in Buchner, *Japan und Heidegger*, 230.

25. See Edmund Husserl, "Philosophy and the Crisis of European Man," in *Phenomenology and the Crisis of Philosophy*, tr. Quentin Lauer (New York: Harper & Row, 1965), 171.

26. From Gadamer's personal correspondence with Graham Parkes, as related in the introduction to Parkes, *Heidegger and Asian Thought*, 5, 7.

27. Winfield E. Nagley, "Introduction to the symposium and reading of a letter from Martin Heidegger," *Philosophy East and West* 20:3 (1970): 221. See also GA 9: 424/321, and Heidegger's statement quoted in Hartig, *Die Lehre des Buddha und Heidegger*, 15–16.

28. Hellmuth Hecker, "Ein Spaziergang mit Heidegger," in Hartig, *Die Lehre des Buddha und Heidegger*, 269.

29. *Nishida Kitarō zenshū* [Complete Works of Nishida Kitarō] (Tokyo: Iwanami, 1987–1989), vol. 12, 281.

Chapter 33

This Is Not a Love Story

Robot Girl and das Rettende *After Heidegger*

Trish Glazebrook

You are my world, you're my robot girl.[1]

In June 2015, Pepper, a non-gender-specific robot designed for use in the home, went on sale. Four thousand sold out in minutes. Pepper is much shorter than adults and does not try to look human. The user agreement asks owners not to engage in sexual or other indecent behavior.[2] Later that year, Hiroshi Ishiguro presented the "most beautiful and intelligent" robot, Erica. Images of thirty "beautiful women" went into facial design so "she should appeal to everyone."[3] His goal is that she be able to guess human intentions and desires, so her response can match them, because then owner and robot "will be able to love each other."[4] That is, she has no desires, but mirrors her owner's. In April 2016, Chen Xiaoping unveiled Jia Jia, nicknamed "robot goddess," in China.[5] When he says hello, she replies, "Yes, my lord, what can I do for you?" She is subservient, and willing to do whatever her owner wants. In this technologization of gender, has woman met her end?

Was the dream of immortality ever possible anyway after Heidegger? I have argued elsewhere that promises of infinite life are not un-Heideggerian.[6] The ideal of immortality does not dispense with the being-toward-death that makes Dasein—or at least Dasein's authenticity, situatedness, here-now-ishness—possible. The infinite of immortality need not be the hypostasis of fixed, unchanging eternity. Rather, it can be Aristotle's infinite, that is, a sequence for which there is always another term. Eternity can be experienced like a day, or the Olympic games,[7] that is, sequentially—not never-dying, but never-now-dying. The posthuman strategy of leap-frogging from one life-extension technology to another, favored by Kurzweil and de Grey,[8] is just such constant deferral toward "the singularity" that is impossible in the

Derridean sense, a cannot-be that must be pregnant with all possibilities, every *telos*-aimed *archē*.

I have also argued that woman is impossible in just this way.[9] She is, *pace* Aristotle, the impossibility of two bodies in one place. She is formlessly inconceivable in Aristotle's "flower-pot theory" of pregnancy:[10] she supplies the matter, while he supplies the form. Accordingly, all children must be male; she can be neither birthed nor thought. And yet, here she stands, ek-sisting, outside herself, or at least beside herself with worry, *Angst*: a *quaestio mihi factA sum*, having become a question, or at least the upside-down question-marking of the *Ursprung-ishness* from which every Dasein springs.

I confess an inverted essentialism: not all women have babies, but all babies have a mother. A posthumanist future that hatches beings in artificial wombs, like the Borg in *Star Trek*,[11] would not be making babies in this account, precisely because they would not have a mother. My point is exactly the appropriation of woman into her ownmost being from her Ge-stellar reduction to egg-donor. For the being whose ownmost possibilities include the possibility beyond which there are no further possibilities, there must be the wholly impossible, inconceivable, grown daughter-Dasein to ground that being's possibilities. How then to think this impossible bearer of any and all possible possibilities, this mothership (in the sense of friendship, or, workmanship, or even scholarship), this meta-Dasein?

Concerning Heidegger, I have also argued that environmental destruction in the *Ge-stell* that is technology is made possible historically by the displacement of Aristotelian teleology to divine intention in Christianity, which is then declared unnecessary in secular humanist, technoscientific modernity where Heidegger's *Ge-stell* holds sway.[12] No wonder nature, made *ateles*, with no ownmost end, appears only reduced to resources on standby to meet human ends. Feminists object that this history renders woman not subject but subjugated, somatically appropriated to man's ends like nature, fully finite in atelic endlessness.

What then of woman's end? After Heidegger, woman's collapse into Robot Girl is an impossibility of *das Rettende*—the saving power—in self-appropriation as endless finitude.

I. Both utopian and dystopian after-Heideggers create a modernist either/or that makes gender inconceivable: woman is culminatingly projected as "Robot Girl."

Anything essential about woman is unsustainable in a world of immortal Dasein, especially when those best affording life-extensions are reduced to wage-earning money-spenders in neoliberal, "late capital," that is consumer culture's outrun of reason by profit. Since woman has always been naturally pointless—*ateles*—except as betrothal resource and son-bearer, and virtually invisible economically, what can it mean for woman's atelicness to become a bad infinite of profligate consumption? What is the point of entering history exactly when Minerva's owl has flown? In a pessimistic, determinist reading of *Ge-stell*, woman arrives just when "*every* history . . . never reaches *history* [*Geschichte*]" (GA 65: 1512/104), when history can only amass facts, so there can be no new beginning except by some *deus* that can only come *ex machina*.

I have argued elsewhere that Heidegger makes an implicit point about capital: calculative reckoning mathematizes nature not just as object, but cold, hard cash.[13] Woman *is* in this world also reduced to pornographic, prostitutional, nuptial exchange value. She remains capital's invisible unpaid labor whose contribution to her community, national food basket, and societal-government possibility cannot be accounted.[14] So I ask here, is the *animal rationale* too repressedly Victorian to admit sexual desire to the human condition? Woman's exchange-ability leaves no room for a female erotic. This remains the case in what MacKinnon calls "rape culture" precisely because denial of female desire precludes consent,[15] of which date rape provides concrete example.[16] Women somehow impossibly arrive into a history of blindness, denial, and genital mutilation—almost 2,000 newly recorded cases in England alone from July to September 2016.[17] Indeed this is not a love story.

Technology also, however, co-grows a saving power: Robot Girl, the perfect solution to fulfill woman's historical function. "Robot" was coined in 1920 by Czech playwright Karel Čapek in *R.U.R. (Rossum's Universal Robots)*, first performed in 1921.[18] *Robota*, literally serf labor, means drudgery, hard work. Čapek's robots prompted debate about exploitation, but seem entirely oblivious. Robot Girl is programmable beyond housework, with no awkward, distracting or labor-intensive ownmost desire, or objection to any of this, or to doing nothing in man's absence. She could be programmed to pine. Seriously, this is not a love story.

Robot Girl might offer a deeper *Rettende*, not *just* maid/sex-toy, but *because* maid/sex-toy, a saving power for women. Reading Heidegger optimistically, she arrives in history in time for the unintelligible singularity, a new beginning. Woman is freed by the third (if unpaid is the first, and underpaid the second) bought daughter of *Bestand*, that I now replace in translation—given language is not a straight trade but an ownmost hermeneutic economy—from "standing reserve" to "patriarcapital." Woman is freed from toolishness by Robot Girl.

If only this were a love story, then women, inconceivable, freed to what can only be impossibly known, too might find in Robot Girl the perfect lover/cleaner/cook, that is to say wife. And yet. Why can women not free themselves from gendered labor division by marrying a robot, or marrying a man and a robot? This nothing-new is more logic of the same, simply labor-passing from one woman to another. Here in this epoch, freed to career-privilege, I hire a woman to care for my house and my child.

Given the genesis of the singularity in patriarcapital, it remains entirely theorized and celebrated in white, educated, industrialized, rich, and democratic (WEIRD) countries. Where does this leave woman? Why should women excitedly with great trepidation, but mostly onanistically, await this WEIRD singularity? How can woman be "posthuman" when she has never been human? To this woman, it looks like a god has only saved man, and not even a Lazarus-raising, third-day inventist, ritually cannibalistic, Marys-loving god. Just Mammon. That's it, then? The culmination of 2,500 years of Western intellects in a few for (overwhelmingly) the most part Richie Riches? The either/or of pess-optimism cannot think woman's arrival outside logics of same. Why should women not rather give up hope and work for change? By "change," I mean *Ereignis* not just after but beyond patriarcapital, a unique but non-totalizing coming-out, not the evening-land singularity project of *Ge-stell.*

II. If *Dasein* is retrievable from the gender-shock of woman's arrival, it is through authenticity without *Jemeinigkeit*. Woman's being-toward-death is un"mine"d ownness.

I have argued elsewhere that *das Rettende*, the saving power, grows in the *Unverborgenheiten* of women subsistence farmers in the global South, whose catastrophic, privileged standpoint within technology's "global conquest" reveals environmental impacts like climate change, resource depletion, and livelihood devastation, language-culture loss, labor exploitation (productive and reproductive).[19] Are women reduced to labor?

In the animated film *Robots*, the protagonist's mother builds a robot in twelve hours of "labor."[20] He grows up and overthrows the evil robot-factory owner who wants to stop making replacement parts, and more profitably sell upgrades. The film is in essence a critique of consumer culture, with particular attention to the dehumanization of workers whose reduction to labor affords disposability when age or broken-downness/illness makes them suboptimal workers. They are "abject": trapped in the no-man's-land between subject and object;[21] but also ab-ject, from *iacio*, *iacere*, *ieci*, *iactum* (to throw), and *ab* (away): projected as disposable, they are thrown away.[22]

Abject labor is especially common in the global South where little regulatory or organized-labor protections exist. Women are doubly vulnerable—to both sexual exploitation, and "termination" when pregnant. In Puerto Rico,

35 percent of childbearing-age women had by 1965 had "the operation," that is sterilization through hysterectomy, in a US population plan to reduce unemployment by reducing the labor force (child resources pre-conceivedly abjected); the island's rural and light industries were being replaced mostly by petrochemical industries requiring fewer workers.[23] This is lived experience of *Ge-stell* (you may have noticed I reject ontological difference) in which people are reduced to instrumental value as standing reserve, denied there-being-hood and only bodies whose labor is controllable and manipulable. For women in the global South, this kind of labor can be preferable to prostitution, often otherwise their best economic option.

So what do women do when they work beyond the logic of the same that is their abjection in patriarchal capital, while self-grounding in a libidinal economy aimed at the individual accumulation of private wealth? Women working in subsistence economies care, in the deepest existential, ontological Heideggerian sense—they work intentionally and ontically to reproduce material conditions of daily living. I have argued that women do not care "essentially," but economically, in their livelihood and labor that is the condition for the possibility of every Dasein. Both within (yet without) the capitalist patriarchy of the global North, women in the global South work to care for family, animals, and community. They work non-subjectivistically, that is not as neoliberal, wage-earning, voters and bearers of rights that contemporary subjects open and are opened by (who both conceal and hide out in) the logic of capital. As I have argued, gynocentric logics of care are relational—being-with is fundamental and constitutive, that is ontological, and always already the impossibility of two bodies in one place.[24] The ownness of women's labor is not "mine," but uniquely determines ontic specifics of her relations. To die is one thing; to be daily responsible for the survival of the child, whose very being you have opened, is an un-"mine"d being-toward-death, not *my* death or *your* death or *her* or *his* death, but death itself, to stand-with in relation to a being and its death-possibility and life possibilities.

Thinking the question of after-Heidegger woman is challenging, as the *Re-reading the Canon* volume *Feminist Readings of Heidegger* makes clear.[25] It can't be right that Dasein is pre-gender, as Heidegger says in the late 1920s—that Dasein has all possibilities of gender (GA 26: §10). Only the hegemon would think gender "possible" and not always already actual, even and especially in a 2,500-year-old tradition of patriarchy. Can woman be authentic without a room of her own? Surely she is bound to the ontic, therefore less than Dasein, in her time-consuming, labor-intensive role of care reproducing daily material conditions of life? Yet if my arguments ring true, woman is the inverted question of end, reason, origin, ground, and Dasein. Not just the being that questions its own being, she is ontico-ontologically the *archē* of any such being-questioner.

Woman is then impossibly inconceivable, an Ursprung unthought that must be thought.

III. Globalization irrupts gender into *Ge-stell* to wreck the homelessness of modernity and open other ways of dwelling.

This section's point can be expressed in one question: before capitalist patriarchs extend their life for in-definitely-ever, might it not be achieved that no child anywhere (but most often, the global South) dies, for example, of malaria before age of two?

Ēthos is Greek for a community bound together by beliefs and practices. It is home in the sense of community-belonging, and the etymology of "ethics." Heidegger analyzes being-in-the-world in terms of what it means to be at home (*zu Hause*) (GA 24: 244–46/172–3). In *Sein und Zeit*, Dasein's un-homeish-ness (*Unheimlichkeit*) is anxiety at "not-being-at-home" in the world (GA 2: 188–89/233), and elsewhere, homelessness is becoming "the destiny of the world" for "modern human beings" (GA 9: 170/258). For Heidegger, homelessness is not a necessary part of the human condition; rather, it is modernity's alienation from nature.[26] The "organized global conquest of the earth" is diagnosed as both a cause and a symptom of human homelessness (GA 6.2: 358/248). The tragedy of many children's death from a disease neglected because their vulnerability is poverty, while diseases of a rich few are major resource sinks, is the ethosless homelessness of modernity: alienation from nature and those who share being-in-the-world.

Heidegger envisions an alternative to homelessness: dwelling. From Hölderlin, he understands *Heimat* as "the power of the earth" (GA 39: 8), which is its capacity as "building bearer, nourishing with its fruits, tending water and rock, plant and animal" (GA 7: 176/178). Accordingly, dwelling is "the manner in which we humans *are* on the earth" (GA 7: 141/147): "to cherish and protect, to preserve and care for, specifically to till the soil, to cultivate the vine . . . in the sense of preserving and nurturing" (GA 7: 141/147). Human dwelling on earth is "sparing and preserving" in which beings are "preserved from harm and danger . . . safeguarded" (GA 7: 143/149).

To express his vision of dwelling in contrast to technology's global conquest, Heidegger borrows from Hölderlin that ". . . poetically man dwells . . .": the "poetic is the basic capacity for human dwelling" (GA 7: 197/228). In the technology essay, he binds together Aristotle's four causes by means of the poetic: *poiēsis* is any creative act, and the four causes are ways that things come into being (GA 7: 11–15/6–10). For Heidegger, "*physis* also . . . is a bringing-forth, *poiēsis*, . . . [in fact] *physis* is indeed *poiēsis* in the highest sense" (GA 7: 15/10). If poetry is creative, nature is the master-poet. *Homo faber* depends upon the generative power of nature because materials used in art and technology have their source there. Part of human dwelling with others in nature is the capacity to make things. Heidegger's argument that humans dwell poetically is the claim that people can be technologically at home in nature thoughtfully, creatively, and symbiotically rather than exploitatively and destructively. But, supposing truth is a woman?

The Chipko women of the Himalayas say "this forest is our mother's home; we will protect it with all our might."[27] Environmentalists argue that control of land should be taken from multinationals that are rapidly destroying the global resource base, and returned to local, indigenous communities whose care for the land promotes sustainability. Weissman argues that because indigenous locals dwell on the land, their practices are sustainable care-taking rather than liquidation for profit.[28] Communities that rely on ecosystem health for their livelihood are in it for the long term, so care for the land. As an after-Heideggerian, I too say, they dwell. They are at home, and understand their ecosystem as a place of care rather than a collection of resources at their disposal. This is not just the care (*Sorge*) of *Sein und Zeit*, though it entails concernful dealings, but later Heidegger's "cultivating and caring [*Pflegen und Hegen*]" (GA 7: 185/217). Another beginning.

Yet this is not a "new beginning"; it is already open. Wangari Maathai's Green Belt Movement (GBM) in 1977 Kenya grew into a nationwide women's environmental organization that empowers communities to conserve their environment and improve livelihoods. In 2015 alone, GBM trained over 20,000 people in eco-management.[29] Under Christiana Figueres's leadership of the United Nations Framework Convention on Climate Change, the Paris Accord was created in 2015 with unanimous agreement from 195 governments who decided "to intentionally change the course of the global economy to protect the most vulnerable and improve life for all." Given years of stalling, deep division between the global North and South, and expiry of the Kyoto Accord with no clear path forward, Figueres's work may be the single-most important achievement of the twenty-first century.[30] Vandana Shiva's activism, theorizing, and policy interventions through protest, argument, and resistance to patenting GMOs and golden rice, have protected seed banks, soil, and water systems, and helped preserve traditional practices of agriculture.[31] In the Niger Delta, the Ogoni women's "gift to humanity" is their fight to keep oil in the ground to prevent greenhouse gases emitted by burning it. Shell Oil did not renew a drilling license that expired after Ogoni women's resistance prevented drilling for ten years. These women took up the struggle after Ken Saro Wiwa and the Ogoni 9 were hanged in 1995 for their resistance.[32] Through their work, the Ogoni women are already world-opening in ways their children may take for granted. This opening is not *Ge-stell*, but dwelling. These displacements of the phallic logic of global capital in labor practices are not the idyll of Heidegger's romanticized peasant. Irrupting into homelessness, they enact care for others, for children, for ecosystems, for the planet.

IV. In conclusion, this message maps after-Heidegger in three points: (1) the "human" does not exist; (2) care is endless but cannot be reconciled with visions of immortality; and (3) being-toward-death makes possible being-toward-life. So the life techno-Dasein takes is always its own; but *das Rettende* and the life *es gibt* are unowned and ownmost.

On this account, "after-Heidegger" is a story, a once-upon-a-time of the "human" that always already is man. History cannot be changed, but the *Ereignis* that is the libidinal economy of this paper is only after-Heidegger because it is after-man, that is, not post men but post capitalist patriarchy. This is Robot Girl upsetting *Her* protagonist.[33] In *Her*, Theodore falls in love with Samantha, a talking AI operating system. He is dismayed to find out she is talking with 8,316 others. Why should love be singular? As care, love is desire for happiness not confined to "mineness." There are many to care with.

Samantha is not, however, the embodied programming of Robot Girl. After-Heidegger Robot Girl bothers not with Haraway's border war between nature and machine.[34] Eyes open, she listens to care from women in yet out of capital. Dasein: she lives her ownmost destiny. Embodied: she has reproductive autonomy. Employed: she is privileged to manage her bank account poorly because she would rather pay for an older brother in Ghana supporting six siblings to go to school than accumulate retirement wealth. She need not marry, because, to quote Neil Young, "when you dance, I can really love."[35] So it turns out to be a love story after all—Robot Girl runs off with the post-man into a better world-opening. Concerning Heidegger, for the time-being, all the time, it was him she was after all.

NOTES

1. Was (Not Was) (1988) Robot Girl. *What Up, Dog?* Chrysalis Records.
2. Justin McCurry, "No Sex, Please, They're Robots, Says Japanese Android Firm," *The Guardian*, September 28, 2015, https://www.theguardian.com/world/2015/sep/28/no-sex-with-robots-says-japanese-android-firm-softbank (Accessed 06/30/2017).
3. Justin McCurry, "Erica, the 'Most Beautiful and Intelligent' Android, Leads Japan's Robot Revolution," *The Guardian*, December 31, 2015, https://www.theguardian.com/technology/2015/dec/31/erica-the-most-beautiful-and-intelligent-android-ever-leads-japans-robot-revolution (Accessed 06/30/2017).
4. McCurry, "Erica, the 'Most Beautiful and Intelligent' Android. . ."

5. Stacy Liberatore, "Meet Jia Jia the 'Robot Goddess': Chinese Inventor Claims AI Humanoid Is the Most Realistic Ever Made (and Has Programmed It to Refer to Him as 'My Lord')," *Daily Mail*, April 18, 2016, http://www.dailymail.co.uk/sciencetech/article-3542621/Meet-Jia-Jia-robot-goddess-Chinese-inventor-claims-humanoid-realistic-programmed-refer-lord.html (Accessed 06/30/2017).

6. Trish Glazebrook, "Architecture against Mortality," *Interfaces* 21/22:1 (2004): 51–58.

7. Aristotle, *Physics 1–4*, tr. P. H. Wicksteed and F. M. Cornford (Cambridge, MA: Harvard University Press, 1929), 3.5.206a20–25.

8. Cf. Extropy Institute, www.extropy.org (accessed 10/02/2016); Greg Klerkx, "Welcome to the Immortals' Club," *New Scientist* 2494 (April 9, 2005), 38–41; Ray Kurzweil and Terry Grossman, *Fantastic Voyage: Live Long Enough to Live Forever* (New York: Rodale Books, 2004).

9. Trish Glazebrook, "What Women Want: An (Eco)feminist in Dialogue with John D. Caputo," in *Cross and Khôra: Deconstruction and Christianity in the Work of John D. Caputo*, ed. Mark Zlomislić and Neal Deroo (Eugene, OR: Pickwick Publications, Wipf and Stock 2010), 230–58.

10. Caroline Whitbeck, "Theories of Sex Difference," in *Women and Values*, ed. Marilyn Pearsall, 2nd ed. (Belmont, CA: Wadsworth, 1993), 34–48.

11. Thanks to Gregory Fried on this point.

12. Trish Glazebrook, "From *Physis* to Nature, *Technê* to Technology: Heidegger on Aristotle, Galileo and Newton," *The Southern Journal of Philosophy* 38:1 (2010): 95–118.

13. Trish Glazebrook and Matt Story, "Heidegger and International Development," in *Heidegger in the Twenty-First Century. Contributions to Phenomenology* 80, ed. Tziovanis Georgakis and Paul J. Ennis (Dordrecht: Springer Science+Business Media, 2015), 121–39. DOI: 10.1007/978–94–017–9769–8_8

14. Cf. Marilyn Waring, *If Women Counted: A New Feminist Economics* (New York: Harper & Row, 1988); Marilyn Waring, *Counting for Nothing: What Men Value and What Women Are Worth* (Toronto: University of Toronto Press, 1999).

15. Catherine MacKinnon, "Rape: On Coercion and Consent," in *Women and Values: Readings in Recent Feminist Philosophy*, ed. Marilyn Pearsall, 2nd ed. (Belmont, CA: Wadsworth, 1993), 214–24.

16. Glazebrook, "From *Physis* to Nature," 231–32.

17. Female genital mutilation (FGM) July 2016 to September 2016, Experimental Statistics report. NHS Digital. http://www.content.digital.nhs.uk/catalogue/PUB22619 (Accessed 04/23/2017).

18. Karel Čapek, *R.U.R. (Rossum's Universal Robots)* (Prague: Aventinum, 1920).

19. Glazebrook and Story, "Heidegger and International Development."

20. Chris Wedge, dir. (2005) *Robots*. Blue Sky Studios/20th Century Fox Animation.

21. Julia Kristeva, *Powers of Horror: An Essay on Abjection* (New York: Columbia University Press, 1982).

22. Jean Genet, *The Thief's Journal*, tr. Bernard Frechtman (New York: Grove Press, 1994 [1949]).

23. Kathey Kraze, History of Forced Sterilization and Current U.S. Abuses, 2014, http://www.ourbodiesourselves.org/health-info/forced-sterilization/ (accessed 10/02/2016).

24. Trish Glazebrook, "Gynocentric Eco-logics," *Ethics and the Environment* 10:2 (2005), Special Issue, ed. Christopher Preston, 75–99.

25. Nancy Holland and Patricia Huntington, ed. *Re-Reading the Canon: Feminist Interpretations of Heidegger* (University Park: The Pennsylvania State University Press, 2001).

26. Trish Glazebrook, "Science," in *The Bloomsbury Companion to Heidegger*, ed. François Raffoul and Eric S. Nelson (London: Continuum, 2013), 337–44: 342.

27. The Chipko Movement: The Women who Hugged Trees. http://www.tottenhamtrees.org/chipko-movement.html (accessed 10/02/2016).

28. Robert Weissman, "Corporate Plundering of Third-World Resources," in *Toxic Struggles: The Theory and Practice of Environmental Justice*, ed. Richard Hofrichter (Gabriola Island, BC: New Society Publishers, 1993), 186–96.

29. See "The Green Belt Movement" at http://www.greenbeltmovement.org/who-we-are and "2015 Annual Report" at http://www.greenbeltmovement.org/who-we-are/annual-reports (accessed 10/02/2016).

30. See http://newsroom.unfccc.int/ and http://www.christianafigueres.com/#/ (accessed 10/02/2016).

31. See http://vandanashiva.com/ (accessed 10/02/2016).

32. See Trish Glazebrook and Anthony Kola-Olusanya, "Justice, Conflict, Capital, and Care: Oil in the Niger Delta," *Environmental Ethics* 33:2 (2011): 163–84.

33. Spike Jonze, dir. (2013) *Her*. Annapurna Pictures/Dist. By Warner Bros. Pictures.

34. Donna Haraway, "A Cyborg Manifesto: Science, Technology, and Socialist-Feminism in the Late Twentieth Century," in *Simians, Cyborgs and Women: The Reinvention of Nature* (London: Routledge, 1991).

35. Neil Young, "When You Dance, I Can Really Love," *After the Gold Rush*, 1970. Reprise Records.

Index

About the Contributors

Kevin Aho is Professor and Chair of the Department of Communication and Philosophy at Florida Gulf Coast University. He has published widely in the areas of existentialism, phenomenology, hermeneutics, and the philosophy of medicine. He is the author of *Body Matters: A Phenomenology of Sickness, Illness, and Disease* (with James Aho, 2008), *Heidegger's Neglect of the Body* (2009), and *Existentialism: An Introduction* (2014). He is the editor of a volume in the New Heidegger Research series entitled *Existential Medicine: Essays on Health and Illness* (2018).

Babette Babich is Professor of Philosophy at Fordham University and specializes in continental philosophy of science and technology. Her recent books include *The Hallelujah Effect: Reflections on Music, Performance Practice and Technology* (2016) and *Un politique brisé: Le souci d'autrui, l'humanisme, et les juifs chez Heidegger* (2016). In addition to editing the journal *New Nietzsche Studies*, she has edited anthologies including *From Phenomenology to Thought, Errancy, and Desire: Essays in Honor of William J. Richardson, S.J.* (1995) and *Hermeneutic Philosophies of Social Science* (2017).

Lee Braver is Professor of Philosophy at the University of South Florida. His main interests are in continental philosophy (especially Heidegger and Foucault), Wittgenstein, realism, and dialogue between continental and analytic philosophy. He is the author of *A Thing of This World: A History of Continental Anti-Realism* (2007), *Heidegger's Later Writings: A Reader's Guide* (2009), *Groundless Grounds: A Study of Wittgenstein and Heidegger* (2012), and *Heidegger: Thinking of Being* (2014); he is the editor of *Division III of "Being and Time": Heidegger's Unanswered Question of Being* (2015). He has also written articles on aesthetics, Davidson, Philip K. Dick, Dilthey, Hubert Dreyfus,

Foucault, Gadamer, Heidegger, Kierkegaard, Levinas, McDowell, Meillassoux, Putnam, Quine, transgressive realism, and Wittgenstein.

Richard Capobianco is the author of *Engaging Heidegger* (2010) and *Heidegger's Way of Being* (2014) and other articles and reviews. He has also co-translated several individual writings, including Heidegger's lecture "On the Question Concerning the Determination of the Matter for Thinking" and Koichi Tsujimura's address "Martin Heidegger's Thinking and Japanese Philosophy." He is Professor of Philosophy at Stonehill College in Massachusetts.

Simon Critchley is Hans Jonas Professor at the New School for Social Research. His books include *Very Little . . . Almost Nothing* (1997), *Infinitely Demanding* (2007), *The Book of Dead Philosophers* (2009), and *The Faith of the Faithless* (2012). Recent works include a novella, *Memory Theatre*, a book-length essay, *Notes on Suicide*, and a book on David Bowie. He is series moderator of The Stone, a philosophy column in *The New York Times*, and coeditor of *The Stone Reader* (2016). He is also fifty percent of an obscure musical combo called Critchley & Simmons. *Ponders End*, their new album, was recently released.

Steven Crowell is Joseph and Joanna Nazro Mullen Professor of Humanities and Professor of Philosophy at Rice University. He is the author of *Husserl, Heidegger, and the Space of Meaning: Paths Toward Transcendental Phenomenology* (2001) and *Normativity and Phenomenology in Husserl and Heidegger* (2013). He edited the *Cambridge Companion to Existentialism* (2012) and, with Jeff Malpas, *Transcendental Heidegger* (2007). With Sonja Rinofner-Kreidl, he edits the journal *Husserl Studies*. He is currently working on the relation between phenomenology and metaphysics.

Daniel O. Dahlstrom, John R. Silber Professor of Philosophy at Boston University, is author of *Das logische Vorurteil* (1994), *Heidegger's Concept of Truth* (2001), *Philosophical Legacies* (2008), *The Heidegger Dictionary* (2013), and *Identity, Authenticity, and Humility* (2017). In addition to translating Heidegger's *Introduction to Phenomenological Research* (2005) and Husserl's *Ideas I* (2014), he served as editor of *Gatherings*, the Heidegger Circle's annual (2010–2014).

Bret W. Davis is Professor of Philosophy at Loyola University Maryland. In addition to receiving a PhD in philosophy from Vanderbilt University, he has spent thirteen years studying and teaching in Japan. He has published more than fifty articles in English and Japanese on Continental, East Asian

Buddhist, and comparative philosophy. His books include the monograph *Heidegger and the Will: On the Way to Gelassenheit* (2007); a translation of Heidegger's *Country Path Conversations* (2010); and the edited volumes *Martin Heidegger: Key Concepts* (2010) and *The Oxford Handbook of Japanese Philosophy* (2018).

Miguel de Beistegui is Professor of Philosophy at the University of Warwick. His books include *Heidegger and the Political: Dystopias* (1998), *Thinking with Heidegger: Displacements* (2003), *Truth and Genesis: Philosophy as Differential Ontology* (2004), *The New Heidegger* (2005), *Immanence and Philosophy: Deleuze* (2010), *Proust as Philosopher: The Art of Metaphor* (2012), and *Aesthetics After Metaphysics: From Mimesis to Metaphor* (2012).

Donatella Di Cesare is Professor of Theoretical Philosophy at Sapienza University, Rome. Her interests include hermeneutics, German philosophy, and Jewish philosophy. Her books include *Utopia of Understanding: Between Babel and Auschwitz* (2012), *Gadamer: A Philosophical Portrait* (2013), *Heidegger, die Juden, die Shoah* (2015), and *Heidegger & Sons: Eredità e futuro di un filosofo* (2015).

Günter Figal is Professor of Philosophy at the University of Freiburg. His books include *Objectivity: The Hermeneutical and Philosophy* (2010), *Martin Heidegger: Phänomenologie der Freiheit* (4th ed., 2013), *Aesthetics and Phenomenology: The Appearance of Things* (2015), and *Heidegger zur Einführung* (7th, rev. ed., 2016). He has edited *The Heidegger Reader* (2009) and is the editor of the *International Yearbook for Hermeneutics*.

Gregory Fried is Professor of Philosophy at Suffolk University. He is the author of *Heidegger's Polemos: From Being to Politics* (2000) and (with Charles Fried) *Because It Is Wrong: Torture, Privacy and Presidential Power in the Age of Terror* (2010). With Richard Polt, he has translated Heidegger's *Introduction to Metaphysics* (2nd ed., 2014), *Being and Truth* (2010), and *Nature, History, State* (2013). Polt and Fried edit the New Heidegger Research series.

Trish Glazebrook is Professor of Philosophy in the School of Politics, Philosophy and Public Affairs at Washington State University. She publishes on Heidegger and science, environment, and sustainability; ecofeminism, capital and care; and gender and climate change. She currently researches women subsistence farmers' adaptations to climate change in Ghana, oil in Africa, and military use of drones.

Peter E. Gordon is the Amabel B. James Professor of History at Harvard University, Faculty Affiliate in the Department of Philosophy, and Faculty Affiliate in the Department of Germanic Languages and Literatures. He is the author of *Rosenzweig and Heidegger: Between Judaism and German Philosophy* (2003); *Continental Divide: Heidegger, Cassirer, Davos* (2010); and *Adorno and Existence* (2016). He is also the coeditor of several volumes in intellectual history and critical theory, including *Weimar Thought: A Contested Legacy* (2013). He is a frequent contributor of essays and reviews to publications such as *The New Republic*, *The New York Review of Books*, and *The Nation*.

Charles Guignon is the author of *Heidegger and the Problem of Knowledge* (1983) and *On Being Authentic* (2004). He is coeditor of *The Existentialists* (2003) and editor of *The Cambridge Companion to Heidegger* (2006). He has coedited a book with Kevin Aho (Dostoevsky's *Notes from the Underground*, 2009) and has also coauthored several papers on psychology.

Lawrence J. Hatab is Louis I. Jaffe Professor of Philosophy and Eminent Scholar Emeritus at Old Dominion University. He is the author of seven books and numerous articles on Heidegger, Nietzsche, and ancient Greek thought, including *Proto-Phenomenology and the Nature of Language* (Rowman & Littlefield International, New Heidegger Research Series, 2017), *Ethics and Finitude: Heideggerian Contributions to Moral Philosophy* (2000), and "The Point of Language in Heidegger's Thinking: A Call for the Revival of Formal Indication" (*Gatherings: The Heidegger Circle Annual*, 2016).

Drew A. Hyland is Charles A. Dana Professor of Philosophy Emeritus at Trinity College, in Hartford, Connecticut, where he taught for forty-seven years. He also has taught graduate courses at the University of Toronto, The New School for Social Research, Boston University, and Suffolk University. He is the author of numerous articles and books on Greek philosophy, Continental philosophy, philosophy of sport, and philosophy of art. Among the books are *Finitude and Transcendence in the Platonic Dialogues* (1995), *Questioning Platonism: Continental Interpretations of Plato* (2004), and *Plato and the Question of Beauty* (2008).

Julia A. Ireland is Associate Professor at Whitman College in Walla Walla, Washington. Together with William McNeill, she is co-translator of Heidegger's three Hölderlin lecture courses, *Hölderlin's Hymns "Germania" and "The Rhine"* (GA 39), *Hölderlin's Hymn "Remembrance"* (GA 52), and *Hölderlin's Hymn "The Ister"* (GA 53). She has published numerous articles on Heidegger and Hölderlin and Heidegger's relationship to National

Socialism, most notably "Naming *Physis* and the 'Inner Truth of National Socialism': A New Archival Discovery." She is completing a monograph on Heidegger and Hölderlin, and recently launched a digital humanities project focused on the *Black Notebooks* called "Heidegger in the Gray Zone."

Arun Iyer, Assistant Professor of Humanities and Social Sciences at the Indian Institute of Technology, Bombay, is the author of *Towards an Epistemology of Ruptures: The Case of Heidegger and Foucault* (2014). With Pol Vandevelde, he is currently coediting and co-translating Gadamer's previously untranslated essays, to be published in three volumes by Bloomsbury. The first of these volumes has appeared under the title *Hermeneutics between History and Philosophy* (2016).

Theodore Kisiel is Distinguished Research Professor Emeritus of philosophy at Northern Illinois University, author of *The Genesis of Heidegger's "Being and Time"* (1993), and coeditor, with Thomas Sheehan, of *Becoming Heidegger: On the Trail of his Early Occasional Writings, 1910–1927* (2007), which has been published in a second, revised edition as *The New Yearbook for Phenomenology and Phenomenological Philosophy IX* (2009).

David Kleinberg-Levin is Professor Emeritus, Department of Philosophy, Northwestern University. His book publications include *The Body's Recollection of Being* (1985), *The Opening of Vision* (1988), *The Listening Self* (1989), *The Philosopher's Gaze: Modernity in the Shadows of Enlightenment* (1999), *Gestures of Ethical Life: Reading Hölderlin's Question of Measure After Heidegger* (2005), *Redeeming Words and the Promise of Happiness: A Critical Theory Approach to Wallace Stevens and Vladimir Nabokov* (2012), *Redeeming Words: Language and the Promise of Happiness in the Stories of Döblin and Sebald* (2014), and *Beckett's Words: The Promise of Happiness in a Time of Mourning* (2015).

John McCumber is Professor in the Department of Germanic Languages at UCLA. His books include *Poetic Interaction: Language, Freedom, Reason* (1989); *The Company of Words: Hegel, Language, and Systematic Philosophy* (1993); *Metaphysics and Oppression: Heidegger's Challenge to Western Philosophy* (1999); *Time in the Ditch: American Philosophy and the McCarthy Era* (2000); *Reshaping Reason: Toward a New Philosophy* (2005); *Time and Philosophy: A History of Continental Thought* (2011); and *On Philosophy: Notes from a Crisis* (2013).

William McNeill is Professor of Philosophy at DePaul University, Chicago. He is the author of two books on Heidegger: *The Glance of the Eye:*

Heidegger, Aristotle, and the Ends of Theory (1999), and *The Time of Life: Heidegger and Ēthos* (2007). He has also translated or co-translated numerous texts by Heidegger, including his lecture courses on Hölderlin.

Andrew J. Mitchell is Winship Distinguished Research Professor of Philosophy at Emory University. He is the author of *Heidegger Among the Sculptors: Body, Space, and the Art of Dwelling* (2010) and *The Fourfold: Reading the Late Heidegger* (2015). He has translated or co-translated several texts by Heidegger, including *Four Seminars* (2003) and *Bremen and Freiburg Lectures* (2012). With Peter Trawny, he has edited *Heidegger's Black Notebooks: Responses to Anti-Semitism* (2017).

Eric S. Nelson is Associate Professor of Philosophy at the Hong Kong University of Science and Technology. He has published over seventy articles and book chapters on Chinese, German, and Jewish philosophy. He is the author of *Chinese and Buddhist Philosophy in Early Twentieth-Century German Thought* (2017) and is currently working on the early modern German reception of Chinese philosophy. He is the coeditor with François Raffoul of *Rethinking Facticity* (2008) and the *Bloomsbury Companion to Heidegger* (expanded ed., 2016). He has also coedited *Addressing Levinas* (2005), *Anthropologie und Geschichte: Studien zu Wilhelm Dilthey aus Anlass seines 100. Todestages* (2013), and *Between Levinas and Heidegger* (2014). He has edited special topic issues of *Frontiers of Philosophy in China* and the *Journal of Chinese Philosophy*.

Richard Polt is Professor of Philosophy at Xavier University in Cincinnati. He is the author of *Heidegger: An Introduction* (1999), *The Emergency of Being: On Heidegger's "Contributions to Philosophy"* (2006), and *The Typewriter Revolution: A Typist's Companion for the 21st Century* (2015). He has edited *Heidegger's "Being and Time": Critical Essays* (2005) and, with Gregory Fried, has translated Heidegger's *Introduction to Metaphysics* (2nd ed., 2014), *Being and Truth* (2010), and *Nature, History, State* (2013). He is currently the editor of *Gatherings: The Heidegger Circle Annual*. Polt and Fried edit the New Heidegger Research series.

François Raffoul is Professor of Philosophy and Section Head of Philosophy at Louisiana State University. He is the author of *Heidegger and the Subject* (1999), *A Chaque fois Mien* (2004), and *The Origins of Responsibility* (2010) and is completing a monograph entitled *Thinking the Event*. He is the coeditor of several volumes: *Disseminating Lacan* (1996), *Heidegger and Practical Philosophy* (2002), *Rethinking Facticity* (2008), *French Interpretations of Heidegger* (2008), and *The Bloomsbury Companion to Heidegger* (2013, 2016). He has co-translated several French philosophers, including

Dominique Janicaud, Jacques Derrida, and Jean-Luc Nancy. He is the coeditor of a book series at SUNY Press entitled Contemporary French Thought.

Robert C. Scharff is Professor of Philosophy Emeritus at the University of New Hampshire and Executive Director of ITERATA, a nonprofit institute for the study of interdisciplinarity in science, industry, and higher education. He is author of *How History Matters to Philosophy: Reconsidering Philosophy's Past After Positivism* (2015), *Comte After Positivism* (2002), and numerous papers on nineteenth- and twentieth-century positivism, post-postivism, and continental philosophy; coeditor (with Val Dusek) of *The Philosophy of Technology: The Technological Condition* (2nd ed., 2014); and former editor of *Continental Philosophy Review* (1994–2005). A new book, *Heidegger Becoming Phenomenological: Reinterpreting Husserl through Dilthey, 1916–1925*, is forthcoming in Rowman and Littlefield's New Heidegger Research series, and he is currently working on another manuscript, *Inheriting Technoscience: Ontological Inquiries and Empirical Turns*.

Dennis J. Schmidt is Research Professor and Head of Philosophy at Western Sydney University. His publications include *Idiome der Wahrheit* (2015), *On Word and Image* (2013), *Lyrical and Ethical Subjects* (2005), *On Germans and Other Greeks* (2001), and *The Ubiquity of the Finite* (1988). He has coedited *Hermeneutische Wege* (2000) and *Difficulties of Ethical Life* (2008). He is the editor of the SUNY Press Series in Continental Philosophy, which now has 164 volumes in print.

Thomas Sheehan teaches religious studies and philosophy at Stanford University. He is the author of *Making Sense of Heidegger: A Paradigm Shift* (Rowman & Littlefield International, New Heidegger Research Series, 2015).

Iain Thomson is Professor of Philosophy at the University of New Mexico, where he received the Gunter Starkey Award for Teaching Excellence. The author of *Heidegger on Ontotheology: Technology and the Politics of Education* (2005) and *Heidegger, Art, and Postmodernity* (2011), Thomson has published dozens of articles on Heidegger in philosophical journals, essay collections, and reference works. He is currently editing a volume on the history of philosophy in the twentieth century and working on a philosophical biography on the troubling and fascinating intersection of Heidegger's life and thought.

Peter Trawny is Director of the Martin-Heidegger-Institut at the University of Wuppertal. His recent books include *Adyton: Heideggers esoterische Philosophie* (2014), *Heidegger and the Myth of a Jewish World Conspiracy* (2015), *Freedom to Fail: Heidegger's Anarchy* (2015), and *On Freedom:*

Technology, Capital, Medium (2017). He has edited numerous volumes of Heidegger's *Gesamtausgabe*, including four volumes of *Black Notebooks* (GA 94–97).

Daniela Vallega-Neu is Associate Professor of Philosophy at the University of Oregon. Her books include *Heidegger's "Contributions to Philosophy": An Introduction* (2003), *The Bodily Dimension in Thinking* (2005), and *Heidegger's Poietic Writings: From "Contributions to Philosophy" to "The Event"* (2018).

Katherine Withy is Associate Professor of Philosophy at Georgetown University. She works on the nature of finitude in Heidegger's philosophy—not only the finitude of human beings (e.g., in moods), but also the finitude of being (e.g., its self-concealing character) and the finitude of meaning (especially in world collapse). She is the author of *Heidegger on Being Uncanny* (2015).

Made in United States
Troutdale, OR
12/18/2024